Learning XSLT

Michael Fitzgerald

O'REILLY®

Beijing · Cambridge · Farnham · Köln · Paris · Sebastopol · Taipei · Tokyo

Learning XSLT

by Michael Fitzgerald

Published by O'Reilly Media, Inc., 1005 Gravenstein Highway North, Sebastopol, CA 95472.

O'Reilly Media, Inc. books may be purchased for educational, business, or sales promotional use. Online editions are also available for most titles (*safari.oreilly.com*). For more information, contact our corporate/institutional sales department: (800) 998-9938 or *corporate@oreilly.com*.

Editor:	Simon St.Laurent
Production Editor:	Marlowe Shaeffer
Cover Designer:	Ellie Volckhausen
Interior Designer:	David Futato

Printing History:

November 2003:	First Edition.

 This book uses RepKover™, a durable and flexible lay-flat binding.

ISBN-10: 0-596-00327-7
ISBN-13: 978-0-596-00327-2
[C]   [7/07]

*To J. Cory Barker—Joe—the guy who got me
started with all this stuff*

Table of Contents

Preface . . . . **ix**

1. Transforming Documents with XSLT **1**
How XSLT Works   2
Using Client-Side XSLT in a Browser   6
Using apply-templates   9

2. Building New Documents with XSLT **16**
Outputting Text   16
Literal Result Elements   23
Using the Element Called element   31
Adding Attributes   33
Outputting Comments   37
Outputting Processing Instructions   38
One Final Example   42

3. Controlling Output **45**
The Output Method   46
Outputting XML   48
Outputting HTML   64
Outputting Text   70
Using a QName Output Method   74
Media Types   75

4. Traversing the Tree **77**
The XPath Data Model   77
Location Paths   82
Expressions   83

What Is a Pattern?   84

Predicates   85

Axes   92

Name and Node Tests   96

Doing the Math with Expressions   99

5. XPath and XSLT Functions **102**

Boolean Functions   104

Node-Set Functions   106

Number Functions   107

String Functions   108

6. Copying Nodes **113**

The copy Element   113

The copy-of Element   118

Copying Nodes from Two Documents   120

7. Using Variables and Parameters **123**

Defining Variables and Parameters   124

Using Variables   127

Using Parameters   130

Invoking Templates with Parameters   132

Using Result Tree Fragments   133

8. Sorting Things Out **137**

Simple Ascending Sort   137

Reversing the Sort   142

By the Numbers   145

Multiple Sorts   148

The lang and case-order Attributes   152

9. Numbering Lists **153**

Numbered Lists   153

Alphabetical Lists   158

Roman Numerals   162

Inserting an Individual Formatted Value   163

Numbering Levels   165

The from Attribute   174

The lang and letter-value Attributes   175

More Help with Formatted Numbers   175

10. Templates **180**

Template Priority 181

Calling a Named Template 186

Using Templates with Parameters 190

Modes 192

Built-in Template Rules 194

11. Using Keys **199**

A Simple Key 199

More Than One Key 202

Using a Parameter with Keys 203

Cross-Referencing with Keys 204

Grouping with Keys 206

12. Conditional Processing **211**

The if Element 212

The choose and when Elements 217

13. Working with Multiple Documents **225**

Including Stylesheets 225

Importing Stylesheets 230

Using the document( ) Function 235

14. Alternative Stylesheets **241**

A Literal Result Element Stylesheet 241

An Embedded Stylesheet 244

Aliasing a Namespace 247

Excluding Namespaces 251

15. Extensions **254**

Xalan, Saxon, and EXSLT Extensions 255

Using a Saxon Extension Attribute 257

Result Tree Fragment to Node-Set 260

Using EXSLT 262

Fallback Behavior 265

Checking for Extension Availability 269

16. XSLT 2.0 and XPath 2.0 . . . . **271**

New XSLT 2.0 Features 272

New XPath 2.0 Features 275

Multiple Result Trees   277
Using Regular Expressions   281
Grouping in XSLT 2.0   286
Extension Functions   288

**17. Writing an XSLT Processor
Interface** **291**
Running an XSLT Processor from Java   291
Writing an XSLT Processor with C#   300

18. Parting Words **306**
The Ox Documentation Tool   307
Signing Off   310

Appendix: XSLT Processors **311**

Glossary **331**

Index **343**

Preface

Extensible Stylesheet Language Transformations (XSLT) and its companion, the XML Path Language (XPath), are arguably the two most widely used XML-related specifications to come out of the World Wide Web Consortium (W3C) since XML 1.0 (*http://www.w3.org/TR/REC-xml.html*).

XSLT 1.0 (*http://www.w3.org/TR/xslt*) and XPath 1.0 (*http://www.w3.org/TR/xpath*) appeared as W3C recommendations in November 1999, about a year and a half after XML. While XSLT and XPath have detractors, they are generally well-accepted in the XML community. One reason why is that XSLT is a relatively easy-to-learn, declarative language. As a declarative language, XSLT relies on an underlying implementation in a programming language such as Java or C++ to get its work done. This book intends to get you doing useful work with XSLT the same day you start reading it.

Who Should Read This Book?

This book is for anyone who wants to get up to speed quickly with XSLT. It is designed around over 200 XML and XSLT examples files—nearly every XSLT feature that this book explores, in fact, is demonstrated by an example that you can run through yourself with the XSLT processor of your choice (Apache's Xalan C++ processor is used with most examples; see *http://xml.apache.org*). It doesn't matter if you're an XML neophyte or a seasoned programmer, this book is designed to help make your learning fast-paced and rewarding.

About the Examples

As a writer, I have labored for about 20 years under the assumption that we all learn best by doing. That's why this book is heavily laden with hands-on examples. All the examples in this book, except for an occasional fragment, are available for download from *http://www.oreilly.com/catalog/learnxslt/*. The examples are organized into directories that are associated with each of the chapters, as in *examples/ch01*, *examples/ch02*, *examples/ch03*, and so on. The XML documents and XSLT stylesheets used in the examples are intentionally simple so as to not obscure the principles they teach with too much distracting markup. These working examples will provide models for you to do about anything you can do with XSLT.

XSLT and XPath Reference

This book doesn't contain reference material for XSLT or XPath. Doug Tidwell's *XSLT* (O'Reilly) does a good job with its reference material, and I recommend you get a copy of that book. The download for this book offers a small Java program called Ox that gives you access to reference information at the command prompt (in *examples/Ox*). For example, if you have a recent Java Runtime Environment (JRE) installed on you computer, you can enter a line such as the following at a command or shell prompt:

```
java -jar ox.jar xsl:text
```

Ox will then return information about the XSLT instruction element text on your screen. You'll learn more about how to use Ox in Chapter 18.

How This Book Is Organized

Learning XSLT is organized into 18 chapters. Here is a brief synopsis of each:

Chapter 1, *Transforming Documents with XSLT*
  Introduces you to some basic XSLT terminology and the process of transforming documents with XSLT processors on the command line, in a browser, and in a graphical application.

Chapter 2, *Building New Documents with XSLT*
  Shows you how to build a new, transformed XML document by adding elements, attributes, and text using XSLT instruction elements or literal result elements. It also shows you how to create comments and processing instructions with XSLT.

Chapter 3, *Controlling Output*
  Explains and demonstrates the differences between XML, XHTML, HTML, and text output. Covers indentation, XML declarations, document type declarations, CDATA sections, and media types. Also discusses whitespace issues.

Chapter 4, *Traversing the Tree*
  Introduces you to XPath, showing you how to use location paths, patterns, and expressions. Explains the seven basic node types, and introduces result tree fragments.

Chapter 5, *XPath and XSLT Functions*
  Shows you how to use XPath and XSLT functions in expressions.

Chapter 6, *Copying Nodes*
Demonstrates how to copy nodes using deep or shallow copy techniques.

Chapter 7, *Using Variables and Parameters*
Talks you through the use of variables and parameters.

Chapter 8, *Sorting Things Out*
Reveals how to sort nodes alphabetically and numerically.

Chapter 9, *Numbering Lists*
Explains how to display formatted numbers in a result tree, including lists that are numbered either alphabetically, with Roman numerals, or numerically.

Chapter 10, *Templates*
Discusses template priority, shows you how to name templates and later invoke them by name, and also shows you how to use parameters and modes with templates and explains what built-in templates are.

Chapter 11, *Using Keys*
With XSLT, you can associate a key with a value and then use this key to find nodes in a document. This chapter explains how to use keys, including a grouping technique.

Chapter 12, *Conditional Processing*
Illustrates how to process nodes with the if and when instructions.

Chapter 13, *Working with Multiple Documents*
Shows how you can use more than one source document for a transformation, as well as how to use more than one stylesheet. Also reveals the difference between including and importing stylesheets.

Chapter 14, *Alternative Stylesheets*
Demonstrates several possible alternative stylesheets, such as a literal result element stylesheet and an embedded stylesheet.

Chapter 15, *Extensions*
Explores the use of extension elements, attributes, and functions made available with some of the more popular processors.

Chapter 16, *XSLT 2.0 and XPath 2.0*
The XSLT 2.0 and XPath 2.0 specifications aren't quite ready for prime time, but they are building momentum and interest, and are nearing completion. This chapter introduces you to some of the more important new features of these new specs.

Chapter 17, *Writing an XSLT Processor Interface*
Using APIs from Java and C#, you can create a custom wrapper for your preferred XSLT processor. This chapter uses code in both languages to show you how.

Chapter 18, *Parting Words*
Reviews important XSLT resources and demonstrates how to use the Ox documentation tool for XSLT and XPath reference.

Appendix, *XSLT Processors*

Helps you find, install, and use a variety of XSLT processors, most of them for free. This appendix also presents some of the basic tenets of using Java processors.

Glossary

A glossary of general XML, XSLT, and XPath terms.

Conventions Used in This Book

The following font conventions are used in this book:

Plain text

Indicates menu titles, menu options, and menu buttons.

Italic

Indicates new terms, URLs, email addresses, filenames, file extensions, pathnames, directories, and Unix activities.

Constant width

Indicates commands, options, switches, variables, attributes, keys, functions, types, classes, namespaces, methods, modules, properties, parameters, values, objects, events, event handlers, XML tags, HTML tags, macros, the contents of files, or the output from commands.

Constant width bold

Shows commands or other text that should be typed literally by the user.

Constant width italic

Shows text that should be replaced with user-supplied values.

 This icon signifies a tip, suggestion, or general note.

 This icon indicates a warning or caution.

Using Examples

This book is here to help you get your job done. In general, you may use the code, stylesheets, or documents in this book in your programs and documentation. You do not need to contact us for permission unless you're reproducing a significant portion of the code. For example, writing a program that uses several chunks of code from this book does not require permission. Selling or distributing a CD-ROM of examples from O'Reilly books *does* require permission. Answering a question by citing this book and quoting example code does not require permission. Incorporating a significant amount of example code from this book into your product's documentation *does* require permission.

We appreciate, but do not require, attribution. An attribution usually includes the title, author, publisher, and ISBN. For example, "*ActionScript: The Definitive Guide*, Second Edition by Colin Moock. Copyright 2001 O'Reilly & Associates, Inc., 0-596-0036-X."

If you feel your use of code examples falls outside fair use or the permission given above, feel free to contact us at *permissions@oreilly.com*.

Comments and Questions

Please address comments and questions concerning this book to the publisher:

O'Reilly & Associates, Inc.
1005 Gravenstein Highway North
Sebastopol, CA 95472
(800) 998-9938 (in the United States or Canada)
(707) 829-0515 (international or local)
(707) 829-0104 (fax)

There is a web page for this book, which lists errata, examples, or any additional information. You can access this page at:

http://www.oreilly.com/catalog/learnxslt/

To comment or ask technical questions about this book, send email to:

bookquestions@oreilly.com

For more information about books, conferences, Resource Centers, and the O'Reilly Network, see the O'Reilly web site at:

http://www.oreilly.com

Acknowledgments

I want to thank the editor of *Learning XSLT*, Simon St. Laurent, for giving me the opportunity to write this book for O'Reilly. I also appreciate the many useful comments provided by the technical reviewers—Michael Kay, Evan Lenz, Jeff Maggard, Sal Mangano, and Dave Pawson. They collectively saved me from a lot of embarrassment! Finally, I want to thank my wife Cristi for her love and support, without which I could not do what I do, nor would I probably want to do what I do.

CHAPTER 1

Transforming Documents with XSLT

Extensible Stylesheet Language Transformations, or XSLT, is a straightforward language that allows you to transform existing XML documents into new XML, Hypertext Markup Language (HTML), Extensible Hypertext Markup Language (XHTML), or plain text documents. XML Path Language, or XPath, is a companion technology to XSLT that helps identify and find nodes in XML documents—elements, attributes, and other structures.

Here are a few ways you can put XSLT to work:

- Transforming an XML document into an HTML or XHTML document for display in a web browser
- Converting from one markup vocabulary to another, such as from Docbook (*http://www.docbook.org*) to XHTML
- Extracting plain text out of an XML document for use in a non-XML application or environment
- Building a new German language document by pulling and repurposing all the German text from a multilingual XML document

This is barely a start. There are many other ways that you can use XSLT, and you'll get acquainted with a number of them in the chapters that follow.

This book assumes that you don't know much about XSLT, but that you are ready to put it to work. Through a series of numerous hands-on examples, *Learning XSLT* guides you through many features of XSLT 1.0 and XPath 1.0, while at the same time introducing you to XSLT 2.0 and XPath 2.0.

If you don't know much about XML yet, it shouldn't be a problem because I'll also cover many of the basics of XML in this book. Technical terms are usually defined when they first appear and in a glossary at the end of the book. The XML specification is located at *http://www.w3.org/TR/REC-xml.html*.

Another specification closely related to XSLT is Extensible Stylesheet Language, or XSL, commonly referred to as XSL-FO (see *http://www.w3.org/TR/xsl/*). XSL-FO is a language for applying styles and formatting to XML documents. It is similar to

Cascading Style Sheets (CSS), but it is written in XML and is somewhat more extensive. (*FO* is short for *formatting objects*.) Initially, XSLT and XSL-FO were developed in a single specification, but they were later split into separate initiatives. This book does not cover XSL-FO; to learn more about this language, I suggest that you pick up a copy of Dave Pawson's *XSL-FO*, also published by O'Reilly.

How XSLT Works

About the quickest way to get you acquainted with how XSLT works is through simple, progressive examples that you can do yourself. The first example walks you through the process of transforming a very brief XML document using a minimal XSLT stylesheet. You transform documents using a processor that complies with the XSLT 1.0 specification.

All the documents and stylesheets discussed in this book can be found in the example archive available for download at *http://examples.oreilly.com/learnxslt*. All example files mentioned in a particular chapter are in the *examples* directory of the archive, under the subdirectory for that chapter (such as *examples/ch01*, *examples/ch02*, and so forth). Throughout the book, I assume that these examples are installed at *C:\LearningXSLT\examples* on Windows or in something like */usr/mike/learningxslt/examples* on a Unix machine.

A Ridiculous XML Document

Now consider the ridiculously brief XML document contained in the file *msg.xml*:

```
<msg/>
```

There isn't much to this document, but it's perfectly legal, well-formed XML. It's just a single, empty element with no content. Technically, it's an *empty element tag*.

Because it is the only element in the document, msg is the *document element*. The document element is sometimes called the *root element*, but this is not to be confused with the *root node*, which will be explained later in this chapter. The first element in any well-formed XML document is always considered the document element, as long as it also contains all other elements in the document (if it has any other elements in it). In order for XML to be *well-formed*, it must follow the syntax rules laid out in the XML specification. I'll highlight well-formedness rules throughout this book, when appropriate.

A document element is the minimum structure needed to have a well-formed XML document, assuming that the characters used for the element name are legal XML name characters, as they are in the case of msg, and that angle brackets (< and >) surround the tag, and the slash (/) shows up in the right place. In an empty element tag, the slash appears after the element name, as in <msg/>. Tags are part of what's called *markup* in XML.

A First XSLT Stylesheet

You can use the XSLT stylesheet *msg.xsl* to transform *msg.xml*:

```
<stylesheet version="1.0"
xmlns="http://www.w3.org/1999/XSL/Transform">
<output method="text"/>

<template match="msg">Found it!</template>

</stylesheet>
```

Before transforming *msg.xml* with *msg.xsl*, I'll discuss what's in this stylesheet. You'll notice that XSLT is written in XML. This allows you to use some of the same tools to process XSLT stylesheets that you would use to process other XML documents.

The stylesheet element

The first element in *msg.xsl* is stylesheet:

```
<stylesheet version="1.0"
xmlns="http://www.w3.org/1999/XSL/Transform">
```

This is the document element for stylesheet, one of two possible document elements in XSLT. The other possible document element is transform, which is actually just a synonym for stylesheet. You can use one or the other, but, for some reason, I see stylesheet used more often than transform, so I'll knuckle under and use it also. Whenever I refer to stylesheet in this book, the same information applies to the transform element as well. You are free to choose either for the stylesheets you write. The stylesheet and transform elements are documented in Section 2.2 of the XSLT specification (this W3C recommendation is available at *http://www.w3.org/TR/xslt*).

The version attribute in stylesheet is required, along with its value of 1.0. (Attributes are explained in the section "Attributes and pseudoattributes," later in this chapter.) An XSLT processor may support Versions 1.1 and 2.0 as the value of version, but this support is only experimental at this point (see Chapter 16). The stylesheet element has other possible attributes beside version, but don't worry about those yet.

The XSLT namespace

The xmlns attribute is a special attribute for declaring a namespace. This attribute, together with a Uniform Resource Identifier (URI) value, is called a *namespace declaration*:

```
xmlns="http://www.w3.org/1999/XSL/Transform"
```

Such a declaration is not peculiar to stylesheet elements, but is more or less universal in XML, meaning that you can use it on any XML element. Nevertheless, an

XSLT stylesheet must always declare a namespace for itself in order for it to work properly with an XSLT processor. The official namespace name, or URI, for XSLT is *http://www.w3.org/1999/XSL/Transform*. A namespace name is always a URI.

The special xmlns attribute is described in the XML namespaces specification, officially, "Namespaces in XML" (*http://www.w3.org/TR/REC-xml-names*). A namespace declaration associates a namespace name with elements and attributes that attempt to make such names unambiguous.

The Namespace Prefix

You can also associate a namespace name with a prefix, and then use the prefix with elements and attributes. More often than not, the XSLT elements are prefixed with xsl, such as in xsl:stylesheet. While the xsl prefix is commonly used in XSLT, these three letters are only a convention, and you are not required to use them. You can use any prefix you want, as long as the characters are legal for XML names. (See Sections 2.2 and 2.3 of the XML specification at *http://www.w3.org/TR/REC-xml.html* for details on what characters are legal for XML names.) For simplicity, I avoid using a prefix in the first few XSLT examples in the book, but I will start using xsl when the stylesheets get a little more complicated because a prefix will help sort out namespaces more readily. You'll learn more about namespaces, including how to use prefixes, in Chapter 2.

The output element

The stylesheet element is followed by an optional output element. This element has 10 possible attributes, but I'll only cover method right now:

```
<output method="text"/>
```

The value text in the method attribute signals that you want the output to be plain text. The default output method for XSLT is xml, and another possible value is html. XSLT 2.0 also offers xhtml (see Chapter 16). There's more to tell about the output element, but I'll leave it at that until Chapter 3. In the XSLT specification, the output element is discussed in Section 16.

The template element

Next up in *msg.xsl* is the template element. This element is really at the heart of what XSLT is and does. A template rule consists of two parts: a pattern to match, and a sequence constructor (so named in XSLT 2.0). The match attribute of template contains a *pattern*, and the pattern in this instance is merely the name of the element msg:

```
<template match="msg">Found it!</template>
```

A pattern attempts to identify nodes in a source document, but has some limitations, which will come more fully to light in Chapter 4. A *sequence constructor* is a list of things telling the processor what to do when a pattern is matched. This very simple sequence constructor just tells the processor to write the text Found it! when the pattern is matched. (I won't use the phrase *sequence constructor* much in this book but will usually just use the term *template* instead.) Put another way, when an XSLT processor finds the msg element in the source document *msg.xml*, it writes the text Found it! from the template to output. When a template writes text from its content to the result tree, or triggers some other sort of output, the template is said to be *instantiated*.

The source document becomes a *source tree* when it is processed by an XSLT processor. Such source documents are usually files containing XML documents, such as *msg.xml*. The result of a transformation becomes a *result tree* within the processor. The result tree is then serialized to standard output (most often the computer's display screen) or to an output file. The source or result of a transformation, however, doesn't have to be a file. A source tree could be built just as easily from an input stream as from a file, and a result tree could be serialized as an output stream.

The output and template elements are called *top-level* elements. They are two of a dozen possible top-level elements that are defined in XSLT 1.0. They are called top-level elements because they are contained within the stylesheet element.

The root node. Another way you could write a location path is with a slash (/). In XPath, a slash by itself indicates the root node or starting point of the document, which comes *before* the first element in the document or document element. A *node* in XPath represents a distinct part of an XML document. A few examples of nodes are the root node, element nodes, and attribute nodes. (You'll get a more complete explanation of nodes in Chapter 4.)

In *root.xsl*, the match attribute in template matches a root node in any source document:

```
<stylesheet version="1.0" xmlns="http://www.w3.org/1999/XSL/Transform">
<output method="text"/>

<template match="/">Found it!</template>

</stylesheet>
```

The msg element is the document element of *msg.xml*, and it is really the only element in *msg.xml*. The template in *root.xsl* only matches the root node (/), which demarcates the point at which processing begins, before the document element. But because the template processes the children of the root node, it finds msg in the source tree as a matter of course.

Because of a feature called *built-in templates*, this stylesheet will produce the same results as *msg.xsl*. Just trust me on this for now: it would be overwhelming at this point to go into all the ramifications of the built-in templates. I will say this, though: built-in templates automatically find nodes that are not specifically matched by a template. This can rattle nerves at first, but you'll get more comfortable with built-in templates soon enough.

Using Client-Side XSLT in a Browser

Now comes the action. An XSLT processor is probably readily available to you on your computer in a browser such as Microsoft Internet Explorer (IE) Version 6 or later, Netscape Navigator (Netscape) Version 7.1 or later, or Mozilla Version 1.4 or later. All three of these browsers have client-side XSLT processing ability already built-in.

A common way to apply an XSLT stylesheet like *msg.xsl* to the document *msg.xml* in a browser is by using a processing instruction. You can see a processing instruction in a slightly altered version of *msg.xml* called *msg-pi.xml*. Open the file *msg-pi.xml* from *examples/ch01* with one of the browsers mentioned. The result tree (a result twig, really) is displayed. Figure 1-1 shows you what the result looks like in IE Version 6, with service pack 1 (SP1). I explain how *msg-pi.xml* works in the section "The XML Stylesheet Processing Instruction" which follows.

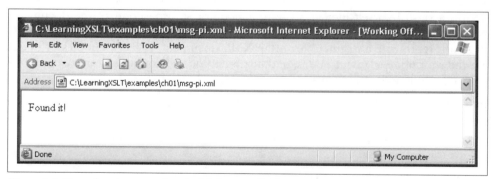

Figure 1-1. Transforming msg-pi.xml with Internet Explorer

When the XSLT processor in the browser found the pattern identified by the template in *msg.xsl*, it wrote the string Found it! onto the browser's canvas or rendering space.

 If you look at the source for the page using View → Source or View → Page Source, you will see that the source tree for the transformation (the document *msg-pi.xml*) is displayed, not the result tree.

The XML Stylesheet Processing Instruction

To apply an XSLT stylesheet to an XML document with a browser, you must first add an XML stylesheet processing instruction to the document. This is the case with *msg-pi.xml*, which is why you can display it in an XSLT-aware browser. A processing instruction, or PI, allows you to include instructions for an application in an XML document.

The document *msg-pi.xml*, which you displayed earlier in a browser, contains an XML stylesheet PI:

```
<?xml-stylesheet href="msg.xsl" type="text/xsl"?>
<msg/>
```

The XML stylesheet PI should always come before the document element (`msg` in this case), and is part of what is called the *prolog* of an XML document. The purpose of this PI is similar to one of the purposes of the `link` tag in HTML, that is, to associate a stylesheet with the document. Usually, there is only one XML stylesheet PI in a document, but under certain circumstances, you can have more than one.

For the official story on PIs in XML, refer to Section 2.6 of the XML specification. The `xml-stylesheet` PI is documented in the W3C Recommendation "Associating Style Sheets with XML Documents" (*http://www.w3.org/TR/xml-stylesheet/*).

In the XML stylesheet PI, the term *xml-stylesheet* is the *target* of the PI. The target identifies the name, purpose, or intent of the PI. This assumes that the application understands what the PI target is. Home-grown PIs are usually application-specific, but the XML stylesheet PI is widely supported and understood. If you invent a new, unique PI target, you also have to write the code to process your PI.

Attributes and pseudoattributes

In XML, attributes may only appear in element start tags or empty element tags, as shown in this element start tag (from *message.xml*):

```
<message priority="low">
```

This `message` element contains an attribute, with `priority` as the attribute name and `low` as the attribute value. The attribute name and value are separated by an equals sign (=). In well-formed XML, attribute values must always be surrounded by either single (') or double (") quotes. The quotes must not be mixed together. You can read more about attributes in Section 3.1 of the XML specification.

The constructs that follow the target in the XML stylesheet PI, `href` and `type`, are not attributes but are *pseudoattributes*. PIs can contain any legal XML characters between the target and the closing `?>`, not just text that looks like attributes. For example, the following PI is perfectly legal:

```
<?do not go gentle into that good night?>
```

The first word following `<?` is `do`. This is the target of the PI, and there must be no space between `<?` and the target. The target is followed by the data `not go gentle into that good night`. This may not be complete nonsense to a Dylan Thomas fan, but a PI will be nonsense to an application unless the PI contains a target and other data that the application understands and knows what to do with it. If an XML processor does not understand the content of a PI, the consequences are not dire. The processor will simply ignore the PI and move on. Pseudoattributes structure the data so processors may have an easier time interpreting it.

The `href` pseudoattribute contains a value that is a URI reference. This URI specifies the relative location of the stylesheet *msg.xsl*. An XSLT processor knows where to find resources relative to its *base URI*. The base URI is usually the directory that holds the source document. The other pseudoattribute, `type`, identifies the content type of the stylesheet, `text/xsl`. The content type identifies the content of the stylesheet as XSL or XSLT text.

A content type of application/xsl or text/xslt may also work with some applications, but text/xsl works consistently. There is some confusion over what content type should be used for XSLT, but let's not get into that brouhaha. Just know that text/xsl is widely accepted and works consistently.

Using apply-templates

One possible element that can be contained inside of a template element is apply-templates. Because apply-templates is contained in template, it is called a *child element* of template. In XSLT, apply-templates is also termed an *instruction element*. An instruction element in XSLT is always contained within something called a *template*. A template is a series of transformation instructions that usually appear within a template element, but not always. A few other elements can contain instructions, as you will see later on. XSLT 1.0 has a number of instruction elements that will eventually be explained and discussed in this book.

The apply-templates element triggers the processing of the *children* of the node in the source document that the template matches. These children (child nodes) can be elements, attributes, text, comments, and processing instructions. If the apply-templates element has a select attribute, the XSLT processor searches exclusively for other nodes that match the value of the select attribute. These nodes are then subject to being processed by other templates in the stylesheet that match those nodes.

Let's not fret about what all that means right now. It's hard to follow exactly what XSLT is doing when you are just starting out. I'll cover more about how apply-templates works in the next chapter.

Analysis of message.xml

To understand how apply-templates works, first take a look at the document *message.xml* in *examples/ch01*:

```
<?xml version="1.0"?>

<message priority="low">Hey, XSLT isn't so hard after all!</message>
```

The message element in *message.xml* has an attribute in its start tag: the priority attribute with a value of low. Also, this element is not empty; it holds the string Hey, XSLT isn't so hard after all! In the terminology of XML, this text is called *parsed character data*, and in the terminology of XPath, this text is called a *text node*.

The XML declaration

Before the message element, at the beginning of this document, is something that looks like a processing instruction, but it's not. It's called an *XML declaration*.

Character Data and Unicode

Character data, indeed any character that appears in an XML document, must be a Unicode character that falls within XML's overall legal subset of Unicode. XML supports ISO/IEC 10646-1 Universal Multi-Octet Character Set, or USC, which is roughly but not strictly interchangeable with Unicode. When referring to the characters that XML supports, most people talk about these characters as Unicode, and so that's what I'll do, too.

Unicode is slowly and surely extending its reach to include, as near as possible, all the character-based writing systems in the world. This obviously goes way beyond the 128-character range of the basic Latin 7-bit ASCII standard. (ASCII, or the American Standard Code for Information Interchange, is a standard of the American National Standards Institute, or ANSI.) Because XML embraces Unicode, it is being used all over the world. In fact, XML is sometimes affectionately referred to as "Unicode with pointy brackets."

It is important to note that a number of Unicode characters are prohibited from XML—for example, most C0 control characters are not allowed characters such as null (0x0000), backspace (0x0008), and form feed (0x000C). The C0 characters comprise the first 32 characters of Unicode, in the hexadecimal range 0000 through 001F. Sections 2.2, 2.3, and 2.4, and Appendix B, of the XML specification go into painstaking detail about what characters can go where in an XML document. You can find out more about Unicode at *http://www.unicode.org* and about ISO/IEC specs at *http://www.iso.ch*.

The XML declaration is optional. You don't have to use one if you don't want to, but it's generally a good idea. If you do use one, however, it must be on the first line to appear in the XML document. Because it must appear before the document element, that also means that an XML declaration is part of the prolog, like the XML stylesheet PI.

If present, an XML declaration must provide version information. Version information appears in the form of a pseudoattribute, `version`, with a value representing a version number, which is almost always `1.0`. Other values are possible, but none are authorized at the moment because an XML version later than 1.0 has not yet been approved.

XML 1.1, which mainly adds more characters to the XML Unicode character repertoire, is currently under consideration, and may become a W3C recommendation by the time you read this book or shortly thereafter. You can see the XML 1.1 spec at *http://www.w3.org/TR/xml11/*.

You can also declare character encoding for a document with an XML declaration, and whether a document stands alone. The XML declaration will be covered in more detail in Chapter 3. See Section 2.8 of the XML specification for more information on XML declarations.

The stylesheet *message.xsl* in *examples/ch01* includes the apply-templates element:

```
<stylesheet version="1.0" xmlns="http://www.w3.org/1999/XSL/Transform">
<output method="text"/>

<template match="message">
 <apply-templates/>
</template>

</stylesheet>
```

Now you'll get a chance to apply this stylesheet to *message.xml* and see what happens. Instead of using a browser as you did earlier, this time you'll have a chance to use Xalan, an open source XSLT processor from Apache, written in both C++ and Java. The C++, command-line version of Xalan runs on Windows plus several flavors of Unix, including Linux. (When I refer to *Unix* in this book, it usually applies to Linux; when I refer to *Xalan*, I mean Xalan C++, unless I mention the Java version specifically.)

Running Xalan

To run Xalan, you also need the C++ version of Xerces, Apache's XML parser. You can find both Xalan C++ and Xerces C++ on *http://xml.apache.org*. After downloading and installing them, you need to add the location of Xalan and Xerces to your path variable. If you are unsure about how to install Xalan or Xerces, or what a path variable is, you'll get help in the appendix.

Once Xalan and Xerces are installed, while still working in *examples/ch01* directory, type the following line in a Unix shell window (use Xalan) or at a Windows command prompt:[*]

```
xalan message.xml message.xsl
```

If successful, the following results should be printed on your screen:

```
Hey, XSLT isn't so hard after all!
```

---

[*] On Unix and its derivatives, xalan installs itself as Xalan. In order for the examples to work, readers can either substitute Xalan for xalan in the examples (because Unix is case sensitive) or create a symbolic link from Xalan to xalan with:

```
cd $XALANCROOT/bin
ln -s Xalan xalan
```

So what just happened? Instead of the processor writing content from the stylesheet into the result tree by using instructions in the stylesheet *message.xsl*, Xalan grabbed content from the document *message.xml*. This is because, once the template found a matching element (the message element), apply-templates processes its children. The only child that message had available to process was a child text node—the string Hey, XSLT isn't so hard after all!

The reason why this works is because of a built-in template that automatically renders text nodes. You'll learn more about how apply-templates and built-in templates work in more detail in later chapters. If you want to go into more depth, you can read about apply-templates in Section 5.4 of the XSLT specification.

More About Xalan C++

If you enter the name *xalan* on a command line, without any arguments, you will see a response like this:

```
Xalan version 1.5.0
Xerces version 2.2.0
Usage: Xalan [options] source stylesheet
Options:
  -a                    Use xml-stylesheet PI, not the 'stylesheet' argument
  -e encoding           Force the specified encoding for the output.
  -i integer            Indent the specified amount.
  -m                    Omit the META tag in HTML output.
  -o filename           Write output to the specified file.
  -p name expression    Sets a stylesheet parameter.
  -u                    Disable escaping of URLs in HTML output.
  -v                    Validates source documents.
  -?                    Display this message.
  -                     A dash as the 'source' argument reads from stdin.
  -                     A dash as the 'stylesheet' argument reads from stdin.
                        '-' cannot be used for both arguments.)
```

The command-line interface for Xalan offers you several options that I want to bring to your attention. For example, if you want to direct the result tree from the processor to a file, you can use the -o option:

```
xalan -o message.txt message.xml message.xsl
```

The result of the transformation is redirected to the file named *message.txt*. Depending on your platform (Unix or Windows), use the cat or type command to display the contents of the file *message.txt*:

```
Hey, XSLT isn't so hard after all!
```

As with a browser, you can also use Xalan with a document that has an XML stylesheet PI, such as *message-pi.xml*:

```
<?xml version="1.0"?>
<?xml-stylesheet href="message.xsl" type="text/xsl"?>
<message priority="low">Hey, XSLT isn't so hard after all!</message>
```

To process this document with the stylesheet in its stylesheet PI, use Xalan's -a option on the command line, like this:

```
xalan -a message-pi.xml
```

The results of the command should be the same as when you specified both the document and the stylesheet as arguments to Xalan.

Using Other XSLT Processors

There are a growing number of XSLT processors available. Many of them are free, and many are available on more than one platform. In this chapter, I have already discussed the Xalan command-line processor, but I will also demonstrate others throughout the book.

Generally, I use Xalan on the command line, which runs on either Windows or Unix, but you can also choose to use a browser if you wish, or another command-line processor, such as Michael Kay's Instant Saxon—a Windows executable, command-line application written in Java. Another option is Microsoft's MSXSL, which also runs in a Windows command prompt. You may prefer to use a processor with a Java interpreter, or you may want to use one of these XSLT processors with a graphical user interface, such as:

- Victor Pavlov's CookTop (*http://www.xmlcooktop.com*)
- Architag's xRay2 (*http://architag.com/xray/*)
- Altova's xmlspy (*http://www.xmlspy.com*)
- SyncRO Soft's <oXygen/> (*http://www.oxygenxml.com*)
- eXcelon's Stylus Studio (*http://www.stylusstudio.com*)

I'll demonstrate here how to use one of these graphical editors: xRay2.

Using xRay2

Architag's xRay2 is a free, graphical XML editor with XSLT processing capability. It is available for download from *http://www.architag.com/xray*. xRay2 runs only on the Windows platform. Assuming that you have successfully downloaded and installed xRay2, follow these steps to process a source document with a stylesheet:

1. Launch the xRay2 application.
2. Open the file *message.xml* with File → Open from your working directory, such as from *C:\LearningXSLT\examples\ch01*.
3. Open the file *message.xsl* with File → Open.
4. Choose File → New XSLT Transform.
5. In the XML Document pull-down menu, select *message.xml* (see the result in Figure 1-2).

6. In the XSLT Program pull-down menu, select *message.xsl* (see what it should look like in Figure 1-3).

7. If it is not already checked, check Auto-update.

8. The result of the transformation should appear in the transform window (see Figure 1-4).

Those are the steps for transforming a file with xRay2. When I suggest transforming a document anywhere in this book, you can use xRay2—or any other XSLT processor you prefer—instead of the one suggested in the example (unless there is a specifically noted feature of the processor used in the example).

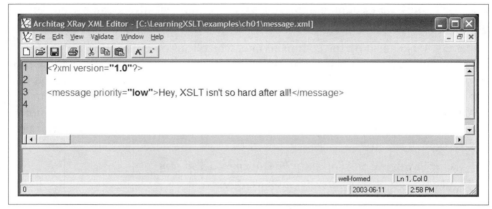

Figure 1-2. message.xml in xRay2

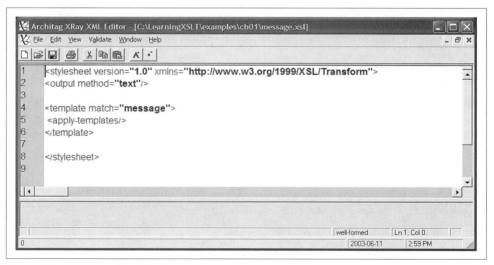

Figure 1-3. message.xsl in xRay2

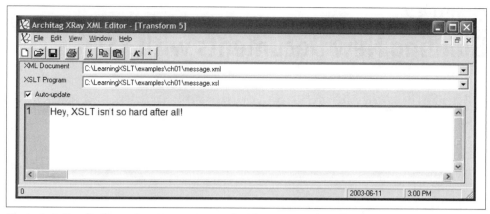

Figure 1-4. Result of transforming message.xml with message.xsl in xRay2

Summary

This chapter has given you a little taste of XSLT—how it works and a few things you can do with it. After reading this introduction, you should understand the ground rules of XSLT stylesheets and the steps involved in transforming documents with a browser, a command-line processor like Xalan, or a processor with a graphical interface, such as xRay2. In the next chapter, you will learn how to create elements, attributes, text, comments, and processing instructions in a result tree using both XSLT instruction elements and literal result elements.

CHAPTER 2
Building New Documents with XSLT

In the first chapter of this book, you got acquainted with the basics of how XSLT works. This chapter will take you a few steps further by showing you how to add text and markup to your result tree with XSLT templates.

First, you'll add literal text to your output. Then you'll work with *literal result elements*, that is, elements that are represented literally in templates. You'll also learn how to add content with the text, element, attribute, attribute-set, comment, and processing-instruction elements. In addition, you'll get your first encounter with attribute value templates, which provide a way to define templates inside attribute values.

Outputting Text

You can put plain, literal text into an XSLT template, and it will be written to a result tree when the template containing the text is processed. You saw this work in the very first example in the book (*msg.xsl* in Chapter 1). I'll go into more detail about adding literal text in this section.

Look at the single-element document *text.xml* in *examples/ch02* (this directory is where all example files mentioned in this chapter can be found):

```
<?xml version="1.0"?>

<message>You can easily add text to your output.</message>
```

With *text.xml* in mind, consider the stylesheet *txt.xsl*:

```
<stylesheet version="1.0" xmlns="http://www.w3.org/1999/XSL/Transform">
<output method="text"/>

<template match="/">Message: <apply-templates/></template>

</stylesheet>
```

When applied to *text.xml*, here is what generally happens, although the actual order of events may vary internally in a processor:

1. The template rule in *txt.xsl* matches the root node (/), the beginning point of the source document.
2. The implicit, built-in template for elements then matches `message`.
3. The text "Message: " (including one space) is written to the result tree.
4. `apply-templates` processes the text child node of a message using the built-in template for text.
5. The built-in template for text picks up the text node "You can easily add text to your output."
6. The output is serialized.

Apply *txt.xsl* to *text.xml* using Xalan:

```
xalan text.xml txt.xsl
```

This gives you the following output:

```
Message: You can easily add text to your output.
```

The *txt.xsl* stylesheet writes the little tidbit of literal text, "Message: ", from its template onto the output, and also grabs some text out of *text.xml*, and then ultimately puts them together in the result tree. You can do the same thing with the XSLT instruction element text.

Using the text Element

Instead of literal text, you can use XSLT's text instruction element to write text to a result tree. Instruction elements, you'll remember, are elements that are legal only inside templates. Using the text element gives you more control over result text than literal text can.

The template rule in *lf.xsl* contains some literal text, including whitespace:

```
<stylesheet version="1.0" xmlns="http://www.w3.org/1999/XSL/Transform">
<output method="text"/>

<template match="/">Message:
  <apply-templates/>
</template>

</stylesheet>
```

When you apply *lf.xsl* to *text.xml* with Xalan like this:

```
xalan text.xml lf.xsl
```

the whitespace—a linefeed and some space—is preserved in the result:

```
Message:
  You can easily add text to your output.
```

The XSLT processor sees the whitespace in the stylesheet as literal text and outputs it as such. The XSLT instruction element text allows you to take control over the whitespace that appears in your template.

In contrast, the stylesheet *text.xsl* uses the text instruction element:

```
<stylesheet version="1.0" xmlns="http://www.w3.org/1999/XSL/Transform">
<output method="text"/>

<template match="/">
 <text>Message: </text>
  <apply-templates/>
</template>

</stylesheet>
```

When you insert text like this, the only whitespace that is preserved is what is contained in the text element—a single space. Try it to see what happens:

```
xalan text.xml text.xsl
```

This gives you the same output you got with *txt.xsl*, with no hidden whitespace:

```
Message: You can easily add text to your output.
```

Back in the stylesheet *txt.xsl*, recall how things are laid out in the template element:

```
<template match="/">Message: <apply-templates/></template>
```

The literal text "Message: " comes immediately after the template start tag. The reason is that if you use any literal text that is not whitespace in a template, an XSLT processor interprets adjacent whitespace in the template element as significant. Any whitespace that is considered significant is preserved and sent along to output.

To see more of how whitespace effects literal text in a result, look at the stylesheet *whitespace.xsl*:

```
<stylesheet version="1.0" xmlns="http://www.w3.org/1999/XSL/Transform">
<output method="text"/>

<template match="/">
Message:

 <apply-templates/>


                               ...including whitespace!

</template>

</stylesheet>
```

Now, process it against *text.xml* to see what happens:

```
xalan text.xml whitespace.xsl
```

Observe how the whitespace is preserved, both from above and below the apply-templates element:

```
Message:

You can easily add text to your output.


                    ...including whitespace!
```

If no nonwhitespace literal text follows apply-templates (that is, if you removed "...including whitespace!" from within template in *whitespace.xsl*), the latter whitespace would not be preserved.

Whitespace is obviously hard to see. I recommend that you make a copy of *whitespace.xsl* and experiment with whitespace to see what happens when you process it.

 Netscape and Mozilla, by the way, preserve the whitespace-only text nodes in output from *whitespace.xsl*, but IE does not. Use *whitespace-pi.xml* to test this in a browser if you like, but keep in mind that such output can vary as browser versions increment upward.

If you use text elements, the other whitespace within template elements becomes insignificant and is discarded when processed. You'll find that whitespace is easier to control if you use text elements. The *control.xsl* stylesheet uses text elements to handle the whitespace in its template:

```
<stylesheet version="1.0" xmlns="http://www.w3.org/1999/XSL/Transform">
<output method="text"/>

<template match="/">
 <text>Message: </text>
 <text>

 </text>
 <text>
 </text>
  <apply-templates/>
 <text>

                ...and whitespace, too!</text>
</template>

</stylesheet>
```

The *control.xsl* stylesheet has four text elements, two of which contain only whitespace, including one that inserts a pair of line breaks. Because you can see the start and end tags of text elements, it becomes easier to judge where the whitespace is, making it easier to control. To see the result, process it with *text.xml*:

```
xalan text.xml control.xsl
```

As an alternative, you could also insert line breaks by using *character references*, like this:

```
<text>&#10;&#10;</text>
```

This instance of the text element contains character references to two line breaks in succession. A character reference begins with an ampersand (&) and ends with a semicolon (;). In XML, you can use decimal or hexadecimal character references. The decimal character reference
 represents the linefeed character using the decimal number 10, preceded by a pound sign (#). A hexadecimal character reference uses a hexadecimal number preceded by a pound sign and the letter *x* (#x). You can also use
 or
, which are equivalent hexadecimal character references to the decimal reference
.

Why Linefeeds?

You might be wondering why I use a linefeed line-end character (
) instead of a carriage return () or carriage return/linefeed combination. The reason is because when a document is processed with a compliant XML processor, the line ends are all changed to linefeeds anyway. In other words, if an XML processor encounters a carriage return or a carriage return/linefeed combination, these characters are converted into linefeeds during processing. You can read about this in Section 2.11 of the XML specification.

The disable-output-escaping attribute

The text element has one optional attribute: `disable-output-escaping`. XSLT does not require processors to support this attribute (see Section 16.4 of the XSLT specification), but most do. This attribute can have one of two values, either yes or no. The default is no, meaning the same whether the `disable-output-escaping` attribute is not present or if its value is no. What does this attribute do? Hang on—this is going to take a bit of explaining.

In XML, some characters are forbidden in certain contexts. Two notable characters that fit into this category are the left angle bracket or less-than sign (<) and the ampersand (&). It's fine to use these characters in markup, such as when beginning a tag with <. You can't, however, use a < in character data (the strings that appear between tags) or in an attribute value. The reason is that the < is a road sign to an XML processor. When an XML processor munches on an XML document, if it sees a <, it says in effect, "Oh. We're starting a new tag here. Branch to the code that handles that." Therefore, you can see why we aren't allowed to use < directly in XML, except in markup.

There is a way out, though. XML provides several ways to represent these characters by escaping them with an entity or character reference whenever you want to use them where they are normally not allowed. Escaping a character essentially hides it from the processor. The most common way to escape characters like < and & is by referencing predefined entities. You'll find XML's built-in, predefined entity references listed in Table 2-1.

Table 2-1. Predefined entities in XML 1.0

Character	Entity reference	Numeric character reference
< (less-than)	&lt;	&#60;
& (ampersand)	&amp;	&#38;
> (greater-than)	&gt;	&#62;
" (quotation)	&quot;	&#34;
' (apostrophe)	&apos;	&#39;

The greater-than entity is provided so that XML can be compatible with Standard Generalized Markup Language (SGML). The > character alone is permissible in character data and in attribute values, escaped or not. (For SGML compatibility, you always need to escape the > character if it appears as part of the sequence]]> , which is used to end CDATA sections. CDATA sections are described in more detail in Chapter 3.)

 XML, by the way, is a legal subset of SGML, an international standard. SGML is a product of the International Organization for Standardization (ISO), and you can find the SGML specifications on the ISO web site, *http://www.iso.ch*. But have your credit card ready: you have to pay for most ISO specifications (sometimes dearly), unlike W3C specifications, which are free to download.

The " and ' entities allow you to include double and single quotes in attribute values. A second matching quote should indicate the close of an attribute value. If not escaped, a misplaced matching quote signals a fatal error, if not followed by well-formed markup. (See Section 1.2 of the XML specification.) I say *matching* because if an attribute value is surrounded by double quotes, it can contain single quotes in its value (as in `"'value'"`). The reverse is also true, that is, single quotes can enclose double quotes (`'"value"'`).

You have to escape an ampersand in character content because the ampersand itself is used to escape characters in entity and character references! If that's confusing, a few examples should clear things up. I'll now show you how the `disable-output-escaping` attribute works.

The little document *escape.xml* contains the name of a famous publisher:

```
<title>O'Reilly</title>
```

The stylesheet *noescape.xsl* adds some new text to this title using the default, which is to *not* disable output escaping:

```
<stylesheet version="1.0" xmlns="http://www.w3.org/1999/XSL/Transform">
<output method="xml" omit-xml-declaration="yes"/>

<template match="/">
 <publisher xmlns="">
  <value-of select="title" xmlns="http://www.w3.org/1999/XSL/Transform"/>
  <text disable-output-escaping="no" xmlns="http://www.w3.org/1999/XSL/Transform">
&amp; Associates</text>
 </publisher>
</template>

</stylesheet>
```

noescape.xsl uses the xml output method. You can't see the effect of output escaping when the output method is text, so you have to use either the xml or html methods. You'll learn more about output methods later in this chapter and in Chapter 3.

This stylesheet also redeclares the XSLT namespace several times (on the value-of and text elements). You'll see how to circumvent this cumbersome practice with a namespace prefix in "Adding a Namespace Prefix," later in this chapter.

To see output escaping in action, process *escape.xml* with this command:

```
xalan escape.xml noescape.xsl
```

Here is the result:

```
<publisher>O'Reilly &amp; Associates</publisher>
```

disable-output-escaping with a value of no has the same effect as having no attribute at all, that is, the output is escaped and & is preserved in the result.

The following stylesheet, *escape.xsl*, disables output escaping:

```
<stylesheet version="1.0" xmlns="http://www.w3.org/1999/XSL/Transform">
<output method="xml" omit-xml-declaration="yes"/>

<template match="/">
 <publisher xmlns="">
  <value-of select="title" xmlns="http://www.w3.org/1999/XSL/Transform"/>
  <text disable-output-escaping="yes" xmlns="http://www.w3.org/1999/XSL/Transform">
&amp; Associates</text>
 </publisher>
</template>

</stylesheet>
```

Process this:

```
xalan escape.xml escape.xsl
```

and you get:

```
<publisher>O'Reilly & Associates</publisher>
```

In *escape.xsl*, escaping is turned off so that & is not preserved. You get only the ampersand in the result. The publisher element, which appears in both *escape.xsl* and *noescape.xsl*, is a literal result element. Let me explain what that is.

Literal Result Elements

A *literal result element* is any XML element that is represented literally in a template, is not in the XSLT namespace, and is written literally onto the result tree when processed. Such elements must be well-formed within the stylesheet, according to the rules in XML 1.0.

The example stylesheet *tedious.xsl*, which produces XML output, contains an instance of the msg literal result element from a different namespace:

```
<stylesheet version="1.0" xmlns="http://www.w3.org/1999/XSL/Transform">
<output method="xml" indent="yes"/>
<template match="/">
 <msg xmlns="http://www.wyeast.net/msg">
  <apply-templates xmlns="http://www.w3.org/1999/XSL/Transform"/>
 </msg>
</template>

</stylesheet>
```

Here is *literal.xml*:

```
<?xml version="1.0"?>

<message>You can use literal result elements in stylesheets.</message>
```

If you apply this stylesheet to *literal.xml*:

```
xalan literal.xml tedious.xsl
```

you will get this output:

```
<?xml version="1.0" encoding="UTF-8"?>
<msg xmlns="http://www.wyeast.net/msg">You can use literal result elements in
stylesheets.</msg>
```

Because this stylesheet uses the XML output method, XML declaration was written to the result tree. The literal result element, along with its namespace declaration, was also written.

Adding a Namespace Prefix

In *tedious.xsl*, the msg element has its own namespace declaration. This is because the XSLT processor would reject the stylesheet if it did not have a namespace declaration. The apply-templates element that follows must also redeclare the XSLT namespace because the processor will produce unexpected results without it. (Try it and you'll see.)

Ok, ok. This is getting a little confusing. If you had to add a namespace declaration to every literal element and then to following XSLT elements, that would add up to a lot of error-prone typing. So, it's time to start using a prefix with the XSLT namespace.

The conventional prefix for XSLT is xsl, but you can choose another one if you like. Here is a rewrite of *tedious.xsl* that uses the xsl prefix with the XSLT namespace declaration. It's called *notsotedious.xsl*:

```
<xsl:stylesheet version="1.0" xmlns:xsl="http://www.w3.org/1999/XSL/Transform">
<xsl:output method="xml" indent="yes"/>

<xsl:template match="/">
 <msg>
  <xsl:apply-templates/>
 </msg>
</xsl:template>

</xsl:stylesheet>
```

This version of the stylesheet drops the namespace declaration for msg because it's no longer required to have one. Likewise, you don't have to redeclare the XSLT namespace for apply-templates either.

If you apply *notsotedious.xsl* to *literal.xml*:

```
xalan literal.xml notsotedious.xsl
```

it produces:

```
<?xml version="1.0" encoding="UTF-8"?>
<msg>You can use literal result elements in stylesheets.</msg>
```

When you use a prefix with a namespace declaration on the XSLT document element stylesheet, as in *notsotedious.xsl*, you don't have to repeat the declaration on any other element in the document that uses the same prefix—you only have to declare it once. Throughout the rest of the book, I'll usually use an xsl prefix in a stylesheet.

Here is another simple example of a literal result element, expanded with a few more details. The template in the stylesheet *literal.xsl* contains a literal result element paragraph:

```
<xsl:stylesheet version="1.0" xmlns:xsl="http://www.w3.org/1999/XSL/Transform">
<xsl:output method="xml" indent="yes"/>
<xsl:template match="/">
 <paragraph><xsl:apply-templates/></paragraph>
</xsl:template>

</xsl:stylesheet>
```

QNames and NCNames

An element or attribute name that is qualified by a namespace is called a *qualified name*, or QName for short. In normal XSLT, two examples of QNames are stylesheet or xsl:stylesheet. Both are (or should be) qualified by the namespace name *http://www.w3.org/1999/XSL/Transform*. A QName may have a prefix, such as xsl, which is separated by a colon from its local part or local name, as in stylesheet. A QName may also consist only of a local part. If a local part is qualified with a namespace, and there is no prefix, it should be qualified by a *default namespace declaration*. You'll learn about default declarations in "Applying namespaces," later in this chapter.

An element or attribute name that is not qualified with a namespace is unofficially called a *non-colonized name*, or, officially, an NCName. As spelled out in XML 1.0, a colon was allowed in XML names, even as the first character of a name. For example, names like doc:type or even :type were and still are legal, even if they are not qualified with a namespace. But there was little notion of namespaces in early 1998 when XML 1.0 came out, so if a colon occurred in a name, it was considered a legal name character. Nevertheless, XML names with colons that are not namespace-qualified are undefined in XSLT and don't work. Avoid them and be happier!

The XML namespaces specification created the term *NCName*. It is an XML name minus the colon, and it makes way for the special treatment of the colon in XML namespace-aware processing. If an XML processor is not up to date and does not support namespaces (most do so now), colons will not be treated specially in names. You can read more about QNames and NCNames in Sections 3 and 4 of the XML namespaces specification.

If namespaces sound somewhat confusing to you, you are in good company. Namespaces in XML are here to stay, but they are admittedly befuddling and difficult to explain.

The output element specifies the xml output method, instead of the text method, and turns indentation on (indent="yes"). When the xml output method is set, XSLT processors will write an XML declaration on the first line of the result tree (as you saw earlier).

When the output element's indent attribute has a value of yes, the processor will add some indentation to make the output more human-readable. The amount of indentation will vary from processor to processor because the XSLT specification states only that, in regard to indentation, an "XSLT processor may add additional whitespace when outputting the result tree" (see Section 16). The modal *may add* gives implementers some free rein on how they put indentation into practice. Some implementers, in fact, don't implement indentation at all, although they are allowed to do so.

Apply *literal.xsl* to *literal.xml* with the command:

```
xalan literal.xml literal.xsl
```

and you will see the following results:

```
<?xml version="1.0" encoding="UTF-8"?>
<paragraph>You can use literal result elements in stylesheets.</paragraph>
```

Using the stylesheet, the processor replaced the document element `message` from the source tree with the literal result element `paragraph` in the result tree. In its output, Xalan also included an encoding declaration in the XML declaration.

The encoding declaration takes the form of an attribute specification (`encoding="UTF-8"`). The encoding declaration provides an encoding name, such as UTF-8, that indicates the intended character encoding for the document. The encoding name is not case sensitive; for example, both `UTF-8` or `utf-8` work fine. Xalan uses uppercase when outputting an encoding declaration, while Saxon uses lowercase. You'll learn more about encoding declarations and character encoding in Chapter 3.

Literal Result Elements for HTML

Taking this a few steps further, the stylesheet *html.xsl* produces HTML output using literal result elements:

```
<xsl:stylesheet version="1.0"
xmlns:xsl="http://www.w3.org/1999/XSL/Transform">
<xsl:output method="html" indent="yes"/>
<xsl:template match="/">
 <html>
  <head>
   <title>HTML Output</title>
  </head>
  <body>
   <p><xsl:apply-templates/></p>
  </body>
 </html>
</xsl:template>

</xsl:stylesheet>
```

The output method is now `html`, so no XML declaration will be written to the output. Indentation is the default for the `html` method, though it is shown explicitly in the output element (`indent="yes"`). The tags for the resulting document are probably familiar to you, and they are near the minimum necessary for an HTML document to display anything. For reference, you can find the current W3C specification for HTML Version 4.01 at *http://www.w3.org/TR/html401/*.

Now, use Xalan to apply the stylesheet to *literal.xml*, and save the result in a file:

```
xalan -o literal.html literal.xml html.xsl
```

This transformation will construct the following result tree and save it to the file *literal.html*:

```
<html>
<head>
<META http-equiv="Content-Type" content="text/html; charset=UTF-8">
```

```
<title>HTML Output</title>
</head>
<body>
<p>You can use literal result elements in stylesheets.</p>
</body>
</html>
```

By default, Xalan's indentation depth is zero, but as a general rule, start tags begin on new lines. Saxon's default indentation depth is three spaces, with start tags on new lines as well.

The META tag

Xalan automatically adds a META tag to the head element. This META tag is an apparent attempt to get Hypertext Transfer Protocol (HTTP) to bind or override the value of the META tag's content attribute (text/html; charset=UTF-8) to the Content-Type field of its response header. In other words, if you request this document with HTTP, such as with a web browser, the server that hosts the document will issue an HTTP response header, and one of the fields or lines in that header should be labeled Content-Type, as shown here:

```
HTTP/1.1 200 OK
Date: Thu, 01 Jan 2003 00:00:01 GMT
Server: Apache/1.3.27
Last-Modified: Thu, 31 Dec 2002 23:59:59 GMT
ETag: "8b6172-c7-3e3878a8"
Accept-Ranges: bytes
Content-Length: 199
Connection: close
Content-Type: text/html; charset=UTF-8
```

I cannot guarantee that the content of the META tag will wind up in the Content-Type header field, though that's what it logically seems to be trying to do. You can tell Xalan to not output the META tag by using the -m option on the command line. For example, the command:

```
xalan -m literal.xml html.xsl
```

will produce HTML output without the META tag:

```
<html>
<head>
<title>HTML Output</title>
</head>
<body>
<p>You can use literal result elements in stylesheets.</p>
</body>
</html>
```

The apply-templates element in *html.xsl* brought the content of message from *literal. xml* into the content of the p element in the resulting HTML. If you open the document *literal.html* in the Mozilla Firefox web browser, it should look like Figure 2-1. (Firefox is a leaner and faster branch of Mozilla.)

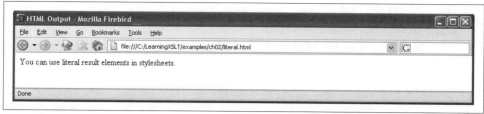

Figure 2-1. Displaying literal.html in Mozilla Firefox

XHTML Literal Result Elements

The XML document *doc.xml* uses a minimal set of elements to express a rather simple document structure:

```
<?xml version="1.0"?>

<doc styletype="text/css">

<css>
 h1 {font-family: sans-serif; font-size: 24pt}
 p {font-size: 16pt}
</css>

<title>Using Literal Result Elements</title>

<heading>What Is a Literal Result Element?</heading>

<paragraph>You can use literal result elements in
stylesheets. A literal result element is any non-XSLT element,
including any attributes, that can be written literally in a
template, and that will be pushed literally onto the
result tree when processed.</paragraph>

</doc>
```

The document element doc in *doc.xml* is the container, so to speak, for the whole document. This element has a single attribute, styletype, that ostensibly provides a content type for a CSS stylesheet. The css element holds a few CSS rules, which don't apply to any elements in *doc.xml*, but they'll come in handy later when you move to XHTML. The title, heading, and paragraph elements that follow have fairly obvious roles. Now look at the stylesheet *doc.xsl*, which you can use to transform *doc.xml* into XHTML:

```
<xsl:stylesheet version="1.0" xmlns:xsl="http://www.w3.org/1999/XSL/Transform">
<xsl:output method="xml" indent="yes"/>

 <xsl:template match="doc">
  <html xmlns="http://www.w3.org/1999/xhtml">
  <head>
   <title><xsl:apply-templates select="title"/></title>
   <style type="{@styletype}">
```

```
   <xsl:apply-templates select="css"/>
  </style>
 </head>
 <body>
  <h1><xsl:apply-templates select="heading"/></h1>
  <p><xsl:apply-templates select="paragraph"/></p>
 </body>
 </html>
 </xsl:template>

</xsl:stylesheet>
```

The output method is XML again, because XHTML is really a vocabulary of XML. (XSLT 1.0 does not support a specific `xhtml` output method, but XSLT 2.0 does.) With indentation on (yes), the output will be more readable. The literal result element for `html` has a namespace declaration for XHTML 1.0.

As a vocabulary of XML, XHTML 1.0 has requirements that go beyond those of HTML, an SGML vocabulary. For example, all XHTML tags must be in lowercase, and must be closed properly, either with an end tag or in the form of an empty element tag. Attribute values must be enclosed in matching double or single quotes. In other words, because XHTML *is* XML, it must be well-formed.

Looking back at *doc.xsl*, what about the braces in the value of style's type attribute? That's called an *attribute value template* in XSLT.

Attribute value templates

An attribute value template provides a way to bring computed data into attribute values. Think for a moment why such a syntax is needed. You know that the markup character < is not allowed in attribute values. That's a rule from the XML 1.0 specification. So, you couldn't use something like a `value-of` element in an attribute value. And you can't use entity references such as `&lt;` as you normally would in an attribute value of a literal result element because an XSLT processor will interpret these references as literal text. These are a few reasons why XSLT provides this special syntax.

The following line in *doc.xsl* contains an attribute value template:

```
<style type="{@styletype}">
```

Because it is processing the doc element, and eventually all its children, the processor uncovers the attribute `styletype` on doc. In the stylesheet, the braces ({ }) enclose the attribute value template. Everything in the braces is computed rather than copied through. The at sign (@) syntax comes from XPath and indicates that the following item in the location path is an attribute you're looking for in the context node. The XSLT processor then picks up the value of the `styletype` attribute from the source tree and places it at this same spot in the output, giving you:

```
<style type="text/css">
```

in the result tree. (You can read more about attribute value templates in Section 7.6.2 of the XSLT specification.)

Now process this transformation and save the result in the file:

```
xalan -o doc.html doc.xml doc.xsl
```

The resulting file *doc.html* will look like this:

```
<?xml version="1.0" encoding="UTF-8"?>
<html xmlns="http://www.w3.org/1999/xhtml">
<head>
<title>Using Literal Result Elements</title>
<style type="text/css">
 h1 {font-family: sans-serif; font-size: 24pt}
 p {font-size: 16pt}
</style>
</head>
<body>
<h1>What Is a Literal Result Element?</h1>
<p>You can use literal result elements in stylesheets.
A literal result element is any non-XSLT element,
including any attributes, that can be written literally in a
template, and that will be pushed literally onto the
result tree when processed.</p>
</body>
</html>
```

Figure 2-2 shows what *doc.html* looks like in Netscape 7.1. Actually, you can either open *doc.html* or *doc-pi.xml* and you'll be looking at essentially the same document.

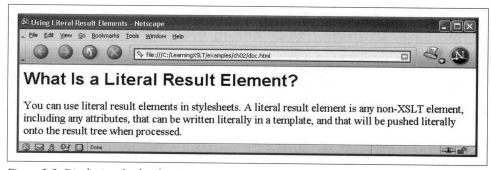

Figure 2-2. Displaying doc.html in Netscape 7.1

Applying namespaces

Before moving on, I want to call your attention to the namespace declaration in *doc. html*. This, which originated in a literal result element in *doc.xsl*, is considered a default namespace declaration:

```
<html xmlns="http://www.w3.org/1999/xhtml">
```

The URI *http://www.w3.org/1999/xhtml*, by the way, is the official namespace for XHTML 1.0. No prefix appears on any element or attribute in the resulting document. A default namespace declaration applies to the element on which it was declared, and also to any child elements that follow that element, but default declarations never apply to attributes.

There is little to no risk of having a name conflict between attribute names. For example, take two elements that both can have an attribute with the same name. With or without a namespace declaration, there won't be a name conflict because an attribute's domain, so to speak, is limited to the element that owns it. You can only use an attribute once on a given element—attribute names must be unique within the element. If, however, two attributes have the same name, and one is qualified with a namespace prefix (a QName with a prefix), those names won't conflict. For example, in the following fragment, the invoice start tag has two attributes:

```
<invoice order="293-7756-11" new:order="2003-08-31-4556">
```

There are two order attributes, but because one is qualified with a prefix, the names won't collide, and you don't break the rule of using an attribute more than once. For more details, see Section 5.2 of the XML namespaces specification.

Using the Element Called element

Literal result elements aren't the only way to create elements on the result tree. You can also use the XSLT instruction element. The following document, *element.xml*, is similar to *literal.xml*, which you saw earlier in this chapter:

```
<?xml version="1.0"?>

<message>You can use the element element to create elements on the result tree.
</message>
```

Unlike *literal.xsl*, the stylesheet *element.xsl* uses element instead of a literal result element to create a new element in the output:

```
<xsl:stylesheet version="1.0" xmlns:xsl="http://www.w3.org/1999/XSL/Transform">
<xsl:output method="xml" indent="yes"/>

  <xsl:template match="message">
    <xsl:element name="{concat('my', name( ))}"><xsl:apply-templates/></xsl:element>
  </xsl:template>

</xsl:stylesheet>
```

element has three attributes. The name attribute is required as it obviously specifies a name for the element. In this example, the name attribute uses an attribute value template to compute a name for the element. In other words, the name of the element is computed by using the concat( ) and name( ) functions to contrive a new name based on the name of the current node. This is useful when you don't have the name of a node until you actually perform the transformation (at runtime).

You don't have to use an attribute value template in the value of name—you could use any legal XML name you want in the value. Computing the name, however, is one justification for using element. Another justification is using attribute sets, which you'll learn about presently. Otherwise, you might as well use a literal result element, but the choice remains yours.

The namespace attribute

element has two other attributes beside name: namespace and use-attribute-sets, which are optional. I'll discuss namespace here, and I'll explain how to work with use-attribute-sets in "Reusing a Set of Attributes," a little later in this chapter.

The namespace attribute identifies a namespace name to associate with the element. If element's name attribute contains a QName with a prefix, the processor will usually associate the namespace name in the namespace attribute with the prefix in the QName, though it is not required to do so (see Section 7.1.2 of the XSLT spec). You can use either a namespace URI in namespace or you can compute the namespace with an attribute value template. The stylesheet *namespace.xsl* uses a namespace URI:

```
<xsl:stylesheet version="1.0" xmlns:xsl="http://www.w3.org/1999/XSL/Transform">
<xsl:output method="xml" indent="yes"/>

<xsl:template match="/">
 <xsl:element name="doc:paragraph" namespace="http://www.example.com/documents">
  <xsl:apply-templates/>
 </xsl:element>
</xsl:template>

</xsl:stylesheet>
```

Apply this stylesheet to *element.xml*:

```
xalan element.xml namespace.xsl
```

and you will see what I'm talking about:

```
<?xml version="1.0" encoding="UTF-8"?>
<doc:paragraph xmlns:doc="http://www.example.com/documents">You can use the element
element to create elements on the result tree.</doc:paragraph>
```

When the XSLT processor encounters the namespace name *http://www.example.com/documents* in namespace and the QName doc:paragraph in name, it associates the prefix doc with the namespace name *http://www.example.com/documents* in the namespace declaration, as you can see. (I should say it *usually* associates the doc prefix with the namespace URI, unless there is a clash.)

Likewise, if you declare this namespace name and prefix on the document element in the stylesheet, as in *rootns.xsl*:

```
<xsl:stylesheet version="1.0" xmlns:xsl="http://www.w3.org/1999/XSL/Transform"
 xmlns:doc="http://www.example.com/documents">
<xsl:output method="xml" indent="yes"/>
```

```
<xsl:template match="/">
 <xsl:element name="doc:paragraph"><xsl:apply-templates/></xsl:element>
</xsl:template>

</xsl:stylesheet>
```

Transforming *element.xml* against *rootns.xsl* using:

```
xalan element.xml rootns.xsl
```

will produce the same result as transforming *element.xml* against *namespace.xsl*:

```
<?xml version="1.0" encoding="UTF-8"?>
<doc:paragraph xmlns:doc="http://www.example.com/documents">You can use the element
element to create elements on the result tree.</doc:paragraph>
```

This section has only covered a few basics about element. You will get to see element at work in a larger example in the later section, "One Final Example." Now let's add an attribute or two to the paragraph element with the attribute instruction.

Adding Attributes

To add a single, nonliteral attribute to paragraph in a result tree, all you have to do is add an XSLT attribute element as a child of element. The stylesheet *attribute.xsl* does just that:

```
<xsl:stylesheet version="1.0" xmlns:xsl="http://www.w3.org/1999/XSL/Transform">
<xsl:output method="xml" indent="yes"/>

<xsl:template match="/">
  <xsl:element name="paragraph">
   <xsl:attribute name="priority">medium</xsl:attribute>
    <xsl:apply-templates/>
  </xsl:element>
</xsl:template>

</xsl:stylesheet>
```

Like element, attribute can have name and namespace attributes. Again, the name attribute, which specifies the name of an attribute for the result tree, is required, while namespace is not. The namespace attribute works pretty much like it does in element. The values of both name and namespace can be computed by using an attribute value template, just as in element.

Apply *attribute.xml* (which contains no attributes) to *attribute.xsl* with:

```
xalan attribute.xml attribute.xsl
```

to produce a result with a priority attribute:

```
<?xml version="1.0" encoding="UTF-8"?>
<paragraph priority="medium">You can use the attribute element to create attributes
on the result tree.</paragraph>
```

The next stylesheet, *attributes.xsl*, adds two more attributes to paragraph for a total of three attributes. One of the additional attributes will have a namespace, and one will not:

```
<xsl:stylesheet version="1.0" xmlns:xsl="http://www.w3.org/1999/XSL/Transform">
<xsl:output method="xml" indent="yes"/>

<xsl:template match="/">
 <xsl:element name="paragraph">
  <xsl:attribute name="priority">medium</xsl:attribute>
  <xsl:attribute name="date">2003-09-23</xsl:attribute>
  <xsl:attribute name="doc:style" namespace="http://www.example.com/documents">
classic</xsl:attribute>
   <xsl:apply-templates/>
  </xsl:element>
 </xsl:template>

</xsl:stylesheet>
```

When transforming *attribute.xml* with *attributes.xsl*:

```
xalan attribute.xml attributes.xsl
```

it produces this result:

```
<?xml version="1.0" encoding="UTF-8"?>
<paragraph priority="medium" date="2003-09-23" xmlns:doc="http://www.example.com/
documents" doc:style="classic">You can use the attribute element to create attributes
on the result tree.</paragraph>
```

There is another way to specify multiple attributes besides listing them one after another: you can use an attribute set.

Reusing a Set of Attributes

The top-level attribute-set element in XSLT allows you to label a group of attributes with a name. Then you can reference and reuse that group of attributes by supplying the name in the use-attribute-sets attribute of element. The attribute element has a required name attribute, and it also has an optional use-attribute-sets attribute (such as element) so that you can chain attribute sets together. The next section, "Chaining attribute sets," shows you how.

The stylesheet *attribute-set.xsl* implements this feature:

```
<xsl:stylesheet version="1.0" xmlns:xsl="http://www.w3.org/1999/XSL/Transform">
<xsl:output method="xml" indent="yes"/>

<xsl:attribute-set name="paragraph">
 <xsl:attribute name="priority">medium</xsl:attribute>
 <xsl:attribute name="date">2003-09-23</xsl:attribute>
 <xsl:attribute name="doc:style" namespace="http://www.example.com/documents">
classic</xsl:attribute>
</xsl:attribute-set>
<xsl:template match="/">
```

```
  <xsl:element name="paragraph" use-attribute-sets="paragraph">
    <xsl:apply-templates/>
  </xsl:element>
</xsl:template>

</xsl:stylesheet>
```

The attribute-set element is a top-level element in XSLT, meaning that it is only allowed as a child of the stylesheet's document element. Also, the attribute-set element allows only attribute elements as children. This named group of attributes is linked to the element paragraph by the use-attribute-sets attribute. You can also see that even though an element and an attribute set have the same name (paragraph), it poses no naming conflict within XSLT.

If you process *attribute-set.xsl* against *attribute.xml* with:

```
xalan attribute.xml attribute-set.xsl
```

you will get about the same result as processing it against *attributes.xsl*:

```
<?xml version="1.0" encoding="UTF-8"?>
<paragraph priority="medium" date="2003-09-23" xmlns:doc="http://www.example.com/
document" doc:style="classic">You can use the attribute element to create attributes
on the result tree.</paragraph>
```

Chaining attribute sets

As I mentioned earlier, you can also chain attribute sets together. The stylesheet *chain.xsl* shows you how to do this:

```
<xsl:stylesheet version="1.0" xmlns:xsl="http://www.w3.org/1999/XSL/Transform">
<xsl:output method="xml" indent="yes"/>

<xsl:attribute-set name="doc" use-attribute-sets="paragraph">
 <xsl:attribute name="doc:style" namespace="http://www.example.com/documents">
classic</xsl:attribute>
</xsl:attribute-set>
<xsl:attribute-set name="paragraph">
 <xsl:attribute name="priority">medium</xsl:attribute>
 <xsl:attribute name="date">2003-09-23</xsl:attribute>
</xsl:attribute-set>

<xsl:template match="/">
 <xsl:element name="paragraph" use-attribute-sets="doc">
  <xsl:apply-templates/>
 </xsl:element>
</xsl:template>

</xsl:stylesheet>
```

This stylesheet has two attribute-set elements that are chained together by means of the use-attribute-sets attribute. The element definition links to the attribute set named doc, which in turn links to the attribute set named paragraph.

When you process these using:

```
xalan attribute.xml chain.xsl
```

the only difference you might see in the result is that the attributes may appear in a different order:

```
<?xml version="1.0" encoding="UTF-8"?>
<paragraph priority="medium" date="2003-09-23" xmlns:doc="http://www.example.com/
documents" doc:style="classic">You can use the element element to create elements on
the result tree.</paragraph>
```

This is not a problem because attributes are unordered in XML. Although a processor may attempt to keep track of the order of attributes, it is not obligated to do so by the XML 1.0 specification.

Finally, an attribute-set element need not have any content, that is, it does not have to have attribute children. This means that you can do the following (*chaining.xsl*):

```
<xsl:stylesheet version="1.0" xmlns:xsl="http://www.w3.org/1999/XSL/Transform">
<xsl:output method="xml" indent="yes"/>

<xsl:attribute-set name="para" use-attribute-sets="paragraph"/>
<xsl:attribute-set name="paragraph">
 <xsl:attribute name="priority">medium</xsl:attribute>
 <xsl:attribute name="date">2003-09-23</xsl:attribute>
 <xsl:attribute name="doc:style" namespace="http://www.example.com/documents">
classic</xsl:attribute>
</xsl:attribute-set>

<xsl:template match="/">
 <xsl:element name="paragraph" use-attribute-sets="para">
  <xsl:apply-templates/>
 </xsl:element>
</xsl:template>

</xsl:stylesheet>
```

The attribute-set element named para does not have any attribute children; however, it links to the attribute-set named paragraph with its use-attribute-sets attribute. This has the effect of, in essence, renaming paragraph to para and producing the same result as *chain.xsl*. Here's the command:

```
xalan attribute.xml chaining.xsl
```

Another thing to keep in mind is that use-attribute-sets is not a required attribute, neither on attribute-set nor on element. So, a stylesheet like *unchain.xsl* is legal:

```
<xsl:stylesheet version="1.0" xmlns:xsl="http://www.w3.org/1999/XSL/Transform">
<xsl:output method="xml" indent="yes"/>

<xsl:attribute-set name="para">
 <xsl:attribute name="doc:style" namespace="http://www.example.com/documents">
classic</xsl:attribute>
</xsl:attribute-set>
```

```
<xsl:attribute-set name="paragraph">
 <xsl:attribute name="priority">medium</xsl:attribute>
 <xsl:attribute name="date">2003-09-23</xsl:attribute>
</xsl:attribute-set>

<xsl:template match="/">
 <xsl:element name="paragraph" use-attribute-sets="para">
  <xsl:apply-templates/>
 </xsl:element>
</xsl:template>

</xsl:stylesheet>
```

And when processed against *attribute.xml* with:

```
xalan attribute.xml unchain.xsl
```

it produces a result with only one attribute:

```
<?xml version="1.0" encoding="UTF-8"?>
<paragraph xmlns:doc="http://www.example.com/documents" doc:style="classic">You can
use the attribute element to create attributes on the result tree.</paragraph>
```

As you may have guessed already, you can use `attribute-sets` creatively to add attributes to, or omit them from, a result tree.

Outputting Comments

Comments allow you to hide advisory text in an XML document. You can also use comments to label documents, or portions of them, which can be useful for debugging. When an XML processor sees a comment, it may ignore or discard it, or it can make the text content of comments available for other kinds of processing. The text in comments is not the same as the text found between element tags, that is, it is not character data. As such, comments can contain characters that are otherwise forbidden, like < and &. XML comments are formed like this:

```
<!-- This element holds the current date & time -->
```

Comments are markup and can go anywhere in an XML document, except directly inside the pointy brackets of other kinds of markup. This means, for example, that you can't place a comment inside of a start tag of an element.

The only legal XML characters that a comment must not contain are the sequence of two hyphen characters (--), as this pair of characters signals the end of a comment. Other than that, you are free to use any legal XML character in a comment. (Again, to check on what characters are legal in XML, and where they are legal, see Sections 2.2 through 2.4 of the XML specification.)

To insert a comment into a result tree, you can use the XSLT instruction element comment, as demonstrated in the *comment.xsl* stylesheet:

```
<xsl:stylesheet version="1.0"
  xmlns:xsl="http://www.w3.org/1999/XSL/Transform">
<xsl:output method="xml" indent="yes"/>

<xsl:template match="/">
 <xsl:comment> comment &amp; msg element </xsl:comment>
 <msg><xsl:apply-templates/></msg>
</xsl:template>

</xsl:stylesheet>
```

The output method is XML. If it were text, the comment would not show up in the output. Because comments in XML can contain markup characters, you can include an ampersand in a comment, among otherwise naughty characters, though it must first be represented by an entity reference (&) in the stylesheet.

Process this stylesheet against *comment.xml* with Xalan:

```
xalan comment.xml comment.xsl
```

You will get the following results:

```
<?xml version="1.0" encoding="UTF-8"?>
<!-- comment & msg element -->
<msg>You can insert comments in your output.</msg>
```

Outputting Processing Instructions

It must come as no surprise that you can add processing instructions, or PIs, to the result tree with the processing-instruction element. This element is formed like this:

```
<xsl:processing-instruction name="xml-stylesheet">href="new.css"
    type="text/css"</xsl:processing-instruction>
```

A processing-instruction element requires one attribute, name, which identifies the target name for the PI. The value of this attribute must be an NCName, and, as such, must not be a QName and cannot contain a colon. In other words, you can't qualify a target name with a namespace.

The content of the processing-instruction element contains the pair of pseudo-attributes href and type that are necessary to apply the CSS stylesheet *processing.css* to the resulting XML document:

```
paragraph {font-size: 24pt; font-family: serif}
code {font-family: monospace}
```

These rules will apply to the paragraph and code elements in the result tree. Provided that you view the result tree in a browser, any paragraph elements will be rendered with a best-fit serif font, in 24-point type, while any code elements will be rendered in a monospace font. (Courier is an example of a monospace font.) You'll get a chance to see the effects of these style rules later on in this section.

In the example that follows, I'll discuss more than just PIs. I'll also talk about a different kind of content in an XML document, and why you have to use more than one template to get at it. Consider for a moment the following XML document, *processing.xml*, which contains mixed content:

```
<?xml version="1.0"?>

<message>You can add processing instructions to a document with the <courier>
processing-instruction</courier> element.</message>
```

Mixed Content

The message element in *processing.xml* contains *mixed content*. Mixed content freely mixes character data and element content together. That's why you see tags for the courier element mixed with text in message. Any elements that appear in mixed content are allowed to appear in any order, although they, of course, must also be well-formed. In this context, well-formed elements must either have both start and end tags or must be empty element tags, and the characters used for text and names must follow XML 1.0 rules. (See Section 3.2.2 of the XML specification for more details about mixed content.)

processing.xsl handles the mixed content in *processing.xml*:

```
<xsl:stylesheet version="1.0" xmlns:xsl="http://www.w3.org/1999/XSL/Transform">
<xsl:output method="xml" indent="yes"/>

<xsl:template match="/">
 <xsl:processing-instruction name="xml-stylesheet">href="processing.css" type="text/
css"</xsl:processing-instruction>
 <xsl:element name="doc">
  <xsl:element name="paragraph"><xsl:apply-templates/></xsl:element>
 </xsl:element>
</xsl:template>

<xsl:template match="courier">
 <xsl:element name="code"><xsl:apply-templates/></xsl:element>
</xsl:template>

</xsl:stylesheet>
```

Using Multiple Template Rules

For the first time in this book, you are seeing a stylesheet (*processing.xsl*) that has more than one template rule. (Remember, a template rule consists of a pattern to match and a constructor telling the processor what to do when the pattern is matched.) The way you design your templates tells the XSLT processor what to look for in a document, and then what to do if and when it finds what you've asked it to find.

In the stylesheet *processing.xsl*, the first template matches the root node in the document using /. When the processor encounters apply-templates in this template, it matches any children of the root node in the source. When applied to *processing.xml*, the built-in templates for elements and text match the message element and its child text content.

The next template rule is invoked whenever it encounters a courier element in the source tree. There is only one courier element in *processing.xml*, so it is only invoked once. If there were more courier elements, it would be invoked for each occurrence of courier. This template also has an apply-templates child, which uses the built-in templates to find the text content of courier (you could try value-of here with the same outcome). As a result, the processor surrounds the character content of courier with code elements, and returns control to the template that invoked it.

The original template, seeing nothing else to do, picks up where the other template left off and takes care of its other work. With the processor holding onto the work that the other template did in a temporary tree, the built-in template for text nodes yanks the character data out of message and surrounds it with paragraph tags.

Somewhere along the way, it surrounds all the elements with the new root element doc. It creates a new PI, too, based on the instructions given by the processing-instruction element. Once that work is done, and the XSLT processor sees that there is nothing left to do, it writes its work out to the result tree, pulls down the shades, locks the door, and calls it quits.

What can go in a template rule?

It's obvious that the template element can hold a template rule, but other XSLT elements can hold templates as well. Generally speaking, a template consists of one or more XSLT elements that can create a result tree. These templates are not template rules *per se* because they don't have to match a pattern—they just contain sequence constructors. Literal result elements and literal text, as well as the apply-templates, attribute, element, comment, processing-instruction, and text elements can all be contained in templates.

The 15 elements that can contain templates (but don't match patterns) are:

- attribute
- comment
- copy
- element
- fallback
- for-each
- if
- message
- otherwise
- param
- processing-instruction
- template
- variable
- when
- with-param

A lot of elements in this list are probably new to you. It would consume pages to tell you what elements can go where in all possible templates, so for now please take this discussion of what templates are on faith. The concept of template rules and templates will continue to unfold throughout the book, all in due time. Meanwhile, Appendix A of Doug Tidwell's *XSLT*, also published by O'Reilly, provides an excellent XSLT reference and lists in detail what elements can contain, including those that follow in the template category.

Creating the PI and Putting It to Work

Now you can run the processor and see for yourself what the result actually is:

```
xalan -o proc.xml processing.xml processing.xsl
```

Here is what *proc.xml* looks like:

```
<?xml version="1.0" encoding="UTF-8"?>
<?xml-stylesheet href="processing.css" type="text/css"?>
<doc>
<paragraph>You can add processing instructions to a document with the <code>
processing-instruction</code> element.</paragraph>
</doc>
```

Xalan placed the XML stylesheet PI in the document prolog (before the document element doc) because of where the processing-instruction element was placed in the first template. PIs can go anywhere in an XML document except inside other markup, so you can move the processing-instruction element to the second template if you want, and see where it comes out in the output.

The problem is, if the stylesheet PI does not appear in the prolog, the rendering engine (a browser in this case) won't apply the *processing.css* stylesheet. The point is that the order of templates, and the order of the content of templates, matters in regard to the output of those templates.

Figure 2-3 shows *proc.xml* displayed in IE.

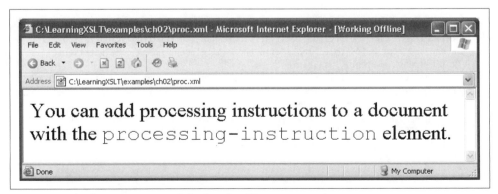

Figure 2-3. The document proc.xml displayed in IE using processing.css

One Final Example

Finally, to wrap things up, here is an example stylesheet that shows you, once again, how to perform most of the techniques discussed in this chapter. The example starts out with the rather short document containing mixed content, *final.xml*:

```
<?xml version="1.0"?>

<message>You can add processing instructions to a document with the <courier>
processing-instruction</courier> element.</message>
```

There isn't much to it, but you can augment *final.xml* with the well-rounded XSLT stylesheet, *final.xsl*:

```
<xsl:stylesheet version="1.0" xmlns:xsl="http://www.w3.org/1999/XSL/Transform">
<xsl:output method="xml" indent="yes"/>

<xsl:attribute-set name="atts">
 <xsl:attribute name="noteworthy">true</xsl:attribute>
 <xsl:attribute name="priority">medium</xsl:attribute>
</xsl:attribute-set>

<xsl:template match="/">
 <xsl:processing-instruction name="xml-stylesheet">href="final.css" type="text/css"
</xsl:processing-instruction>
 <xsl:comment> final.xml as processed with final.xsl </xsl:comment>
 <doc>
  <heading>Final Summary</heading>
  <paragraph>Following is a summary of how you can build documents with XSLT:
</paragraph>
  <paragraph>You can add text either literally or with the <code>text</code> element.
</paragraph>
  <paragraph>You can use literal result elements in stylesheets.</paragraph>
  <xsl:element name="paragraph">You can use <xsl:element name="code">element
</xsl:element> elements in stylesheets.</xsl:element>
  <xsl:comment> you can add a line break &amp; some spaces with the text element
</xsl:comment>
  <xsl:text>

  </xsl:text>
  <xsl:element name="paragraph"><xsl:attribute name="noteworthy">true</xsl:attribute>
You can add attributes to elements with the <xsl:element name="code">attribute
</xsl:element> element.</xsl:element>
  <xsl:element name="paragraph" use-attribute-sets="atts">You can even add sets of
attributes to elements with the <xsl:element name="code">attribute-set</xsl:element>
top-level element.</xsl:element>
  <paragraph>You can add comments with the <code>comment</code> element.</paragraph>
  <xsl:element name="paragraph"><xsl:text>And last but not least: </xsl:text>
<xsl:apply-templates select="message"/></xsl:element>
 </doc>
</xsl:template>
```

```
<xsl:template match="courier">
 <xsl:element name="code"><xsl:apply-templates/></xsl:element>
</xsl:template>

</xsl:stylesheet>
```

Processing *final.xml* with *final.xsl*, you can serialize the result tree and place it in a file:

```
xalan -o finally.xml final.xml final.xsl
```

The XML document *finally.xml* turns out like this:

```
<?xml version="1.0" encoding="UTF-8"?>
<?xml-stylesheet href="final.css" type="text/css"?>

<!-- final.xml as processed with final.xsl -->
<doc>
<heading>Final Summary</heading>
<paragraph>Following is a summary of how you can build documents with XSLT:
</paragraph>
<paragraph>You can add text either literally or with the <code>text</code> element.
</paragraph>
<paragraph>You can use literal result elements in stylesheets.</paragraph>
<paragraph>You can use <code>element</code> elements in stylesheets.</paragraph>
<!-- you can add a line break & some spaces with the text element -->

    <paragraph noteworthy="true">You can add attributes to elements with the <code>
attribute</code> element.</paragraph>
<paragraph noteworthy="true" priority="medium">You can even add sets of attributes to
elements with the <code>attribute-set</code> top-level element.</paragraph>
<paragraph>You can add comments with the <code>comment</code> element.</paragraph>
<paragraph>And last but not least: You can add processing instructions to a document
with the <code>processing-instruction</code> element.</paragraph>
</doc>
```

When *finally.xml* is displayed in Mozilla, it depends on the CSS stylesheet *final.css* to figure out how to render heading, paragraph, and code elements:

```
heading {display: block; font-size: 16pt; font-family: sans-serif; margin: 8pt 15pt}
paragraph {display: block; font-size: 12pt; font-family: serif; margin: 5pt 15pt}
code {display: inline; font-size: 11pt; font-family: monospace}
```

The display property with value of block gives the heading and paragraph elements a block- or box-like appearance on the browser canvas or rendering space. The display value of inline for code means that elements should be displayed inline with other text. The sans-serif font family for heading indicates that you want the browser to select a sans-serif font on a best-match basis, just as with monospace for code elements. The margin property sets the top and right margins for the element to either 8 and 15 points, or 5 and 15 points, respectively.

With this CSS applied in Mozilla, *finally.xml* is displayed in Figure 2-4.

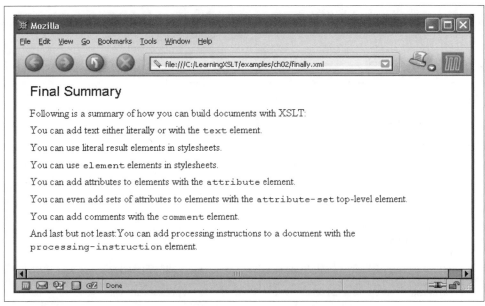

Figure 2-4. The document finally.xml displayed in Mozilla with final.css

Summary

In this chapter, you have learned the techniques that allow you to build a new result tree document. You learned about literal result elements and the XSLT instruction elements text, element, attribute, attribute-set, comment, and processing-instruction. You also learned about XHTML's relationship to HTML, and came to grips with some of the fundamentals of how template rules are evaluated and processed (more to come on that topic). You are now ready to explore ways that you can finely tune a result tree with the output element. You'll find out how in Chapter 3.

Controlling Output

Chapter 3 shows you how to control the XML, HTML, and text output of an XSLT processor using the XSLT top-level element output. You have seen the output element in previous examples, but I have only discussed 2 of output's 10 attributes so far. I'll talk about each of output's attributes in this chapter.

In this chapter, I'll talk about the results you can expect from different output methods in XML, HTML, text, or custom output. I'll also cover indentation, how to manage XML declarations, document type declarations, CDATA sections, and media types. For more detail, cross-reference this chapter with Section 16 of the XSLT specification.

 Be aware that not all XSLT processors adhere strictly to the output element. There are models in which the XSLT processor has no control over the final serialization of the output because the output values are overridden. You will see an example of this type of model when you use the Moxie processor, discussed in Chapter 17.

Multiple Output Elements

You can use multiple instances of the output element in a stylesheet. If there is more than one occurrence, all the attributes of the output elements are combined when the stylesheet is processed, as if there were only one instance of output. If any of the attributes conflict—for example, there were more than one method attribute, each with a different value—the value that is in the last occurrence of the attribute wins. This holds true unless other stylesheets are imported into your current stylesheet. XSLT has a mechanism for importing other stylesheets and then assigning priorities for the imported stylesheets. Don't worry about that now. I'll discuss what happens when you import documents in Chapter 13.

The Output Method

As you have already seen, the output element has a method attribute. This attribute indicates explicitly the kind of output you want the XSLT processor to produce, namely, XML, HTML, or plain text. These three amigos—the attribute values xml, html, and text—should always be lowercase when used as values for method. (Again, XSLT 2.0 will also support the xhtml output method.)

The Default Output Methods

If you don't assign a value to method, you get a default output method depending on what a stylesheet produces. The default output method for XSLT is XML unless the document element in the result is html. In such a case, the default output method is HTML. The tag name html can be in uppercase, lowercase, or mixed case, but it must not have a namespace URI associated with it (no xmlns attribute).

Default HTML output

To understand how default HTML works, consider the document *name.xml* found in *examples/ch03* (this is where all the examples files mentioned in this chapter are found):

```
<name>
 <last>Churchill</last>
 <first>Winston</first>
</name>
```

Then look at *default-html.xsl* that produces HTML using literal result elements:

```
<xsl:stylesheet version="1.0" xmlns:xsl="http://www.w3.org/1999/XSL/Transform">


<xsl:template match="name">
 <html>
  <body>
  <p><xsl:apply-templates select="last"/></p>
  <p><xsl:apply-templates select="first"/></p>
  </body>
 </html>
</xsl:template>

</xsl:stylesheet>
```

Notice that there is no output element in *default-html.xsl* to tell the processor explicitly what the output method is. Apply this stylesheet to *name.xml* with Xalan:

```
xalan -m name.xml default-html.xsl
```

and it will produce a default HTML result:

```
<html>
<head>
</head>
<body>
<p>Churchill</p>
<p>Winston</p>
</body>
</html>
```

The -m command-line option suppresses the META tag that Xalan would normally produce. The result does not have an XML declaration because Xalan evaluated the result as HTML, as it should. The result is also indented (line breaks at start tags, but zero space) because if the output method is HTML, a default value of yes for indent is assumed as if an output element with indent="yes" attribute were present.

With Xalan, you can also control the amount of indentation from the command line by using the -i option with an integer. For example, if you want to indent the output by three spaces, type this command:

```
xalan -i 3 -m name.xml default-html.xsl
```

The indented output will look like this:

```
<html>
    <body>
        <p>Churchill</p>
        <p>Winston</p>
    </body>
</html>
```

The child elements body and p are nicely indented by three spaces. This indentation feature of Xalan is not specified by XSLT itself, but it is nice to have nevertheless. You can read more about the default HTML output method in Section 16.2 of the XSLT specification.

Default XML output

Now, check out *default-xml.xsl*, which produces a default XML result using literal result elements:

```
<xsl:stylesheet version="1.0" xmlns:xsl="http://www.w3.org/1999/XSL/Transform">


<xsl:template match="name">
 <name>
  <family><xsl:apply-templates select="last"/></family>
  <given><xsl:apply-templates select="first"/></given>
 </name>
</xsl:template>

</xsl:stylesheet>
```

Applying *default-xml.xsl* to *name.xml* with Xalan:

```
xalan name.xml default-xml.xsl
```

will produce the following result:

```
<?xml version="1.0" encoding="UTF-8"?>
<name><family>Churchill</family><given>Winston</given></name>
```

The default XML output method for Xalan kicks out an XML declaration with an encoding declaration for UTF-8 (more about this in the later section "The encoding declaration"). The elements are output with no indentation added because the default for indent is no for XML output (as if an output element were present with indent="no").

You can use the default methods for HTML and XML, but it is always cleaner, and more apparent to other humans reading your stylesheet, if you specify the method attribute explicitly with a value of xml or html. (You can read even more about the default XML output method in Section 16.1 of the XSLT specification.)

Outputting XML

With the XML output method, whether declared explicitly or by default, a compliant XSLT processor produces well-formed XML as output. As you already know, well-formed XML follows the syntax rules outlined in the XML specification—rules such as matching start and end tags, matching quotes around attribute values, proper nesting of elements, and so forth. For example, if you create XML as you did in Chapter 2, the processor will make sure that the XML is well-formed. If it is not, the XSLT processor will report any errors.

The output element helps you to control a number of features relating XML output, including the XML declaration, document type declarations, and CDATA sections, all of which are discussed in the sections that follow.

The XML Declaration

As explained in Chapter 1, the XML declaration is optional. You don't have to use it, except under certain circumstances, such as when an encoding declaration is imperative. XSLT allows you to have control over the XML declaration with the output element. With output, you can keep XML declarations from being written to output, change version information, control the encoding declaration, and monitor the standalone declaration. I'll cover all of these features step-by-step in the sections that follow.

Omitting the XML declaration

Most XSLT processors automatically write an XML declaration at the top of the result. If the XML declaration is not essential to your output, you can turn this behavior off by giving output's omit-xml-declaration attribute a value of yes; by default, the value is no when the attribute is not present. The `omit-xml-declaration` attribute is used in *omit.xsl*:

```
<xsl:stylesheet version="1.0" xmlns:xsl="http://www.w3.org/1999/XSL/Transform">
<xsl:output method="xml" indent="yes"/>
<xsl:output omit-xml-declaration="yes"/>
<xsl:template match="name">
 <name>
  <family><xsl:apply-templates select="last"/></family>
  <given><xsl:apply-templates select="first"/></given>
 </name>
</xsl:template>

</xsl:stylesheet>
```

This stylesheet uses two output elements. You could merge them into one output element if you wish. The only reason I use two output elements in this example is because it makes a cleaner line break this way!

When applied to *name.xml* using:

```
xalan name.xml omit.xsl
```

the XML declaration is dropped, as you can see in the output:

```
<name>
<family>Churchill</family>
<given>Winston</given>
</name>
```

The encoding declaration

XML 1.0 supports characters or atomic units of text as described in ISO/IEC 10646-1:1993 Information technology—Universal Multiple-Octet Coded Character Set (UCS)—Part 1: Architecture and Basic Multilingual Plane, plus its seven amendments (see *http://www.iso.ch*). The mission of the UCS standard is to identify all characters in all writing systems in the world. Since XML 1.0 became a W3C recommendation, ISO/IEC 10646-1:1993 has advanced to ISO/IEC 10646-1:2000.

Unicode is a parallel standard developed by the Unicode Consortium (see *http://www.unicode.org*). XML 1.0 likewise supports Unicode Version 2.0, but Unicode has recently advanced to Version 4.0, so there are some differences in what XML 1.0 supports and in what the latest version of Unicode supports.

Both ISO/IEC 10646-1 and Unicode assign the same values and descriptions for each character, but Unicode defines some semantics for the characters that ISO/IEC 10646-1 does not. In this book, I'll generally refer to Unicode, although Unicode and ISO/IEC 10646-1 are an inexact synonym.

Good background reading on Unicode and character sets is Mike Brown's XML tutorial at *http://www.skew.org/xml/tutorial*. To look up character charts, see Kosta Kostis' charts at *http://www.kostis.net/charsets/*.

Each character in Unicode is represented by a unique, hexadecimal (base 16) number. The first 128 characters in Unicode are the same characters in US-ASCII or Latin-1 (ISO-8859-1), which surely makes the transition to Unicode easier to follow. The numbers that represent these characters are called *code points*.

Code Points

You got a very brief introduction to the concept of character encoding in Chapter 2. An XML document, whether in a file or in a stream, is really just a series of bytes. A byte is a chunk of bits (ones and zeroes)—usually eight. When you assign a character encoding to a document, you express an intent to the processing software to transform the bytes in the document into a sequence of characters that another processor can recognize.

Character encoding is the mapping of binary values to code points or character positions. Let me explain what code points are. Back in the 1960s, ANSI created the ASCII or US-ASCII character-encoding format. US-ASCII represents only 128 characters, numbered 0–127, with each numbered position representing a code point. In their binary forms, every US-ASCII character is represented by only 7 bits—a 7-bit byte rather than an 8-bit byte (octet). Other 7-bit encoding forms were created in other parts of the world at this time as well, not just in the U.S.

The uppercase letter *A* in US-ASCII, for example, is represented by the 7 bits 1000001 and is mapped to the code point 65 (decimal or integer) or 41 in hexadecimal. So the character-encoding scheme we call US-ASCII maps the code point 65 to the 7-bit binary representation 1000001. Character sets map integers to graphic character representations—the US-ASCII character set maps the integer 65 to the character A, for example.

But 7-bits can only represent 128 distinct values (the highest 7-bit binary number 1111111 equals the decimal equivalent 127). There are thousands of characters in human writing systems beyond ordinary, provincial 128-character US-ASCII. So if you want more characters, such as 256 rather than 128, you need to bump up your binary numbers from 7 bits to 8 bits.

ISO/IEC 8859. ISO-8859-1, commonly called Latin-1, represents 256 Western European characters, numbered 0–255, using 8-bit bytes or octets. It was originally specified by the European Computer Manufacturers Association (ECMA) in the 1980s and is currently defined there as ECMA-94 (see *http://www.ecma-international.org*). This standard is also endorsed by ISO and is specified in ISO/IEC 8859-1:1998 Information technology—8-bit single-byte graphic character sets—Part 1: Latin alphabet No. 1 (see *http://www.iso.ch*). ISO-8859-1 is only the beginning: there are actually 15 character sets in this family. These character sets helped to unify earlier 7-bit efforts. All 15 of these 8-bit character sets are specified by ISO and are listed in Table 3-1.

Table 3-1. ISO 8859 specifications

ISO standard	Description	Character set name
ISO/IEC 8859-1:1998	Part 1, Latin 1	ISO-8859-1
ISO/IEC 8859-2:1999	Part 2, Latin 2	ISO-8859-2
ISO/IEC 8859-3:1999	Part 3, Latin 3	ISO-8859-3
ISO/IEC 8859-4:1998	Part 4, Latin 4	ISO-8859-4
ISO/IEC 8859-5:1998	Part 5, Cyrillic	ISO-8859-5
ISO/IEC 8859-6:1996	Part 6, Arabic	ISO-8859-6
ISO 8859-7:1987	Part 7, Greek	ISO-8859-7
ISO/IEC 8859-8:1999	Part 8, Hebrew	ISO-8859-8
ISO/IEC 8859-9:1999	Part 9, Latin 5	ISO-8859-9
ISO/IEC 8859-10:1998	Part 10, Latin 6	ISO-8859-10
ISO/IEC 8859-11:2001	Part 11, Thai	ISO-8859-11
ISO/IEC 8859-13:1998	Part 13, Latin 7	ISO-8859-13
ISO/IEC 8859-14:1998	Part 14, Latin 8 (Celtic)	ISO-8859-14
ISO/IEC 8859-15:1999	Part 15, Latin 9	ISO-8859-15
ISO/IEC 8859-16:2001	Part 16, Latin 10	ISO-8859-16

Using octets to represent single characters expands the limit to 256 characters. The ISO 8859 character sets reuse the code points 0–255 for each part. Part 1 assigns the small Latin letter ÿ (y with dieresis) to code point 255 but the same code point 255 is assigned to the ѕ (Cyrillic small letter *dzhe*) in Part 5. Unicode avoids code point conflicts by assigning a unique number to each character. Unicode accomplishes this by not limiting character definitions to a single octet.

UTF-8 and UTF-16. XML processors are required to support both UTF-8 and UTF-16 character encodings. These encodings provide different ways of representing Unicode characters in binary form. (UTF stands for *UCS Transformation Format.*) UTF-8 is not limited to a fixed-length character encoding but can use between one and six bytes to represent Unicode characters. Unicode code points in the range of 0–255 are represented with one octet, those in the range of 256–2047 are represented with two octets, those in the range of 2048–65535 are represented with three octets, and so forth. It uses a special encoding scheme to get the most out of the least bits, using the first octet of a sequence of more than one octet to indicate how many octets are in the sequence. (See *http://www.ietf.org/rfc/rfc2279.txt.*)

UTF-16 uses a minimum of two octets to represent characters and, if the character cannot be represented with two octets, it uses four octets. It also uses a special encoding scheme (see *http://www.ietf.org/rfc/rfc2279.txt*), but if you are using only Latin characters, UTF-16 characters can take up more space when they don't need to. For example, the letter *A* would only take one octet in UTF-8 but would take two in UTF-16. On the other hand, a character in the higher ranges that might take six octets in UTF-8 would take at most four octets in UTF-16. UTF-8 is a good choice for Latin alphabets, and UTF-16 is good for other than the simplest Chinese, Japanese, and Korean characters.

The Byte Order Mark. A Byte Order Mark, or BOM, is a special space character (Unicode character FEFF) that is used only as an encoding signature. If an XML document is UTF-16, it must begin with a BOM; if it is UTF-8, it may begin with a BOM. If the document is not UTF-8 or UTF-16, the character encoding must be declared. You can also declare UTF-8 or UTF-16 encoding explicitly in an XML declaration. (See Section 4.3.3 of the XML specification.)

XML processors may support other encodings such as US-ASCII, ISO-8859-1, or Shift_JIS (Japanese). The Internet Assigned Numbers Authority keeps track of encoding names and publishes them at *http://www.iana.org/assignments/character-sets*. You can use your own private encoding name if you start it with x-, but you would have to write your own code to process it.

Unicode and the Command Shell Window

In a shell or command prompt window, it's difficult, if not impossible, to see the difference between one kind of character encoding and another. To show you the effect of this, apply the stylesheet *encoding.xsl* to *name.xml* with Xalan:

```
xalan name.xml encoding.xsl
```

Here's *encoding.xsl*:

```
<xsl:stylesheet version="1.0" xmlns:xsl="http://www.w3.org/1999/XSL/Transform">

<xsl:output method="xml" indent="yes"/>
<xsl:output encoding="UTF-16"/>

<xsl:template match="name">
 <name>
  <family><xsl:apply-templates select="last"/></family>
  <given><xsl:apply-templates select="first"/></given>
 </name>
</xsl:template>

</xsl:stylesheet>
```

The result in a Windows command prompt window, which doesn't handle UTF-16 properly, will look something like this:

```
■< ? x m l   v e r s i o n = " 1 . 0 "   e n c o d i n g = " U T F - 1 6 " ? >
< n a m e >
< f a m i l y > A s a m i < / f a m i l y >
< g i v e n > T o m o h a r u < / g i v e n >
< / n a m e >
```

The dark block at the beginning of the document shows you where the BOM is. Even though the BOM is a zero-width space, the code page used by the Windows command prompt represents it differently. A code page is a Microsoft character set, and if your computer is configured for U.S. English, the code page is likely to be 437. Code page 437, using the Lucida Console font, interprets 8 bits of the character (FE in hexadecimal, 11111110 in binary, and 254 in decimal) as a black square. That is what is mapped to the character in the code page (see *http://www.kostis.net/charsets/cp437.htm*). In Unicode, the black square is 25A0 in hexadecimal (see Figure 3-1), and it is 9632 in decimal.

Changing the Code Page in Windows

Here is how to test what code page your window is using at a Windows command prompt (such as on Windows XP Professional). Enter the command:

```
mode con: cp
```

You can use the mode command to display the status of your system, among other things. If you change the code page to 850 (multilingual Latin 1) with this command:

```
mode con: cp select=850
```

you then transform *name.xml* with *encoding.xsl*. The result in your command prompt window will look different. To change your code page back to 437, type this command:

```
mode con: cp select=437
```

Where did that extra space come from in the output of *encoding.xsl*? Because you are using UTF-16 encoding, each character in the output is represented by two octets. Code page 437 interprets the other 8 bits (FF in hexadecimal, 11111111 in binary, and 255 in decimal) as nonbreaking space. Unicode numbers the nonbreaking space as A0 in hexadecimal and as 160 in decimal. That's where the extra space is coming from. This incompatibility between encoding schemes and the display of characters in a shell window or text editor is the cause of a lot of confusion. It is good to be aware of it. Character Map and UniPad are tools that can help analyze Unicode characters.

Using Character Map and UniPad

The Windows Character Map utility allows you to select and copy characters in available fonts for use in other applications, but it also helps you quickly identify the Unicode code point and names for characters. Notice the lower-left corner in Figure 3-1, which identifies the Unicode code point in hexadecimal (U+25A0), plus the character name (Black Square). Figure 3-1 shows what the Character Map looks like in Windows XP Professional.

Looking at a File with xxd

If you are running Linux or Cygwin on a Windows box (see *http://www.cygwin.com*), you probably have the *xxd* utility available to you on the command line. This utility can examine a file and let you see it in hexadecimal or binary form, which may be of use to you with regard to encoding as you can look at a file character-by-character. For example, if you execute the following transformation:

```
xalan -o dump.xml name.xml encoding.xsl
```

the result of the transformation is saved to the file *dump.xml*. You can look at *dump.xml* with *xxd* using this command line:

```
xxd -g 1 dump.xml
```

By default, each line of output from *xxd* is numbered in hexadecimal, with the first line beginning with an octet numbered 0000000 and the last one numbered 000000f (0–15 in decimal). Following that, each character is printed in hexadecimal, with the normal Latin characters shown on the far right. If the character can't be represented in ASCII, it is represented by a dot (.) on the right side.

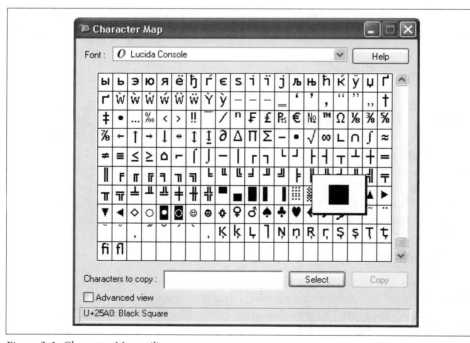

Figure 3-1. Character Map utility

Another useful program is Sharmahd Computing's SC UniPad, a Unicode text editor available for free download from *http://www.unipad.org*. Among other things, Uni-Pad shows you the Unicode value of a character based on the position of the cursor in the edit window. Figure 3-2 shows you *dump.xml* in a UniPad window. Note the Unicode character information in the status bar. A few things the status bar tells you is the Unicode code point for the character where the cursor is located (U+003C) and the character's descriptive name (LESS-THAN SIGN). It indicates the encoding (UTF-16 (L) for little endian), and tells you that the byte-order mark is present (BOM).

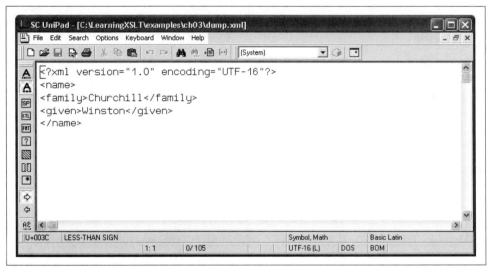

Figure 3-2. dump.xml in UniPad

Entities and text declarations

A text declaration is similar to an XML declaration, but it does not have to provide version information. Text declarations are used for separate, external documents called *entities*. If an external entity is not in UTF-8 or UTF-16, the external entity must have a text declaration (see Section 4.3.3 of the XML specification). To understand what an external entity is, look at the document *entity.xml*:

```
<?xml version="1.0" encoding="ISO-8859-1"?>
<?xml-stylesheet href="entity.css" type="text/css"?>
<!DOCTYPE name [
<!ENTITY first SYSTEM "name.ent">
]>

<name>
 <last>Churchill</last>
 <first>&first;</first>
</name>
```

This document contains an internal document type definition, or DTD, called an *internal subset*. It's internal to the XML document that it qualifies. The entity is declared in the internal subset (note the keyword ENTITY). You'll learn about DTDs in "Controlling Document Type Declarations," later in this chapter. For right now, I'll focus only on the entity.

The entity is an external, parsed entity. *External* means that the content of the entity is stored in an external file. *Parsed* means that the entity is made of text that may be parsed. The name of this entity is first. The SYSTEM keyword indicates that the entity is in a named file, and the name of that file is *name.ent*. The first element contains a (&first;) that, when processed, will be expanded or replaced with the contents of the file *name.ent*:

```
<?xml encoding="ISO-8859-1"?>Randolph
```

The external entity *name.ent* contains a text declaration that has an encoding declaration with the encoding name ISO-8859-1. It looks like an XML declaration, but the version information is not required (nor is it forbidden). If you display *entity.xml* in IE, at least in Version 6.0 or greater, the entity will be expanded so that the content of the first element will be *Randolph*.

Figure 3-3 shows what *entity.xml* looks like in IE when using the stylesheet *entity.css*:

```
name {font-size: 18pt}
last {display:inline}
```

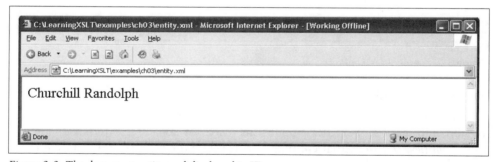

Figure 3-3. The document entity.xml displayed in IE

You'll read more about entities in "The standalone declaration" to follow. For more information on text declarations, see Section 4.3.1 of the XML specification.

The standalone declaration

The *standalone declaration* in an XML declaration indicates explicitly whether an XML document depends on external markup declarations. An element type declaration, such as <!ELEMENT family (#PCDATA)>, is an example of a markup declaration.

Markup declarations are stored in DTDs. The following document, *standalone.xml*, states bluntly that it does not depend on external documents:

```
<?xml version="1.0" encoding="UTF-8" standalone="yes"?>

<name>
 <last>Churchill</last>
 <first>Winston</first>
</name>
```

If, however, you apply the stylesheet *notalone.xsl*:

```
<xsl:stylesheet version="1.0" xmlns:xsl="http://www.w3.org/1999/XSL/Transform">

<xsl:output method="xml" indent="yes"/>
<xsl:output doctype-system="notalone.dtd"/>
<xsl:output standalone="no"/>

<xsl:template match="name">
 <name>
  <family><xsl:apply-templates select="last"/></family>
  <given><xsl:apply-templates select="first"/></given>
 </name>
</xsl:template>

</xsl:stylesheet>
```

to *standalone.xml*, using:

```
xalan -o notalone.xml standalone.xml notalone.xsl
```

the value of the standalone declaration is changed from yes to no in the output document *notalone.xml*, and a document type declaration is also added:

```
<?xml version="1.0" encoding="UTF-8" standalone="no"?>
<!DOCTYPE name SYSTEM "notalone.dtd">
<name>
<family>Churchill</family>
<given>Winston</given>
</name>
```

The DTD *notalone.dtd* contains three markup declarations, all for elements:

```
<!ELEMENT name (family, given)>
<!ELEMENT family (#PCDATA)>
<!ELEMENT given (#PCDATA)>
```

You'll learn more about the document type declaration later in this chapter in "Controlling Document Type Declarations."

It is important for you to know—though you have probably already realized it—that standalone declarations are not required. They may be useful in some applications because the XML declaration must be on the first line in a document, and so information about whether the document has dependencies is available to applications early on.

If a document declares standalone="no", but actually has dependencies nonetheless, an XML processor will ignore the declaration. If a document does have dependencies, declaring standalone="yes" will generate an error. If a document doesn't have a standalone declaration in an XML declaration, it usually doesn't matter much anyway: an XML processor will find the external markup declarations nevertheless. Again, for more insight, see "Controlling Document Type Declarations."

XML version information

Version 1.0 of XML was approved as a W3C recommendation in February 1998. While the 1.0 specification has held its ground for over five years, it is likely that the W3C will deliver XML 1.1 as a recommendation in 2003. If so, XSLT is ready in at least one respect: you can control XML version information in an XML declaration with output's version attribute.

Here is an example of how it works. The stylesheet *version.xsl* uses the version attribute on the output element:

```
<xsl:stylesheet version="1.0" xmlns:xsl="http://www.w3.org/1999/XSL/Transform">
<xsl:output method="xml" indent="yes" encoding="UTF-8"/>
<xsl:output version="1.1"/>

<xsl:template match="name">
 <name>
  <family><xsl:apply-templates select="last"/></family>
  <given><xsl:apply-templates select="first"/></given>
 </name>
</xsl:template>

</xsl:stylesheet>
```

When applied to *name.xml* like:

```
xalan name.xml version.xsl
```

this stylesheet will produce the following result with an altered XML declaration:

```
<?xml version="1.1" encoding="UTF-8"?>
<name>
<family>Churchill</family>
<given>Winston</given>
</name>
```

The XML version is changed from 1.0 to 1.1.

 Xalan and Saxon both support the version attribute of output.

Controlling Document Type Declarations

A document type declaration associates document type definitions (DTDs) with an XML document. In essence, it helps an XML validator find where DTDs exist. The DTD can be either internal to an XML document, external to it, or both. To illustrate, the document *name-int.xml* has an internal subset:

```
<?xml version="1.0" encoding="UTF-8"?>
<!DOCTYPE name [
<!ELEMENT name (last, first)>
<!ELEMENT last (#PCDATA)>
<!ELEMENT first (#PCDATA)>
]>

<name>
 <last>Churchill</last>
 <first>Winston</first>
</name>
```

DTDs, as you already can see, have a different syntax than ordinary XML. DOCTYPE is the keyword for the document type declaration. Following that keyword is the name of the document element for the XML document called name. Inside the square brackets ([ ]) are three element declarations that begin with the keyword ELEMENT.

According to this internal subset, a name element must be followed by exactly one last element, which is followed by exactly one first element. Both last and first must contain parsed character data (#PCDATA). The document contained in *internal.xml* is valid with regard to its internal subset.

The document *external.xml* references an external DTD called the *external subset*. It is in a file called *external.dtd*; *external.xml* is valid with regard to it:

```
<?xml version="1.0" encoding="UTF-8"?>
<!DOCTYPE name SYSTEM "external.dtd">

<name>
 <last>Churchill</last>
 <first>Winston</first>
</name>
```

The SYSTEM keyword indicates that the following value will be a system identifier or URI. Here is *external.dtd* that has the same declarations as *internal.dtd*, but in a document separate from the instance:

```
<!ELEMENT name (last, first)>
<!ELEMENT last (#PCDATA)>
<!ELEMENT first (#PCDATA)>
```

The document *both.xml* contains an internal subset and also refers to an external subset:

```
<?xml version="1.0" encoding="UTF-8"?>
<!DOCTYPE name SYSTEM "both.dtd" [
<!ELEMENT last (#PCDATA)>
```

```
]>
<name>
 <last>Churchill</last>
 <first>Winston</first>
</name>
```

The document type declaration encloses an internal subset and also points to the external subset *both.dtd* with a system identifier:

```
<!ELEMENT name (last, first)>
<!ELEMENT first (#PCDATA)>
```

The external subset contains declarations for the name and first elements, and the internal subset holds a declaration for last only. Both the internal and external subsets are needed to validate the document.

Validation with transformation

You can validate a source document at the same time that you transform it by using the -v (validate) command-line option. For example, the following command line performs validation on *both.xml* before the document is transformed with *both.xsl*:

```
xalan -v both.xml both.xsl
```

The validate option works with Saxon and MSXSL as well. MSXSL is a fast, Windows-native command-line processor available free from Microsoft (see the appendix for more information on MSXSL).

Adding a document type declaration with a system identifier

XSLT won't let you add markup declarations such as <!ELEMENT name (last, first)> to an internal subset through a transformation, but it will let you add document type declarations to a result. The document *name.xml*, for example, doesn't have a document type declaration. You can add one with XSLT by using the doctype-system attribute on output. The following stylesheet, *doctype-system.xsl*, shows you how:

```
<xsl:stylesheet version="1.0" xmlns:xsl="http://www.w3.org/1999/XSL/Transform">
<xsl:output method="xml" indent="yes" encoding="UTF-8"/>
<xsl:output doctype-system="name.dtd"/>

<xsl:template match="name">
 <name>
  <family><xsl:apply-templates select="last"/></family>
  <given><xsl:apply-templates select="first"/></given>
 </name>
</xsl:template>

</xsl:stylesheet>
```

When *name.xml* is transformed with this stylesheet:

```
xalan name.xml doctype-system.xsl
```

the *doctype-system* attribute triggers the creation of a document type declaration in the result that references the system identifier *name.dtd*:

```
<?xml version="1.0" encoding="UTF-8"?>
<!DOCTYPE name SYSTEM "name.dtd">
<name>
<family>Churchill</family>
<given>Winston</given>
</name>
```

Adding a document type declaration with a public identifier

Public identifiers are often associated with widely accepted DTDs—the strict DTD associated with XHTML, for example. In some situations, software can resolve the names of public identifiers with local copies of a DTD, rather than by using a remote DTD over a network. Finding and using local DTDs can save processing time, especially when you have many files to validate.

Following is a public identifier for strict XHTML 1.0:

```
-//W3C//DTD XHTML 1.0 Strict//EN
```

The leading - indicates that the public identifier is not registered with ISO. The name of the identifier's owner is preceded by a pair of slashes (//W3C), followed by a pair of slashes and the description of the DTD (//DTD XHTML 1.0 Strict), followed by a pair of slashes and a language code (//EN).

The stylesheet *doctype-public.xsl* adds a public identifier for strict XHTML 1.0 to a result:

```
<xsl:stylesheet version="1.0" xmlns:xsl="http://www.w3.org/1999/XSL/Transform">
<xsl:output method="xml" indent="yes" encoding="UTF-8"/>
<xsl:output doctype-public="-//W3C//DTD XHTML 1.0 Strict//EN"/>
<xsl:output doctype-system="http://www.w3.org/TR/xhtml1/DTD/xhtml1-strict.dtd"/>

<xsl:template match="name">
<html xmlns="http://www.w3.org/1999/xhtml">
<head>
 <title><xsl:value-of select="name( )"/></title>
</head>
<body>
  <p><xsl:apply-templates select="last"/></p>
  <p><xsl:apply-templates select="first"/></p>
</body>
</html>
</xsl:template>

</xsl:stylesheet>
```

In addition to a public identifier, this stylesheet also specifies a system identifier URI for an XHTML DTD. The value-of element's select attribute contains an expression that calls the XPath name( ) function that returns the name of a node, rather than its content. You'll learn more about XPath functions such as name( ) in Chapter 5.

When applied to *name.xml* with:

```
xalan name.xml doctype-public.xsl
```

doctype-public.xsl produces the following output:

```
<?xml version="1.0" encoding="UTF-8"?>
<!DOCTYPE html PUBLIC "-//W3C//DTD XHTML 1.0 Strict//EN" "http://www.w3.org/TR/
xhtml1/DTD/xhtml1-strict.dtd">
<html xmlns="http://www.w3.org/1999/xhtml">
<head>
<title>name</title>
</head>
<body>
<p>Churchill</p>
<p>Winston</p>
</body>
</html>
```

Validating XHTML

This output is valid, strict XHTML 1.0. Save the output to a file, for example, with the command:

```
xalan -o name.html name.xml doctype-public.xsl
```

As XHTML, you can validate *name.html* just as you would any XML document. One easy way to do this is with W3C's online validation tool. If you go to the W3C Markup Validation Service page at *http://validator.w3.org*, you can upload a local file, such as *name.html*, using the Browse button (see Figure 3-4). Then you can click the Validate File button, and the service will attempt to validate the file. One of the nice things about the W3C service is that it provides diagnostics if there are errors present on the page, making it easier to correct the errors. This online tool also works as an XML and HTML validator.

Outputting CDATA Sections

CDATA sections in XML allow you to hide characters like < and & from the XSLT processor. The difference between a CDATA section and an individual entity reference is that you hide a section of characters rather than just one at a time.

A CDATA section begins with the characters `<![CDATA[` and ends with `]]>`. For example, the company element in this fragment contains a CDATA section:

```
<company><![CDATA[<pub>O'Reilly & Associates</pub>]]></company>
```

The & and < characters in the CDATA section are hidden so that they aren't interpreted as markup (such as the start of an entity or character reference). The `cdata-section-elements` attribute on output lets you tell the XSLT processor which elements you want to contain CDATA sections in the result.

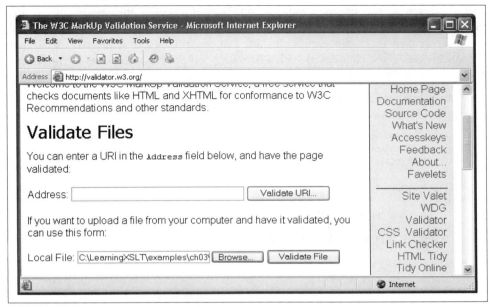

Figure 3-4. The W3C Markup Validation Service

To see how it's done, consider the stylesheet *cdata.xsl*:

```
<xsl:stylesheet version="1.0" xmlns:xsl="http://www.w3.org/1999/XSL/Transform">
<xsl:output method="xml" indent="yes"/>
<xsl:output cdata-section-elements="notes"/>

<xsl:template match="name">
 <name>
  <family><xsl:apply-templates select="last"/></family>
  <given><xsl:apply-templates select="first"/></given>
  <notes>Author &amp; British prime minister</notes>
 </name>
</xsl:template>

</xsl:stylesheet>
```

In this example, the cdata-section-elements attribute of output contains the name of an element (notes) whose content you want to enclose in a CDATA section. If you process *name.xml* with *cdata.xsl*:

```
xalan name.xml cdata.xsl
```

you will see the following result:

```
<?xml version="1.0" encoding="UTF-8"?>
<name>
<family>Churchill</family>
<given>Winston</given>
<notes><![CDATA[Author & British prime minister]]></notes>
</name>
```

The character data content of *notes* (from the template in the stylesheet) is surrounded by a CDATA section in the result, and the entity reference & is changed into &. The cdata-section-elements attribute can contain a list of whitespace-separated element names. Each element in such a list must contain character data in the source document, as *notes* does.

You can also serialize CDATA sections by using literal text. To do this, use literal text such as shown in *literal-cdata.xsl*:

```
<xsl:stylesheet version="1.0" xmlns:xsl="http://www.w3.org/1999/XSL/Transform">
<xsl:output method="xml" indent="yes"/>
<xsl:output cdata-section-elements="notes"/>

<xsl:template match="name">
 <name>
   <family><xsl:apply-templates select="last"/></family>
   <given><xsl:apply-templates select="first"/></given>
   <notes><![CDATA[Author & British prime minister]]></notes>
 </name>
</xsl:template>

</xsl:stylesheet>
```

When you transform *name.xml* with this stylesheet using:

```
xalan name.xml literal-cdata.xsl
```

you will see the CDATA section passed on literally to the result:

```
<?xml version="1.0" encoding="UTF-8"?>
<name>
<family>Churchill</family>
<given>Winston</given>
<notes><![CDATA[Author & British prime minister]]></notes>
</name>
```

You can find more about CDATA sections in Section 2.7 of the XML specification.

Outputting HTML

You have seen a few examples that produce HTML output. The following HTML example is more complicated than ones you have seen before. This section covers explicit, presentation-oriented HTML output, discussed in Section 16.2 of the XSLT specification. The XML document, *wg.xml* (Example 3-1), contains the names of the former and current W3C XML Working Group (WG) members at the time of the publication of the first edition of XML 1.0.

Example 3-1. XML document listing the names of the XML Working Group members

```
<?xml version="1.0"?>

<!--
names of persons acknowledged as current and past members
of the W3C XML Working Group at the time of the publication
```

```
 of the first edition of the XML specification on 1998-02-10
 -->

<names>
 <name>
  <last>Angerstein</last>
  <first>Paula</first>
 </name>
 <name>
  <last>Bosak</last>
  <first>Jon</first>
 </name>
 <name>
  <last>Bray</last>
  <first>Tim</first>
 </name>
 <name>
  <last>Clark</last>
  <first>James</first>
 </name>
 <name>
  <last>Connolly</last>
  <first>Dan</first>
 </name>
 <name>
  <last>DeRose</last>
  <first>Steve</first>
 </name>
 <name>
  <last>Hollander</last>
  <first>Dave</first>
 </name>
 <name>
  <last>Kimber</last>
  <first>Eliot</first>
 </name>
 <name>
  <last>Magliery</last>
  <first>Tom</first>
 </name>
<name>
  <last>Maler</last>
  <first>Eve</first>
 </name>
 <name>
  <last>Maloney</last>
  <first>Murray</first>
 </name>
<name>
  <last>Murata</last>
  <first>Makoto</first>
 </name>
```

```
<name>
 <last>Nava</last>
 <first>Joel</first>
</name>
<name>
 <last>O'Connell</last>
 <first>Conleth</first>
</name>
<name>
 <last>Paoli</last>
 <first>Jean</first>
</name>
<name>
 <last>Sharpe</last>
 <first>Peter</first>
</name>
<name>
 <last>Sperberg-McQueen</last>
 <first>C. M.</first>
</name>
<name>
 <last>Tigue</last>
 <first>John</first>
</name>
</names>
```

 The element names last and first fit Western-oriented names, which admittedly is a problem when you are dealing with international names. In other examples in this chapter, last is transformed to family and first is transformed to given, which is more generalized for international names. But because this example is only concerned with presentation-oriented HTML, changing the element names to more descriptive names is extraneous.

Along with the names of the individual in alphabetical order, the document contains an informative comment in the prolog (near the top). You can use the stylesheet *wg.xsl*, shown in Example 3-2, to transform this document into the HTML shown in Example 3-3.

Example 3-2. A stylesheet to convert the list of members from Example 3-1 into the HTML shown in Example 3-3

```
<xsl:stylesheet version="1.0" xmlns:xsl="http://www.w3.org/1999/XSL/Transform">

<xsl:output method="html" version="4.01"/>
<xsl:output doctype-system="http://www.w3.org/TR/html4/strict.dtd"/>

<xsl:output doctype-public="-//W3C//DTD HTML 4.01//EN"/>

<xsl:template match="/">
```

Example 3-2. A stylesheet to convert the list of members from Example 3-1 into the HTML shown in Example 3-3 (continued)

```
<html>
 <head>
 <title>Original W3C XML Working Group Members</title>
 <style type="text/css">
 body {font-family: sans-serif}
 h1 {font-size: 20pt}
 lu {font-size: 16pt}
 </style>
 </head>
 <body>
 <h1>Original W3C XML Working Group Members</h1>
 <p>Following are the
  <xsl:value-of select="substring(comment( ),2,string-length(comment( ))-12)"/>
   10 February 1998:</p>
  <ul><xsl:apply-templates/></ul>
 </body>
 </html>
</xsl:template>

<xsl:template match="name">
 <li><xsl:apply-templates/></li>
</xsl:template>

<xsl:template match="last">
 <xsl:comment> family name </xsl:comment>
 <xsl:apply-templates/><xsl:text>, </xsl:text>
</xsl:template>

<xsl:template match="first">
 <xsl:comment> given name </xsl:comment>
 <xsl:apply-templates/>
</xsl:template>

</xsl:stylesheet>
```

The stylesheet sets the output method to html unambiguously, that is, it does not depend on the default HTML output method. The version attribute indicates the HTML version number. This won't show up in the output, but it is available should any application want the information (rare). The stylesheet will also produce a public and system identifier for HTML 4.01.

The first template matches on the root of the document and starts building the outer layers of an HTML document, including some CSS style rules. Following that, there is an interesting line of gobbledy-gook that I want to draw your attention to:

```
<xsl:value-of select="substring(comment( ),2,string-length(comment( ))-12)"/>
```

This instance of value-of returns a substring or shortened version of the comment in the prolog by using the substring( ) function. The first argument of the substring( ) function is comment( ), which looks like a function, but it isn't—it's something called a *node-test* (you'll learn about node-tests in Chapter 4). The expression in the select attribute uses substring( ) to subtract 14 characters from the comment—2 characters at the beginning of the comment (skips characters 0 and 1, and starts at character 2) and 12 at the end of the comment.

 Processing comments blindly without knowing their exact content will probably result in a good deal of frustration on your part.

The string-length( ) function, which appears as the third argument of the function substring( ), returns the length of the comment (181 characters) and subtracts 12 from 181. This removes the ISO 8601 date from the returned comment and allows the stylesheet to add a differently formatted date (10 February 1998), which is specified as literal text. The returned comment is preceded by the text *Following are the*. You will learn more about expressions and functions in Chapter 5.

The first template, the one that matches the document root (/), calls apply-templates, which in turn finds the template that reaches each occurrence of the child element name. This name template instantiates the HTML element li (list item) and then calls apply-templates, which finds template rules for its children last and first. The templates for last and first add comments to the result, and the template for last adds a comma. After each template is invoked, it returns control to the template that invoked it. The XSLT processor munches through the whole document until it can't find any more nodes in the source.

Go ahead and process *wg.xml* with *wg.xsl*, saving the result to *wg.html*:

```
xalan -o wg.html wg.xml wg.xsl
```

The resulting file *wg.html* follows in Example 3-3.

Example 3-3. The HTML results of processing Example 3-1 using the XSLT stylesheet shown in Example 3-2

```
<!DOCTYPE HTML PUBLIC "-//W3C//DTD HTML 4.01//EN" "http://www.w3.org/TR/html4/strict.dtd">
<html>
<head>
<META http-equiv="Content-Type" content="text/html; charset=UTF-8">
<title>Original W3C XML Working Group Members</title>
<style type="text/css">
  body {font-family: sans-serif}
  h1 {font-size: 20pt}
  lu {font-size: 16pt}
  </style>
</head>
<body>
<h1>Original W3C XML Working Group Members</h1>
<p>Following are the
    names of persons acknowledged as current and past members
 of the W3C XML Working Group at the time of the publication
 of the first edition of the XML specification on
```

```
    10 February 1998:</p>
<ul>
 <li>
  <!-- family name -->Angerstein,
  <!-- given name -->Paula
 </li>
 <li>
  <!-- family name -->Bosak,
  <!-- given name -->Jon
 </li>
 <li>
  <!-- family name -->Bray,
  <!-- given name -->Tim
 </li>
 <li>
  <!-- family name -->Clark,
  <!-- given name -->James
 </li>
 <li>
  <!-- family name -->Connolly,
  <!-- given name -->Dan
 </li>
 <li>
  <!-- family name -->DeRose,
  <!-- given name -->Steve
 </li>
 <li>
  <!-- family name -->Hollander,
  <!-- given name -->Dave
 </li>
 <li>
  <!-- family name -->Kimber,
  <!-- given name -->Eliot
 </li>
 <li>
  <!-- family name -->Magliery,
  <!-- given name -->Tom
 </li>
 <li>
  <!-- family name -->Maler,
  <!-- given name -->Eve
 </li>
 <li>
  <!-- family name -->Maloney,
  <!-- given name -->Murray
 </li>
 <li>
  <!-- family name -->Murata,
  <!-- given name -->Makoto
 </li>
 <li>
```

Example 3-3. The HTML results of processing Example 3-1 using the XSLT stylesheet shown in Example 3-2 (continued)

```
  <!-- family name -->Nava,
  <!-- given name -->Joel
</li>
<li>
  <!-- family name -->O'Connell,
  <!-- given name -->Conleth
</li>
<li>
  <!-- family name -->Paoli,
  <!-- given name -->Jean
</li>
<li>
  <!-- family name -->Sharpe,
  <!-- given name -->Peter
</li>
<li>
  <!-- family name -->Sperberg-McQueen,
  <!-- given name -->C. M.
</li>
<li>
  <!-- family name -->Tigue,
  <!-- given name -->John
</li>
</ul>
</body>
</html>
```

Figure 3-5 shows what *wg.html* looks like in Mozilla.

You can easily validate *wg.html* using Mozilla's built-in link to the W3C Markup Validation Service. To do so, follow these steps:

1. Choose File → Edit Page (or CTRL+E) in Mozilla.

2. When the Composer window appears, choose Tools → Validate HTML.

3. When the W3C Markup Validation Service window appears, click the Browse button and select *wg.html*.

4. Click the button Validate this file.

5. The successful result should appear as Figure 3-6.

Outputting Text

The text output method lets an XSLT processor know that you intend to output plain text to the result. You have already seen simple examples that do this previously in the book. This example shows you how to output programming language text using the text method. If you are not a programmer, this section may be a little

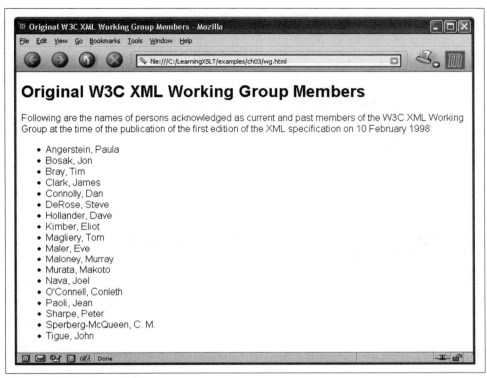

Figure 3-5. wg.html in Mozilla

tough to follow. You can skip it if programming makes you queasy or if you aren't interested in .NET, although the same approach can be used to generate Java, Visual-Basic, COBOL, or the language of your choice.

Now, I'll show you how you can use XSLT to write a program in the C# programming language. The stylesheet *csharp.xsl* uses the text output method:

```
<xsl:stylesheet version="1.0" xmlns:xsl="http://www.w3.org/1999/XSL/Transform">
<xsl:output method="text"/>

<xsl:template match="name">
using System;
using System.Xml;

class Name {

    static void Main( ) {
        XmlTextWriter w = new XmlTextWriter(Console.Out);
        w.Formatting = Formatting.Indented;
        w.Indentation = 1;
        w.WriteStartDocument( );
        w.WriteStartElement("<xsl:value-of select="name( )"/>");
        w.WriteAttributeString("title", "Mr.");
```

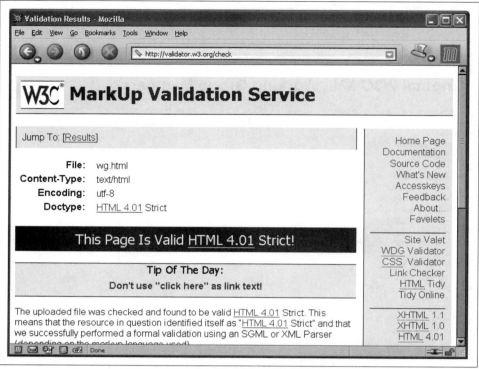

Figure 3-6. W3C Validation Service report on wg.html

```
            w.WriteElementString("family", "<xsl:value-of select="last"/>");
            w.WriteElementString("given", "<xsl:value-of select="first"/>");
            w.WriteEndElement( );
            w.Close( );

        }

    }
    </xsl:template>

    </xsl:stylesheet>
```

This stylesheet uses value-of instruction elements to grab string values from the source tree. The first occurrence of value-of uses the XPath function name( ) to grab the name of the element that the template matches. The template actually matches not just the name of an element node, but a *node-set*, that is, the set of nodes including the element name and its children. The value-of element, however, returns only the string value of the first node of this node-set. The next two occurrences of value-of capture the text node children of the last and first elements in the source tree, respectively. (You'll learn more about nodes and node-sets in Chapter 4.)

When *name.xml* is processed with this stylesheet, it outputs a C# program. C# is part of the .NET Framework and offers many conveniences for a programmer that must handle XML. You can download .NET for Windows from Microsoft at *http://www.microsoft.com/net/*. You can also download Ximian's open source implementation of .NET at *http://www.go-mono.com/*, which runs on Linux and Windows, as well as FreeBSD and Mac OS X.

To transform *name.xml* with *csharp.xsl*, use this command to save the program to a file:

```
xalan -o name.cs name.xml csharp.xsl
```

After the transformation, the program is saved to the file *name.cs*:

```
using System;
using System.Xml;

class Name {

    static void Main( ) {
        XmlTextWriter w = new XmlTextWriter(Console.Out);
        w.Formatting = Formatting.Indented;
        w.Indentation = 1;
        w.WriteStartDocument( );
        w.WriteStartElement("name");
        w.WriteAttributeString("title", "Mr.");
         w.WriteElementString("family", "Churchill");
         w.WriteElementString("given", "Winston");
        w.WriteEndElement( );
        w.Close( );

    }

}
```

The XmlTextWriter object allows C# programs to write well-formed XML to the console, file, or stream. The output of this particular program is written to the console (standard output), and the output will be indented. This is set by the Formatting and Indentation properties. The document element name is created by the WriteStartElement( ) method of XmlTextWriter, and it has a single attribute, title, created with WriteAttributeString( ). This element also has two children, family and given, produced by a pair of WriteElementString( ) methods.

You can compile and run this program if you have the .NET Framework downloaded and installed. Compile the program with the Microsoft C# compiler by typing the following at a command prompt:

```
csc name.cs
```

Or with the Mono compiler using:

```
mcs name.cs
```

It should report no errors—all you should see are some copyright messages. The output of the compilation is an executable file called *name.exe*. If you have the Windows implementation, type:

```
name
```

If you have the Mono implementation, type:

```
mono name.exe
```

Again, this example works only if you have .NET installed. When you successfully run this program on Windows, for example, it produces the following well-formed XML output:

```
<?xml version="1.0" encoding="IBM437"?>
<name title="Mr.">
 <family>Churchill</family>
 <given>Winston</given>
</name>
```

IBM437 is an IANA-registered character set name for the Windows code page 437. XML processors are not required to support this character set, but they are permitted to support any character sets registered at IANA (which IBM437 is), plus any private character sets (they must be prefixed with x-).

Using a QName Output Method

I have explained the xml, html, and text output methods. You can also use a QName for a value of the method attribute. But there's a catch: if you use a QName, it must be supported as an extension by the XSLT processor that you use with it. (This mechanism allows you to invoke a user-written serializer, such as with a SAX ContentHandler.) This can be useful if you want to produce non-XML formats as your output.

Johannes Döbler's XSLT processor jd.xslt offers several QName values for the method attribute by way of extension. One of them is jd:empty.

The value of method must be a QName, not an NCName. Any value other than xml, html, or text is considered an extension and must be qualified with a namespace.

The jd:empty output method, when used together with the jd.xslt processor, produces a result tree but doesn't serialize it. This is useful when you are interested only in measuring the performance of the processor with a given stylesheet. The stylesheet *empty.xsl* uses output with a method of jd:empty:

```
<xsl:stylesheet version="1.0" xmlns:xsl="http://www.w3.org/1999/XSL/Transform">
<xsl:output method="jd:empty" xmlns:jd="http://www.aztecrider.com/xslt"/>

<xsl:template match="name">
```

```
<name>
 <family><xsl:apply-templates select="last"/></family>
 <given><xsl:apply-templates select="first"/></given>
</name>
</xsl:template>

</xsl:stylesheet>
```

The QName jd:empty is associated with the namespace name *http://www.aztecrider.com/xslt*. You can process *empty.xsl* against the document *name.xml* with jd.xslt to see what happens. (For details of how to download, install, and run jd.xslt, see the appendix.) To run it, enter the following at a command or shell prompt using the -verbose switch:

```
java -jar jdxslt.jar -verbose name.xml empty.xsl
```

You won't see a result, but the processor will deliver the following information:

```
jd.xslt processor version 1.4.0

java vm              = Sun Microsystems Inc., 1.4.1_01
parser               = org.apache.crimson.parser.XMLReaderImpl
modelbuilder factory = jd.xml.xpath.model.build.ModelBuilderFactory
read stylesheet      = file:C:/LearningXSLT/examples/ch03/empty.xsl
prepare stylesheet   = 180 ms
read xml input       = 10 ms (using normal tree model)
transform input      = 10 ms
max memory usage     = 1.937 MB
```

With -verbose, the processor reports the transformation performance results.

Media Types

The last attribute I'll mention is media-type. This attribute allows you to set the media type for the result. Media types are also sometimes called MIME types (MIME is short for Multipurpose Internet Mail Extensions), but since the types apply to more than just email, the term *media type* is more encompassing.

Here is one example fragment. A media type of application/xml may be specified in an output element like this:

```
<xsl:output output="xml" media-type="application/xml"/>
```

The value of this attribute, if you use it, will not be reflected explicitly in the result. In fact, the specification makes no stipulations about whether a processor needs to provide this information to an application. Nevertheless, an application might possibly make the media type information available to a server running HTTP, which could then use it in the Content-Type field of an HTTP header. This was probably the intent of this obscure attribute.

Table 3-2 lists the default media types for the three built-in output methods of XSLT.

Table 3-2. Default media types

Method	Default media type
XML	text/xml
HTML	text/html
Text	text/plain

Summary

This chapter covered the results you get from different output methods, including default and unambiguous XML, HTML, text, or custom output. It also talked about indentation, working with XML declarations, document type declarations, CDATA sections, and media types. In the next chapter, you will learn more details about using XPath to look at XML documents as trees of nodes.

CHAPTER 4

Traversing the Tree

In the previous three chapters, you have seen a number of examples that use the XML Path Language (XPath). This chapter discusses XPath topics, such as the XPath data model, the difference between patterns and expressions, predicates, the difference between abbreviated and unabbreviated location paths, axes, and node and name tests. (XPath and XSLT functions will be discussed in the next chapter.)

 Though it is not exactly light reading, you may want to print a copy of the XPath 1.0 specification. It is a little over 30 pages. You can find it at *http://www.w3.org/TR/xpath*.

The XPath Data Model

The foundation of XPath is its view of the XML document as a tree with branches called nodes. XPath's data model is a tree data model. The tree model comes to us from traditional computer science. It is a way of organizing or imagining the order of data in a hierarchical or structured way. To illustrate the tree model, Figure 4-1 represents roughly the XML document *nodes.xml* found in *examples/ch04* as a tree of nodes.

Each box in Figure 4-1 represents a node or point in the tree structure of the document. In the XPath data model, a node represents part of an XML document such as the root or starting point of the document, elements, attributes, text, and so on. In the traditional tree model, the lines connecting the nodes are called *edges*. If a node does not have children, it is called a *leaf node*. (The terms *edge* and *leaf node* are not used in the XPath spec.) If you follow the edges, you are following a path. The nodes in a tree have family relationships: parent-child, ancestor-descendant, sibling, and so forth.

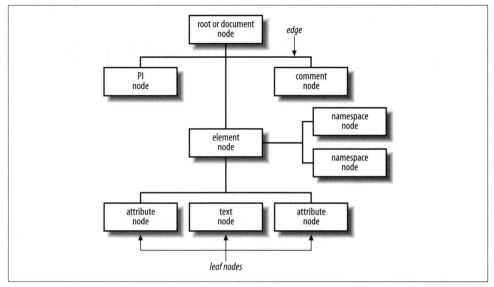

Figure 4-1. A tree of nodes

XPath Nodes

An XML document, according to the XPath 1.0 data model, can be conceptually described as having seven possible node types:

- Root (called the *document node* in XPath 2.0)
- Element
- Attribute
- Text
- Namespace
- Comment
- Processing instruction

You have already encountered nodes of all these types earlier in the book. For further illustration, the file *nodes.xml* contains at least one occurrence of each of these nodes:

```
<?xml-stylesheet href="tree-view.xsl" type="text/xsl"?>

<!-- Last invoice of day's batch -->

<amount vendor="314" xml:lang="en"
 xmlns="urn:wyeast-net:invoice">7598.00</amount>
```

Each node is labeled with its appropriate XPath 1.0 node type in Figure 4-2, and Table 4-1 describes each of the XPath node types.

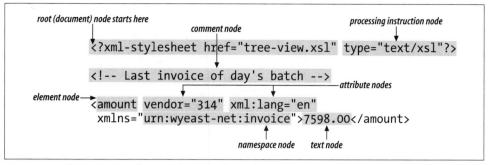

Figure 4-2. The seven XPath 1.0 nodes in nodes.xml

Table 4-1. XPath nodes types

Node type	Description
Root (document) node	The whole document, starting conceptually at the beginning of the document, before the document or root element. The root node must have at least (and at most) one element child: the document element. In the XPath model, a root node may also have processing instruction and comment children. Other children are ignored.
Element node	An element, such as amount, which is also the document element in *nodes.xml*.
Attribute node	An attribute, such as vendor="314" or xml:lang="en".
Text node	Text inside of an element, such as 7598.00 inside amount (yes, it looks like a real number, but XPath just sees it as text here).
Namespace node	A namespace name, a URI such as the URN urn:wyeast-net:invoice (also includes a prefix, if applicable).
Comment node	A comment, such as <!-- Last invoice of day's batch -->.
Processing instruction node	A processing instruction, such as <?xml-stylesheet href="tree-view.xsl" type="text/css"?>.

XPath 2.0, which is not yet an approved recommendation of the W3C, takes a slightly different approach in regard to nodes and types, at least at this book's level of detail. You will be introduced to XPath 2.0 in Chapter 16. For more information, see *http://www.w3.org/TR/xpath20/*

A View of the Tree

To get a good idea of the how the XPath 1.0 data model views an XML document as a tree, you can use the ASCII Tree Viewer (the stylesheet *ascii-treeview.xsl*) created by Mike Brown and Jeni Tennison. This stylesheet labels all seven node types using plain text or ASCII output. An edited version of this stylesheet is available in *examples/ch04*.

When you process *nodes.xml* with *ascii-treeview.xsl* using Xalan, as follows:

```
xalan nodes.xml ascii-treeview.xsl
```

you will see each of the nodes labeled in the output:

```
root
 |___processing instruction target='xml-stylesheet' instruction=
'href="tree-view.xsl" type="text/xsl"'
 |___comment ' Last invoice of day's batch '
 |___element 'amount' in ns 'urn:wyeast-net:invoice' ('amount')
       | \___attribute 'vendor' = '314'
       | \___attribute 'lang' in ns 'http://www.w3.org/XML/1998/namespace' ('xml:
lang') = 'en'
       | \___namespace 'xml' = 'http://www.w3.org/XML/1998/namespace'
       | \___namespace '' = 'urn:wyeast-net:invoice'
       |___text '7598.00'
```

 You can download the original, unedited version of *ascii-treeview.xsl* from *http://skew.org/xml/stylesheets/treeview/ascii/*. I have edited this stylesheet so that it will find and label namespace nodes and ignore insignificant whitespace.

The stylesheet referenced at the top of *nodes.xml* is *tree-view.xsl*. It is the Pretty XML Tree Viewer, also developed by Mike Brown and Jeni Tennison. It produces HTML output rather than ASCII. You can get *tree-view.xsl*, along with its required companion stylesheet *tree-view.css*, from *http://skew.org/xml/stylesheets/treeview/html/*. There already are edited copies of these stylesheets in *examples/ch04*.

If you open and view *nodes.xml* with IE, you will see the result shown in Figure 4-3. The seven node types are all represented, as you can see from the labels.

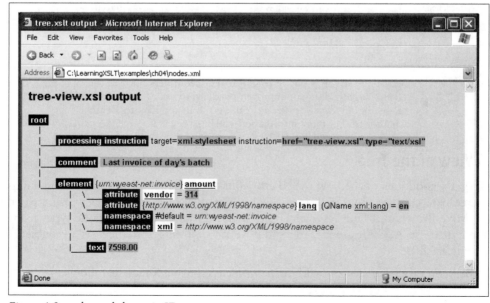

Figure 4-3. nodes.xml shown in IE

As with *ascii-treeview.xsl*, I have made a few small edits to *tree-view.xsl*. The edit changes a parameter value to a nonzero value, switching on the behavior that makes the stylesheet show namespace nodes. I have also uncommented a line so that insignificant whitespace is stripped using the `strip-space` element. You will learn more about parameters in Chapter 7. You will learn about stripping and preserving insignificant space later in the book.

The xml:lang Attribute

The document *nodes.xml* uses the `xml:lang` attribute. This attribute indicates that the content of the element that specifies it, and any of its associated attribute values, are given in the language defined by the value of `xml:lang`. This attribute is a special attribute from the XML namespace, *http://www.w3.org/XML/1998/namespace*, and is associated with the `xml` prefix. This attribute takes a token value that represents a language according to IETF RFC 1766, Tags for the Identification of Languages (see *http://www.ietf.org/rfc/rfc1766.txt*), in conjunction with the ISO/IEC 639 standards (see *http://www.iso.ch*). (IETF RFC, by the way, stands for *Internet Engineering Task Force Request for Comments*; see *http://www.ietf.org/rfc.html*.) Some examples of these tokens are *en* for English, *fr* for French, *de* for German (Deutsch), and *es* for Spanish (Español). These can also include tokens with subtags such as *en-US* for United States English and *en-GB* for Great Britain English.

What's a Context?

In order to work properly, XPath and XSLT have to keep track of where processing occurs in the source document and what node it's working on at any particular moment. XPath and XSLT have developed a vocabulary to describe such things. The more familiar you are with the terms described in the following paragraphs, the better off you will be when working with XSLT. You will get more and more exposure to these terms throughout the remainder of this book.

Most of the terms revolve around something called a *context*. In XPath, the *context node* is the node that is currently selected and being processed. The context node is usually the node addressed by a `select` attribute, such as with the `apply-templates` element. The XSLT spec also refers to a *current node*, which is almost always the same thing as the context node. You can retrieve the current node with the `current( )` function, an XSLT function that I'll discuss in Chapter 5.

The only time the context node and the current node are not the same thing is when a predicate is being evaluated. A predicate is a filter for nodes, contained in square brackets, such as in `amount[@xml:lang='en']`. When a node is being evaluated within the square brackets or predicate, it temporarily becomes the current node. This is the only time that the context node and the current node are not identical. You'll learn about predicates in the section "Predicates," later in this chapter.

A *node-set* is a set of unordered nodes that can be of different kinds. A node-set can consist of an unordered group of element, attribute, and text nodes, for example. The *current node list* is an XSLT term and refers to an ordered set of nodes, obtained when, for example, the `select` attribute of the `apply-templates` element is processed.

The *context position*, represented by a nonzero, positive integer, is an XPath term that indicates the node at which processing is positioned, something like the current position when iterating through an array or vector in a programming language. The *context size* represents the number of nodes in the current list, and is also a nonzero, positive integer. This is like an array size, though numbering starts at 1, not 0.

The term *document order* refers to the order in which nodes actually appear as they are encountered in a source document. The current node list can be a subset of the nodes found in document order in a source tree. Document order can be in forward or reverse, along a given axis such as the child or parent axis (see the section "Axes," later in the chapter for a more thorough explanation).

If you don't feel like you've got your arms around all these terms, that's okay: you'll get more exposure to them over time and they'll eventually sink in. Now that you have a basic understanding of the XPath data model and some of its essential terminology, I'll start exploring expressions and patterns after a brief discussion of location paths.

Location Paths

The basic syntax of XPath is the *location path*. A location path consists of one or more items that identify nodes in a tree using the XPath data model and syntax. For example, looking back at *nodes.xml*, the following simple location path identifies the sole element node in that document:

```
amount
```

This is actually XPath's abbreviated syntax form, which you've seen a lot of already (you'll learn more about XPath's unabbreviated syntax a little later). This path assumes that the node will be found along the child axis (discussed in "Axes," later in this chapter).

Now, I'll add another *location step* to the location path:

```
amount/@vendor
```

Location steps are separated by a slash (/). This location path has two steps. The first step identifies the amount element, and the second step identifies the vendor attribute. This path assumes that the node will be found along the child axis followed by the attribute axis.

Another location path might be:

```
/amount/@xml:lang
```

Notice that this location path is *preceded* by a slash. The slash at the beginning of the location path indicates the root or document node, so this path tells the processor that the amount element must be the document element because it is the element child of the root node. The next step locates the xml:lang attribute that is associated with amount. Now here is another one:

```
/comment( )
```

This path will locate a comment that is a child of the root or document node. comment( ) is a node test. A *node test* checks whether a node matches a particular kind of node such as comment( ), text( ), processing-instruction( ), or node( ) for any node.

Now, I'll go into more detail about location paths by describing XPath expressions.

Expressions

An XPath expression allows you to go beyond the basic location of an element or attribute in a document by name, as you have just seen. Expressions let you:

- Specify location paths using names with either an abbreviated syntax, such as name/family, or unabbreviated syntax, such as child::name/child::family.
- Use XPath axes such as parent, as in .. in abbreviated syntax, or parent::name in unabbreviated.
- Perform basic arithmetic such as addition (+), subtraction (-), multiplication (*), division (div), and modulo (mod)—using parentheses optionally—such as 3 + (5 * 5).
- Perform Boolean logic using the operators and, or, =, !=, <=, <, >= and > such as 2 < 3 (because expressions occur in attribute values, you must use < instead of <).
- Reference variables defined elsewhere, such as $var = 3 (= in XPath tests for equivalence, and doesn't perform assignment; Chapter 7 describes variables).
- Call functions such as current( ), local-name( ), or position( ) (Chapter 5 discusses functions).
- Perform name and node tests such as rng:* (name test) or text( ) (node test).

When an XPath expression is evaluated, it can return an object of one of four types:

node-set
> An unordered collection of zero or more nodes without duplicates.

boolean
> A value of either true or false.

number
> A floating-point number.

string
> A string that is a sequence of legal Unicode characters.

By *return*, I mean that the XSLT processor hands back a node to the processing stream, in this case, one that has a particular type.

An XSLT processor can also return a type added by the XSLT spec called a *result tree fragment*. This is a portion of the result tree that may or may not be well-formed XML and is treated like a string. A result tree fragment is not an XPath type but was added to the four XPath types by the XSLT spec.

 XPath, by the way, isn't locked into XSLT alone. Beyond XSLT, XPath is also used in other W3C specifications such as the XPointer scheme (see *http://www.w3.org/TR/xptr-xpointer/*), in XQuery (see *http://www.w3.org/TR/xquery*), and in XForms (see *http://www.w3.org/TR/xforms/*). The W3C is also working on integrating XPath with DOM, the Document Object Model (see *http://www.w3.org/TR/DOM-Level-3-XPath/*).

Expressions occur in certain attribute values in XSLT. These features will be explored later in the chapter, but before moving any further, it's important that you understand what patterns are and how they work.

What Is a Pattern?

An XSLT *pattern* is a subset of an XPath expression. It is part of a template rule that allows the template to test whether a node matches certain criteria. This subset of expressions called a pattern is defined by XSLT, not by XPath.

A pattern can only evaluate a node-set, meaning a group of zero or more nodes. A node-set type is the only thing a pattern can evaluate or return. A pattern can match elements and attributes and use node tests (see "Name and Node Tests," later in this chapter) and predicates (see the next section, "Predicates"). It can also use the id( ) function (demonstrated in Chapter 5) and the key( ) function (described in Chapter 11), but that's about the sum of it.

There are four places in XSLT where you can identify a pattern, each time as a value of an attribute. The places that specify a pattern are in the match attribute of template and key elements, and in the count and from attributes of the number element. You can read more about patterns in Section 5.2 of the XSLT specification.

A pattern is one of two parts of a *template rule*, which, according to XSLT 2.0, consists of a pattern described in an attribute value and a sequence constructor, which tells the processor what to do—what items to produce—when it encounters the pattern and therefore is instantiated (see Section 2.4.1 of the XSLT 2.0 spec available at *http://www.w3.org/TR/xslt20/*).

Predicates

A predicate is a filter that can be used with a pattern as well as an expression. It checks to see whether a node-set matches an expression contained in square brackets. Again harking back to *nodes.xml*, here is an example of a pattern with a predicate:

```
amount[@vendor = '314']
```

One way to think about predicates is in terms of the word *where*—in other words, this pattern matches an amount element *where* the vendor attribute associated with amount has a value of 314. (As I mentioned earlier in the chapter, when the predicate is evaluated, the node in the predicate temporarily becomes the current node.)

The content between the square brackets is actually an expression. This is the only way that a pattern makes use of an expression. You can, of course, use predicates with expressions, as well as with patterns. If a predicate matches a given criteria, the predicate returns a Boolean value of true, or false if otherwise. In other words, if the expression in a predicate matches a node-set in a pattern, it returns true, and the template that matches the pattern is instantiated; if there is no match, the template is skipped.

Look at another example of a predicate:

```
amount[current() = '7598.00']
```

This one checks to see whether the content of amount is 7598.00 and returns true if it is. This could also be written as:

```
amount[. = '7598.00']
```

Here is yet another example:

```
amount[position()=1]
```

This tests to see whether amount is the first node in the set. This could also be written as:

```
amount[1]
```

To illustrate these concepts further, Example 4-1 shows the document *names.xml*. It's a slightly different version of *wg.xml*, which you worked with in the last chapter. The `last` and `first` elements have been changed to `family` and `given`, respectively. Several attributes and an encoding declaration have been added.

Example 4-1. An XML list of contributors to XML 1.0

```
<?xml version="1.0" encoding="ISO-8859-1"?>

<!--
names of persons acknowledged as current and past members
of the W3C XML Working Group at the time of the publication
of the first edition of the XML specification on 1998-02-10
-->

<names>
 <name>
  <family>Angerstein</family>
  <given>Paula</given>
 </name>
 <name title="chair">
  <family>Bosak</family>
  <given>Jon</given>
 </name>
 <name title="editor">
  <family>Bray</family>
  <given>Tim</given>
 </name>
 <name title="technical lead">
  <family>Clark</family>
  <given>James</given>
 </name>
 <name>
  <family>Connolly</family>
  <given>Dan</given>
 </name>
 <name>
  <family>DeRose</family>
  <given>Steve</given>
 </name>
 <name>
  <family>Hollander</family>
  <given>Dave</given>
 </name>
 <name>
  <family>Kimber</family>
  <given>Eliot</given>
 </name>
 <name>
  <family>Magliery</family>
  <given>Tom</given>
 </name>
 <name>
```

Example 4-1. An XML list of contributors to XML 1.0 (continued)

```
  <family>Maler</family>
  <given>Eve</given>
 </name>
 <name>
  <family>Maloney</family>
  <given>Murray</given>
 </name>
 <name>
  <family>Murata</family>
  <given>Makoto</given>
 </name>
 <name>
  <family>Nava</family>
  <given>Joel</given>
 </name>
 <name>
  <family>O'Connell</family>
  <given>Conleth</given>
 </name>
 <name title="editor">
  <family>Paoli</family>
  <given>Jean</given>
 </name>
 <name>
  <family>Sharpe</family>
  <given>Peter</given>
 </name>
 <name title="editor">
  <family>Sperberg-McQueen</family>
  <given>C. M.</given>
 </name>
 <name>
  <family>Tigue</family>
  <given>John</given>
 </name>
</names>
```

Now consider the stylesheet *pattern.xsl*, shown in Example 4-2.

Example 4-2. A stylesheet extracting the fourth listed member of the XML team

```
<xsl:stylesheet version="1.0" xmlns:xsl="http://www.w3.org/1999/XSL/Transform">
<xsl:output method="text"/>

<xsl:template match="/">
 <xsl:apply-templates select="names"/>
</xsl:template>

<xsl:template match="names">
 <xsl:apply-templates select="name[4]/@title"/>
</xsl:template>

<xsl:template match="name[4]/@title">
```

```
<xsl:text>The XML 1.0 WG's </xsl:text>
<xsl:value-of select="."/>
<xsl:text> was </xsl:text>
<xsl:value-of select="../given"/>
<xsl:text> </xsl:text>
<xsl:value-of select="../family"/>
<xsl:text>.</xsl:text>
</xsl:template>

</xsl:stylesheet>
```

Apply this stylesheet to *names.xml* with Xalan:

```
xalan names.xml pattern.xsl
```

and you'll see this one-line result:

```
The XML 1.0 WG's technical lead was James Clark.
```

There are other, more efficient ways to write this stylesheet, but this version suffices for the moment. Each match attribute in each of the three templates contains a pattern:

- The pattern in the first template rule, /, matches the root or document node and then applies the template that matches names.
- The pattern in the second template rule matches the document element names, and then applies the template that matches the title attribute (@title) of the fourth name child (name[4]) of names.
- The third and final pattern matches the title attribute of the fourth name element.

When the final template is instantiated, it uses several value-of elements to take information out of the source document, and also uses four text elements to put text on the result tree. The period (.) in the select attribute of the first value-of selects the current node.

Matching Multiple Nodes with a Pattern

You can match a union of multiple nodes by using the union operator (|) in a pattern or expression. The union operator denotes alternatives, that is, when you see the union operator separating node names, read the word *or*. To see what I mean, I'll show you *union.xsl*, which produces valid, string HTML 4.01 output. But first, Example 4-3 shows *provinces.xml*, along with an internal subset DTD, which contains a list of Canadian provinces.

Example 4-3. An XML list of contributors to XML 1.0

```
<?xml version="1.0" encoding="UTF-8"?>
<?xml-stylesheet href="union.xsl" type="text/xsl"?>
<!DOCTYPE provinces [
<!ELEMENT provinces (province)+>
<!ELEMENT province (name, abbreviation)>
```

Example 4-3. An XML list of contributors to XML 1.0 (continued)

```
<!ATTLIST province id ID #REQUIRED>
<!ELEMENT name (#PCDATA)>
<!ELEMENT abbreviation (#PCDATA)>
]>

<provinces>
 <province id="AB">
  <name>Alberta</name>
  <abbreviation>AB</abbreviation>
 </province>
 <province id="BC">
  <name>British Columbia</name>
  <abbreviation>BC</abbreviation>
 </province>
 <province id="MB">
  <name>Manitoba</name>
  <abbreviation>MB</abbreviation>
 </province>
 <province id="NB">
  <name>New Brunswick</name>
  <abbreviation>NB</abbreviation>
 </province>
 <province id="NL">
  <name>Newfoundland and Labrador</name>
  <abbreviation>NL</abbreviation>
 </province>
 <province id="NT">
  <name>Northwest Territories</name>
  <abbreviation>NT</abbreviation>
 </province>
 <province id="NS">
  <name>Nova Scotia</name>
  <abbreviation>NS</abbreviation>
 </province>
 <province id="NU">
  <name>Nunavut</name>
  <abbreviation>NU</abbreviation>
 </province>
 <province id="ON">
  <name>Ontario</name>
  <abbreviation>ON</abbreviation>
 </province>
 <province id="PE">
  <name>Prince Edward Island</name>
  <abbreviation>PE</abbreviation>
 </province>
 <province id="QC">
  <name>Quebec</name>
  <abbreviation>QC</abbreviation>
 </province>
 <province id="SK">
  <name>Saskatchewan</name>
  <abbreviation>SK</abbreviation>
```

Example 4-3. An XML list of contributors to XML 1.0 (continued)

```
 </province>
 <province id="YT">
  <name>Yukon</name>
  <abbreviation>YT</abbreviation>
 </province>
</provinces>
```

This document has an internal subset DTD. The only attribute declared is the required attribute id, which is of type ID. This attribute type is explained further in Chapter 5.

This document may be transformed into HTML with *union.xsl*, shown in Example 4-4.

Example 4-4. A stylesheet that applies the same rule to multiple nodes

```
<xsl:stylesheet version="1.0" xmlns:xsl="http://www.w3.org/1999/XSL/Transform">
<xsl:output method="html"/>
<xsl:output doctype-system="http://www.w3.org/TR/html4/strict.dtd"/>
<xsl:output doctype-public="-//W3C//DTD HTML 4.01//EN"/>

<xsl:template match="provinces">
 <html>
 <head><title>Provinces of Canada and Abbreviations</title></head>
 <body style="text-align:center">
 <h3 style="text-align:center">Provinces of Canada and Abbreviations</h3>
 <table style="margin-left:auto;margin-right:auto" rules="all" border="4">
 <thead style="background-color:black;color:white">
  <tr>
   <th style="width:230">Province</th>
   <th style="width:230">Abbreviation</th>
  </tr>
 </thead>
 <tbody align="center">
 <xsl:apply-templates select="province"/>
 </tbody>
 </table>
 </body>
 </html>
</xsl:template>

<xsl:template match="province">
 <tr>
  <xsl:apply-templates select="name|abbreviation"/>
 </tr>
</xsl:template>

<xsl:template match="name|abbreviation">
 <td>
 <xsl:apply-templates/>
 </td>
</xsl:template>

</xsl:stylesheet>
```

After the first template rule matches provinces, it generates the main body of HTML markup, which includes table-related elements such as table, thead, and tbody, plus CSS rules in style attributes.

The second template rule matches province nodes and then applies templates to the name or abbreviation children of province. (name | abbreviation) surrounds the output with tr (table row) tags. The final template rule matches on the pattern of name or abbreviation nodes, enclosing that output with td (table data) tags.

When you process *provinces.xml* with *union.xsl*:

```
xalan provinces.xml union.xsl
```

you see the following outcome from processing the union of name and abbreviation nodes. Note how the text content of both name and abbreviation nodes are contained in td elements, which are children of tr elements. This allows the columns of the table to line up properly. The resulting HTML document, listed in Example 4-5, is shown in Figure 4-4.

Example 4-5. An HTML table created by the stylesheet in Example 4-4

```
<!DOCTYPE HTML PUBLIC "-//W3C//DTD HTML 4.01//EN" "http://www.w3.org/TR/html4/
strict.dtd">
<html>
<head>
<META http-equiv="Content-Type" content="text/html; charset=UTF-8">
<title>Provinces of Canada and Abbreviations</title>
</head>
<body style="text-align:center">
<h3 style="text-align:center">Provinces of Canada and Abbreviations</h3>
<table style="margin-left:auto;margin-right:auto" rules="all" border="4">
<thead style="background-color:black;color:white">
<tr>
<th style="width:230">Province</th><th style="width:230">Abbreviation</th>
</tr>
</thead>
<tbody align="center">
<tr>
<td>Alberta</td><td>AB</td>
</tr>
<tr>
<td>British Columbia</td><td>BC</td>
</tr>
<tr>
<td>Manitoba</td><td>MB</td>
</tr>
<tr>
<td>New Brunswick</td><td>NB</td>
</tr>
<tr>
<td>Newfoundland and Labrador</td><td>NL</td>
</tr>
<tr>
```

```
<td>Northwest Territories</td><td>NT</td>
</tr>
<tr>
<td>Nova Scotia</td><td>NS</td>
</tr>
<tr>
<td>Nunavut</td><td>NU</td>
</tr>
<tr>
<td>Ontario</td><td>ON</td>
</tr>
<tr>
<td>Prince Edward Island</td><td>PE</td>
</tr>
<tr>
<td>Quebec</td><td>QC</td>
</tr>
<tr>
<td>Saskatchewan</td><td>SK</td>
</tr>
<tr>
<td>Yukon</td><td>YT</td>
</tr>
</tbody>
</table>
</body>
</html>
```

Axes

XPath views nodes along axes. An *axis* refers to various ways that you can locate nodes along the edges (branches) of a tree structure, either forward or backward. For example, the *parent* axis refers to the parent of a node, and the *self* axis refers only to a node itself. You can specify a few of the axes by using the abbreviated syntax, such as the parent (`../given`), child (`given`), and self (`.`) axes, but you can also specify them using the unabbreviated syntax, as in `parent::given`, `child::given`, and `self::node()`. One of the reasons you would want to use unabbreviated axes specifiers is because they allow you to find and access nodes that are not in the current node list.

Axes are oriented along a forward or reverse direction. Only 4 of the 13 axes have a reverse orientation. For example, the *ancestor* axis refers to nodes that come before the context node in the reverse direction, up to and including the root node. The descendant axis, on the other hand, includes nodes that come after the context node in the forward direction.

XPath defines 13 different axes, which are all listed and described in Table 4-2.

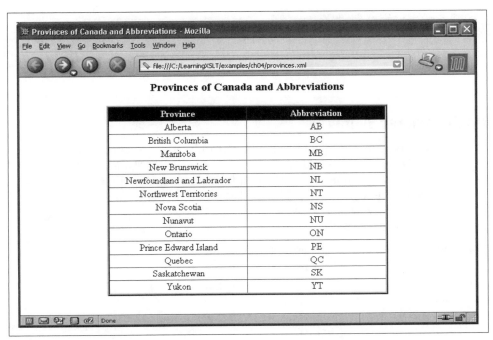

Figure 4-4. An HTML table in Mozilla

Table 4-2. XPath axes

Axis	Direction	Description
Ancestor	Reverse	Ancestors of the context node, up to and including the root or document node. This includes the parent node.
Ancestor-or-self	Reverse	Ancestors of the context node, including the context node itself and the root node.
Attribute	Forward	Attributes of the element context node.
Child	Forward	Children of the context node.
Descendant	Forward	Descendants of the context node.
Descendant-or-self	Forward	Descendants of the context node, up to and including the root node.
Following	Forward	All nodes that follow the context node in the same document, in document order, excluding descendants, attribute nodes, and namespace nodes.
Following-sibling	Forward	All sibling nodes that follow the context node, excluding attribute and namespace nodes.
Namespace	Forward	Namespace nodes of the current context.
Parent	Forward	Parent of the context node.
Preceding	Reverse	All nodes that precede the context node in the same document, in document order, excluding descendants, attribute nodes, and namespace nodes.

Table 4-2. XPath axes (continued)

Axis	Direction	Description
Preceding-sibling	Reverse	All sibling nodes that precede the context node, excluding attribute and namespace nodes.
Self	Not applicable	The context node itself.

Unabbreviated Syntax

The axes can be explicitly expressed using XPath's unabbreviated syntax, by connecting an axis name with a node name or a node test (see "Name and Node Tests," later in this chapter). Table 4-3 compares a few abbreviated and unabbreviated syntax examples to help you understand the relationship between the two.

Table 4-3. Abbreviated and unabbreviated syntax examples

Abbreviated	Unabbreviated
../given	parent::given
given	child::given
//given	descendant::given
.	self::node( )
*	child::*
text( )	child::text( )
@vendor	attribute::vendor

The following stylesheet shows you how axes and the unabbreviated syntax work together. The stylesheet, shown in Example 4-6, is called *unabbreviated.xsl* and is similar to *pattern.xsl*, which you saw earlier in this chapter.

Example 4-6. A stylesheet using the full axis syntax

```
<xsl:stylesheet version="1.0" xmlns:xsl="http://www.w3.org/1999/XSL/Transform">
<xsl:output method="text"/>

<xsl:template match="/">
 <xsl:apply-templates select="child::names"/>
</xsl:template>

<xsl:template match="child::names">
 <xsl:apply-templates select="child::name[4]/attribute::title"/>
</xsl:template>

<xsl:template match="child::name[4]/attribute::title">
 <xsl:text>The XML 1.0 WG's </xsl:text>
 <xsl:value-of select="self::node( )"/>
 <xsl:text> was </xsl:text>
 <xsl:value-of select="parent::name/child::given"/>
 <xsl:text> </xsl:text>
```

Example 4-6. A stylesheet using the full axis syntax (continued)

```
<xsl:value-of select="parent::name/child::family"/>
<xsl:text>.</xsl:text>
</xsl:template>

</xsl:stylesheet>
```

Lines in the stylesheet that use unabbreviated syntax are highlighted in bold. The *parent*, *child*, *self*, and *attribute* axes are connected to node names using a connector (::). The *parent* axis may be abbreviated as .., so that parent::name/child::given could be ../given.

The *self* axis is connected to node( ). This syntax looks like a function call, but it's really not. It's a *node test* that tests to see whether a node matches a particular criterion. The node( ) test matches any node and is sometimes called a *wildcard* (though the word *wildcard* doesn't appear in the XPath 1.0 spec).

If you apply *unabbreviated.xsl* to *names.xml*, using:

```
xalan names.xml unabbreviated.xsl
```

you get the following line as a result:

```
The XML 1.0 WG's technical lead was James Clark.
```

Reaching Out of Context with Unabbreviated Syntax

As I mentioned earlier, you can use axes to reach for nodes that are not in context. As usual, I'll illustrate how to do this with an example. When the stylesheet shown in Example 4-7, *ancestor.xsl*, processes the last name node in *names.xml*, it also processes the first name node in the document by using the *ancestor* axis.

Example 4-7. A stylesheet using the ancestor axis

```
<xsl:stylesheet version="1.0" xmlns:xsl="http://www.w3.org/1999/XSL/Transform">
<xsl:output method="text"/>

<xsl:template match="/">
 <xsl:apply-templates select="child::names"/>
</xsl:template>

<xsl:template match="child::names">
 <xsl:apply-templates select="child::name[18]"/>
</xsl:template>

<xsl:template match="child::name[18]">
 <xsl:value-of select="ancestor::names/child::name[1]/child::given"/>
 <xsl:text> </xsl:text>
 <xsl:value-of select="ancestor::names/child::name[1]/child::family"/>
 <xsl:text> is first on the list, and </xsl:text>
 <xsl:value-of select="child::given"/>
 <xsl:text> </xsl:text>
```

Example 4-7. A stylesheet using the ancestor axis (continued)

```
<xsl:value-of select="child::family"/>
<xsl:text> is last.</xsl:text>
</xsl:template>

</xsl:stylesheet>
```

The node processed by the last template in the stylesheet is the last (child::name[18]) name node in *names.xml*. While this template processes the last name node, it also finds an ancestor, the names node, and then processes the first name child of names called given (ancestor::names/child::name[1]/child::given) and the first name child of names called family (ancestor::names/child::name[1]/child::family). Apply it with:

```
xalan names.xml ancestor.xsl
```

The result of processing *names.xml* with this stylesheet is as follows:

```
Paula Angerstein is first on the list, and John Tigue is last.
```

Name and Node Tests

You can match a variety of nodes with XPath using name and node tests. A name test can match any element name, any element name with a given prefix, or a QName (a namespace-qualified name, with or without a prefix). Node tests can match text, comment, processing instruction nodes, or any node. You can use abbreviated or unabbreviated syntax with name and node tests. Table 4-4 describes each of the tests.

Table 4-4. Name and node tests

Test	Test type	Description
*	Name	Matches any element name (or attribute name if using the attribute axis).
rng:*	Name	Matches any element name with an rng prefix (or any other prefix you choose).
rng:text	Name	Matches the QName rng:text.
text( )	Node	Matches text nodes.
comment( )	Node	Matches comment nodes.
processing-instruction( )	Node	Matches processing instruction nodes.
processing-instruction('xml-stylesheet')	Node	Matches processing instruction nodes with the target name xml-stylesheet.
node( )	Node	Matches any node.

node( ) matches only nodes along the specified axis; if no axis is specified, the child axis is assumed, and you won't get attributes!

Example 4-8 shows a RELAX NG schema for *provinces.xml* called *provinces.rng*.

Example 4-8. A RELAX NG schema for provinces.xml

```
<?xml version="1.0"?>
<!--Relax NG schema for provinces.xml-->
<rng:element name="provinces" xmlns:rng="http://relaxng.org/ns/structure/1.0"
 datatypeLibrary="http://www.w3.org/2001/XMLSchema-datatypes">
 <rng:oneOrMore>
  <rng:element name="province">
   <rng:attribute name="id">
    <rng:data type="ID"/>
   </rng:attribute>
   <rng:element name="name">
    <rng:text/>
   </rng:element>
   <rng:element name="abbreviation">
    <rng:text/>
   </rng:element>
  </rng:element>
 </rng:oneOrMore>
</rng:element>
```

RELAX NG is a simple yet elegant schema language for XML (see *http://www.relaxng.org*). The document *provinces.xml* is valid with regard to this schema, which defines the instance document with a natural, structured hierarchy of definitions. RELAX NG adopts XML Schema datatypes as a datatype library (note the datatypeLibrary attribute on the first element and the rng:data element as a child of rng:attribute).

Example 4-9, *splat.xsl*, is a simple stylesheet that uses name and node tests to analyze the RELAX NG schema.

Example 4-9. A stylesheet for analyzing the RELAX NG schema

```
<xsl:stylesheet version="1.0"
 xmlns:xsl="http://www.w3.org/1999/XSL/Transform"
 xmlns:rng="http://relaxng.org/ns/structure/1.0">
<xsl:output method="text"/>

<xsl:template match="/">
 <xsl:value-of select="comment( )"/>
 <xsl:text>&#10;</xsl:text>
 <xsl:apply-templates select="rng:*"/>
</xsl:template>

<xsl:template match="rng:*">
 <xsl:value-of select="local-name( )"/>
 <xsl:text>, </xsl:text>
 <xsl:value-of select="name(@*)"/>
 <xsl:text> = </xsl:text>
 <xsl:value-of select="@*"/>
 <xsl:text>&#10;</xsl:text>
```

Example 4-9. A stylesheet for analyzing the RELAX NG schema (continued)

```
<xsl:apply-templates select="rng:*"/>
</xsl:template>

</xsl:stylesheet>
```

Because the elements in the schema are namespace-qualified and use a prefix (rng:), the stylesheet must declare the namespace and prefix as well (xmlns:rng="http://relaxng.org/ns/structure/1.0"). The template that matches the root uses a comment( ) node test to return the text content of a comment in the source. It then applies templates to any element qualified with the RELAX NG namespace (rng:*).

> Don't make the mistake of using a location path like rng:element/attribute instead of rng:element/rng:attribute. The first location path searches for rng:element followed by an attribute element in no namespace! The second location example uses a prefix with the element name. Take care to use namespace prefixes where needed in location paths.

The next template matches on rng:* and reports the names of these elements using the XPath local-name( ) function, which returns the element name without the prefix. The name( ) function returns the names of attributes, if any, using name( ) with @* as an argument; @* is used by itself to return an attribute value. This template uses apply-templates with rng:* again and thereby reports on all RELAX NG elements in the source tree.

When applied like this:

```
xalan provinces.rng splat.xsl
```

the text output is:

```
Relax NG schema for provinces.xml
element, name = provinces
oneOrMore,  =
element, name = province
attribute, name = id
data, type = ID
element, name = name
text,  =
element, name = abbreviation
text,  =
```

The first line of the result is the comment at the top of *provinces.rng*. The remaining lines report the RELAX NG element names followed by the names and values of any attributes the element might have.

For more information on name and node tests, see Section 2.3 of the XPath specification.

Doing the Math with Expressions

Expressions allow you to perform simple arithmetic and Boolean logic when processing nodes. Here's an example of some simple addition and multiplication. The document *math.xml* contains a group of operand elements, each containing an integer:

```
<math>
 <operand>12</operand>
 <operand>23</operand>
 <operand>45</operand>
 <operand>56</operand>
 <operand>75</operand>
</math>
```

You can use an expression to add and multiply 25 with these operands, as shown in Example 4-10, the stylesheet *math.xsl*.

Example 4-10. A stylesheet that does simple math

```
<xsl:stylesheet version="1.0" xmlns:xsl="http://www.w3.org/1999/XSL/Transform">
<xsl:output method="text"/>

<xsl:template match="math">
 <xsl:apply-templates select="operand"/>
</xsl:template>

<xsl:template match="operand">
 <xsl:value-of select="."/>
 <xsl:text> + 25 = </xsl:text>
 <xsl:value-of select=". + 25"/>
 <xsl:text>&#10;</xsl:text>
 <xsl:value-of select="."/>
 <xsl:text> * 25 = </xsl:text>
 <xsl:value-of select=". * 25"/>
 <xsl:text>&#10;</xsl:text>
</xsl:template>

</xsl:stylesheet>
```

The expression is the value of several select attributes of value-of that add and multiply the content of each operand element with 25. The value-of element returns a string value, but the presence of + or * automatically converts the content of operand to a number, if possible. If the content of operand were a nonnumerical string, however, the number conversion wouldn't take place. This won't cause an error, but you will get NaN (Not a Number) in response.

When you process *math.xsl* against *math.xml* using:

```
xalan math.xml math.xsl
```

you get this result:

```
12 + 25 = 37
12 * 25 = 300
23 + 25 = 48
23 * 25 = 575
45 + 25 = 70
45 * 25 = 1125
56 + 25 = 81
56 * 25 = 1400
75 + 25 = 100
75 * 25 = 1875
```

The stylesheet shown in Example 4-11, *boolean.xsl*, combines addition and multiplication with some Boolean logic. It uses expressions in predicates to test whether the content of operand nodes are both greater-than and less-than a value.

Example 4-11. A stylesheet demonstrating more mathematical capability

```
<xsl:stylesheet version="1.0" xmlns:xsl="http://www.w3.org/1999/XSL/Transform">
<xsl:output method="text"/>

<xsl:template match="/">
 <xsl:apply-templates select="math"/>
</xsl:template>

<xsl:template match="math">
 <xsl:apply-templates select="operand[(. &lt; 50) and (. &gt; 30)]"/>
</xsl:template>

<xsl:template match="operand[(. &lt; 50) and (. &gt; 30)]">
 <xsl:value-of select="."/>
 <xsl:text> + 25 = </xsl:text>
 <xsl:value-of select=". + 25"/>
 <xsl:text>&#10;</xsl:text>
 <xsl:value-of select="."/>
 <xsl:text> * 25 = </xsl:text>
 <xsl:value-of select=". * 25"/>
 <xsl:text>&#10;</xsl:text>
</xsl:template>

</xsl:stylesheet>
```

In ordinary English, the expression:

```
(. &lt; 50) and (. &gt; 30)
```

tests whether the operand is less than 50 and greater than 30. The entity references < and > are used in the predicates instead of < and > because < is forbidden in attribute values in XML (see Section 3.1 of the XML specification). To balance this limitation, XML uses entity references for both symbols, even though > is legal in attribute values. The parentheses distinguish the greater-than and less-than tests, which are compared with the and operator. For a complete list of Boolean and math operators in XPath, see Table 4-5.

Table 4-5. XPath operators

Operator	Type	Description
and	Boolean	Boolean AND
or	Boolean	Boolean OR
=	Boolean	Equals
!=	Boolean	Not equal
< (<)	Boolean	Less than
<=(<=)	Boolean	Less than or equal to
>(>)	Boolean	Greater than
>=(>=)	Boolean	Greater than or equal to
+	Number	Addition
-	Number	Subtraction
*	Number	Multiplication
div	Number	Division
mod	Number	Modulo (remainder of division)

This concludes your mini math lesson in XPath and XSLT. To learn more about math in XPath, see Sections 3.4 and 3.5 in the XPath specification.

Summary

This chapter discussed the XPath data model with its seven node types. It also explained location paths, expressions and patterns, predicates, abbreviated and unabbreviated location paths, and axes. You learned how to do simple arithmetic and name and node tests, as well. For additional light on this subject, see Chapter 9 of O'Reilly's *XML in a Nutshell* by Elliotte Rusty Harold and W. Scott Means, and Chapter 3 from O'Reilly's *XSLT* by Doug Tidwell.

The next chapter continues the theme by exploring XPath and XSLT functions used in expressions.

CHAPTER 5
XPath and XSLT Functions

XPath defines 27 functions that may be called in expressions, including predicates. XSLT adds 9 functions to the XPath mix. You have already seen a number of these functions at work in previous examples in this book, such as name( ), string-length( ), and substring( ).

Table 5-1 briefly documents all of the XPath 1.0 functions, including arguments. Similarly, Table 5-2 describes the XSLT 1.0 functions. XPath functions are divided into 4 types: Boolean, node-set, number, and string.

 Node tests such as text( ) and comment( ) look like functions but they are not really functions. Node tests simply test whether a given node matches a node type.

I'll demonstrate a number of functions in this chapter, but other chapters in this book will expose you to more examples of functions. For additional details on XPath functions, see Section 4 of the XPath specification. You can read more about XSLT functions in Sections 12 through 15 of the XSLT specification.

 This is an introductory book and it does not provide exhaustive explanations of all of the XPath functions, though it will give you a chance to use many of them. John Simpson's *XPath and XPointer* (O'Reilly) explores XPath (and its derivative XPointer) in greater detail. Doug Tidwell's *XSLT* (O'Reilly), provides an excellent reference that demonstrates all these functions, as does Michael Kay's *XSLT Programmer's Reference* (Wrox). Another resource is Mulberry Technologies' XSLT and XPath Quick Reference at *http://www.mulberrytech.com/quickref/ XSLTquickref.pdf*.

Table 5-1. XPath functions

XPath function signature	Type	Returns	Description
`boolean(object)`	Boolean	Boolean	Converts the argument to a Boolean.
`ceiling(number)`	Number	Number	Returns the smallest integer (closest to negative infinity) that is not less than the argument.
`concat(string, string, string*)`	String	String	Returns a concatenation of two or more string arguments.
`contains(string, string)`	String	Boolean	Returns true if the first argument contains the string in the second argument.
`count(node-set)`	Node-set	Number	Returns the number of nodes in a node-set.
`false()`	Boolean	Boolean	Returns false.
`floor(number)`	Number	Number	Returns the largest integer (closest to positive infinity) that is not more than the argument.
`id(object)`	Node-set	Node-set	Selects elements by unique ID.
`lang(string)`	Boolean	Boolean	Returns true if the argument matches the context node's `xml:lang` value.
`last()`	Node-set	Number	Returns the context size (the node position of the last node).
`local-name(node-set?)`	Node-set	String	Returns the local part of an expanded QName (without a prefix).
`name(node-set?)`	Node-set	String	Returns a QName.
`namespace-uri(node-set?)`	Node-set	String	Returns a namespace URI.
`normalize-space(string?)`	String	String	Returns a string with its whitespace normalized.
`not(boolean)`	Boolean	Boolean	Returns true if the argument is false.
`number(object?)`	Number	Number	Converts an object to a number.
`position()`	Node-set	Number	Returns the context position (of the current node).
`round(number)`	Number	Number	Returns an integer, rounded closest to the value of the argument.
`starts-with(string, string)`	String	Boolean	Returns true if the first string starts with the second; otherwise it returns false.
`string(object?)`	String	String	Converts an object into a string.
`string-length(string?)`	String	Number	Returns the length of a string.
`substring(string, number, number?)`	String	String	Returns a substring of the first argument, based on the starting position in the second argument, and the optional length in the third.
`substring-after(string, string)`	String	String	Returns the substring of the first argument that follows the first occurrence of the second argument in the first.

Table 5-1. XPath functions (continued)

XPath function signature	Type	Returns	Description
substring-before(string, string)	String	String	Returns the substring of the first argument that precedes the first occurrence of the second argument in the first.
sum(node-set)	Number	Number	Returns a sum of nodes.
translate(string, string, string)	String	String	Returns the first argument string with occurrences of characters in the second replaced by corresponding characters in the third.
true( )	Boolean	Boolean	Returns true.

Table 5-2. XSLT functions

XSLT function signature	Returns	Description
document(object, node-set?)	Node-set	Loads additional documents, allowing a transformation to have more than one input document.
key(string, object)	Node-set	Applies the key in the first argument using the second argument.
format-number(number, string, string?)	String	Converts a number to a string using the format pattern in the second argument and the decimal format identified by the third argument, if present.
current( )	Node-set	Returns the current node.
unparsed-entity-uri(string)	String	Returns a URI for an unparsed entity.
generate-id(node-set?)	String	Generates a unique ID for an element in the result tree.
system-property(string)	Object	Returns an XSLT system property.
element-available(string)	Boolean	Returns true if the named element is available.
function-available(string)	Boolean	Returns true if the named function is available.

If you need even more functions, consider exploring the EXSLT extensions library, explained in Chapter 15.

Boolean Functions

Boolean functions return true or false and are used in stylesheet logic that tests whether something is true. In XPath, the Boolean functions are boolean( ), false( ), lang( ), not( ), and true( ). In XSLT, the functions that return Booleans are element-available( ) and function-available( ). You'll learn to use element-available( ) and function-available( ) in Chapter 15, as well as how to use the system-property( ) function that returns an object. The strings functions contains( ) and starts-with( ) also return Booleans.

The lang( ) Function

The XPath Boolean functions include lang( ), which returns true if an xml:lang attribute exists with a given language token—its only argument. This token must be quoted with single quotes. (By the way, the value of xml:lang is inherited by child elements, though this isn't shown in the following example.)

The brief document *greet.xml* in *examples/ch05* contains greetings in four languages— English, French, Spanish, and German:

```
<?xml version="1.0"?>

<greet>
 <greeting xml:lang="en">Welcome</greeting>
 <greeting xml:lang="fr">Bienvenue</greeting>
 <greeting xml:lang="es">Bienvenida</greeting>
 <greeting xml:lang="de">Willkommen</greeting>
</greet>
```

The stylesheet *greet.xsl* uses the lang( ) function to select the greeting element that has an xml:lang attribute with a value of fr:

```
<xsl:stylesheet version="1.0" xmlns:xsl="http://www.w3.org/1999/XSL/Transform">
<xsl:output method="text"/>

<xsl:template match="greet">
 <xsl:apply-templates select="greeting[lang('fr')]"/>
</xsl:template>

<xsl:template match="greeting[lang('fr')]">
 <xsl:text>French: </xsl:text>
 <xsl:value-of select="."/>
</xsl:template>

</xsl:stylesheet>
```

When you process *greet.xml* with *greet.xsl* using Xalan as shown:

```
xalan greet.xml greet.xsl
```

you get the following output:

```
French: Bienvenue
```

When this stylesheet processes greeting elements in the source tree, it tests whether the element has an xml:lang attribute with the specified value fr. When the pattern matches such an element, the lang( ) function returns true, and the template is instantiated.

Now, I'll move on to XPath node-set functions.

Node-Set Functions

The node-set functions return node-sets, strings, or numbers. From XPath, the node-set functions include count( ), id( ), last( ), local-name( ), name( ), namespace-uri( ), and position( ). The count( ), last( ), and position( ) functions return numbers, and local-name( ), name( ), and namespace-uri( ) return strings. The following additional functions from XSLT return node-sets: document( ), key( ), and current( ).

You saw the name( ) and local-name( ) functions several times in earlier chapters, and you'll see it in later chapters, too. You'll get a chance to explore the document( ) function in Chapter 13 and the key( ) function in Chapter 11. The current( ) function is used in an example in the section "String Functions," later in this chapter.

The id( ) Function

Here's how the id( ) function works. In valid XML 1.0, an ID is a unique identifier held in an attribute value. The attribute must be declared in a DTD to be recognized as being of type ID. If this identifier of type ID is duplicated in the document, the document is invalid. An ID must not start with a number. IDs can uniquely identify an element, which helps you to find and isolate parts of documents that may be of interest.

A document you saw in the last chapter, *provinces.xml*, has id attributes of type ID. The id( ) function can help you find a given ID in a document and then return some bit of information. The stylesheet *id.xsl* uses id( ):

```
<xsl:stylesheet version="1.0" xmlns:xsl="http://www.w3.org/1999/XSL/Transform">
<xsl:output method="text"/>

<xsl:template match="provinces">
 <xsl:apply-templates select="id('NU')"/>
</xsl:template>

<xsl:template match="id('NU')">
 <xsl:value-of select="name"/>
</xsl:template>

</xsl:stylesheet>
```

The id( ) function may be used in patterns as well as expressions. The pattern that matches id('NU') finds an element node with an attribute of type ID that has a value of NU. The following is a fragment from *provinces.xml*:

```
<province id="NU">
 <name>Nunavut</name>
 <abbreviation>NU</abbreviation>
 </province>
```

When applied to *provinces.xml*, *id.xsl* finds this instance of the province element and returns the string value of the text in the name element that is a child of province. This is what the processor will return:

```
Nunavut
```

Now, I'll introduce some number functions.

Number Functions

The XPath number functions all return numbers. However, none of the XSLT functions return numbers. The number functions are ceiling( ), floor( ), number( ), round( ), and sum( ). The node-set functions count( ), last( ), and position( ) also return numbers, as does the string function string-length( ).

The sum( ) Function

The sum( ) function takes a single node-set as an argument and returns or adds up a sum of numbers from that node-set. The document *math.xml* contains a group of operand elements, each with numeric content:

```
<math>
  <operand>12</operand>
  <operand>23</operand>
  <operand>45</operand>
  <operand>56</operand>
  <operand>75</operand>
</math>
```

You can use the sum( ) function in *sum.xsl* to add these numbers and return the sum:

```
<xsl:stylesheet version="1.0" xmlns:xsl="http://www.w3.org/1999/XSL/Transform">
<xsl:output method="text"/>

<xsl:template match="math">
 <xsl:value-of select="sum(operand)"/>
</xsl:template>

</xsl:stylesheet>
```

If applied to *math.xml*, this stylesheet will produce a sum of the numbers in all the operand children of math:

```
211
```

The round( ) Function

Taking a number as an argument, the round( ) function returns an integer that is rounded closest to the value of the function's argument. Consider *round.xml*:

```
<math>
 <down>
```

```
  <operand>12.12</operand>
  <operand>23.22</operand>
 </down>
 <up>
  <operand>12.15</operand>
  <operand>23.73</operand>
 </up>
</math>
```

Then apply the stylesheet *round.xsl*:

```
<xsl:stylesheet version="1.0" xmlns:xsl="http://www.w3.org/1999/XSL/Transform">
<xsl:output method="text"/>

<xsl:template match="math">
 <xsl:apply-templates select="up|down"/>
</xsl:template>

<xsl:template match="up|down">
 <xsl:value-of select="round(sum(operand))"/>
 <xsl:text> </xsl:text>
</xsl:template>

</xsl:stylesheet>
```

The sum( ) function returns a number to round( ). The stylesheet finds the up or down children of operand. When it finds them, it outputs the rounded sum of the operands:

```
35 36
```

The content of the operand children of down, 12.12, and 23.22 is converted to numbers, summed, and then rounded down to 35. On the other hand, the content of the operand children of up, 12.15, and 23.73 is converted to numbers, summed, and then rounded up to 36.

I'll wrap up with string functions.

String Functions

The string functions return strings and Booleans. The XPath string functions are concat( ), contains( ) (returns a Boolean), normalize-space( ), starts-with( ) (also returns a Boolean), string( ), string-length( ), substring( ), substring-after( ), substring-before( ), and translate( ). The XSLT functions format-number( ), unparsed-entity-uri( ), and generate-id( ) also return strings. You saw substring( ) and string-length( ) in action in Chapter 3.

The concat( ) Function

I'll demonstrate how to use concat( ) here. The file *poem.xml* holds a limerick written by XML mensch John Cowan:

```
<?xml version="1.0" encoding="UTF-8"?>
```

```
<poem>
 <line>My corporate data's a mess!</line>
 <line>It's all semi-structured, no less.</line>
 <line>But I'll be carefree</line>
 <line>Using XSLT</line>
 <line>In an XML DBMS.</line>
 <attribution>John Cowan</attribution>
</poem>
```

You could format the poem in any number of ways, but I'll show you one way to do it with concat( ). The stylesheet *limerick.xsl* does most of its work with the concat( ) function:

```
<xsl:stylesheet version="1.0" xmlns:xsl="http://www.w3.org/1999/XSL/Transform">
<xsl:output method="text"/>

<xsl:template match="poem">
 <xsl:value-of select="concat(line[1], '&#10;',
                              line[2], '&#10;',
                              '&#32;&#32;&#32;',
                              line[3], '&#10;',
                              '&#32;&#32;&#32;',
                              line[4], '&#10;',
                              line[5], '&#10;',
                              '&#9;&#9;-',
                              attribution)"/>
</xsl:template>

</xsl:stylesheet>
```

The concat( ) function takes two or more strings as arguments and concatenates them together. In this stylesheet, concat( ) concatenates 14 strings together, collecting 5 of them from line elements. It inserts whitespace directly—linefeeds, spaces, and tabs—and picks up one last string from the attribution element.

The result of processing *poem.xml* with *limerick.xsl* produces a nicely formatted limerick:

```
My corporate data's a mess!
It's all semi-structured, no less.
   But I'll be carefree
   Using XSLT
In an XML DBMS.
            -John Cowan
```

The normalize-space( ), translate( ), and substring( ) Functions

Now let's use normalize-space( ), translate( ), and substring( ) together to help perform a conversion of a Microsoft file path with a Unix one. The document *path.xml* contains a Microsoft path that includes a filename:

```
<ms>
```

```
C:\LearningXSLT\examples\ch05\path.xml
```

```
</ms>
```

Let's suppose you want to convert this path to Unix and get rid of linefeeds that surround the path. The *fix.xsl* stylesheet can do this with a single expression:

```
<xsl:stylesheet version="1.0" xmlns:xsl="http://www.w3.org/1999/XSL/Transform">
<xsl:output method="xml"/>

<xsl:template match="ms">
 <unix>/usr/mike<xsl:value-of select="normalize-space(translate(substring(.,5),'\','/
'))"/></unix>
</xsl:template>

</xsl:stylesheet>
```

The result of processing *path.xml* with *fix.xsl* with:

```
xalan path.xml fix.xsl
```

produces:

```
<?xml version="1.0" encoding="UTF-8"?>
<unix>/usr/mike/LearningXSLT/examples/ch05/path.xml</unix>
```

The innermost XSLT function called is substring(.,5). This call refers to the string value of the current node, that is, the child text node of ms, using the single period (.). (The single period is generally a synonym for the current() function, which returns the current node.) The second argument is 5, which indicates what character will begin the text node of the substring (because it is preceded by two linefeeds, the fifth character immediately follows the colon). substring() has an optional third argument (not shown in this example), which is a number that determines the overall length of the substring.

The translate() function takes three arguments. The first is the string to be translated. In the case of this example, it is the lopped-off string produced by the substring() function. The next argument is the character (it could be a list of characters) that you want to translate. You can list more than one character to translate, but this example only uses one, that is, \. The third argument tells what the second argument \ will translate into, namely, /. If the second and third arguments list more than one character, each character in the second argument list is translated with the corresponding character in the third argument list.

You have to use caution with translate(), as it is easy to swap characters that you do not intend to swap. The conversion takes place for every instance of the character in the source tree, not just the first one.

Finally, the normalize-space() function normalizes space in ms by trimming leading and trailing whitespace.

The generate-id( ) Function

As discussed earlier in "The id( ) Function," an ID is a unique identifier in XML. The generate-id( ) function creates IDs that are guaranteed to be unique within a document. The stylesheet *generate-id.xsl* generates a unique ID for each new welcome element that it creates:

```
<xsl:stylesheet version="1.0" xmlns:xsl="http://www.w3.org/1999/XSL/Transform">
<xsl:output method="xml" indent="yes"/>
<xsl:output doctype-system="welcome.dtd"/>

<xsl:template match="greet">
 <xsl:element name="greeting">
  <xsl:apply-templates select="greeting"/>
 </xsl:element>
</xsl:template>

<xsl:template match="greeting">
 <xsl:element name="welcome">
  <xsl:attribute name="xml:lang"><xsl:value-of select="@xml:lang"/></xsl:attribute>
  <xsl:attribute name="id"><xsl:value-of select="generate-id(.)"/></xsl:attribute>
  <xsl:value-of select="current( )"/>
 </xsl:element>
</xsl:template>

</xsl:stylesheet>
```

The stylesheet also passes on the xml:lang attributes with its values from the source to the result. It also creates a document type declaration that associates the result document with the DTD called *welcome.dtd*. It's shown here:

```
<!ELEMENT greeting (welcome+)>
<!ELEMENT welcome (#PCDATA)>
<!ATTLIST welcome id ID #REQUIRED
                  xml:lang CDATA #REQUIRED>
```

This DTD declares an id attribute of type ID for the generated, unique ID values. Create the result document with this command:

```
xalan -i 1 -o welcome.xml greet.xml generate-id.xsl
```

welcome.xml looks like this:

```
<?xml version="1.0" encoding="UTF-8"?>
<!DOCTYPE greeting SYSTEM "welcome.dtd">
<greeting>
 <welcome xml:lang="en" id="N003EBD80.004836F4">Welcome</welcome>
 <welcome xml:lang="fr" id="N003EBD80.00483720">Bienvenue</welcome>
 <welcome xml:lang="es" id="N003EBD80.0048374C">Bienvenido</welcome>
 <welcome xml:lang="de" id="N003EBD80.00483778">Willkommen</welcome>
</greeting>
```

welcome.xml is valid with regard to *welcome.dtd*. The id attributes are of type ID in the DTD, and each of the id values is unique.

welcome.xsl extracts a German welcome from *welcome.xml* while showing its ID:

```
<xsl:stylesheet version="1.0" xmlns:xsl="http://www.w3.org/1999/XSL/Transform">
<xsl:output method="text"/>

<xsl:template match="greeting">
 <xsl:apply-templates select="welcome[lang('de')]"/>
</xsl:template>

<xsl:template match="welcome[lang('de')]">
 <xsl:text>German: </xsl:text>
 <xsl:value-of select="."/>
 <xsl:text> (ID: </xsl:text>
 <xsl:value-of select="@id"/>
 <xsl:text>)</xsl:text>
</xsl:template>

</xsl:stylesheet>
```

Now validate *welcome.xml* by using the -v option with Xalan while you transform it with *welcome.xsl*:

```
xalan -v welcome.xml welcome.xsl
```

Here is the result of the transformation:

```
German: Willkommen (ID: N003EBD80.00483778)
```

Summary

This concludes your introduction to XPath and XSLT functions. I've hardly introduced you to all the functions, but by the time you finish reading this book, you'll have encountered many of them in working examples.

In the next chapter, you'll learn how to use the copy and copy-of instructions.

CHAPTER 6

Copying Nodes

Sometimes when you are building a result tree, you just want to copy nodes out of an XML document without altering them. You can do this with the copy and copy-of instruction elements. You will learn about the differences in these two elements and how to use them in this chapter. I'll start with the copy element.

The copy Element

You'll be working with several XML documents relating to the European Union (EU) in the examples that follow. You can read more about the EU—in at least 12 different languages—at *http://europa.eu.int/*. The document *eu.xml*, Example 6-1, found in the directory *examples/ch06*, represents member states, founding member states, and candidate member states from the EU.

Example 6-1. An XML document listing EU member and candidate states

```
<?xml version="1.0" encoding="UTF-8"?>

<!-- European Union member states and candidate states -->

<eu>
 <member>
  <state>Austria</state>
  <state founding="yes">Belgium</state>
  <state>Denmark</state>
  <state>Finland</state>
  <state founding="yes">France</state>
  <state founding="yes">Germany</state>
  <state>Greece</state>
  <state>Ireland</state>
  <state founding="yes">Italy</state>
  <state founding="yes">Luxembourg</state>
  <state founding="yes">The Netherlands</state>
  <state>Portugal</state>
  <state>Spain</state>
```

```
  <state>Sweden</state>
  <state>United Kingdom</state>
 </member>
 <candidate>
  <state>Bulgaria</state>
  <state>Cyprus</state>
  <state>Czech Republic</state>
  <state>Estonia</state>
  <state>Hungary</state>
  <state>Latvia</state>
  <state>Lithuania</state>
  <state>Malta</state>
  <state>Poland</state>
  <state>Romania</state>
  <state>Slovenia</state>
  <state>Slovakia</state>
  <state>Turkey</state>
 </candidate>
</eu>
```

There are currently, as of early 2003, 15 member states in the EU, and 13 candidate member states. If you wanted to duplicate element nodes from this document, you could use the XSLT copy instruction element, though it has certain limitations.

First, consider this inadequate stylesheet, *copy.xsl*:

```
<xsl:stylesheet version="1.0" xmlns:xsl="http://www.w3.org/1999/XSL/Transform">
<xsl:output method="xml" indent="yes"/>

<xsl:template match="eu">
 <xsl:apply-templates select="member"/>
</xsl:template>

<xsl:template match="member">
  <xsl:apply-templates select="state[2]"/>
</xsl:template>

<xsl:template match="state">
 <xsl:copy/>
</xsl:template>

</xsl:stylesheet>
```

The output method is explicitly XML because that's really the only output method that makes any sense with copy. This stylesheet targets the second state element in *eu.xml* for copying. This state element has the word Belgium as content, and also has a founding attribute, indicating that Belgium is one of the founding members of the EU. If you apply the stylesheet to *eu.xml*, however, with:

```
xalan eu.xml copy.xsl
```

you get this result:

```
<?xml version="1.0" encoding="UTF-8"?>
<state/>
```

Where's the attribute value and the element content? Surprise! The copy element doesn't get it for you. It copies the current node, but only if it is an element and has any namespace nodes associated with that element. That's it. This is sometimes called a *shallow copy*. A shallow copy does not copy any attribute nodes or child nodes, including text nodes. This is a good thing, though, because sometimes that's exactly what you want. I'll show you why.

Suppose, for example, that you wanted to pull all the elements that represent the six founding states of the EU out of *eu.xml*. You could do this with the stylesheet *founding.xsl*:

```
<xsl:stylesheet version="1.0" xmlns:xsl="http://www.w3.org/1999/XSL/Transform">
<xsl:output method="xml" indent="yes"/>

 <xsl:template match="eu">
  <xsl:apply-templates select="member"/>
 </xsl:template>

 <xsl:template match="member">
 <eu-members>
   <xsl:apply-templates select="state[@founding]"/>
 </eu-members>
 </xsl:template>

 <xsl:template match="state">
  <xsl:copy>
   <xsl:apply-templates/>
  </xsl:copy>
 </xsl:template>

</xsl:stylesheet>
```

This stylesheet finds all the state elements that are children of member, and that also have founding attributes, and wraps them all in an eu-members document element. The addition of the apply-templates element as a child of copy means that the template will process all children of the matched nodes, including text, invoking the built-in templates whenever there is a match. When you process *eu.xml* against *founding.xsl*:

```
xalan -i 1 eu.xml founding.xsl
```

you will get the following:

```
<?xml version="1.0" encoding="UTF-8"?>
<eu-members>
 <state>Belgium</state>
 <state>France</state>
 <state>Germany</state>
```

```
<state>Italy</state>
<state>Luxembourg</state>
<state>The Netherlands</state>
</eu-members>
```

The copy element outputs the state element, and apply-templates picks up the text content of the state elements through the built-in template for text. Because attributes are not considered children of elements, apply-templates does not return their values. Attributes have parents, however, which are always elements.

Adding Attributes with copy

The copy element has one optional attribute, use-attribute-sets. In Chapter 2, you saw this attribute in action. It allows you to invoke a named set of attributes stored in an attribute-set element, adding them to an element in the result tree. The following stylesheet, *notfounding.xsl*, shown in Example 6-2, shows you how it's done.

Example 6-2. An XSLT stylesheet that adds attributes in the course of a copy

```
<xsl:stylesheet version="1.0" xmlns:xsl="http://www.w3.org/1999/XSL/Transform">
<xsl:output method="xml" indent="yes"/>

<xsl:attribute-set name="new">
 <xsl:attribute name="founding">no</xsl:attribute>
</xsl:attribute-set>

<xsl:template match="eu">
 <xsl:apply-templates select="member"/>
</xsl:template>

<xsl:template match="member">
<eu>
 <members>
  <xsl:apply-templates select="state[not(@founding)]"/>
 </members>
</eu>
</xsl:template>

<xsl:template match="state">
 <xsl:copy use-attribute-sets="new">
  <xsl:apply-templates/>
 </xsl:copy>
</xsl:template>

</xsl:stylesheet>
```

In contrast to *founding.xsl*, this stylesheet finds state elements that do not have founding attributes by using the XPath Boolean function not( ). When it finds these elements, it uses the attribute set named new to add a new founding attribute to the resulting element. Apply it with:

```
xalan -i 1 eu.xml notfounding.xsl
```

and you'll get this result:

```
<?xml version="1.0" encoding="UTF-8"?>
<eu>
 <members>
  <state founding="no">Austria</state>
  <state founding="no">Denmark</state>
  <state founding="no">Finland</state>
  <state founding="no">Greece</state>
  <state founding="no">Ireland</state>
  <state founding="no">Portugal</state>
  <state founding="no">Spain</state>
  <state founding="no">Sweden</state>
  <state founding="no">United Kingdom</state>
 </members>
</eu>
```

As you can see, the XSLT processor grabbed all state elements that did not have a founding attribute and then added a new founding attribute with a value of no to each of them. The stylesheet also duplicated the eu and members elements using literal result elements.

One other thing: the copy element can contain a template. That's why it can have an apply-templates child, as shown in the following example, *identity.xsl*. A copy element can even contain other copy elements.

The Identity Transform

You can create an identity transform that copies nodes by using the copy element. The stylesheet *identity.xsl* matches all nodes and then copies each of them:

```
<xsl:stylesheet version="1.0" xmlns:xsl="http://www.w3.org/1999/XSL/Transform">
<xsl:output method="xml" indent="yes" encoding="US-ASCII"/>

<xsl:template match="@*|node()">
 <xsl:copy>
  <xsl:apply-templates select="@*|node()"/>
 </xsl:copy>
</xsl:template>

</xsl:stylesheet>
```

The XPath syntax @* matches attributes, or (|) node() matches all other nodes. apply-templates then triggers the built-in templates for any node it finds.

The document *identity.xml* contains an example of each of the seven node types in the XPath data model (root, element, attribute, text, comment, processing instruction, and namespace):

```
<?xml-stylesheet href="identity.xsl" type="text/xsl"?>

<!-- EU state: Belgium -->

<state member="true" xmlns="urn:wyeast-net:eu">Belgium</state>
```

Because *identity.xml* contains an XML stylesheet PI, you can transform it using:

```
xalan -a identity.xml
```

The copy looks very much like the original, except Xalan adds an XML declaration:

```
<?xml version="1.0" encoding="US-ASCII"?>
<?xml-stylesheet href="identity.xsl" type="text/xsl"?>

<!-- EU state: Belgium -->
<state xmlns="urn:wyeast-net:eu" member="true">Belgium</state>
```

The copy element works fine in some situations, but in other instances, you may prefer to copy an element's attributes and children automatically, as a matter of course. You can do that with copy-of.

The copy-of Element

The copy-of element goes further than its counterpart copy. Where copy by itself only copies element nodes and their associated namespace nodes, copy-of copies element and namespace nodes, plus attribute nodes and children. This is called a *deep copy*.

The stylesheet *copy-of.xsl* demonstrates the difference between a shallow copy and a deep copy (note bold):

```
<xsl:stylesheet version="1.0" xmlns:xsl="http://www.w3.org/1999/XSL/Transform">
<xsl:output method="xml"/>

<xsl:template match="eu">
 <xsl:apply-templates select="member"/>
</xsl:template>

<xsl:template match="member">
  <xsl:apply-templates select="state[2]"/>
</xsl:template>

<xsl:template match="state">
 <xsl:copy-of select="."/>
</xsl:template>

</xsl:stylesheet>
```

The only difference between *copy.xsl* and *copy-of.xsl* is that *copy.xsl* uses copy with no attributes, and *copy-of.xsl* uses copy-of with a select attribute. You will see the real evidence when you process *eu.xml* against *copy-of.xsl*:

```
xalan eu.xml copy-of.xsl
```

This produces:

```
<?xml version="1.0" encoding="UTF-8"?>
<state founding="yes">Belgium</state>
```

Instead of just copying the element node as with copy, copy-of copies the element node state, its attribute founding with its value, and its text node child Belgium.

The copy-of element can also copy other kinds of child nodes. The stylesheet *candidate.xsl* copies all the state children of candidate in *eu.xml* with the deep copy method using copy-of, and it grabs the eu and candidate elements using a shallow copy method with copy:

```
<xsl:stylesheet version="1.0" xmlns:xsl="http://www.w3.org/1999/XSL/Transform">
<xsl:output method="xml" indent="yes"/>

 <xsl:template match="eu">
  <xsl:copy>
   <xsl:apply-templates select="candidate"/>
  </xsl:copy>
 </xsl:template>

 <xsl:template match="candidate">
  <xsl:copy>
   <xsl:copy-of select="state"/>
  </xsl:copy>
 </xsl:template>

</xsl:stylesheet>
```

Apply the stylesheet using this line:

```
xalan -i 1 eu.xml candidate.xsl
```

and you will get the following output:

```
<?xml version="1.0" encoding="UTF-8"?>
<eu>
 <candidate>
  <state>Bulgaria</state>
  <state>Cyprus</state>
  <state>Czech Republic</state>
  <state>Estonia</state>
  <state>Hungary</state>
  <state>Latvia</state>
  <state>Lithuania</state>
  <state>Malta</state>
  <state>Poland</state>
  <state>Romania</state>
  <state>Slovakia</state>
  <state>Slovenia</state>
  <state>Turkey</state>
 </candidate>
</eu>
```

This creates a new document that contains only the names of the 13 European state candidates.

Copying Nodes from Two Documents

Using copy-of, you can piece together new documents by copying the nodes you want wholesale. So far, you have only seen how to copy nodes out of one document as, customarily, an XSLT processor handles only one input document or source tree. This example will show you how to process more than one input document with the XSLT function document( ). You caught a glimpse of document( ) in Chapter 4; Chapter 13 will cover document( ) in more detail.

In addition to *eu.xml*, you will also find *other.xml* in *examples/ch06*, which contains a list of non-EU states, shown in Example 6-3.

Example 6-3. An XML document listing non-EU states

```
<?xml version="1.0" encoding="UTF-8"?>

<!-- Other non-EU, European states  -->

<eu>
 <other>
  <state>Albania</state>
  <state>Andorra</state>
  <state>Belarus</state>
  <state>Estonia</state>
  <state>Bosnia-Herzegovina</state>
  <state>Croatia</state>
  <state>Iceland</state>
  <state>Liechtenstein</state>
  <state>Macedonia, Former Yugoslav Republic of</state>
  <state>Moldova</state>
  <state>Monaco</state>
  <state>Norway</state>
  <state>Russia</state>
  <state>San Marino</state>
  <state>Serbia and Montenegro</state>
  <state>Switzerland</state>
  <state>Ukraine</state>
  <state>Vatican City</state>
 </other>
</eu>
```

Using the document( ) function, the stylesheet *two.xsl* takes nodes out of *other.xml* in addition to *eu.xml*:

```
<xsl:stylesheet version="1.0" xmlns:xsl="http://www.w3.org/1999/XSL/Transform">
<xsl:output method="xml" indent="yes"/>

<xsl:template match="eu">
 <xsl:copy>
  <xsl:comment>
   <xsl:text>Member states: </xsl:text>
   <xsl:value-of select="count(member/state)"/>
```

```
     </xsl:comment>
     <xsl:copy-of select="member"/>
     <xsl:comment>
      <xsl:text>Candidate states: </xsl:text>
      <xsl:value-of select="count(candidate/state)"/>
     </xsl:comment>
     <xsl:copy-of select="candidate"/>
     <xsl:comment>
      <xsl:text>Other states: </xsl:text>
      <xsl:value-of select="count(document('other.xml')/eu/other/state)"/>
     </xsl:comment>
     <xsl:copy-of select="document('other.xml')/eu/other"/>
    </xsl:copy>
   </xsl:template>

  </xsl:stylesheet>
```

The nodes in the first source tree contained in the file *eu.xml* are fed to the XSLT
processor via the command line. The document( ) function picks up the source in
other.xml at the stylesheet level. This stylesheet also uses the count( ) function to
count state elements, arriving at the number of countries in each category: member,
candidate, and other. With this command:

```
   xalan -i 1 eu.xml two.xsl
```

the processor will produce the following result, shown in Example 6-4.

Example 6-4. An XML document listing European countries and their relation to the EU

```
<?xml version="1.0" encoding="UTF-8"?>
<eu>
 <!--Member states: 15-->
 <member>
  <state>Austria</state>
  <state founding="yes">Belgium</state>
  <state>Denmark</state>
  <state>Finland</state>
  <state founding="yes">France</state>
  <state founding="yes">Germany</state>
  <state>Greece</state>
  <state>Ireland</state>
  <state founding="yes">Italy</state>
  <state founding="yes">Luxembourg</state>
  <state founding="yes">The Netherlands</state>
  <state>Portugal</state>
  <state>Spain</state>
  <state>Sweden</state>
  <state>United Kingdom</state>
 </member>
 <!--Candidate states: 13-->
 <candidate>
  <state>Bulgaria</state>
  <state>Cyprus</state>
  <state>Czech Republic</state>
```

```
  <state>Estonia</state>
  <state>Hungary</state>
  <state>Latvia</state>
  <state>Lithuania</state>
  <state>Malta</state>
  <state>Poland</state>
  <state>Romania</state>
  <state>Slovakia</state>
  <state>Slovenia</state>
  <state>Turkey</state>
 </candidate>
 <!--Other states: 18-->
 <other>
  <state>Albania</state>
  <state>Andorra</state>
  <state>Belarus</state>
  <state>Estonia</state>
  <state>Bosnia-Herzegovina</state>
  <state>Croatia</state>
  <state>Iceland</state>
  <state>Liechtenstein</state>
  <state>Macedonia, Former Yugoslav Republic of</state>
  <state>Moldova</state>
  <state>Monaco</state>
  <state>Norway</state>
  <state>Russia</state>
  <state>San Marino</state>
  <state>Serbia and Montenegro</state>
  <state>Switzerland</state>
  <state>Ukraine</state>
  <state>Vatican City</state>
 </other>
</eu>
```

Summary

In this chapter, you have learned how to copy nodes using the copy element for shallow copies and the copy-of element for deep copies. You also learned how to merge nodes from more than one source tree with the document( ) function (more on this in Chapter 13). In the next chapter, you'll learn how to use variables and parameters.

CHAPTER 7

Using Variables and Parameters

XSLT offers several ways to bind a name to a value so that the value can be later referenced by name any number of times in a stylesheet. The variable element binds a name to an immutable value once it's been evaluated, while the param element binds a name to a default value, but it's a value you can change. You can define a default value with param and then pass a new value into the stylesheet or to a template. The with-param element allows you to apply or call a template from another template with a new value for one or more parameters, like a method or function call with arguments.

Variables in XSLT are limited in what they can do. They are not like variables in programming languages that you can reassign over and over again. Generally, you will define a variable once and then reference it as often as you want. You will also generally change the default value of a parameter just when you pass a value to a stylesheet or template. There are ways around this, but, by and large, that is how you use them. In this way, XSLT variables are more similar to constants in a programming language than to variables.

You can use the variable and param elements globally on the top-level as stylesheet-wide values, or locally within templates. If a variable is global, its scope is the entire stylesheet; if it is local, its scope is restricted to the template where it is defined or passed in. The with-param element may appear only as an immediate child of an apply-templates template (for processing child templates) or of a call-template element (for processing named templates—more on this in Chapter 10). A variable can be of any type—Boolean, node-set, number, string, or result tree fragment.

In XSLT 2.0, you will also be able to use with-param as a child of the apply-imports element. You can't do that in XSLT 1.0.

This chapter introduces you to using variables and parameters in stylesheets, both globally and locally. I'll use the general term *variable* to refer to the values of variable, param, and with-param in this chapter and throughout the book.

You can read about variables and parameters in Section 11 of the XSLT specification.

Defining Variables and Parameters

Before going any deeper into the subject, there are a few things I'd like to discuss that apply to the variable, param, and with-param elements. To begin with, all three elements have just two attributes:

1. The required name attribute that binds a name to a value of the variable. This is a QName.

2. The optional select attribute that can contain an expression that defines the value of the variable.

In addition, all three elements also provide two general ways to define a value:

1. You can define a value using an expression in the select attribute.

2. You can also define a value using something called a *result tree fragment* with a template in the content of the element. As discussed in Chapter 4, a result tree fragment is an XSLT 1.0 datatype that defines a fragment of text or markup.

After you define a variable, you can reference its value by preceding the variable name with a dollar sign, such as in $discount. I'll cover both ways to define a value and discuss the differences.

 By the way, you can't use circular definitions when defining a variable. This means that you can't define a variable by referencing itself.

Defining Default Values for Parameters

Unlike a value defined with the variable element, a value defined with the param element can have a default value that you can change. Nevertheless, a parameter is not required to have an explicit, default value; it can just be empty. Said another way, if a parameter does not have an explicitly defined value, the processor will give it a value of a zero-length string.

When you define a global parameter on the top level, you can pass in a new value when the transformation is performed that replaces the default value using a mechanism provided by the XSLT processor; and when you define a local parameter in a template, you can pass in a new value from another template by using with-param. You will see examples of how this works in the later sections, "Using Parameters" for global variables, and "Invoking Templates with Parameters" for local variables.

Defining Values with Expressions and Templates

As I mentioned earlier, you can define a variable value with an expression in a select attribute or with a template in element content (as you will soon see in the section "Using result tree fragments to define variables"). However, you cannot define a value using both an expression and a template at the same time. In other words, you cannot use the select attribute together with element content to define a single variable, as they are mutually exclusive.

Using the select attribute to define variables

For example, the following declaration defines a value using an expression in a select attribute:

```
<xsl:variable name="discount" select="0.40 + 0.30"/>
```

The expression adds the numbers 0.40 and 0.30 and the resulting number value of 0.70 is bound to the discount variable. An XSLT processor automatically knows that this variable is a number. Likewise, the following variable would be interpreted containing the number 50:

```
<xsl:variable name="discount" select="50"/>
```

You can also bind a string to a variable explicitly using embedded quotation marks:

```
<xsl:variable name="discount" select="'n/a'"/>
```

Notice the single quotes inside the double quotes in the value of select. This binds the string value n/a to discount. You could also write the declaration in this way, with double quotes inside of single quotes:

```
<xsl:variable name='discount' select='"n/a"'/>
```

Either single or double quotes are fine, but you aren't allowed to mix them (that is, name='discount" is illegal).

 If you enclose the value of select in just double or single quotes, without any internal quotes, the value is interpreted as a node-set and not as a string. Because / is not a legal XML name character, n/a would be interpreted as a location path—the element n with a child a—probably not what you are after.

Because select contains an expression, you can use arithmetic, functions, even references to other variables, when defining a value for a variable with select. Here's yet another example showing a slightly more complex expression that defines a parameter:

```
<xsl:param name="discount" select="floor($option)+0.05"/>
```

You can also specify a location path in select, as in:

```
<xsl:param name="discount" select="catalog/value"/>
```

This variable would extract the content of the value element for its value. Another possibility is to use the document( ) function in select like this:

```
<xsl:param name="discount" select="document('discount.xml')"/>
```

With this, the value of discount is picked up from the external document *discount.xml*:

```
<value>0.10</value>
```

Though it is discussed elsewhere in the book, you'll learn more about the document( ) function in Chapter 13.

Using result tree fragments to define variables

When you define a variable using a template in element content, such content is a result tree fragment. Because it is defined as a template, a result tree fragment can be a node-set consisting of markup, which has its own root element. The following declaration uses a result tree fragment to define a variable:

```
<xsl:variable name="discount">
<xsl:element name="discount">0.10</xsl:element>
</xsl:variable>
```

Here element is used to create an element named discount with the content 0.10 for the result tree.

The result tree fragment type is defined by XSLT, not by XPath. It is called a temporary tree in XSLT 2.0, and it can be manipulated by an XSLT 2.0 processor in more sophisticated ways than a result tree fragment can be manipulated by an XSLT 1.0 processor. (An XSLT 2.0 temporary tree, however, cannot be manipulated by an XSLT 1.0 processor.) See the section "Using Result Tree Fragments," later in this chapter for a working example.

Using Variables

Variables in XSLT allow you to associate a name with a value, making it easier to use a given value more than once. I'll start the series of examples in this chapter with a single, global variable that contains a numeric value that is available in every template in the stylesheet, if needed. The following document, *price.xml*, in *examples/ch07*, represents a single catalog entry:

```
<?xml version="1.0"?>
<!DOCTYPE catalog SYSTEM "price.dtd">

<catalog>
 <item id="SC-0001">
  <maker>Scratchmore</maker>
  <description>Wool sweater</description>
  <size>L</size>
  <price>120.00</price>
  <currency>USD</currency>
 </item>
</catalog>
```

price.xml happens to be valid with regard to the DTD *price.dtd*, also in *examples/ch07*. The stylesheet *variable.xsl* derives a discounted price from *price.xml* and outputs new content for the catalog:

```
<xsl:stylesheet version="1.0" xmlns:xsl="http://www.w3.org/1999/XSL/Transform">
<xsl:output method="xml" indent="yes"/>
<xsl:output doctype-system="catalog.dtd"/>
<xsl:variable name="discount" select="0.10"/>

<xsl:template match="catalog">
 <xsl:copy>
  <xsl:apply-templates select="item"/>
 </xsl:copy>
</xsl:template>

<xsl:template match="item">
 <xsl:copy>
  <xsl:attribute name="id"><xsl:value-of select="@id"/></xsl:attribute>
  <xsl:copy-of select="maker|description|size|price"/>
  <discount><xsl:value-of select="$discount"/></discount>
  <discountPrice><xsl:value-of select="price - (price * $discount)"/></discountPrice>
  <xsl:copy-of select="currency"/>
 </xsl:copy>
</xsl:template>

</xsl:stylesheet>
```

The stylesheet outputs XML that includes a new document type declaration referencing *catalog.dtd* (available in *examples/ch07*). Because the variable element is at the top level, it declares a global variable, discount, that is available or visible to all templates in the stylesheet. This variable is referenced later in the stylesheet with the variable reference $discount. A variable reference is preceded by a dollar sign ($).

There is no internal conflict, by the way, between the element name discount and the variable name discount. There is also no name conflict between a variable defined on the top level and one with the same name defined in a template. However, there will be a name conflict if two or more variables share the same name and are defined on the top level (unless they have a different import precedence; see Chapter 13 for an explanation), or if they share the same name and are defined locally in a template.

The stylesheet makes copies of the maker, description, size, and price elements (maker|description|size|price). In Chapter 4, the | operator was said to imply *or*. In this instance, the | operator implies *and*. In other words, the elements maker *and* description *and* size *and* price are all copied. (| can generally be read as *union*.)

The stylesheet creates two new elements in the result tree, discount and discountPrice. The content of these elements is formed with the aid of the discount variable, which contains a discount percentage of 10 percent (0.10). The discount and discountPrice elements will contain content that is computed with the value of the discount variable.

To see the result, transform *price.xml* with *variable.xsl* with the following command:

```
xalan -v -i 1 price.xml variable.xsl
```

The -v option instructs Xalan to validate the source document *price.xml* against the DTD it references in its document type declaration (*price.dtd*), not the DTD output document references (*catalog.dtd*). The -i option indicates that child elements should be indented by one space per child. This command will give you the following output:

```
<?xml version="1.0" encoding="UTF-8"?>
<!DOCTYPE catalog SYSTEM "catalog.dtd">
<catalog>
 <item id="SC-0001">
  <maker>Scratchmore</maker>
  <description>Wool sweater</description>
  <size>L</size>
  <price>120.00</price>
  <discount>0.1</discount>
  <discountPrice>108</discountPrice>
  <currency>USD</currency>
 </item>
</catalog>
```

The added discount element reports the discount percentage, and the new discountPrice element contains the calculated discounted price. You can improve the appearance of numbers in the discount and discountPrice elements by using the format-number( ) function in the stylesheet. (format-number( ) was mentioned in Chapter 5 and you will learn more about it in Chapter 9.) variable-alt.xsl uses both the format-number( ) and document( ) functions:

```
<xsl:stylesheet version="1.0" xmlns:xsl="http://www.w3.org/1999/XSL/Transform">
<xsl:output method="xml" indent="yes"/>
<xsl:variable name="discount" select="document('discount.xml')"/>
<xsl:template match="catalog">
 <xsl:copy>
  <xsl:apply-templates select="item"/>
 </xsl:copy>
</xsl:template>

<xsl:template match="item">
 <xsl:copy>
  <xsl:attribute name="id"><xsl:value-of select="@id"/></xsl:attribute>
  <xsl:copy-of select="maker|description|size|price"/>
  <discount><xsl:value-of select="$discount"/></discount>
  <discountPrice><xsl:value-of select="format-number(price -
(price*$discount),'###.00')"/></discountPrice>
  <xsl:copy-of select="currency"/>
 </xsl:copy>
</xsl:template>

</xsl:stylesheet>
```

Xalan reports that it does not support the format-number( ) function, so I'll use the Instant Saxon processor for this example instead. Instant Saxon 6.5.3, the last version of Instant Saxon, runs on the Windows platform and is available for download from *http://saxon.sourceforge.net*. (Or just use *saxon.exe* in *examples/ch07*). After Instant Saxon is installed, apply *variable-alt.xsl* to *price.xml* with this line:

```
saxon price.xml variable-alt.xsl
```

You will see a difference from the output of *variable.xsl* with that of the output of *variable-alt.xsl*:

```
<?xml version="1.0" encoding="utf-8"?>
<catalog>
   <item id="SC-0001">
      <maker>Scratchmore</maker>
      <description>Wool sweater</description>
      <size>L</size>
      <price>120.00</price>
      <discount>0.10</discount>
      <discountPrice>108.00</discountPrice>
      <currency>USD</currency>
   </item>
</catalog>
```

The content of discount was taken from the content of the value element in *discount. xml* via the document( ) function. Because of this, the content in the output is 0.10 rather than 0.1 (it was 0.1 with *variable.xsl*). Because of format-number( ), the content of discountPrice is 108.00 rather than just 108. The second argument of format-number( ) (###.00) specifies that the number is to be formatted in the output with two places after the decimal point.

As you know, you can't change a value defined with variable, so what do you do if you want to change the value of the discount? You can use the param element.

Using Parameters

The following stylesheet, *param.xsl*, is only a little different than *variable.xsl*—the top-level element variable is switched with a param element—but what a difference that small change makes:

```
<xsl:stylesheet version="1.0" xmlns:xsl="http://www.w3.org/1999/XSL/Transform">
<xsl:output method="xml" indent="yes"/>
<xsl:output doctype-system="catalog.dtd"/>
<xsl:param name="discount" select="0.10"/>
<xsl:template match="catalog">
 <xsl:copy>
  <xsl:apply-templates select="item"/>
 </xsl:copy>
</xsl:template>

<xsl:template match="item">
 <xsl:copy>
  <xsl:attribute name="id"><xsl:value-of select="@id"/></xsl:attribute>
  <xsl:copy-of select="maker|description|size|price"/>
  <discount><xsl:value-of select="$discount"/></discount>
  <discountPrice><xsl:value-of select="price - (price * discount)"/></discountPrice>
  <xsl:copy-of select="currency"/>
 </xsl:copy>
</xsl:template>

</xsl:stylesheet>
```

This stylesheet defines a global parameter (it's global because it is defined on the top level of the stylesheet). This means that the parameter discount is available throughout the stylesheet, wherever it might be needed. Given this stylesheet, the default value of discount is 0.10, and you can change the value of discount using a mechanism provided by the XSLT processor on the command line.

This book focuses mostly on XSLT processors that have command-line interfaces. For XSLT processors written in Java and based on Sun's Java API for XML Processing (JAXP), for example, APIs provide programmatic methods for setting parameter values, namely javax.xml.transform.setParameter(String name, Object value). You will get a chance to use JAXP in a programming example in Chapter 17.

Passing in a Parameter with Xalan

The Xalan processor has a -p command-line option. This option allows you to associate a parameter name with a new value, which is in turn handed to the processor to produce a different result tree. To increase the amount of the discount from 10 percent (0.10) to 20 percent (0.20), enter the following command line:

```
xalan -i 1 -p discount '0.20' price.xml param.xsl
```

This transformation will produce the following result:

```
<?xml version="1.0" encoding="UTF-8"?>
<!DOCTYPE catalog SYSTEM "catalog.dtd">
<catalog>
 <item id="SC-0001">
  <maker>Scratchmore</maker>
  <description>Wool sweater</description>
  <size>L</size>
  <price>120.00</price>
  <discount>0.20</discount>
  <discountPrice>96</discountPrice>
  <currency>USD</currency>
 </item>
</catalog>
```

Notice the new content of the discount and discountPrice elements. This was a result of passing in a parameter value. You can use the -p option for as many parameters as you wish to change, provided that those parameters are defined in the stylesheet you are processing. Other processors, such as Instant Saxon, use a different syntax to pass in parameter values.

Passing in a Parameter with Instant Saxon

The Instant Saxon processor uses a simpler command-line syntax than Xalan's syntax. To associate a parameter name with a new value, increasing the discount from 10 percent (0.10) to 30 percent (0.30), enter this line:

```
saxon price.xml param.xsl discount="0.3"
```

The parameter discount is coupled with a new value just by using the equals sign (=). Here is the output:

```
<?xml version="1.0" encoding="utf-8"?>

<!DOCTYPE catalog
  SYSTEM "catalog.dtd">
<catalog>
    <item id="SC-0001">
        <maker>Scratchmore</maker>
        <description>Wool sweater</description>
        <size>L</size>
        <price>120.00</price>
        <discount>0.3</discount>
```

```
            <discountPrice>84</discountPrice>
            <currency>USD</currency>
        </item>
    </catalog>
```

Other XSLT processors, such as James Clark's XT and Microsoft's MSXSL, also use this simple syntax for associating a parameter with a new value.

So far, you have seen a global variable and parameter. Next you'll see how to define and use a local one.

Invoking Templates with Parameters

The *with-param.xsl* stylesheet shown in Example 7-1 doesn't define a global parameter on the top level, but it does define a local variable within a template.

Example 7-1. A stylesheet using a locally scoped variable

```
<xsl:stylesheet version="1.0" xmlns:xsl="http://www.w3.org/1999/XSL/Transform">
<xsl:output method="xml" indent="yes"/>
<xsl:output doctype-system="catalog.dtd"/>

<xsl:template match="catalog">
 <xsl:copy>
  <xsl:apply-templates select="item">
   <xsl:with-param name="discount" select="'0.50'"/>
  </xsl:apply-templates>
 </xsl:copy>
</xsl:template>

<xsl:template match="item">
 <xsl:param name="discount"/>
 <xsl:copy>
  <xsl:attribute name="id"><xsl:value-of select="@id"/></xsl:attribute>
  <xsl:copy-of select="maker|description|size|price"/>
  <discount><xsl:value-of select="$discount"/></discount>
  <discountPrice><xsl:value-of select="price - (price * $discount)"/></discountPrice>
  <xsl:copy-of select="currency"/>
 </xsl:copy>
</xsl:template>

</xsl:stylesheet>
```

The first child element of the template that matches item is the param element, which just happens to be empty by default. When you use local parameters defined with param, the param element must appear as the first child element in a template. This was probably so that their values are taken into account *before* the template is processed. You can also define local variables in a template with the variable element, but these can appear anywhere in a template. They don't have to be first in line.

The template that matches catalog applies templates to item elements, but as it does so, it adds a child to apply-templates called with-param. This element passes a new value for the local discount parameter to the template that matches item. To see how it works, enter the following line at a prompt:

```
xalan -i 1 price.xml with-param.xsl
```

The processor yields the following deeply discounted results:

```
<?xml version="1.0" encoding="UTF-8"?>
<!DOCTYPE catalog SYSTEM "catalog.dtd">
<catalog>
 <item id="SC-0001">
  <maker>Scratchmore</maker>
  <description>Wool sweater</description>
  <size>L</size>
  <price>120.00</price>
  <discount>0.50</discount>
  <discountPrice>60</discountPrice>
  <currency>USD</currency>
 </item>
</catalog>
```

You can use the with-param element in two places, either as a child of apply-templates or as a child of call-template. You will see how you can use with-param with call-template in Chapter 10.

 In XSLT 1.0, parameters are not passed through by built-in templates. XSLT 2.0, however, does pass through parameters via built-in templates.

In the final examples in this chapter, I'll show you how to create a variable value with a result tree fragment, and then how to use that fragment later in the stylesheet.

Using Result Tree Fragments

As you saw earlier, a variable value, created with a template as element content, creates a result tree fragment. The stylesheet in Example 7-2, *fragment.xsl*, constructs a variable value for discount using a template with a variable element, and then later accesses that value with copy-of.

Example 7-2. Copying a variable

```
<xsl:stylesheet version="1.0" xmlns:xsl="http://www.w3.org/1999/XSL/Transform">
<xsl:output method="xml" indent="yes"/>
<xsl:output doctype-system="catalog.dtd"/>
<xsl:variable name="discount">
<discount>0.40</discount>
<discountPrice><xsl:value-of select="format-number(catalog/item/price * 0.60, '###.00')"/>
</discountPrice>
</xsl:variable>
```

Example 7-2. Copying a variable (continued)

```
<xsl:template match="catalog">
 <xsl:copy>
  <xsl:apply-templates select="item"/>
 </xsl:copy>
</xsl:template>

<xsl:template match="item">
 <xsl:copy>
  <xsl:copy-of select="@id"/>
  <xsl:copy-of select="maker|description|size|price"/>
  <xsl:copy-of select="$discount"/>
  <xsl:copy-of select="currency"/>
 </xsl:copy>
</xsl:template>

</xsl:stylesheet>
```

Notice the `value-of` contained in `discountPrice` in variable. The first argument of `format-number()` uses a location path to address the content of the price element in the source tree. The context node for evaluating a global variable is the root node of the original source document; that's why the location path uses `catalog/item/price` instead of `/catalog/item/price`, an absolute location path.

Later, in the template for `item`, `copy-of` elements copy the `id` attribute from the source `item` and the nodes contained in discount's result tree fragment.

To test it out, enter this command line:

```
saxon price.xml fragment.xsl
```

You will get this outcome:

```
<?xml version="1.0" encoding="utf-8"?>

<!DOCTYPE catalog
  SYSTEM "catalog.dtd">
<catalog>
   <item id="SC-0001">
      <maker>Scratchmore</maker>
      <description>Wool sweater</description>
      <size>L</size>
      <price>120.00</price>
      <discount>0.40</discount>
      <discountPrice>72.00</discountPrice>
      <currency>USD</currency>
   </item>
</catalog>
```

A result tree fragment does not have to be well-formed XML. For example, you could also just use a bit of text in a result tree fragment, as shown in the variable definition for discount in Example 7-3, *frag.xsl*.

Example 7-3. Using text as a result tree fragment

```
<xsl:stylesheet version="1.0" xmlns:xsl="http://www.w3.org/1999/XSL/Transform">
<xsl:output method="xml" indent="yes"/>
<xsl:output doctype-system="catalog.dtd"/>
<xsl:variable name="discount">0.70</xsl:variable>
<xsl:variable name="discountPrice" select="format-number(catalog/item/price - (catalog/
item/price) * $discount, '###.00')"/>

<xsl:template match="catalog">
 <xsl:copy>
  <xsl:apply-templates select="item"/>
 </xsl:copy>
</xsl:template>

<xsl:template match="item">
 <xsl:copy>
  <xsl:copy-of select="@id"/>
  <xsl:copy-of select="maker|description|size|price"/>
  <discount><xsl:value-of select="$discount"/></discount>
  <discountPrice><xsl:value-of select="$discountPrice"/></discountPrice>
  <xsl:copy-of select="currency"/>
 </xsl:copy>
</xsl:template>

</xsl:stylesheet>
```

The variable discount contains only the text 0.70. (It's not best to define a simple value like 0.70 as a tree fragment, as it is somewhat more costly processing-wise to do so.) When the discountPrice variable is defined, it contains a reference to discount as part of its definition. The two variables are referenced later in the stylesheet by instances of value-of.

 You can reference a global variable before you define it, but you must define a local variable before you reference it.

Watch what happens with this command:

```
saxon price.xml frag.xsl
```

Here is the result:

```
<?xml version="1.0" encoding="UTF-8"?>
<!DOCTYPE catalog SYSTEM "catalog.dtd">
<catalog>
 <item id="SC-0001">
  <maker>Scratchmore</maker>
  <description>Wool sweater</description>
  <size>L</size>
  <price>120.00</price>
```

```
      <discount>0.70</discount>
      <discountPrice>36.00</discountPrice>
      <currency>USD</currency>
    </item>
  </catalog>
```

Before concluding, I should mention a few more things about result tree fragments. Only XSLT 1.0 allows you to copy result tree fragments or use them as strings. However, the node-set( ) extension function offered by many XSLT 1.0 processors allows you to use a result tree fragment as a tree of temporary nodes. node-set( ) is not actually part of XSLT 1.0, but it is a useful extension added by many XSLT processors. You will learn how to use two versions of node-set( ) in Chapter 15. XSLT 2.0 uses temporary trees rather than result tree fragments, which are stricter. Unlike its 1.0 predecessor, XSLT 2.0 is a tree of XML nodes and cannot contain mere fragments of text.

Summary

In this chapter, you have learned how to define variables and parameters using variable and param. You have also learned how to pass parameters into a stylesheet using XSLT processor mechanisms and to pass them within a stylesheet using with-param. Result tree fragments now should be a little less mysterious. You will have other encounters with variables and parameters in the chapters that follow.

In the next chapter, you'll learn how to sort nodes with the XSLT sort instruction.

CHAPTER 8

Sorting Things Out

Sometimes nodes don't come to you in a convenient order. XSLT's sort instruction element allows you to sort nodes in alphabetical or numerical order. You can also use sort to sort nodes in ascending (a, b, c) or descending (z, y, x) order.

This chapter walks you through a brief exploration of sort. You can also read about sorting in Section 10 of the XSLT specification. I'll start, as usual, with a simple example.

Simple Ascending Sort

If you look at Example 8-1, the document *europe.xml* in *examples/ch08*, you'll notice that the European states are not listed in alphabetical order.

Example 8-1. Unalphabetized European countries

```
<?xml version="1.0" encoding="UTF-8"?>
<?xml-stylesheet href="pretty.xsl" type="text/xsl"?>

<europe>
  <state>Belgium</state>
  <state>Germany</state>
  <state>Finland</state>
  <state>Greece</state>
  <state>Ireland</state>
  <state>Luxembourg</state>
  <state>Portugal</state>
  <state>Spain</state>
  <state>Andorra</state>
  <state>Belarus</state>
  <state>Monaco</state>
  <state>Sweden</state>
  <state>United Kingdom</state>
  <state>Austria</state>
  <state>Malta</state>
  <state>Vatican City</state>
```

Example 8-1. Unalphabetized European countries (continued)

```
    <state>Bulgaria</state>
    <state>Bosnia-Herzegovina</state>
    <state>Cyprus</state>
    <state>France</state>
    <state>Estonia</state>
    <state>Italy</state>
    <state>Hungary</state>
    <state>Latvia</state>
    <state>Ukraine</state>
    <state>Lithuania</state>
    <state>Moldova</state>
    <state>Denmark</state>
    <state>Poland</state>
    <state>Romania</state>
    <state>Slovenia</state>
    <state>The Netherlands</state>
    <state>Turkey</state>
    <state>Albania</state>
    <state>Serbia and Montenegro</state>
    <state>Croatia</state>
    <state>Slovakia</state>
    <state>Iceland</state>
    <state>Czech Republic</state>
    <state>Liechtenstein</state>
    <state>Macedonia, Former Yugoslav Republic of</state>
    <state>Norway</state>
    <state>Russia</state>
    <state>San Marino</state>
    <state>Switzerland</state>
</europe>
```

You can sort the names of the European states in ascending order (that is, in English as *a*, *b*, *c*, and so on) by using the sort element with no attributes, as a child of apply-templates.

The sort element is used in the stylesheet shown in Example 8-2, *sort.xsl*.

Example 8-2. Creating a sorted list of countries as text

```
<xsl:stylesheet version="1.0" xmlns:xsl="http://www.w3.org/1999/XSL/Transform">
<xsl:output method="text"/>

 <xsl:template match="europe">
   <xsl:text>Alphabetical List of European States</xsl:text>
   <xsl:text>&#10;Total Number of States: </xsl:text>
   <xsl:value-of select="count(state)"/>
   <xsl:text>&#10;&#10;</xsl:text>
   <xsl:apply-templates select="state">
    <xsl:sort/>
   </xsl:apply-templates>
 </xsl:template>
```

Example 8-2. Creating a sorted list of countries as text (continued)

```
<xsl:template match="state">
  <xsl:text> - </xsl:text>
  <xsl:apply-templates/>
  <xsl:text>&#10;</xsl:text>
</xsl:template>

</xsl:stylesheet>
```

This stylesheet produces plain text output (it uses the text method of output), as shown in Example 8-3. A few text instruction elements are sprinkled here and there to label the output or add a line feed (using the
 character reference). The count( ) function is also used to count the number of state elements in the source tree, and the return value of this function is displayed using value-of.

The sort element appears as a child of apply-templates. It may only appear as a child of either apply-templates or for-each.

 The XSLT instruction element for-each is like a template within a template that selects a node-set and then instantiates its template for each node in the set. You will see this element demonstrated in several places in this book.

In this stylesheet, when state elements are selected with apply-templates, the processor will also apply a sort.

To see what happens, apply the *sort.xsl* stylesheet to *europe.xml* using this command:

```
xalan europe.xml sort.xsl
```

The plain text, lexicographically alphabetized result tree shown in Example 8-3 will be output to your screen.

Example 8-3. A sorted text list produced by sort.xsl

```
Alphabetical List of European States
Total Number of States: 45

  - Albania
  - Andorra
  - Austria
  - Belarus
  - Belgium
  - Bosnia-Herzegovina
  - Bulgaria
  - Croatia
  - Cyprus
  - Czech Republic
  - Denmark
  - Estonia
  - Finland
```

Example 8-3. A sorted text list produced by sort.xsl (continued)

- France
- Germany
- Greece
- Hungary
- Iceland
- Ireland
- Italy
- Latvia
- Liechtenstein
- Lithuania
- Luxembourg
- Macedonia, Former Yugoslav Republic of
- Malta
- Moldova
- Monaco
- Norway
- Poland
- Portugal
- Romania
- Russia
- San Marino
- Serbia and Montenegro
- Slovakia
- Slovenia
- Spain
- Sweden
- Switzerland
- The Netherlands
- Turkey
- Ukraine
- United Kingdom
- Vatican City

If you would like pretty output worthy of a browser, you could also create an HTML wrapper with the stylesheet shown in Example 8-4, *pretty.xsl*.

Example 8-4. A stylesheet for producing a sorted list of states presented in HTML

```
<xsl:stylesheet version="1.0" xmlns:xsl="http://www.w3.org/1999/XSL/Transform">

 <xsl:template match="europe">
  <html>
  <head><title>European States</title></head>
  <style type="text/css">body {font-family: sans-serif}</style>
  <body>
  <h3>Alphabetical List of European States</h3>
  <p><b>Total Number of States:</b><xsl:text> </xsl:text>
   <xsl:value-of select="count(state)"/></p>
  <ul>
   <xsl:apply-templates select="state">
    <xsl:sort/>
   </xsl:apply-templates>
```

```
  </ul>
  </body>
  </html>
</xsl:template>

<xsl:template match="state">
 <li><xsl:apply-templates/></li>
</xsl:template>

</xsl:stylesheet>
```

This stylesheet produces indented HTML output by default (without explicitly stating so in an output element), because the first element in the result tree is html and there is no output element to define the method.

Process the stylesheet with Xalan:

```
    xalan -i 1 europe.xml pretty.xsl
```

Once again, the -i option followed by 1 tells the processor to indent the output by one space. You will see output like Example 8-5.

Example 8-5. The HTML results of using pretty.xsl

```
<html>
 <head>
  <META http-equiv="Content-Type" content="text/html; charset=UTF-8">
  <title>European States</title>
 </head>
 <style type="text/css">body {font-family: sans-serif}</style>
 <body>
  <h3>Alphabetical List of European States</h3>
  <p>
  <b>Total Number of States:</b> 45</p>
  <ul>
  <li>Albania</li>
  <li>Andorra</li>
  <li>Austria</li>
  <li>Belarus</li>
  <li>Belgium</li>
  <li>Bosnia-Herzegovina</li>
  <li>Bulgaria</li>
  <li>Croatia</li>
  <li>Cyprus</li>
  <li>Czech Republic</li>
  <li>Denmark</li>
  <li>Estonia</li>
  <li>Finland</li>
  <li>France</li>
  <li>Germany</li>
  <li>Greece</li>
  <li>Hungary</li>
  <li>Iceland</li>
```

Example 8-5. The HTML results of using pretty.xsl (continued)

```
    <li>Ireland</li>
    <li>Italy</li>
    <li>Latvia</li>
    <li>Liechtenstein</li>
    <li>Lithuania</li>
    <li>Luxembourg</li>
    <li>Macedonia, Former Yugoslav Republic of</li>
    <li>Malta</li>
    <li>Moldova</li>
    <li>Monaco</li>
    <li>Norway</li>
    <li>Poland</li>
    <li>Portugal</li>
    <li>Romania</li>
    <li>Russia</li>
    <li>San Marino</li>
    <li>Serbia and Montenegro</li>
    <li>Slovakia</li>
    <li>Slovenia</li>
    <li>Spain</li>
    <li>Sweden</li>
    <li>Switzerland</li>
    <li>The Netherlands</li>
    <li>Turkey</li>
    <li>Ukraine</li>
    <li>United Kingdom</li>
    <li>Vatican City</li>
  </ul>
 </body>
</html>
```

If you simply open *europe.xml* with a browser such as Netscape 7.1, the browser will apply the stylesheet *pretty.xsl* referenced in the XML stylesheet PI, and the result will appear in the browser as shown in Figure 8-1.

Reversing the Sort

The sort element uses ascending order by default, as if the order attribute were present with a value of ascending, like so:

```
<xsl:sort order="ascending"/>
```

This order follows the normal *a*, *b*, *c* order of the English alphabet. You can also sort in descending order, that is, using English, in the order *z*, *y*, *x*. To do this, you have to add an order attribute to sort, as does the stylesheet *descending.xsl*, shown in Example 8-6.

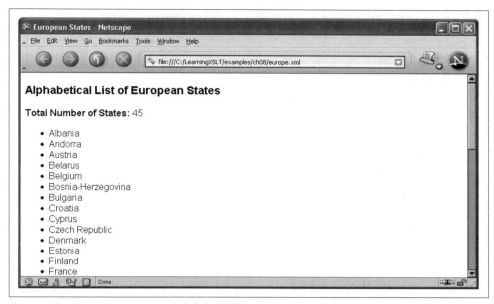

Figure 8-1. European states sorted alphabetically in Netscape 7.1

Example 8-6. A stylesheet for sorting country names backward

```
<xsl:stylesheet version="1.0" xmlns:xsl="http://www.w3.org/1999/XSL/Transform">
<xsl:output method="text"/>

 <xsl:template match="europe">
   <xsl:apply-templates select="state">
    <xsl:sort order="descending"/>
   </xsl:apply-templates>
   <xsl:text>Number of European States: </xsl:text>
   <xsl:value-of select="count(state)"/>
   <xsl:text>&#10;</xsl:text>
 </xsl:template>

 <xsl:template match="state">
   <xsl:text> - </xsl:text>
   <xsl:apply-templates/>
   <xsl:text>&#10;</xsl:text>
 </xsl:template>

</xsl:stylesheet>
```

Now apply it with:

```
xalan europe.xml descending.xsl
```

to get the output shown in Example 8-7.

Example 8-7. A reverse-sorted list of countries produced using descending.xsl

```
 - Vatican City
 - United Kingdom
 - Ukraine
 - Turkey
 - The Netherlands
 - Switzerland
 - Sweden
 - Spain
 - Slovenia
 - Slovakia
 - Serbia and Montenegro
 - San Marino
 - Russia
 - Romania
 - Portugal
 - Poland
 - Norway
 - Monaco
 - Moldova
 - Malta
 - Macedonia, Former Yugoslav Republic of
 - Luxembourg
 - Lithuania
 - Liechtenstein
 - Latvia
 - Italy
 - Ireland
 - Iceland
 - Hungary
 - Greece
 - Germany
 - France
 - Finland
 - Estonia
 - Denmark
 - Czech Republic
 - Cyprus
 - Croatia
 - Bulgaria
 - Bosnia-Herzegovina
 - Belgium
 - Belarus
 - Austria
 - Andorra
 - Albania
Number of European States: 45
```

The output is in reverse, or descending, order in English.

By the Numbers

So far, you have sorted nodes alphabetically (actually, lexicographically). You can also sort nodes numerically by specifying the sort element's data-type attribute with a value of number. By default, sort works as if data-type were present and had a value of text, which indicates that you want to sort text alphabetically.

To see how it works, have a look at Example 8-8, the document *member.xml*.

Example 8-8. An XML list of EU member states

```
<?xml version="1.0" encoding="UTF-8"?>
<?xml-stylesheet href="year.xsl" type="text/xsl"?>

<!-- European Union member states -->

<member>
 <state joined="1995">Austria</state>
 <state joined="1950">Belgium</state>
 <state joined="1973">Denmark</state>
 <state joined="1995">Finland</state>
 <state joined="1950">France</state>
 <state joined="1950">Germany</state>
 <state joined="1981">Greece</state>
 <state joined="1973">Ireland</state>
 <state joined="1950">Italy</state>
 <state joined="1950">Luxembourg</state>
 <state joined="1950">The Netherlands</state>
 <state joined="1986">Portugal</state>
 <state joined="1986">Spain</state>
 <state joined="1995">Sweden</state>
 <state joined="1973">United Kingdom</state>
</member>
```

Example 8-8 holds state elements, each containing the name of a European Union (EU) member state, in alphabetical order. Each of the 15 state elements also has a joined attribute with a number value, indicating the year the country joined the EU.

If you want to sort by year rather than name, you could use the stylesheet shown in Example 8-9, *numeric.xsl*.

Example 8-9. A stylesheet for sorting countries by year of EU membership

```
<xsl:stylesheet version="1.0" xmlns:xsl="http://www.w3.org/1999/XSL/Transform">
<xsl:output method="text"/>

 <xsl:template match="member">
   <xsl:text>Number of EU Member States: </xsl:text>
   <xsl:value-of select="count(state)"/>
   <xsl:text>&#10;</xsl:text>
   <xsl:apply-templates select="state/@joined">
    <xsl:sort data-type="number"/>
```

```
    </xsl:apply-templates>
    <xsl:text>&#10;</xsl:text>
  </xsl:template>

  <xsl:template match="state/@joined">
    <xsl:text> - </xsl:text>
    <xsl:apply-templates select=".."/>
    <xsl:text> (</xsl:text>
    <xsl:value-of select="."/>
    <xsl:text>)&#10;</xsl:text>
  </xsl:template>

</xsl:stylesheet>
```

The sort element in Example 8-9 has a data-type attribute with a value of number and sorts by the year in the attribute joined. The template that matches state/@joined may seem a little obscure, but it gets exactly what it's after, namely, the name of the European state (obtained with ..), followed by a year (obtained with .), placing the year in parentheses.

To see what happens, apply the stylesheet with:

```
    xalan member.xml numeric.xsl
```

and you will get the output shown in Example 8-10.

Example 8-10. The sorted list of countries produced by running numeric.xsl

```
Number of EU Member States: 15
 - Belgium (1950)
 - France (1950)
 - Germany (1950)
 - Italy (1950)
 - Luxembourg (1950)
 - The Netherlands (1950)
 - Denmark (1973)
 - Ireland (1973)
 - United Kingdom (1973)
 - Greece (1981)
 - Portugal (1986)
 - Spain (1986)
 - Austria (1995)
 - Finland (1995)
 - Sweden (1995)
```

You can see from the output that the state nodes were sorted according to the year in the joined attribute, not alphabetically according to the name of the European state. Because the states are already in alphabetical order in the source tree, they also come out in alphabetical order in the result tree, after being sorted by year.

If you want to list the most recent year first, you can do so by adding the order attribute, as seen in Example 8-11, the stylesheet *recent.xsl*.

Example 8-11. A stylesheet for reverse-sorting countries by year of EU membership

```
<xsl:stylesheet version="1.0" xmlns:xsl="http://www.w3.org/1999/XSL/Transform">
<xsl:output method="text"/>

<xsl:template match="member">
  <xsl:text>Number of EU Member States: </xsl:text>
  <xsl:value-of select="count(state)"/>
  <xsl:text>&#10;</xsl:text>
  <xsl:apply-templates select="state/@joined">
    <xsl:sort data-type="number" order="descending"/>
  </xsl:apply-templates>
  <xsl:text>&#10;</xsl:text>
</xsl:template>

<xsl:template match="state/@joined">
  <xsl:text> - </xsl:text>
  <xsl:apply-templates select=".."/>
  <xsl:text> (</xsl:text>
  <xsl:value-of select="."/>
  <xsl:text>)&#10;</xsl:text>
</xsl:template>

</xsl:stylesheet>
```

In *recent.xsl*, the order attribute is added to sort and has a value of descending. Now apply it with this command:

```
xalan member.xml recent.xsl
```

and your results will look like Example 8-12.

Example 8-12. The reverse-sorted list of countries produced by running recent.xsl

```
Number of EU Member States: 15
 - Austria (1995)
 - Finland (1995)
 - Sweden (1995)
 - Portugal (1986)
 - Spain (1986)
 - Greece (1981)
 - Denmark (1973)
 - Ireland (1973)
 - United Kingdom (1973)
 - Belgium (1950)
 - France (1950)
 - Germany (1950)
 - Italy (1950)
 - Luxembourg (1950)
 - The Netherlands (1950)
```

If you open *member.xml* with a browser, the stylesheet *year.xsl* (shown in Example 8-13) will be applied.

Example 8-13. A stylesheet for sorting countries by year into an XHTML representation

```
<xsl:stylesheet version="1.0" xmlns:xsl="http://www.w3.org/1999/XSL/Transform">
<xsl:output method="xml" indent="yes"/>
<xsl:output doctype-public="-//W3C//DTD XHTML 1.0 Strict//EN"/>
<xsl:output doctype-system="http://www.w3.org/TR/xhtml1/DTD/xhtml1-strict.dtd"/>

 <xsl:template match="member">
   <html xmlns="http://www.w3.org/1999/xhtml">
   <head><title>EU Member States</title>
   <style type="text/css">
   h3 {font-size: 16pt}
   body {font-size: 13pt}</style>
   </head>
   <body>
   <h3>EU Member States</h3>
   <p>There are <xsl:text> </xsl:text>
    <xsl:value-of select="count(state)"/>
   member states, listed starting from the most recent year:</p>
   <ul>
   <xsl:apply-templates select="state">
   <xsl:sort select="@joined" data-type="number" order="descending"/>
   </xsl:apply-templates>
   </ul>
   </body>
   </html>
 </xsl:template>

 <xsl:template match="state">
   <xsl:element name="li" namespace="http://www.w3.org/1999/xhtml">
   <xsl:apply-templates/>
   <xsl:text> (</xsl:text>
   <xsl:value-of select="@joined"/>
   <xsl:text>)</xsl:text>
   </xsl:element>
 </xsl:template>

</xsl:stylesheet>
```

The stylesheet presents the same results as *recent.xsl* but in strict XHTML 1.0, as shown in Mozilla Firefox in Figure 8-2.

Multiple Sorts

You can sort nodes more than once, if needed, and you can also sort child nodes a different way than you sort their parent nodes. The select attribute of sort can help you do the job, as will be demonstrated in this section. Example 8-14, the document *shopping.xml*, represents a short, disorderly shopping list.

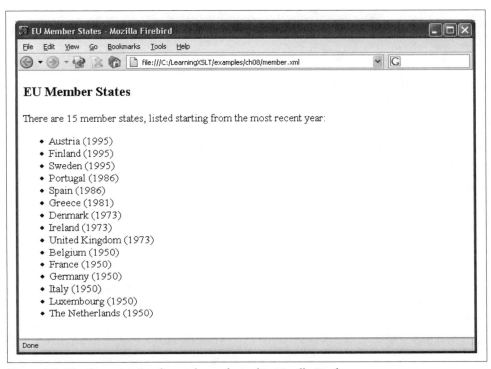

Figure 8-2. The document member.xml transformed in Mozilla Firefox

Example 8-14. An XML shopping list

```
<list>
 <freezer>
  <item>peas</item>
  <item>green beans</item>
  <item>pot pie</item>
  <item>ice cream</item>
 </freezer>
 <bakery>
  <item>rolls</item>
  <item>jelly doughnuts</item>
  <item>bread</item>
 </bakery>
 <produce>
  <item>bananas</item>
  <item>kumquats</item>
  <item>apples</item>
 </produce>
</list>
```

To help get things in better shape, Example 8-15, the stylesheet *shopping.xsl*, uses sort twice to sort different node-sets.

Example 8-15. A stylesheet for sorting the grocery list on two levels

```
<xsl:stylesheet version="1.0" xmlns:xsl="http://www.w3.org/1999/XSL/Transform">
<xsl:output method="text"/>

  <xsl:template match="list">
    <xsl:apply-templates select="*">
      <xsl:sort select="name( )"/>
    </xsl:apply-templates>
  </xsl:template>

  <xsl:template match="*">
    <xsl:text>Section: </xsl:text>
    <xsl:value-of select="name( )"/>
    <xsl:text>&#10;</xsl:text>
    <xsl:apply-templates select="item">
      <xsl:sort/>
    </xsl:apply-templates>
  </xsl:template>

  <xsl:template match="item">
    <xsl:text> * </xsl:text>
    <xsl:apply-templates/>
    <xsl:text>&#10;</xsl:text>
  </xsl:template>

</xsl:stylesheet>
```

Example 8-15 outputs plain text. The first template in this stylesheet matches `list` and then sorts on the names (using `name( )`) of the element children (using `*`) of `list`. This is the first sort. The second template matches only on the element children of `list`, again using `*`. After inserting some text (such as `Section:`) and the name of the element (again with `name( )`), the template sorts the text node content of `item` children. This is the second sort.

Finally, the last template matches `item` elements, prefixing text nodes with an asterisk (a bullet) in the result tree, and throwing in a line break after the text.

To see the results, type the command:

```
xalan shopping.xml shopping.xsl
```

and you will see Example 8-16.

Example 8-16. The sorted list of groceries produced by running shopping.xsl

```
Section: bakery
 * bread
 * jelly doughnuts
 * rolls
Section: freezer
 * green beans
 * ice cream
 * peas
```

```
 * pot pie
Section: produce
 * apples
 * bananas
 * kumquats
```

Originally, in the source document, the child elements of list were ordered freezer, bakery, and produce. Now they are alphabetically correct, that is, bakery, freezer, and produce. The children of each of these elements—all item elements—are correctly ordered as well.

Using copy and copy-of, the stylesheet in Example 8-17 (*list.xsl*) generates an XML result.

Example 8-17. A stylesheet for produce XML alphabetized by its content

```
<xsl:stylesheet version="1.0" xmlns:xsl="http://www.w3.org/1999/XSL/Transform">
<xsl:output method="xml" indent="yes"/>

 <xsl:template match="list">
  <xsl:copy>
   <xsl:apply-templates select="*">
    <xsl:sort select="name( )"/>
   </xsl:apply-templates>
  </xsl:copy>
 </xsl:template>

 <xsl:template match="*">
  <xsl:copy>
   <xsl:apply-templates select="item">
    <xsl:sort/>
   </xsl:apply-templates>
  </xsl:copy>
 </xsl:template>

 <xsl:template match="item">
  <xsl:copy-of select="."/>
 </xsl:template>

</xsl:stylesheet>
```

As a result of the following command:

```
    xalan -i 1 shopping.xml list.xsl
```

you'll get nicely alphabetized nodes, as shown in Example 8-18.

Example 8-18. The sorted list of groceries produced by running list.xsl

```
<?xml version="1.0" encoding="UTF-8"?>
<list>
 <bakery>
  <item>bread</item>
```

```
<item>jelly doughnuts</item>
<item>rolls</item>
</bakery>
<freezer>
<item>green beans</item>
<item>ice cream</item>
<item>peas</item>
<item>pot pie</item>
</freezer>
<produce>
<item>apples</item>
<item>bananas</item>
<item>kumquats</item>
</produce>
</list>
```

The lang and case-order Attributes

One attribute of sort that I haven't discussed is lang. This optional attribute lets you specify a language token, such as jp or ru, so that sorting rules will be determined by the alphabet of a language such as Japanese or Russian (Cyrillic). If the lang attribute is absent, an XSLT processor is supposed to determine the language from the system environment. This attribute does not yet appear to be supported by all processors, but the structure for that support is in place and over time, as demand arises for XSLT in more languages, support for lang will broaden.

Another missing attribute is the optional case-order. This attribute is supposed to allow you to sort by uppercase first using an attribute value of upper-first, or to sort by lowercase first with lower-first. The XSLT specification, however, allows for this to be language dependent, and so there are varying interpretations of how this is supposed to work. In some languages, a word may have a different meaning based on capitalization rather than spelling. In such cases, case-order will be useful.

Summary

You've learned how to sort alphabetically, in ascending and descending order, and by numbers. With this foundation, you may already have an appetite for advanced information on sorting, which you can find in Chapter 4 of Michael Kay's *XSLT Programmer's Reference* (Wrox) or in Chapter 6 of Doug Tidwell's *XSLT* (O'Reilly). In the next chapter, you'll learn how to add formatted numbers to the result tree.

CHAPTER 9

Numbering Lists

If you would like to add numbered lists to a result tree, you can use the XSLT instruction element number. The number element allows you to do simple number formatting, generate alphabetical lists, use Roman numerals, insert individual formatted numbers, and number lists at various levels. (Before actually using number, however, you'll first learn how to do numbering with the position( ) function.)

You can also format numbers with the XSLT function format-number( ), used optionally with the decimal-format instruction element. You can read more about the number element in Section 7.7 of the XSLT specification, and more about format-number( ) and decimal-format in Section 12.3 of the same spec.

Numbering with the number element can be complex and sometimes confusing with the possible combinations of all nine of its optional attributes. I won't touch on all possible numbering schemes in XSLT in this chapter, as I don't think it would be reasonable to do so, even in an advanced book. Rest assured, though, that by the time you finish reading this chapter, you'll understand most of what you need to know to order numbered lists with XSLT.

Numbered Lists

As usual, to illustrate a concept, I'll begin with a simple example. In the directory *examples/ch09*, you'll find the document *canada.xml*, which contains a list of all the Canadian provinces, in alphabetical order, as shown in Example 9-1.

Example 9-1. An XML list of Canadian provinces and territories

```
<?xml version="1.0" encoding="UTF-8"?>

<provinces>
 <name>Alberta</name>
 <name>British Columbia</name>
 <name>Manitoba</name>
 <name>New Brunswick</name>
```

Example 9-1. An XML list of Canadian provinces and territories (continued)

```
<name>Newfoundland and Labrador</name>
<name>Northwest Territories</name>
<name>Nova Scotia</name>
<name>Nunavut</name>
<name>Ontario</name>
<name>Prince Edward Island</name>
<name>Quebec</name>
<name>Saskatchewan</name>
<name>Yukon</name>
</provinces>
```

You can generate numbers manually from the XPath function position( ) to number a list from *canada.xml*. Example 9-2, *position.xsl*, shows you one way to do this.

Example 9-2. A stylesheet using node position for numbering

```
<xsl:stylesheet version="1.0" xmlns:xsl="http://www.w3.org/1999/XSL/Transform">
<xsl:output method="text"/>

 <xsl:template match="provinces">
   <xsl:apply-templates select="name"/>
 </xsl:template>

 <xsl:template match="name">
 <xsl:value-of select="position( )"/>
 <xsl:text>. </xsl:text>
 <xsl:value-of select="."/>
 <xsl:text>&#10;</xsl:text>
 </xsl:template>

</xsl:stylesheet>
```

In the first value-of element in the template rule that matches name, the position( ) function returns an integer reflecting the current position in the current node list. The current node list at this point consists of all the name nodes in the source tree. After giving you the position, the template inserts some text, then the text node child of the current name, then a linefeed. When you apply the stylesheet like this:

```
xalan canada.xml position.xsl
```

you will get the output shown in Example 9-3.

Example 9-3. A list of numbered provinces, produced by running position.xsl

```
1. Alberta
2. British Columbia
3. Manitoba
4. New Brunswick
5. Newfoundland and Labrador
6. Northwest Territories
7. Nova Scotia
8. Nunavut
```

Example 9-3. A list of numbered provinces, produced by running position.xsl (continued)

```
9. Ontario
10. Prince Edward Island
11. Quebec
12. Saskatchewan
13. Yukon
```

One pitfall of using position( ) is that if you use apply-templates without a select attribute, the whitespace text nodes are numbered as well. position( ) is actually counting nodes—that is, it is counting the nodes in processing order, regardless of where they are in the tree. Don't be surprised if you get strange numbers in output as a result of position( ) quietly counting whitespace nodes!

 If you are producing HTML or XHTML output, remember that you can also generate numbered lists using the ol and li elements.

The number Element

You can get by just using position( ), but XSLT's number instruction element is far more powerful. Example 9-4, the stylesheet *number.xsl*, is similar to Example 8-2, *sort.xsl* in *examples/ch08*, but with at least one obvious difference—the presence of the number instruction element.

Example 9-4. An XSLT stylesheet using the number element

```
<xsl:stylesheet version="1.0" xmlns:xsl="http://www.w3.org/1999/XSL/Transform">
<xsl:output method="text"/>

 <xsl:template match="provinces">
   <xsl:apply-templates select="name"/>
 </xsl:template>

 <xsl:template match="name">
  <xsl:number format=" 1. "/>
  <xsl:value-of select="."/>
  <xsl:text>&#10;</xsl:text>
 </xsl:template>

</xsl:stylesheet>
```

The template that matches name inserts a formatted number into the result tree using number, followed by the string value of each text node child of name that it finds. This is followed by a line break (
). Without using position( ), the number is derived from the position of the node in the source tree, not the current node list. When number is instantiated, it numbers all the name elements in the source document.

The inserted number is formatted according to the contents of the optional format attribute. The format attribute does the job that the first text element in *position.xsl* did. All of the attributes of number are optional, by the way, but if you don't use format, you might find that your numbers don't look very good.

The content of format is a string that describes how you want the number formatted in output. In the case of *number.xsl*, format contains first a space followed by the digit 1, followed by a period (.), and ending with another space. The digit 1 will be replaced by an incremented number when the transformation takes place.

To see how this looks, transform *canada.xml* with *number.xsl* with:

```
xalan canada.xml number.xsl
```

and you will get the results shown in Example 9-5.

Example 9-5. The results of using the number.xsl stylesheet

```
 1. Alberta
 2. British Columbia
 3. Manitoba
 4. New Brunswick
 5. Newfoundland and Labrador
 6. Northwest Territories
 7. Nova Scotia
 8. Nunavut
 9. Ontario
10. Prince Edward Island
11. Quebec
12. Saskatchewan
13. Yukon
```

The count Attribute

Without the count attribute, by default, only the nodes of the same name and type as the current node are counted. If the count attribute is present, however, the nodes that match the pattern in count are counted. For example, when applied to *canada.xml*, the stylesheet *count.xsl*, in Example 9-6, produces the same result as *number.xsl*, though the nodes you want to count are made explicit in the count attribute.

Example 9-6. Making the count explicit

```
<xsl:stylesheet version="1.0" xmlns:xsl="http://www.w3.org/1999/XSL/Transform">
<xsl:output method="text"/>

<xsl:template match="provinces">
  <xsl:apply-templates select="name"/>
</xsl:template>

<xsl:template match="name">
 <xsl:number count="name" format=" 1. "/>
 <xsl:value-of select="."/>
 <xsl:text>&#10;</xsl:text>
</xsl:template>

</xsl:stylesheet>
```

More on Formatting

The output from *number.xsl* and *count.xsl* looks very similar to what you get with *position.xsl*, but you can line things up a bit better by adding a tab to the format attribute, as shown in Example 9-7, the stylesheet *tab.xsl*.

Example 9-7. Modifying number formatting

```
<xsl:stylesheet version="1.0" xmlns:xsl="http://www.w3.org/1999/XSL/Transform">
<xsl:output method="text"/>

 <xsl:template match="provinces">
   <xsl:apply-templates select="name"/>
 </xsl:template>

 <xsl:template match="name">
  <xsl:number format=" 01.&#09;"/>
  <xsl:value-of select="."/>
  <xsl:text>&#10;</xsl:text>
 </xsl:template>

</xsl:stylesheet>
```

The value of the format attribute in *tab.xsl* is a little different than what you saw earlier. Instead of following the period with a space, there is a decimal character reference (	) for a horizontal tab. (You could also write this as a hexadecimal reference, that is, 	.) As you'll see, the tab will help line up the output.

The digit 1 has also been replaced by 01. This indicates that you want to use at least two places for your numbers instead of one. To see what I mean, transform *canada.xml* with *tab.xsl* with this command:

```
xalan canada.xml tab.xsl
```

Example 9-8 shows the result.

Example 9-8. The results of explicit formatting using tab.xsl

```
01.    Alberta
02.    British Columbia
03.    Manitoba
04.    New Brunswick
05.    Newfoundland and Labrador
06.    Northwest Territories
07.    Nova Scotia
08.    Nunavut
09.    Ontario
10.    Prince Edward Island
11.    Quebec
12.    Saskatchewan
13.    Yukon
```

Because *tab.xsl* formats the number with two places, you will get a leading zero for the numbers 1–9. Notice also that, because of the addition of the tab, all the text lines up nicely.

Alphabetical Lists

Instead of decimal numbers, you can also use alphabetical characters in lists generated by the `number` element. To get this to work, just change the digit in the `format` attribute value to a single letter—*a* for lowercase and *A* for uppercase. For example, *alpha.xsl*, shown in Example 9-9, uses a lowercase *a*.

Example 9-9. A stylesheet for alphabetical formatting

```
<xsl:stylesheet version="1.0" xmlns:xsl="http://www.w3.org/1999/XSL/Transform">
<xsl:output method="text"/>

 <xsl:template match="provinces">
   <xsl:apply-templates select="name"/>
 </xsl:template>

 <xsl:template match="name">
  <xsl:number format="&#32;a.&#32;&#32;"/>
  <xsl:value-of select="."/>
  <xsl:text>&#10;</xsl:text>
 </xsl:template>

</xsl:stylesheet>
```

Preceding and following the lowercase letter *a* are spaces defined by decimal character references ( ). You also could have used literal characters (just plain spaces) or hexadecimal character references (the hex reference for a space is). I use character references here in `format` because I think it's easier to see where the whitespaces are rather than the literal spaces, but you're free to choose which way you want to do it—it's a matter of personal style.

When you transform *canada.xml* against *alpha.xsl* with:

```
xalan canada.xml alpha.xsl
```

you get Example 9-10.

Example 9-10. The results of using the number element with alphabetical formatting

```
a.  Alberta
b.  British Columbia
c.  Manitoba
d.  New Brunswick
e.  Newfoundland and Labrador
f.  Northwest Territories
g.  Nova Scotia
h.  Nunavut
i.  Ontario
```

```
j.  Prince Edward Island
k.  Quebec
l.  Saskatchewan
m.  Yukon
```

Using Uppercase

If you prefer uppercase characters in your list, use an uppercase *A* in format instead of a lowercase *a*, as shown in *upper-alpha.xsl*, which is not shown here but is in *examples/ch09*. When you transform *canada.xml* with *upper-alpha.xsl*, you will see this generate a list ordered with uppercase letters rather than lowercase.

Longer Alphabetical Lists

What happens when an alphabetical list is longer than the English alphabet, that is, longer than 26 items? XSLT generates repeat characters, that is, lowercase, *a*, *b*, *c*...*x*, *y*, *z* is followed by *aa*, *ab*, *ac*, then followed by *ba*, *bb*, *bc*, then *ca*, *cb*, *cc*, and so on.

In Example 9-11, the document *us.xml* alphabetically lists all 50 states of the United States of America.

Example 9-11. A list of all the United States in XML

```xml
<?xml version="1.0"?>

<us>
 <state>Alabama</state>
 <state>Alaska</state>
 <state>Arizona</state>
 <state>Arkansas</state>
 <state>California</state>
 <state>Colorado</state>
 <state>Connecticut</state>
 <state>Delaware</state>
 <state>Florida</state>
 <state>Georgia</state>
 <state>Hawaii</state>
 <state>Idaho</state>
 <state>Illinois</state>
 <state>Indiana</state>
 <state>Iowa</state>
 <state>Kansas</state>
 <state>Kentucky</state>
 <state>Louisiana</state>
 <state>Maine</state>
 <state>Maryland</state>
 <state>Massachusetts</state>
 <state>Minnesota</state>
 <state>Michigan</state>
 <state>Mississippi</state>
```

Example 9-11. A list of all the United States in XML (continued)

```
<state>Missouri</state>
<state>Montana</state>
<state>Nebraska</state>
<state>Nevada</state>
<state>New Hampshire</state>
<state>New Jersey</state>
<state>New Mexico</state>
<state>New York</state>
<state>North Carolina</state>
<state>North Dakota</state>
<state>Oklahoma</state>
<state>Oregon</state>
<state>Ohio</state>
<state>Pennsylvania</state>
<state>Rhode Island</state>
<state>South Carolina</state>
<state>South Dakota</state>
<state>Tennessee</state>
<state>Texas</state>
<state>Utah</state>
<state>Vermont</state>
<state>Virginia</state>
<state>Washington</state>
<state>West Virginia</state>
<state>Wisconsin</state>
<state>Wyoming</state>
</us>
```

The stylesheet *us.xsl* uses number to list the states in *us.xml* using lowercase letters:

```
<xsl:stylesheet version="1.0" xmlns:xsl="http://www.w3.org/1999/XSL/Transform">
<xsl:output method="text"/>

  <xsl:template match="us">
    <xsl:apply-templates select="state"/>
  </xsl:template>

  <xsl:template match="state">
    <xsl:number format="&#x0020;a.&#x0009;"/>
    <xsl:value-of select="."/>
    <xsl:text>&#10;</xsl:text>
  </xsl:template>

</xsl:stylesheet>
```

The format attribute in this stylesheet uses two longer hexadecimal character references, one for space ( ) and another for tab (	). The number 32 in decimal is equivalent to 20 in hexadecimal; the numbers 0 through 9 are represented identically in decimal and hexadecimal. You can drop the leading zeros if you want, and write the references as and 	.

Apply the stylesheet *us.xsl* to the document *us.xml* with:

```
xalan us.xml us.xsl
```

and you will see the following results in Example 9-12.

Example 9-12. An alphabetically ordered list of all the U.S. states

a. Alabama
b. Alaska
c. Arizona
d. Arkansas
e. California
f. Colorado
g. Connecticut
h. Delaware
i. Florida
j. Georgia
k. Hawaii
l. Idaho
m. Illinois
n. Indiana
o. Iowa
p. Kansas
q. Kentucky
r. Louisiana
s. Maine
t. Maryland
u. Massachusetts
v. Minnesota
w. Michigan
x. Mississippi
y. Missouri
z. Montana
aa. Nebraska
ab. Nevada
ac. New Hampshire
ad. New Jersey
ae. New Mexico
af. New York
ag. North Carolina
ah. North Dakota
ai. Oklahoma
aj. Oregon
ak. Ohio
al. Pennsylvania
am. Rhode Island
an. South Carolina
ao. South Dakota
ap. Tennessee
aq. Texas
ar. Utah
as. Vermont
at. Virginia
au. Washington
av. West Virginia
aw. Wisconsin
ax. Wyoming

Roman Numerals

XSLT also supports numbering with Roman numerals in either upper- or lower-case—with *I, II, III, IV,* or *i, ii, iii, iv,* and so forth. To get Roman numerals in your output, just supply an upper- or lowercase letter *I* or *i* in the format attribute.

The *roman.xsl* stylesheet, shown in Example 9-13, formats its output with lowercase Roman numerals.

Example 9-13. A stylesheet for numbering with Roman numerals

```
<xsl:stylesheet version="1.0" xmlns:xsl="http://www.w3.org/1999/XSL/Transform">
<xsl:output method="text"/>

 <xsl:template match="us">
   <xsl:apply-templates select="state"/>
 </xsl:template>

 <xsl:template match="state">
 <xsl:number format="i&#x9;"/>
 <xsl:value-of select="."/>
 <xsl:text>&#10;</xsl:text>
 </xsl:template>

</xsl:stylesheet>
```

In this example, the lowercase letter *i* isn't preceded by any character, and it is followed by a single tab (	). Apply this stylesheet to *us.xml* with:

```
xalan us.xml roman.xsl
```

and you get the results shown in Example 9-14.

Example 9-14. U.S. states listed with Roman numerals

```
i       Alabama
ii      Alaska
iii     Arizona
iv      Arkansas
v       California
vi      Colorado
vii     Connecticut
viii    Delaware
ix      Florida
x       Georgia
xi      Hawaii
xii     Idaho
xiii    Illinois
xiv     Indiana
xv      Iowa
xvi     Kansas
xvii    Kentucky
xviii   Louisiana
xix     Maine
```

Example 9-14. U.S. states listed with Roman numerals (continued)

```
xx        Maryland
xxi       Massachusetts
xxii      Minnesota
xxiii     Michigan
xxiv      Mississippi
xxv       Missouri
xxvi      Montana
xxvii     Nebraska
xxviii    Nevada
xxix      New Hampshire
xxx       New Jersey
xxxi      New Mexico
xxxii     New York
xxxiii    North Carolina
xxxiv     North Dakota
xxxv      Oklahoma
xxxvi     Oregon
xxxvii    Ohio
xxxviii   Pennsylvania
xxxix     Rhode Island
xl        South Carolina
xli       South Dakota
xlii      Tennessee
xliii     Texas
xliv      Utah
xlv       Vermont
xlvi      Virginia
xlvii     Washington
xlviii    West Virginia
xlix      Wisconsin
l         Wyoming
```

Uppercase Roman Numerals

For uppercase Roman numerals, do the same thing as you do with alphabetical lists. The stylesheet *upper-roman.xsl* replaces the lowercase *i* with an uppercase *I*, followed by a decimal character reference for a tab (	). (This stylesheet is not shown here but is in *examples/ch09*.) If you transform *us.xml* with *upper-roman.xsl*, it will give you uppercase Roman numerals rather than lowercase.

Inserting an Individual Formatted Value

The value attribute of the number elements can be an individual value that you can format and then insert into the output. As a single value, it will also be a fixed value that isn't based on the position of the current node in the source document.

However, the value attribute can contain an expression whose result is a number that is not fixed. If, for example, the expression in value consists only of the position( ) function, numbering will be sequential and not fixed. See the stylesheet *value.xsl* in *examples/ch09* for an example of this (not shown here). You can apply this stylesheet to *canada.xml* if you want to try it. This stylesheet also sorts the content of *canada.xml* in reverse, or descending, order.

If you want to insert the single number *1,000,000* into a result tree, you could do so with the value attribute on number. Given the little document *thanks.xml*:

```
<thank>Thanks a </thanks>
```

you could insert a single number into it with *thanks.xsl*, as shown in Example 9-15.

Example 9-15. Inserting a single formatted number

```
<xsl:stylesheet version="1.0" xmlns:xsl="http://www.w3.org/1999/XSL/Transform">
<xsl:output method="text"/>

 <xsl:template match="thanks">
  <xsl:value-of select="."/>
  <xsl:number value="1000000" grouping-size="3" grouping-separator=","/>
  <xsl:text>!</xsl:text>
 </xsl:template>

</xsl:stylesheet>
```

The value attribute holds the desired number, 1000000. The grouping-size attribute indicates that you want to group the number at the thousands place. The grouping-separator attribute specifies a separator character (a comma [,]) that will occur at the thousands place. In order to work, the two grouping attributes must be used together.

Process *thanks.xml* with *thanks.xsl* for this result:

```
Thanks a 1,000,000!
```

Without the two grouping attributes used on number in *thanks.xsl*, the commas wouldn't appear in this output.

If you live in a locale that uses a period or dot (.) instead of a comma (,) as a group separator, you will prefer to use the stylesheet in Example 9-16, *dot.xsl*.

Example 9-16. Formatting the number with a dot separator

```
<xsl:stylesheet version="1.0" xmlns:xsl="http://www.w3.org/1999/XSL/Transform">
<xsl:output method="text"/>

 <xsl:template match="thanks">
  <xsl:value-of select="."/>
  <xsl:number value="1000000" grouping-size="3" grouping-separator="."/>
  <xsl:text>!</xsl:text>
 </xsl:template>

</xsl:stylesheet>
```

The only difference between *thanks.xsl* and *dot.xsl* is the value of the grouping-separator attribute. When used against *thanks.xml*, this stylesheet generates:

```
Thanks a 1.000.000!
```

The grouping attributes grouping-size and grouping-separator also work with numbers generated in the ordinary way by the number element, not just with a number supplied by the value attribute, as shown in *dot.xsl*. For example, if you have a document that has several thousand nodes that you want to count, the following instance of the number element with no value attribute would place a comma at the thousands place:

```
<xsl:number format="&#10;" grouping-size="3" grouping-separator=","/>
```

If you want to see this in action, generate the numbers 1 through 2,000 by applying *generator.xsl* to *generator.xml*, which contains 2,000 num nodes (not shown here but available in *examples/ch09*). These files—a trivial pair—exist among the examples only to demonstrate how the grouping attributes work with ordinary numbering. As you might have guessed, listing 2,000 nodes is impractical to print in a book!

Numbering Levels

An XSLT processor analyzes a source tree before any processing takes place. This makes it reasonably easy for the processor to determine how many nodes lie along a given axis, and makes it possible to produce different numbering levels when transforming a document. You can control this with number's level attribute.

The level attribute lets you set the level at which numbering takes place with one of three values: single, multiple, and any. So far, you have only seen numbering single level, which is the default. Here is a brief explanation of the three numbering levels, assuming that you don't use the from attribute and that the count attribute matches the current node:

- By default, the value of level is single, meaning that numbering takes place only with regard to sibling nodes on *one* level. More precisely, nodes on the single (one) level are counted along the preceding-sibling axis, and include all the preceding sibling nodes that match count or the current node.
- If the value of level is multiple, this means that all nodes on the ancestor-or-self axis, that match count or the current node, are counted.
- If the level attribute has a value of any, all nodes on the preceding or ancestor axes before the current node, that match count or the current node, are counted as they appear in document order.

That's the technical explanation. The different numbering levels will be clearer to you after you get a chance to go through a couple of examples.

Counting on Multiple Levels

To start out, take a look at Example 9-17, *outline.xml*, which lists some information about money in the United States.

Example 9-17. An XML document about U.S. currency

```xml
<?xml version="1.0"?>

<outline>
 <section title="US coin denominations">
  <item>cent</item>
  <item>nickel</item>
  <item>dime</item>
  <item>quarter</item>
  <item>half dollar</item>
  <item>dollar</item>
 </section>
 <section title="Persons on US coins">
  <item>Abraham Lincoln (cent)</item>
  <item>Thomas Jefferson (nickel)</item>
  <item>Franklin Roosevelt (dime)</item>
  <item>George Washington (quarter)</item>
  <item>John Kennedy (half dollar)</item>
  <item>Sacagawea (dollar)</item>
 </section>
 <section title="US currency in bills">
  <item>$1 dollar bill</item>
  <item>$2 dollar bill</item>
  <item>$5 dollar bill</item>
  <item>$10 dollar bill</item>
  <item>$20 dollar bill</item>
  <item>$50 dollar bill</item>
  <item>$100 dollar bill</item>
 </section>
 <section title="Persons on US bills">
  <item>George Washington ($1)</item>
  <item>Thomas Jefferson ($2)</item>
  <item>Abraham Lincoln ($5)</item>
  <item>Alexander Hamilton $10</item>
  <item>Andrew Jackson ($20)</item>
  <item>Ulysses Grant ($50)</item>
  <item>Benjamin Franklin ($100)</item>
 </section>
</outline>
```

There are two levels to count in *outline.xml*, namely, section and item nodes. The following stylesheet, *outline.xsl*, counts on both levels because it uses multiple as the value of the level attribute on number.

This stylesheet also introduces the for-each instruction element. As stated earlier, the for-each element works like a template within a template, and it is instantiated each time the node in the required select attribute is matched.

Example 9-18 shows *outline.xsl*.

Example 9-18. Using for-each for numbering

```
<xsl:stylesheet version="1.0" xmlns:xsl="http://www.w3.org/1999/XSL/Transform">
<xsl:output method="text"/>

<xsl:template match="outline">
 <xsl:for-each select="section|//item">
  <xsl:number level="multiple" count="section | item" format="i. a. "/>
  <xsl:value-of select="@title | text()"/>
  <xsl:text>&#10;</xsl:text>
 </xsl:for-each>
 <xsl:text>&#10; see http://www.usmint.gov and http://www.bep.treas.gov&#10;</xsl:text>
</xsl:template>

</xsl:stylesheet>
```

The select attribute of for-each can contain an expression. In *outline.xsl*, the select attribute instructs the processor to iterate through the section elements *and* (signified by |) all item elements in *outline.xml*. The two slashes (//) preceding item in the select attribute refer to all item elements that are descendants of the root node—in other words, *all* item elements in the *entire* source document.

The number element specifies a multilevel count for section and item elements by using the value of multiple for level, meaning that all ancestors will be counted. number also formats the numbers with lowercase Roman numerals on one level and with lowercase letters on another. After the appropriate number is inserted, a value-of grabs title attributes and text nodes. When for-each is done iterating through the nodes, the template adds a couple of URLs on to the end of the result to show where the information came from.

The result of applying *outline.xsl* to *outline.xml* with:

```
xalan outline.xml outline.xsl
```

is shown in Example 9-19.

Example 9-19. The results of using the stylesheet on multiple levels

```
i. US coin denominations
i. a. cent
i. b. nickel
i. c. dime
i. d. quarter
i. e. half dollar
i. f. dollar
ii. Persons on US coins
ii. a. Abraham Lincoln (cent)
ii. b. Thomas Jefferson (nickel)
ii. c. Franklin Roosevelt (dime)
ii. d. George Washington (quarter)
ii. e. John Kennedy (half dollar)
```

Example 9-19. The results of using the stylesheet on multiple levels (continued)

```
ii. f. Sacagawea (dollar)
iii. US currency in bills
iii. a. $1 dollar bill
iii. b. $2 dollar bill
iii. c. $5 dollar bill
iii. d. $10 dollar bill
iii. e. $20 dollar bill
iii. f. $50 dollar bill
iii. g. $100 dollar bill
iv. Persons on US bills
iv. a. George Washington ($1)
iv. b. Thomas Jefferson ($2)
iv. c. Abraham Lincoln ($5)
iv. d. Alexander Hamilton $10
iv. e. Andrew Jackson ($20)
iv. f. Ulysses Grant ($50)
iv. g. Benjamin Franklin ($100)

see http://www.usmint.gov and http://www.bep.treas.gov
```

As a result of using `level="multiple"`, the section nodes are counted at one level with Roman numerals, and the `item` nodes are counted at another level, alphabetically.

Now I'll clean up the Roman numerals that repeat in the previous example. I want to see the Roman numerals only on the section nodes, and the alphabetical numbering only on the item nodes. The way to make this happen is to number each node-set differently, in separate templates that don't use `level="multiple"`, which is what is done in Example 9-20, *better.xsl*.

Example 9-20. A cleaner method for numbering on multiple levels manually

```
<xsl:stylesheet version="1.0" xmlns:xsl="http://www.w3.org/1999/XSL/Transform">
<xsl:output method="text"/>

<xsl:template match="outline">
 <xsl:apply-templates select="section"/>
 <xsl:text>&#10;</xsl:text>
 <xsl:text>see http://www.usmint.gov and http://www.bep.treas.gov</xsl:text>
 <xsl:text>&#10;</xsl:text>
</xsl:template>

<xsl:template match="section">
 <xsl:number format="I. "/>
 <xsl:value-of select="@title"/>
 <xsl:text>&#10;</xsl:text>
 <xsl:apply-templates select="item"/>
</xsl:template>

<xsl:template match="item">
 <xsl:number format=" a. "/>
 <xsl:value-of select="text()"/>
```

```
<xsl:text>&#10;</xsl:text>
</xsl:template>

</xsl:stylesheet>
```

The template that matches the `outline` node applies templates to `section` nodes, and the template that matches `section` nodes applies templates to `item` nodes, in that order. The template that matches `section` nodes numbers the `section` nodes on the single level (the default) using one format, and the template that matches `item` nodes numbers `item` nodes also on the single level using a different format. I think the result is more attractive than the previous, multilevel example. When applied to *outline.xml*, using:

```
xalan outline.xml better.xsl
```

better.xsl creates the output shown in Example 9-21.

Example 9-21. A cleaner result

```
I. US coin denominations
 a. cent
 b. nickel
 c. dime
 d. quarter
 e. half dollar
 f. dollar
II. Persons on US coins
 a. Abraham Lincoln (cent)
 b. Thomas Jefferson (nickel)
 c. Franklin Roosevelt (dime)
 d. George Washington (quarter)
 e. John Kennedy (half dollar)
 f. Sacagawea (dollar)
III. US currency in bills
 a. $1 dollar bill
 b. $2 dollar bill
 c. $5 dollar bill
 d. $10 dollar bill
 e. $20 dollar bill
 f. $50 dollar bill
 g. $100 dollar bill
IV. Persons on US bills
 a. George Washington ($1)
 b. Thomas Jefferson ($2)
 c. Abraham Lincoln ($5)
 d. Alexander Hamilton $10
 e. Andrew Jackson ($20)
 f. Ulysses Grant ($50)
 g. Benjamin Franklin ($100)

see http://www.usmint.gov and http://www.bep.treas.gov
```

That looks better. If you increased the depth of the outline by adding child elements to item elements, you could add another template to *better.xsl* that numbers the new level of nodes and is invoked from the template that processes nodes just above this new level.

More Depth

Now, let's look at a document that has a little more depth, where you can see a varied hierarchy in the elements. Example 9-22, the document *data.xml*, contains some contact information for several standards organizations headquartered in the United States.

Example 9-22. Information about standards organizations

```
<?xml version="1.0" encoding="US-ASCII"?>
<data locale="us">
 <record>
  <name>
   <full>Internet Assigned Numbers Authority</full>
   <brief>IANA</brief>
  </name>
  <address>
   <street>4676 Admiralty Way, Suite 330</street>
   <city>Marina del Rey</city>
   <state>CA</state>
   <code>90292</code>
   <nation>USA</nation>
  </address>
  <tel>
   <phone>+1 310 823 9358</phone>
   <fax>+1 310 823 8649</fax>
   <email>iana@iana.org</email>
  </tel>
 </record>
 <record>
  <name>
   <full>Internet Society</full>
   <brief>ISOC</brief>
  </name>
  <address>
   <street>1775 Wiehle Ave., Suite 102</street>
   <city>Reston</city>
   <state>VA</state>
   <code>20190</code>
   <nation>USA</nation>
  </address>
  <tel>
   <phone>+1 703 326 9880</phone>
   <fax>+1 703 326 9881</fax>
   <email>info@ison.org</email>
  </tel>
```

Example 9-22. Information about standards organizations (continued)

```
 </record>
 <record>
  <name>
   <full>Organization for the Advancement of Structured Information Standards</full>
   <brief>OASIS</brief>
  </name>
  <address>
   <street>630 Boston Rd.</street>
   <city>Billerica</city>
   <state>MA</state>
   <code>01821</code>
   <nation>USA</nation>
  </address>
  <tel>
   <phone>+1 978 667 5115</phone>
   <fax>+1 978 667 5114</fax>
   <email>info@oasis-open.org</email>
  </tel>
 </record>
</data>
```

The stylesheet shown in Example 9-23, *data.xsl*, counts all elements on the multiple level *from* the data element.

Example 9-23. A stylesheet numbering with the from element

```
<xsl:stylesheet version="1.0" xmlns:xsl="http://www.w3.org/1999/XSL/Transform">
<xsl:output method="text"/>
<xsl:strip-space elements="*"/>

<xsl:template match="/">
 <xsl:apply-templates select="data//*"/>
</xsl:template>

<xsl:template match="data//*">
 <xsl:number level="multiple" count="*" from="data" format="1.1.1 "/>
 <xsl:value-of select="name( )"/>
 <xsl:text>: </xsl:text>
 <xsl:text>&#9;</xsl:text>
 <xsl:value-of select="text( )"/>
 <xsl:text>&#10;</xsl:text>
</xsl:template>

</xsl:stylesheet>
```

I'll discuss the from attribute in a moment. *data.xsl* prints each element's name with its immediate text node children, with each name preceded by a formatted section number and interspersed with a colon and whitespace. The result of processing *data.xml* with *data.xsl* with:

```
    xalan data.xml data.xsl
```

is shown in Example 9-24.

Example 9-24. Results with section numbering

```
1 record:
1.1 name:
1.1.1 full:     Internet Assigned Numbers Authority
1.1.2 brief:    IANA
1.2 address:
1.2.1 street:   4676 Admiralty Way, Suite 330
1.2.2 city:     Marina del Rey
1.2.3 state:    CA
1.2.4 code:     90292
1.2.5 nation:   USA
1.3 tel:
1.3.1 phone:    +1 310 823 9358
1.3.2 fax:      +1 310 823 8649
1.3.3 email:    iana@iana.org
2 record:
2.1 name:
2.1.1 full:     Internet Society
2.1.2 brief:    ISOC
2.2 address:
2.2.1 street:   1775 Wiehle Ave., Suite 102
2.2.2 city:     Reston
2.2.3 state:    VA
2.2.4 code:     20190
2.2.5 nation:   USA
2.3 tel:
2.3.1 phone:    +1 703 326 9880
2.3.2 fax:      +1 703 326 9881
2.3.3 email:    info@ison.org
3 record:
3.1 name:
3.1.1 full:     Organization for the Advancement of Structured Information Standards
3.1.2 brief:    OASIS
3.2 address:
3.2.1 street:   630 Boston Rd.
3.2.2 city:     Billerica
3.2.3 state:    MA
3.2.4 code:     01821
3.2.5 nation:   USA
3.3 tel:
3.3.1 phone:    +1 978 667 5115
3.3.2 fax:      +1 978 667 5114
3.3.3 email:    info@oasis-open.org
```

The numbering in Example 9-24 shows the structure of the elements and the hierarchical relationship of these elements to each other. It also shows how markup can be structured into numbered sections that technical or legal documents sometimes require.

Counting on Any Level

I'll now show you the difference between counting with multiple levels compared to counting on any level. The stylesheet *any.xsl* is a little different than *outline.xsl*: the value of level is any instead of multiple, and the value of format is also changed (i. a. becomes 1.). When you process *outline.xml* with *any.xsl*:

```
xalan outline.xml any.xsl
```

you get the result shown in Example 9-25.

Example 9-25. Results of numbering using the any level

```
1.  US coin denominations
2.  cent
3.  nickel
4.  dime
5.  quarter
6.  half dollar
7.  dollar
8.  Persons on US coins
9.  Abraham Lincoln (cent)
10. Thomas Jefferson (nickel)
11. Franklin Roosevelt (dime)
12. George Washington (quarter)
13. John Kennedy (half dollar)
14. Sacagawea (dollar)
15. US currency in bills
16. $1 dollar bill
17. $2 dollar bill
18. $5 dollar bill
19. $10 dollar bill
20. $20 dollar bill
21. $50 dollar bill
22. $100 dollar bill
23. Persons on US bills
24. George Washington ($1)
25. Thomas Jefferson ($2)
26. Abraham Lincoln ($5)
27. Alexander Hamilton $10
28. Andrew Jackson ($20)
29. Ulysses Grant ($50)
30. Benjamin Franklin ($100)

see http://www.usmint.gov and http://www.bep.treas.gov
```

Using the any level produces a sequential numbering of all nodes—no matter what level they are on. This could be useful, for example, when numbering diagrams in a document.

The from Attribute

The from attribute was shown earlier in *data.xsl*. This attribute tells the XSLT processor the node where you want the counting to start *from*. Example 9-26, the stylesheet *from.xsl*, uses the from attribute.

Example 9-26. A stylesheet using from

```
<xsl:stylesheet version="1.0" xmlns:xsl="http://www.w3.org/1999/XSL/Transform">
<xsl:output method="text"/>

<xsl:template match="outline">
 <xsl:for-each select="section|//item">
  <xsl:number from="section" level="multiple" count="section | item" format=" a "/>
  <xsl:value-of select="@title | text( )"/>
  <xsl:text>&#10;</xsl:text>
 </xsl:for-each>
 <xsl:text>&#10; see http://www.usmint.gov and http://www.bep.treas.gov&#10;</xsl:text>
</xsl:template>

</xsl:stylesheet>
```

When you count using from="section", the processor counts the nodes *after* the section nodes in the source tree, that is, all the item nodes. The result of this is that item nodes are counted, but the section nodes are not, as Example 9-27 shows.

Example 9-27. A stylesheet for counting from section elements

```
US coin denominations
 a cent
 b nickel
 c dime
 d quarter
 e half dollar
 f dollar
Persons on US coins
 a Abraham Lincoln (cent)
 b Thomas Jefferson (nickel)
 c Franklin Roosevelt (dime)
 d George Washington (quarter)
 e John Kennedy (half dollar)
 f Sacagawea (dollar)
US currency in bills
 a $1 dollar bill
 b $2 dollar bill
 c $5 dollar bill
 d $10 dollar bill
 e $20 dollar bill
 f $50 dollar bill
 g $100 dollar bill
Persons on US bills
 a George Washington ($1)
 b Thomas Jefferson ($2)
 c Abraham Lincoln ($5)
```

Example 9-27. A stylesheet for counting from section elements (continued)

```
d Alexander Hamilton $10
e Andrew Jackson ($20)
f Ulysses Grant ($50)
g Benjamin Franklin ($100)

see http://www.usmint.gov and http://www.bep.treas.gov
```

Notice that no number precedes the section text (U.S. coin denominations and so forth). Now that you've seen several examples of multilevel numbering, I hope you can find at least one of them that meets your needs.

The lang and letter-value Attributes

I'll mention a pair of attributes from number that I haven't yet discussed, but without concrete examples. These attributes have to do with the different way numbering is handled in different human languages. Speakers of English and other European languages are accustomed to numbering with so-called Arabic numerals, that is, with the ten digits 0–9. Some languages, such as Hebrew and Greek, use letters from their alphabets as numbers.

The lang attribute, like xml:lang, takes a language token as a value, such as *en, fr, de*, or *es*. This language token is supposed to signal to the XSLT processor what language is in use with regard to numbering. Another attribute, letter-value, takes the values alphabetic or traditional. These values are there to help distinguish between language-specific numbering systems that assign numerical values to alphabetical sequences or assign numerical values to letters in a traditional way. Unless you are familiar with a given language, such as Hebrew or Greek, some of these numbering schemes can be elusive.

The specification is somewhat loose in regard to this aspect of numbering, probably because the variations and ambiguities of numbering could make implementing number an overwhelming task. If you need to use traditional numbering, check the documentation provided with your XSLT processor of choice to find out how the processor handles these cases.

More Help with Formatted Numbers

The format attribute of the number element isn't the only place to turn for help with formatting numbers in XSLT. You can also use the format-number( ) function coupled optionally with the decimal-format element. The top-level decimal-format element has 10 attributes that define number characteristics, such as the decimal separator and percent sign used when formatting a number. Table 9-1 lists these 10 attributes with their default values.

The default values of decimal-format are assumed if the element is not present; if decimal-format is present, the default values are assumed if a given attribute is not used.

Table 9-1. Decimal format attributes

Attribute	Default	Description	Example
decimal-separator	.	Symbol that acts as a decimal point	100.00
digit	#	Symbol that represents any digit in number patterns	,###.00
grouping-separator	,	Symbol that separates groups of digits	1,000.00
infinity	Infinity	Symbol that represents infinity	∞ (∞)
minus-sign	-	Symbol that represents a minus sign	− (−)
name		Name for a decimal format	us
NaN	NaN	Symbol for Not a Number	?
pattern-separator	;	Symbol for separating pattern definitions	,###.00; (-,###.00)
percent	%	Symbol for percent sign	percent
per-mille	‰	Symbol for per mille sign	permille

The number characteristics defined by decimal-format are used with the format-number( ) function. The decimal-format element has no effect unless used with the format-number( ) function.

Example 9-28, the document *format.xml*, provides a list of eight positive integers that will be formatted in this example.

Example 9-28. Integers for formatting

```
<?xml version="1.0"?>
<?xml-stylesheet href="format.xsl" type="text/xsl"?>

<format>
 <number>100</number>
 <number>1000</number>
 <number>10000</number>
 <number>100000</number>
 <number>1000000</number>
 <number>10000000</number>
 <number>100000000</number>
 <number>1000000000</number>
</format>
```

The XML stylesheet PI references the *format.xsl* stylesheet shown in Example 9-29.

Example 9-29. A stylesheet with named formats for numbers

```
<xsl:stylesheet version="1.0" xmlns:xsl="http://www.w3.org/1999/XSL/Transform">
<xsl:output method="html"/>
<xsl:decimal-format name="de" decimal-separator=","
    grouping-separator="."/>
<xsl:decimal-format name="fr" decimal-separator=","
    grouping-separator=" "/>
<xsl:decimal-format name="ru" decimal-separator=","
    grouping-separator=" "/>
<xsl:decimal-format name="uk" decimal-separator="."
    grouping-separator=","/>
<xsl:decimal-format name="us" decimal-separator="."
    grouping-separator=","/>

<xsl:template match="convert">
 <html>
 <head>
 <title>Number Formatter</title>
 <style type="text/css">
 table {margin-left:auto;margin-right:auto}
 td {text-align:right;padding: 5px 5px 5px 5px}
 h3 {text-align:center}
 </style>
 </head>
 <body>
 <h3>Number Formatter</h3>
 <table rules="all">
 <thead>
 <tr>
  <th>Deutschland</th>
  <th>France</th>
  <th>&#x420;&#x43E;&#x441;&#x441;&#x438;&#x44f;</th> <!-- Russia -->
  <th>United Kingdom</th>
  <th>United States</th>
 </tr>
 </thead>
 <tbody>
 <xsl:apply-templates select="number"/>
 </tbody>
 </table>
 </body>
 </html>
</xsl:template>

<xsl:template match="number">
 <tr>
 <td><xsl:value-of select="format-number(.,'.###,00&#x20AC;','de')"/></td>
 <td><xsl:value-of select="format-number(.,' ###,00&#x20AC;','fr')"/></td>
 <td><xsl:value-of select="format-number(.,' ###,00p.','ru')"/></td>
 <td><xsl:value-of select="format-number(.,'&#xA3;,###.00','uk')"/></td>
 <td><xsl:value-of select="format-number(.,'&#x24;,###.00','us')"/></td>
 </tr>
</xsl:template>

</xsl:stylesheet>
```

Each of the five instances of the decimal-format element at the top of the stylesheet define a number format, each with its own name. These formats define currency patterns for Germany (Deutschland), France, **Россия** (Russia), the United Kingdom, and the United States. The currency patterns identify the decimal and grouping separators that are formally used when describing currency in those countries.

The stylesheet creates some HTML and CSS for the result tree. The headings (th) include the name *Russia* spelled in Cyrillic **Россия** using character references. As the table rows are formed with the second template, each number element in *format.xml* is processed with each of the five named number formats by calling the format-number( ) function. I'll pick apart the first function call so you can better understand what's going on with all five:

```
format-number(.,'.###,00&#x20AC;','de')
```

The format-number( ) function can take three arguments (as this call does), but only two arguments are required. The first argument in this call is a period (.). This is a synonym for the current node (current( ) and self::node( ) also work here). The current node is a node from the node list containing all the number nodes in the source tree.

The second argument is a number pattern for formatting the number, as follows:

- The period (.) represents a grouping separator.
- The three hashes, or pound signs (###), each represent digits. (You could change this to some other symbol with the digit attribute in decimal-format; the default is #.)
- The comma (,) after the ### represents a decimal point or separator.
- The character reference (€) is for the Euro currency symbol €.
- This pattern can produce a formatted number such as 1.000,00 €.

The third and final argument for format-number( ) references a named number format (as in de) that is defined by a decimal-format element.

The result of formatting *format.xml* with *format.xsl* is shown in Figure 9-1 in Mozilla Firefox. One reason I did this example in HTML is so that I could show the Cyrillic characters and currency symbols. They don't show well in a command prompt window!

I researched the currency formats using IBM's open source International Components for Unicode (ICU) project. ICU provides libraries of services that use the latest versions of Unicode, including international number formats (see *http://oss.software. ibm.com/icu/*). For information on these currency patterns discussed here, check out the ICU LocaleExplorer at *http://oss.software.ibm.com/cgi-bin/icu/lx/en/utf-8/*.

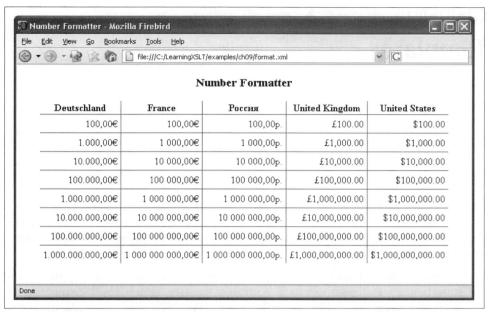

Deutschland	France	Россия	United Kingdom	United States
100,00€	100,00€	100,00p.	£100.00	$100.00
1.000,00€	1 000,00€	1 000,00p.	£1,000.00	$1,000.00
10.000,00€	10 000,00€	10 000,00p.	£10,000.00	$10,000.00
100.000,00€	100 000,00€	100 000,00p.	£100,000.00	$100,000.00
1.000.000,00€	1 000 000,00€	1 000 000,00p.	£1,000,000.00	$1,000,000.00
10.000.000,00€	10 000 000,00€	10 000 000,00p.	£10,000,000.00	$10,000,000.00
100.000.000,00€	100 000 000,00€	100 000 000,00p.	£100,000,000.00	$100,000,000.00
1.000.000.000,00€	1 000 000 000,00€	1 000 000 000,00p.	£1,000,000,000.00	$1,000,000,000.00

Figure 9-1. Displaying format.xml in Mozilla Firefox

 Though it is well-researched, ICU might not always reflect the common street practice of native speakers or users of a given language.

Summary

In this chapter, you learned how to create numbered lists for a result tree. You learned how to format numbers, create alphabetical and Roman numeral lists, insert single, formatted numbers into the result, and number lists at different levels. You also learned how to format numbers with the format-number( ) function coupled with the decimal-format element.

You can put numbering behind you for now—it's time to learn more about templates.

CHAPTER 10

Templates

You've learned a lot about template rules—how to create them, how to write patterns that trigger them, and how to generate results from them. You should be familiar with the following concepts about templates:

- Template rules attempt to match patterns in a source document. A pattern is a subset of an expression, which is mostly used to match child elements and attributes using the child and attribute axes. (You can also use predicates, plus the id( ) and key( ) functions. You learned about predicates in Chapter 4 and about id( ) in Chapter 5, and you will learn about key( ) in the next chapter.)

- When a pattern is matched in a source document, the content of the template (called a sequence constructor in XSLT 2.0) is instantiated or written out to the result tree.

- When apply-templates is used in a template element, it processes the children of the matched pattern, searching for other template rules that match those children.

- If the select attribute is used on apply-templates, it processes the children of the matched pattern that are specifically named in the attribute, searching for template rules that match those nodes so named. The select attribute can contain an expression.

- Built-in templates do behind-the-scenes work in processing nodes that may not be explicitly identified in templates rules, such as text nodes.

This chapter discusses additional issues related to templates, namely, what template priority is, how to create and call named templates, how to use parameters with templates using with-param, what modes are and how to use them (the mode attribute), and finally some additional details on built-in templates.

Template Priority

What happens if you have more than one template rule that matches the exact same pattern, or more than one template rule with different patterns that happen to match the exact same nodes? Which template, if any, gets instantiated? Multiple templates matching the same node present a problem. When this happens, an XSLT processor has the option to stop processing and recover from the error, or recover from the error after issuing a warning. The way a processor recovers from conflicting templates is to instantiate only the last template in a stylesheet that matches the pattern. I'll show you what I mean.

Example 10-1, the document *ri.xml* in *examples/ch10*, lists the five counties in the state of Rhode Island in the U.S.

Example 10-1. An XML document listing Rhode Island counties

```
<?xml version="1.0" encoding="US-ASCII"?>

<state name="Rhode Island">
 <county>Bristol</county>
 <county>Kent</county>
 <county>Newport</county>
 <county>Providence</county>
 <county>Washington</county>
</state>
```

The stylesheet *last.xsl*, shown in Example 10-2, has two templates that match the pattern for the state element node, each producing a different result.

Example 10-2. A stylesheet that matches a state twice

```
<xsl:stylesheet version="1.0" xmlns:xsl="http://www.w3.org/1999/XSL/Transform">
<xsl:output method="xml" indent="yes"/>

 <xsl:template match="/">
  <county state="{state/@name}">
   <xsl:apply-templates select="state"/>
  </county>
 </xsl:template>

 <xsl:template match="state">
   <xsl:apply-templates select="county"/>
 </xsl:template>

 <xsl:template match="state">
  <xsl:apply-templates select="county[starts-with(.,'K')]"/>
 </xsl:template>
 <xsl:template match="county">
  <name><xsl:apply-templates/></name>
 </xsl:template>

</xsl:stylesheet>
```

In order of appearance, the first template that matches state elements selects all the county children of state. The second template that matches state selects only the county child whose text content starts with the letter *K* (using the starts-with( ) function). Both templates invoke the last template, which matches county elements. Process *ri.xml* with *last.xsl* like this:

```
xalan -i 1 ri.xml last.xsl
```

Because an XSLT processor uses the last template when a match conflict arises, the stylesheet *last.xsl* produces this output:

```
<?xml version="1.0" encoding="UTF-8"?>
<county state="Rhode Island">
  <name>Kent</name>
</county>
```

Only the state node containing Kent is instantiated because that is what the last template matching state instructed the processor to do.

 Notice that the encoding for the document is UTF-8 even though the source document has an encoding of US-ASCII. To change the encoding US-ASCII in the output, you'd have to add an encoding attribute with a value of US-ASCII to the output element.

Now in contrast, if you apply *last.xsl* to *ri.xml* with Instant Saxon, as follows:

```
saxon ri.xml last.xsl
```

you will see the following error report:

```
Recoverable error
Ambiguous rule match for /state[1]
Matches both "state" on line 14 of file:/C:/LearningXSLT/examples/ch08/last.xsl
and "state" on line 10 of file:/C:/LearningXSLT/examples/ch08/last.xsl
<?xml version="1.0" encoding="utf-8"?>
<county state="Rhode Island">
    <name>Kent</name>
</county>
```

An XSLT processor is not required to report multiple templates matching one template rule, but processors may report such an error and may recover from the error. Either way, the processor must either stop or recover from the error by applying the last template that matches the rule. (See the last paragraph in Section 5.5 of the XSLT specification.)

The priority Attribute

Now compare *last.xsl* with *priority.xsl*, which is a very similar stylesheet shown in Example 10-3.

Example 10-3. A stylesheet using priorities

```
<xsl:stylesheet version="1.0" xmlns:xsl="http://www.w3.org/1999/XSL/Transform">
<xsl:output method="xml" indent="yes"/>

 <xsl:template match="/">
  <county state="{state/@name}">
   <xsl:apply-templates select="state"/>
  </county>
 </xsl:template>

 <xsl:template match="state" priority="2">
  <xsl:apply-templates select="county"/>
 </xsl:template>

 <xsl:template match="state" priority="1">
  <xsl:apply-templates select="county[starts-with(.,'K')]"/>
 </xsl:template>
 <xsl:template match="county">
  <name><xsl:apply-templates/></name>
 </xsl:template>

</xsl:stylesheet>
```

The only difference between *last.xsl* and *priority.xsl* is that the two templates matching state elements each have priority attributes. The priority attribute can explicitly set which of two or more conflicting templates gets used first. The higher the value of the priority attribute, the higher the priority of the template; in other words, a template with a priority of 2 trumps a template with a priority of 1.

When applied to *ri.xml*, *priority.xsl* produces the following output:

```
<?xml version="1.0" encoding="UTF-8"?>
<county state="Rhode Island">
 <name>Bristol</name>
 <name>Kent</name>
 <name>Newport</name>
 <name>Providence</name>
 <name>Washington</name>
</county>
```

The template with a priority of 2 is invoked (the first template of the two that matches state), but the template with the priority of 1 is not. Trivially, using the priority attribute can allow you to switch templates on and off, which can be useful for testing.

More formally, however, the priority attribute's reason for being is to help distinguish the patterns that match the same node but use different patterns. Example 10-4, *same.xsl*, shows you an example of this.

Example 10-4. A stylesheet that matches the same node with different patterns

```
<xsl:stylesheet version="1.0" xmlns:xsl="http://www.w3.org/1999/XSL/Transform">
<xsl:output method="xml" indent="yes"/>

 <xsl:template match="/">
  <county state="{state/@name}">
   <xsl:apply-templates select="state"/>
  </county>
 </xsl:template>

 <xsl:template match="state">
  <xsl:apply-templates select="county"/>
 </xsl:template>

 <xsl:template match="county[starts-with(.,'K')]">
  <first-match><xsl:apply-templates/></first-match>
 </xsl:template>

 <xsl:template match="county[2]">
  <last-match><xsl:apply-templates/></last-match>
 </xsl:template>

 <xsl:template match="county">
  <name><xsl:apply-templates/></name>
 </xsl:template>

</xsl:stylesheet>
```

The template rule matching county[starts-with(.,'K')] and the one matching county[2] both match the same node count, but each uses a different pattern (in that each uses a different predicate) to identify the node. This results in a recoverable error.

As with *last.xsl*, when *ri.xml* is processed with *same.xsl*:

```
xalan -i 1 ri.xml same.xsl
```

Xalan recovers from the error silently by using the last matching rule:

```
<?xml version="1.0" encoding="UTF-8"?>
<county state="Rhode Island">
 <name>Bristol</name>
 <last-match>Kent</last-match>
 <name>Newport</name>
 <name>Providence</name>
 <name>Washington</name>
</county>
```

When *ri.xml* is processed with Instant Saxon, using:

```
saxon ri.xml same.xsl
```

it issues a warning about the error before recovering and using the last template rule:

```
Recoverable error
Ambiguous rule match for /state[1]/county[2]
Matches both "county[2]" on line 18 of file:/C:/LearningXSLT/examples/ch10/same.xsl
and "county[starts-with(.,'K')]" on line 14 of file:/C:/LearningXSLT/examples/ch10/
same.xsl
<?xml version="1.0" encoding="utf-8"?>
<county state="Rhode Island">
    <name>Bristol</name>
    <last-match>Kent</last-match>
    <name>Newport</name>
    <name>Providence</name>
    <name>Washington</name>
</county>
```

prior.xsl, as shown in Example 10-5, changes the priority of these conflicting rules by using the priority attribute.

Example 10-5. Avoiding a conflict with the priority attribute

```
<xsl:stylesheet version="1.0" xmlns:xsl="http://www.w3.org/1999/XSL/Transform">
<xsl:output method="xml" indent="yes"/>

<xsl:template match="/">
 <county state="{state/@name}">
  <xsl:apply-templates select="state"/>
 </county>
</xsl:template>

<xsl:template match="state">
 <xsl:apply-templates select="county"/>
</xsl:template>

<xsl:template match="county[starts-with(.,'K')]" priority="2">
 <first-match><xsl:apply-templates/></first-match>
</xsl:template>

<xsl:template match="county[2]" priority="1">
 <last-match><xsl:apply-templates/></last-match>
</xsl:template>

<xsl:template match="county">
 <name><xsl:apply-templates/></name>
</xsl:template>

</xsl:stylesheet>
```

Process it with:

```
saxon ri.xml prior.xsl
```

and the error is avoided:

```
<?xml version="1.0" encoding="utf-8"?>
<county state="Rhode Island">
    <name>Bristol</name>
    <first-match>Kent</first-match>
    <name>Newport</name>
    <name>Providence</name>
    <name>Washington</name>
</county>
```

The template matching county[starts-with(.,'K')] is instantiated because it has a priority of 2 while the one matching county[2] is not because it has a lower priority value (1).

Another feature that affects template priority is *import precedence*. Using the top-level XSLT element import, you can import other stylesheets into a given stylesheet. Import precedence is determined by the order in which stylesheets are imported, which has an influence over template priority. This topic is explored in Chapter 13.

 The XSLT specification spells out the default priorities—what template has priority over another by default with no priority attribute—in Section 5.5. In general, the more specific the pattern, the higher its priority. For example, county[1] has a higher default priority than county because it is more specific.

Calling a Named Template

It's possible to have templates in a stylesheet that don't overtly match any node pattern: you can invoke such templates by name. You assign a template a name by giving it a name attribute. In fact, if a template element does not use a match attribute, it must have a name attribute instead (though it is also permissible for a template to have both match and name attributes).

The call-template instruction element has one required attribute, also called name. The value of the name attribute on a call-template element must match the value of a name attribute on a template element. It's an error to have more than one template with the same name.

When you want to instantiate a named template, ring it up with a call-template element. The advantage of calling named templates is that you can instantiate them on demand rather than only when a given pattern is encountered in a source tree. Also, the context does not change when you call a template by name. Calling a template is similar to calling a function or method in a programming language such as C or Java, but without a return value.

Example 10-6 is a stylesheet that uses the call-template element named *call.xsl*.

Example 10-6. A stylesheet using call-template

```
<xsl:stylesheet version="1.0" xmlns:xsl="http://www.w3.org/1999/XSL/Transform">
<xsl:output method="text"/>

<xsl:template match="state">
Counties of <xsl:value-of select="@name"/>:
 <xsl:call-template name="nl"/>
 <xsl:apply-templates select="county"/>
</xsl:template>

<xsl:template match="county">
 <xsl:text> - </xsl:text>
 <xsl:value-of select="."/>
 <xsl:call-template name="nl"/>
</xsl:template>

<xsl:template name="nl">
 <xsl:text>&#10;</xsl:text>
</xsl:template>

</xsl:stylesheet>
```

In *call.xsl*, the template named *nl* (short for *newline*) contains a text element that holds a decimal character reference for a single linefeed character (
). The other two templates in the stylesheet call the *nl* template to insert on demand a single line-feed into the result tree. When applied to *ri.xml* with:

```
xalan ri.xml call.xsl
```

this stylesheet produces:

```
Counties of Rhode Island:

 - Bristol
 - Kent
 - Newport
 - Providence
 - Washington
```

Using the name and match Attributes Together

A template element can have both a name and a match attribute at the same time. This does not happen often, but you might want to do this because you could instantiate a template upon finding a pattern, or you could call the template when desired. I'll give you an example of how this works.

Look at the following similar XML documents in Examples 10-7 and 10-8. These documents show the estimated populations of the respective states, by county, as of July 1, 2001. (This information was garnered from the United States Census Bureau web site, *http://www.census.gov*.) The first is Example 10-7, *delaware.xml*.

Example 10-7. Delaware information in XML

```
<?xml version="1.0"?>

<state name="Delaware">
 <description>July 1, 2001 population estimates<description>
 <from>U.S. Census Bureau</from>
 <url>http://www.census.gov</url>
 <county name="Kent">
  <population>129066</population>
 </county>
 <county name="New Castle">
  <population>505829</population>
 </county>
 <county name="Sussex">
  <population>161270</population>
 </county>
</state>
```

The second document is *rhodeisland.xml*, shown in Example 10-8.

Example 10-8. Rhode Island information in XML

```
<?xml version="1.0"?>

<state name="Rhode Island">
 <description>July 1, 2001 population estimates<description>
 <from>U.S. Census Bureau</from>
 <url>http://www.census.gov</url>
 <county name="Bristol">
  <population>51173</population>
 </county>
 <county name="Kent">
  <population>169224</population>
 </county>
 <county name="Newport">
  <population>85218</population>
 </county>
 <county name="Providence">
  <population>627314</population>
 </county>
 <county name="Washington">
  <population>125991</population>
 </county>
</state>
```

The stylesheet in Example 10-9, *both.xsl*, employs a template that uses both the match and name attributes.

Example 10-9. A stylesheet that uses both match and name attributes on template

```
<xsl:stylesheet version="1.0" xmlns:xsl="http://www.w3.org/1999/XSL/Transform">
<xsl:output method="text"/>

<xsl:template match="state">
```

```
<xsl:call-template name="nl"/>
<xsl:text>Counties of </xsl:text>
<xsl:value-of select="@name"/>
<xsl:call-template name="nl"/>
<xsl:text>Description: </xsl:text>
<xsl:value-of select="description"/>
<xsl:call-template name="nl"/>
<xsl:text>Source: </xsl:text>
<xsl:value-of select="from"/>
<xsl:call-template name="nl"/>
<xsl:text>URL: </xsl:text>
<xsl:value-of select="url"/>
<xsl:call-template name="nl"/>
<xsl:apply-templates select="county"/>
<xsl:text>Estimated state population: </xsl:text>
<xsl:value-of select="sum(county/population)"/>
<xsl:call-template name="nl"/>
</xsl:template>

<xsl:template match="county">
<xsl:text> - </xsl:text>
<xsl:value-of select="@name"/>
<xsl:text>: </xsl:text>
<xsl:value-of select="population"/>
<xsl:apply-templates select="population"/>
</xsl:template>

<xsl:template match="population" name="nl">
<xsl:text>&#10;</xsl:text>
</xsl:template>
</xsl:stylesheet>
```

This stylesheet creates a simple text report when used to process documents such as *delaware.xml* and *rhodeisland.xml*. As part of the report, it also sums the content of population nodes using the XPath function sum( ).

Like *call.xsl*, this stylesheet also has a template named *nl*. The difference is that the template also matches on population nodes. This means that the template is invoked both when a population element is processed (see apply-templates in the template that matches county) and directly by call-template.

The following example processes *delaware.xml* and *rhodeisland.xml* with *both.xsl* using xsltproc, an XSLT processor written in C and based on the C libraries libxslt and libxml2. It runs in a Unix environment such as Linux or—as I use it—as part of Cygwin on Windows. This processor is available for download from *http://xmlsoft.org* or as part of the Cygwin distribution available at *http://www.cygwin.com*.

I'm showing you xsltproc because it allows you to process one or more XML documents against a stylesheet at one time. Here is the command line:

```
xsltproc both.xsl delaware.xml rhodeisland.xml
```

The stylesheet comes first, followed by a list of XML documents that you want to process. The outcome of this command is:

```
Counties of Delaware
Description: July 1, 2001 population estimates
Source: U.S. Census Bureau
URL: http://www.census.gov
  - Kent: 129066
  - New Castle: 505829
  - Sussex: 161270
Estimated state population: 796165

Counties of Rhode Island
Description: July 1, 2001 population estimates
Source: U.S. Census Bureau
URL: http://www.census.gov
  - Bristol: 51173
  - Kent: 169224
  - Newport: 85218
  - Providence: 627314
  - Washington: 125991
Estimated state population: 1058920
```

Looking back at the stylesheet, notice where the *nl* template is invoked directly with multiple instances of call-template. After the stylesheet processes the name and population data of each county by invoking the template that matches county nodes, it then applies templates for population nodes, inserting a linefeed after each node.

Using Templates with Parameters

For the purposes of XSLT, a parameter is a name that can be bound to a value and then later referenced by name. You learned about this in Chapter 7. You can use the with-param element as a child element of either apply-templates or call-template to pass a parameter into a template. For example, a template could be invoked several times, each time with a different parameter value, thus changing what happens when the template is invoked. Watch what happens when a stylesheet calls a template with four different parameter values.

Example 10-10, *yukon.xml*, lists cities in Canada's Yukon Territory.

Example 10-10. A list of cities in the Yukon

```
<?xml version="1.0" encoding="UTF-8"?>

<province name="Yukon Territory">
 <city>Beaver Creek</city>
 <city>Carcross</city>
 <city>Carmacks</city>
 <city>Dawson</city>
 <city>Faro</city>
 <city>Haines Junction</city>
 <city>Mayo</city>
```

Example 10-10. A list of cities in the Yukon (continued)

```
<city>Ross River</city>
<city>Teslin</city>
<city>Watson Lake</city>
<city>Whitehorse</city>
</province>
```

The stylesheet in Example 10-11, *yukon.xsl*, processes *yukon.xml* with each instance of call-template passing a different value for the parameter *nl*.

Example 10-11. Processing cities with call-template

```
<xsl:stylesheet version="1.0" xmlns:xsl="http://www.w3.org/1999/XSL/Transform">
<xsl:output method="text"/>

<xsl:template match="province">
 <xsl:text>Yukon Territory Cities</xsl:text>
 <xsl:call-template name="nl">
  <xsl:with-param name="nl" select="'&#10;&#10;'"/>
 </xsl:call-template>
 <xsl:apply-templates select="city"/>
</xsl:template>

<xsl:template match="city">
 <xsl:text> -> </xsl:text>
 <xsl:value-of select="."/>
 <xsl:call-template name="nl">
  <xsl:with-param name="nl" select="'&#10;'"/>
 </xsl:call-template>
</xsl:template>

<xsl:template match="city[.='Dawson']">
 <xsl:text> -> </xsl:text>
 <xsl:value-of select="."/>
 <xsl:call-template name="nl">
  <xsl:with-param name="nl" select="' (second largest city in the Yukon)&#10;'"/>
 </xsl:call-template>
</xsl:template>

<xsl:template match="city[.='Whitehorse']">
 <xsl:text> -> </xsl:text>
 <xsl:value-of select="."/>
 <xsl:call-template name="nl">
  <xsl:with-param name="nl" select="' (largest city in the Yukon)&#10;'"/>
 </xsl:call-template>
</xsl:template>

<xsl:template name="nl">
 <xsl:param name="nl"/>
 <xsl:value-of select="$nl"/>
</xsl:template>

</xsl:stylesheet>
```

When you apply *yukon.xsl* to *yukon.xml* with:

```
xalan yukon.xml yukon.xsl
```

you produce this result:

```
Yukon Territory Cities

   -> Beaver Creek
   -> Carcross
   -> Carmacks
   -> Dawson (second largest city in the Yukon)
   -> Faro
   -> Haines Junction
   -> Mayo
   -> Ross River
   -> Teslin
   -> Watson Lake
   -> Whitehorse (largest city in the Yukon)
```

When the first template is invoked, it inserts the heading text Yukon Territory Cities and then calls the template named *nl* with the parameter *nl* containing a value of two linefeed character references. (In XSLT, there are no name conflicts between the names of templates and the names of parameters or variables.)

As each instance of city is encountered in the source, the stylesheet invokes the template that matches city, each time with the parameter *nl* containing only one linefeed. However, when the stylesheet finds city nodes that contain the text nodes Dawson or Whitehorse, it calls the template with distinct parameter values for *nl*—a line of text followed by a linefeed.

You could produce the same results as *yukon.xsl* without using with-param; however, *yukon.xsl* illustrates how to use with-param. You can read more about with-param in Section 11.6 of the XSLT specification.

 You can also use with-param as a child of apply-templates, as demonstrated in the stylesheet *with-param.xsl*, explained in Chapter 7. Nevertheless, with-param is more commonly used with call-template.

Modes

You already know what happens when more than one template matches an identical pattern—a conflict arises that may be overcome by template priority. There is also another workaround for template pattern conflicts: modes. Modes are useful when a stylesheet needs to visit a given node many times with varying results, such as when producing a table of contents or a list of authorities, to name a few examples.

The mode attribute is an optional attribute for both the template and apply-templates elements. If you modify these elements each with a matching mode attribute and value, you can match identical patterns with templates, without generating an error. Following is an example of how it works.

Example 10-12, the document *hawaii.xml*, lists each of the counties in the state of Hawaii in the U.S., along with the largest city in each county.

Example 10-12. Hawaii counties and their largest cities

```xml
<?xml version="1.0" encoding="UTF-8"?>
<?xml-stylesheet href="mode.xsl" type="text/xsl"?>

<us>
 <state name="Hawaii">
  <county name="Hawaii">
   <city class="largest">Hilo</city>
  </county>
  <county name="Honolulu">
   <city class="largest">Honolulu</city>
  </county>
  <county name="Kauai">
   <city class="largest">Kapaa</city>
  </county>
  <county name="Maui">
   <city class="largest">Kahului</city>
  </county>
 </state>
</us>
```

Using an XML stylesheet PI, the document references the stylesheet *mode.xsl*, shown in Example 10-13, which produces HTML output.

Example 10-13. A stylesheet for processing counties in different modes

```xml
<xsl:stylesheet version="1.0" xmlns:xsl="http://www.w3.org/1999/XSL/Transform">
<xsl:output method="html"/>

<xsl:template match="us/state">
 <html>
 <head>
 <title>State: <xsl:value-of select="@name"/></title>
 <style type="text/css">
 h1, h2 {font-family: sans-serif;color: blue}
 ul {font-size: 16pt}
 </style>
 </head>
 <body>
 <h1>State: <xsl:value-of select="@name"/></h1>
 <h2>All Counties</h2>
 <ul><xsl:apply-templates select="county" mode="county"/></ul>
 <h2>Largest Cities (by County)</h2>
 <ul><xsl:apply-templates select="county" mode="city"/></ul>
 </body>
```

Example 10-13. A stylesheet for processing counties in different modes (continued)

```
  </html>
</xsl:template>

<xsl:template match="county" mode="county">
 <li><xsl:value-of select="@name"/></li>
</xsl:template>

<xsl:template match="county" mode="city">
 <li>
  <xsl:value-of select="city"/> (<xsl:value-of select="@name"/>)
 </li>
</xsl:template>

</xsl:stylesheet>
```

There are two templates in this stylesheet that match county elements. Because each of the two is invoked in a different mode, no conflict occurs. In the first template in the stylesheet, there are two instances of the apply-templates element, each matching the county pattern and each with a mode attribute that has a unique value (one has a value of county, the other city). There are no name conflicts in XSLT between the values of match and mode attributes.

Later in the stylesheet, there are two templates that also have mode attributes, matching the values used earlier (county and city). In order to work, the value of mode on a template element must match the value of mode in one or more instances of apply-templates.

The outcome of applying *mode.xsl* to *hawaii.xml* in Mozilla is shown in Figure 10-1.

There are several paragraphs about modes in Section 5.7 of the XSLT specification.

Built-in Template Rules

XSLT processors have a feature known as *built-in template rules*. The built-in template rules were discussed in various places earlier in the book. Because of the built-in templates, an XSLT processor will process nodes in a source document, even though there are no explicit, matching template rules present in the stylesheet used to process the source document.

To illustrate how built-in templates work, here is a ridiculously simple example. The source document *mammals.xml*, shown in Example 10-14, lists a few mammals that are native to North America.

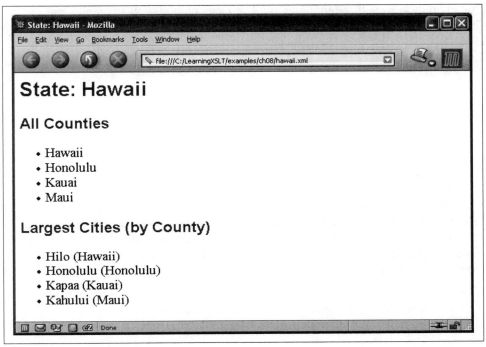

Figure 10-1. Displaying hawaii.xml in Mozilla

Example 10-14. A list of some native North American mammals

```
<?xml version="1.0"?>

<mammals locale="North America">
 <mammal>American Bison</mammal>
 <mammal>American black bear</mammal>
 <mammal>Bighorn sheep</mammal>
 <mammal>Bobcat</mammal>
 <mammal>Common gray fox</mammal>
 <mammal>Cougar</mammal>
 <mammal>Coyote</mammal>
 <mammal>Gray wolf</mammal>
 <mammal>Mule deer</mammal>
 <mammal>Pronghorn</mammal>
 <mammal>White-tailed deer</mammal>
</mammals>
```

The rather boring stylesheet *blank.xsl* has only one line and no template rules:

```
<stylesheet version="1.0" xmlns="http://www.w3.org/1999/XSL/Transform"/>
```

When you process *mammals.xml* with this stylesheet:

```
xalan mammals.xml blank.xsl
```

Xalan finds no explicit templates for the element nodes in *mammals.xml*, so the built-in template rules kick in, producing the following result:

```
<?xml version="1.0" encoding="UTF-8"?>

    American Bison
    American black bear
    Bighorn sheep
    Bobcat
    Common gray fox
    Cougar
    Coyote
    Gray wolf
    Mule deer
    Pronghorn
    White-tailed deer
```

The built-in rules processed the root node, the element nodes, and all the text nodes that it found in *mammals.xml*. If you use an explicit template for just one of the nodes, that node will be processed with that template, but all the other nodes will be processed with the built-in templates.

The stylesheet *built-in.xsl* has only one template, and that template matches only one element node, the sixth `mammal` child of `mammals`, in *mammals.xml*:

```
<xsl:stylesheet version="1.0" xmlns:xsl="http://www.w3.org/1999/XSL/Transform">
<xsl:output method="text"/>

<xsl:template match="mammals/mammal[6]">
 Found <xsl:value-of select="."/>!
</xsl:template>

</xsl:stylesheet>
```

Process *mammals.xml* with *built-in.xsl* with:

```
xalan mammals.xml built-in.xsl
```

and you will get this output:

```
    American Bison
    American black bear
    Bighorn sheep
    Bobcat
    Common gray fox

    Found Cougar!

    Coyote
    Gray wolf
    Mule deer
    Pronghorn
    White-tailed deer
```

When the processor encounters the node pattern matched in the template, it instantiates the template (including whitespace), but it also applies the built-in rules. You can, in effect, shut off the built-in rules by matching the unwanted nodes with an empty template matching mammal, as does *shutoff.xsl*, shown in Example 10-15.

Example 10-15. A stylesheet that shuts off a rule

```
<xsl:stylesheet version="1.0" xmlns:xsl="http://www.w3.org/1999/XSL/Transform">
<xsl:output method="text"/>

<xsl:template match="mammals">
 <xsl:apply-templates select="mammal"/>
</xsl:template>

<xsl:template match="mammal"/>

<xsl:template match="mammal[6]">
 Found <xsl:value-of select="."/>!
</xsl:template>

</xsl:stylesheet>
```

When applied to *mammals.xml*:

```
xalan mammals.xml built-in.xsl
```

the result is just:

```
Found Cougar!
```

The difference is that when the processor encounters the first template, it searches for all templates that match mammal. Although both templates in the stylesheet match mammal, they are distinct because only one has a predicate that matches the sixth mammal node and instantiates some literal text. The other template instructs the processor to do nothing with all mammal nodes. (This does not cause an error because the more specific template that matches mammal[6] has priority over the template that matches only mammal.)

Notice the difference in the final stylesheet in this section, *cougar.xsl*, shown in Example 10-16.

Example 10-16. A stylesheet that only reports the cougar

```
<xsl:stylesheet version="1.0" xmlns:xsl="http://www.w3.org/1999/XSL/Transform">
<xsl:output method="xml" indent="yes"/>

<xsl:template match="mammals">
<north.american>
 <mammal>
  <cat><xsl:apply-templates select="mammal[6]"/></cat>
 </mammal>
</north.american>
</xsl:template>

</xsl:stylesheet>
```

This single template processes the children of mammals, but it selects only the sixth mammal element, in document order, and discards the others. When processed with *mammals.xml*, like this:

```
xalan -i 1 mammals.xml cougar.xsl
```

you get the following result:

```
<?xml version="1.0" encoding="UTF-8"?>
<north.american>
 <mammal>
  <cat>Cougar</cat>
 </mammal>
</north.american>
```

I have mostly shown examples of the built-in rules working with element nodes, text nodes, and the root node. Table 10-1 summarizes what all the behaviors of the built-in template rules are when they encounter each of the seven nodes.

Table 10-1. Built-in template rule behavior

Node	Behavior
Root	Processes all children
Element	Processes all children, including the text nodes; the built-in rule for text copies text through
Attribute	Copies text through
Text	Copies text through
Comment	Nothing
Processing-instruction	Nothing
Namespace	Nothing

Section 5.8 of the XSLT specification discusses built-in template rules in greater detail. (Information on North American mammals was taken from the web site of the Smithsonian Institution's National Museum of Natural History at *http://web6.si.edu/np_mammals/index.htm*.)

Summary

You've discovered several new ways to use templates in this chapter. You learned about template priority, how to call named templates with call-template, and how to call or apply templates with parameters. You also learned how to use modes, and became more aware of built-in templates and what they do in absence of working templates.

In the next chapter, you will learn what a key is, how to define keys with the key element, and then how to process those keys with the key( ) function.

CHAPTER 11

Using Keys

A *key* provides a means of identifying some of the data that is associated with it. A key might identify a record in a database, for example, or an element in a collection, as in Java. XSLT also uses keys.

XSLT's support for keys is provided through the key element and the key( ) function in tandem. The key element declares the key, and the key( ) function invokes it. The examples that follow in this chapter will show you how to declare and apply keys in several ways, including grouping.

These examples are simple by design, but they don't clearly demonstrate the main benefit of keys, which is better performance. One way you could see a performance hike would be to call a key repeatedly on a document with many nodes. The reason for improved performance is that an XSLT processor creates an internal index for nodes that makes finding those nodes much faster.

By the way, you can read about keys in Section 12.2 of the XSLT specification.

A Simple Key

Following is part of the valid XML document *un.xml* (found in *examples/ch11*), which stores information about the 190 member states of the United Nations (UN). Example 11-1 is just a fragment of the document as, at over 700 lines, it's too long to list in its entirety.

Example 11-1. Information about countries that belong to the UN

```
<?xml version="1.0" encoding="ISO-8859-1"?>

<un>
 <state cc="af">
  <name>Afghanistan</name>
  <admitted>19 Nov. 1946</admitted>
 </state>
 <state cc="al">
  <name>Albania</name>
```

```
<admitted>14 Dec. 1955</admitted>
</state>
<state cc="dz">
 <name>Algeria</name>
 <admitted>8 Oct. 1962</admitted>
</state>
<state cc="ad">
 <name>Andorra</name>
 <admitted>28 July 1993</admitted>
</state>
<state cc="ao">
 <name>Angola</name>
 <admitted>1 Dec. 1976</admitted>
</state>
<state cc="ag">
 <name>Antigua and Barbuda</name>
 <admitted>11 Nov. 1981</admitted>
</state>
<state cc="ar">
 <name>Argentina</name>
 <admitted>24 Oct. 1945</admitted>
</state>
<state cc="am">
 <name>Armenia</name>
 <admitted>2 Mar. 1992</admitted>
</state>
<state cc="au">
 <name>Australia</name>
 <admitted>1 Nov. 1945</admitted>
</state>
```

This document holds three pieces of information for each member state:

1. The member state's country code, stored as the value of the cc attribute on the state element.

2. The name of the member state, stored in the name element.

3. The date that the member state was admitted to the UN, stored in the admitted element.

The following stylesheet, *un.xsl*, declares a key on the top level and then uses it in the template to pick up information about Australia (au) from *un.xml* (note bold):

```
<xsl:stylesheet version="1.0" xmlns:xsl="http://www.w3.org/1999/XSL/Transform">
<xsl:output method="text"/>
<xsl:key name="UN" match="state" use="@cc"/>

<xsl:template match="/">
 <xsl:value-of select="key('UN', 'au')/name"/>
</xsl:template>

</xsl:stylesheet>
```

The following two sections explain the interrelationship between the key element and the key( ) function.

The key Element

The key element is a top-level element, meaning that it must be a child of the stylesheet element and is not allowed inside templates. It has three required attributes. The first is the name attribute, which provides the name by which a key( ) function may refer to the declared key. The name of the key in *un.xsl* is UN.

The second attribute, match, contains a pattern that the key matches, just as the match attribute on the template element matches a pattern. The pattern that the key declaration matches in *un.xsl* is the location path state.

The third and final attribute, use, contains an expression that is applied to every node that matches the pattern in match. The value of use in this declaration is @cc, which corresponds to the cc attribute on state elements.

This key declaration won't do you any good unless you use a key( ) function in the stylesheet to find and exploit the key. You can call the key( ) function in an expression, such as in the select attribute of value-of.

The key( ) Function

In order to do its work, the key( ) function depends on a top-level key declaration. This function returns a node-set. Its signature indicates that it has two required arguments:

```
key(string, object)
```

The first argument to key( ) is a string enclosed in single quotes that matches the name of a declared key. In the *un.xsl* stylesheet, the name is UN, also in single quotes. The second argument is an object that will be converted to a string and applied to the key. This value must match the node defined in the expression contained in the use attribute of the key element. So, in *un.xsl*, the argument au in single quotes matches the state element in *un.xml* that has a cc attribute with a value of au.

Following the function call to key( ) is the location path /name. This path refers to a child node of the node returned as a result of calling key( ). As with the document( ) function, you can add location paths after the key( ) function call.

To see how it works, apply the stylesheet to the document:

```
xalan un.xml un.xsl
```

and you will get this result:

```
Australia
```

The expression in the select attribute of value-of calls the key( ) function using the key declaration named UN. The single quotes (') around the function arguments are necessary. During the transformation, the expression found a state node in *un.xml* that had a cc attribute whose value was au. Then value-of returned the text node in the name child of the matching node, that is, the text Australia.

The interesting thing about keys in XSLT is that they don't rely on context to do their work. Keys establish their own context, based on the value of the match attribute in the key element. (Keys also select only nodes that exist in the same document as the context node.) This makes keys appropriate for use in situations where you don't want to rely on a current context to do processing. This characteristic, likewise, makes keys suitable for cross-referencing nodes in entirely different contexts, as you will see in the section "Cross-Referencing with Keys," later in this chapter.

More Than One Key

You can, of course, declare and invoke more than one key in a stylesheet. *keys.xsl* makes use of two keys, each using a different expression to find a value:

```
<xsl:stylesheet version="1.0" xmlns:xsl="http://www.w3.org/1999/XSL/Transform">
<xsl:output method="text"/>
<xsl:key name="State" match="state" use="name"/>
<xsl:key name="UN" match="state" use="@cc"/>

<xsl:template match="/">
 <xsl:value-of select="key('State', 'Germany')/name"/>
 <xsl:text> </xsl:text>
 <xsl:value-of select="key('UN', 'de')/admitted"/>
</xsl:template>

</xsl:stylesheet>
```

The declared key named State helps find a node that matches the text nodes in state elements, such as Germany; the key named UN finds a node that matches the value of cc attributes, such as de.

Apply the stylesheet *keys.xsl* to *un.xml* with:

```
xalan un.xml keys.xsl
```

and you get this output:

```
Germany 18 Sep. 1973
```

It may seem odd that the call to key( ) in the first value-of is followed by the path /name because the key itself matches a name element. If you leave off the path /name, the pattern in the match attribute of the key declaration will be matched, and all children of the matched node will be processed, not just the name node. Adding the location step /name at the end of the key( ) function call refines what gets returned by the expression.

Using a Parameter with Keys

Instead of using stationary keys as in the previous two stylesheets, what if you want to vary a key? You can use parameters to do this. Once again, a parameter is a value bound to a name that you can also pass into a template or stylesheet to change the outcome of a transformation. (Parameters were discussed in Chapter 7.) The *kp.xsl* stylesheet uses a parameter named kp to change the result of a call to key( ):

```
<xsl:stylesheet version="1.0" xmlns:xsl="http://www.w3.org/1999/XSL/Transform">
<xsl:output method="text"/>
<xsl:key name="UN" match="state" use="@cc"/>
<xsl:param name="kp">af</xsl:param>

<xsl:template match="/">
 <xsl:text>The member state </xsl:text>
 <xsl:value-of select="key('UN', $kp)/name"/>
 <xsl:text> was admitted to the UN on </xsl:text>
 <xsl:value-of select="key('UN', $kp)/admitted"/>
 <xsl:text>.</xsl:text>
</xsl:template>

</xsl:stylesheet>
```

The key named UN is the same as the key with the same name in both *un.xsl* and *keys.xsl*. Immediately following that key declaration is the top-level element, param. This element binds a name to a value for later reference in the stylesheet. The default value of the parameter kp is af, the country code for Afghanistan, which is the first member state in *un.xml*.

Later on in the stylesheet, in the two key( ) calls, the parameter kp is referenced with $kp. Each time the stylesheet calls key( ), the reference to kp is replaced by the value af. Now you'll get a chance to apply this stylesheet in a couple of different ways to see how this parameter makes a difference.

First, apply the stylesheet to *un.xml* the way you normally would:

```
xalan un.xml kp.xsl
```

and you will get the following result:

```
The member state Afghanistan was admitted to the UN on 19 Nov. 1946.
```

Passing in a Parameter to the Stylesheet

Now, in the following command, you can pass in a new parameter value for kp into the stylesheet and produce a different outcome to the transformation:

```
xalan -p kp  "'es' un.xml kp.xsl
```

The single quotes are important. With this command line, the processor passes the value es for the kp parameter into *kp.xsl*. The default value of kp is af, which is replaced with the value es during the transformation, giving you this somewhat different result:

```
The member state Spain was admitted to the UN on 14 Dec. 1955.
```

Select other country codes of your choice from the cc attributes in *un.xml*, and pass them into the stylesheet to see what happens. Instant Saxon uses a little simpler syntax on the command line for passing in parameters. Note the end of this command line:

```
saxon un.xml kp.xsl kp=ls
```

Or:

```
saxon un.xml kp.xsl kp="ls"
```

Instant Saxon associates the parameter/value pair with an equals sign (=). This command gives you results like this:

```
The member state Lesotho was admitted to the UN on 17 Oct. 1966.
```

Because the parameter kp is used by both keys, its value is a sort of cross-reference that establishes a relationship between the value of an attribute and the content of an element. In the next example, you'll see how this can be expanded to touch more than one XML document at a time.

Cross-Referencing with Keys

In the final example of this chapter, you'll cross-reference identical content in two separate documents. To do this, you'll use a parameter and the document( ) function. The following two XML documents share some identical content. The first, *states.xml*, lists the names of eight western states in the continental United States:

```
<?xml version="1.0" encoding="US-ASCII"?>

<usstates>
 <western>
  <usstate>Arizona</usstate>
  <usstate>California</usstate>
  <usstate>Idaho</usstate>
  <usstate>Montana</usstate>
  <usstate>Nevada</usstate>
  <usstate>Oregon</usstate>
  <usstate>Washington</usstate>
  <usstate>Utah</usstate>
 </western>
</usstates>
```

The second document, *capitals.xml*, lists the capitals of these states:

```
<?xml version="1.0" encoding="US-ASCII"?>

<capitals>
 <capital usstate="Arizona">Phoenix</capital>
 <capital usstate="California">Sacramento</capital>
```

```
<capital usstate="Idaho">Boise</capital>
<capital usstate="Montana">Helena</capital>
<capital usstate="Nevada">Carson City</capital>
<capital usstate="Oregon">Salem</capital>
<capital usstate="Washington">Olympia</capital>
<capital usstate="Utah">Salt Lake City</capital>
</capitals>
```

The value of the usstate attributes in this document is the same as the content of the usstate elements in *states.xml*. The stylesheet *cross.xsl* takes advantage of this relationship by bringing this information together in a result tree:

```
<xsl:stylesheet version="1.0" xmlns:xsl="http://www.w3.org/1999/XSL/Transform">
<xsl:output method="text"/>
<xsl:key name="Capital" match="capitals/capital" use="@usstate"/>
<xsl:key name="State" match="usstates/western/usstate" use="."/>
<xsl:param name="cr">Arizona</xsl:param>

<xsl:template match="/">
 <xsl:apply-templates select="document('capitals.xml')/capitals"/>
 <xsl:text>, </xsl:text>
 <xsl:value-of select="key('State', $cr)"/>
</xsl:template>

<xsl:template match="capitals">
 <xsl:value-of select="key('Capital', $cr)"/>
</xsl:template>

</xsl:stylesheet>
```

The stylesheet declares two keys, Capital and State, and a parameter, cr. The first template matches the document root (/) of the main document it intended to process, *states.xml*. It also applies templates to the capitals node in *capitals.xml* using the document( ) function.

When templates are applied to the capitals node, the template that matches capitals is invoked, and the key( ) function is called for the key named Capital. The template returns the string value using the key Capital key. Control is then returned to the invoking template after this is accomplished.

After all this takes place, a comma and space are inserted into the result tree by a text element from the first template, and the key( ) function is called again for the key named State. Using Arizona as the default value of cr, the stylesheet, when applied to *states.xml*, gives you the following answer:

```
Phoenix, Arizona
```

Try it with other states, such as Oregon, like this:

```
xalan -p cr "'Oregon' states.xml cross.xsl
```

The result you will get is:

```
Salem, Oregon
```

Or, you can get the same output using Instant Saxon this way:

```
saxon states.xml cross.xsl cr="Oregon"
```

This example demonstrates how keys, combined with other functionality, can be a powerful tool in searching for, and establishing, a relationship between that content, as well as matching, verifying, and extracting content from one or more documents.

Grouping with Keys

An interesting problem that you can solve with keys comes under the rubric of *grouping*. Grouping in XSLT refers to the process of grouping nodes logically with related nodes in the output. The problem that grouping solves is that nodes may not be grouped to your liking in the source document. For an example, look at *group.xml*:

```
<?xml version="1.0" encoding="US-ASCII"?>
<?xml-stylesheet href="group.xsl" type="text/xsl"?>

<uscities>
 <western>
  <uscity state="Nevada">Las Vegas</uscity>
  <uscity state="Arizona">Phoenix</uscity>
  <uscity state="California">San Francisco</uscity>
  <uscity state="Nevada">Silver City</uscity>
  <uscity state="Washington">Seattle</uscity>
  <uscity state="Montana">Missoula</uscity>
  <uscity state="Washington">Spokane</uscity>
  <uscity state="California">Los Angeles</uscity>
  <uscity state="Utah">Salt Lake City</uscity>
  <uscity state="California">Sacramento</uscity>
  <uscity state="Idaho">Boise</uscity>
  <uscity state="Montana">Butte</uscity>
  <uscity state="Washington">Tacoma</uscity>
  <uscity state="Montana">Helena</uscity>
  <uscity state="Oregon">Portland</uscity>
  <uscity state="Nevada">Reno</uscity>
  <uscity state="Oregon">Salem</uscity>
  <uscity state="Oregon">Eugene</uscity>
  <uscity state="Utah">Provo</uscity>
  <uscity state="Idaho">Twin Falls</uscity>
  <uscity state="Utah">Ogden</uscity>
  <uscity state="Arizona">Flagstaff</uscity>
  <uscity state="Idaho">Idaho Falls</uscity>
  <uscity state="Arizona">Tucson</uscity>
 </western>
</uscities>
```

The uscity nodes in *group.xml* list western U.S. cities at random, not in an organized way as you might prefer. One feature that can help is that each uscity node has a state attribute. The XSLT grouping technique I'll show you can organize the output according to state, also listing each appropriate city with the given state. This grouping technique is popularly known as the Muenchian method, after Steve Muench (*http://www.oreillynet.com/pub/au/609*), the really smart guy who discovered the method.

The Muenchian method of grouping employs keys together with the generate-id() function (you learned about generate-id() back in Chapter 5). There are other grouping methods in XSLT, such as one that uses the preceding-sibling axis, but I've chosen to show you only the Muenchian method here for two reasons: it is the most efficient or fastest method of grouping; and it is the most similar to the new grouping method using the XSLT 2.0 element for-each-group, which you will see in Chapter 16.

 You can find discussions of other grouping methods in Michael Kay's *XSLT Programmer's Reference* (Wrox) or Doug Tidwell's *XSLT* (O'Reilly), but both authors also recommend the Muenchian method as being the most efficient.

The stylesheet *group.xsl* assembles its output according to the Muenchian method, which I will explain in a moment:

```
<xsl:stylesheet version="1.0" xmlns:xsl="http://www.w3.org/1999/XSL/Transform">
<xsl:output method="html"/>
<xsl:key name="list" match="uscity" use="@state"/>

<xsl:template match="/">
<html>
<head>
<title>Western State Cities</title></head>
<style type="text/css">
h2 {font-family:verdana,helvetica,sans-serif;font-size:13pt}
li {font-family:verdana,helvetica,sans-serif;font-size:11pt}
</style>
<body>
<xsl:for-each select="/uscities/western/uscity[generate-id(.)=generate-id(key('list',
@state))]/@state">
<xsl:sort/>
<h2><xsl:value-of select="."/></h2>
<ul>
 <xsl:for-each select="key('list', .)">
  <xsl:sort/>
  <li><xsl:value-of select="."/></li>
 </xsl:for-each>
</ul>
</xsl:for-each>
</body>
</html>
</xsl:template>

</xsl:stylesheet>
```

The secret to understanding the Muenchian method lies in its use of keys and the generate-id() function. Near the beginning of *group.xsl*, the key named list is defined. This key is used to efficiently find state attributes on uscity elements. The generate-id() function is used with the key() function in for-each to process the first node in a set. In this example, it finds the first node whose state attribute identifies a given state and outputs the name of the state found in the attribute.

Following that, another for-each processes each other node in the document matching the previous for-each, also using key(). The value-of under this for-each outputs the name of the given city. The sort element under the for-each elements sorts the nodes in alphabetical order.

It's a little complicated, but it works well. Test it with the command:

```
xalan -m -i 1 group.xml group.xsl
```

and you will get nicely grouped HTML output that looks like this:

```
<html>
 <head>
  <title>Western State Cities</title>
 </head>
 <style type="text/css">
h2 {font-family:verdana,helvetica,sans-serif;font-size:13pt}
li {font-family:verdana,helvetica,sans-serif;font-size:11pt}
</style>
 <body>
  <h2>Arizona</h2>
  <ul>
   <li>Flagstaff</li>
   <li>Phoenix</li>
   <li>Tucson</li>
  </ul>
  <h2>California</h2>
  <ul>
   <li>Los Angeles</li>
   <li>Sacramento</li>
   <li>San Francisco</li>
  </ul>
  <h2>Idaho</h2>
  <ul>
   <li>Boise</li>
   <li>Idaho Falls</li>
   <li>Twin Falls</li>
  </ul>
  <h2>Montana</h2>
  <ul>
   <li>Butte</li>
   <li>Helena</li>
   <li>Missoula</li>
  </ul>
  <h2>Nevada</h2>
  <ul>
   <li>Las Vegas</li>
   <li>Reno</li>
```

```
   <li>Silver City</li>
  </ul>
  <h2>Oregon</h2>
  <ul>
   <li>Eugene</li>
   <li>Portland</li>
   <li>Salem</li>
  </ul>
  <h2>Utah</h2>
  <ul>
   <li>Ogden</li>
   <li>Provo</li>
   <li>Salt Lake City</li>
  </ul>
  <h2>Washington</h2>
  <ul>
   <li>Seattle</li>
   <li>Spokane</li>
   <li>Tacoma</li>
  </ul>
 </body>
</html>
```

In the output, under each alphabetically listed state, comes an alphabetical list of cities. That's what grouping can do for you. Because it has an XML stylesheet PI, you can also open *group.xml* in a browser to see the output. Figure 11-1 shows *group.xml* transformed by *group.xsl* in the Mozilla Firefox browser that appears with the Mozillazine (MZ) theme.

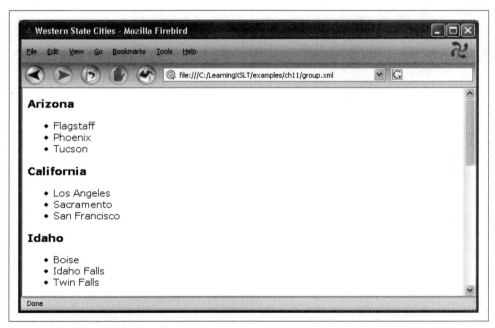

Figure 11-1. group.xml in Mozilla Firefox

Summary

You learned how to declare and invoke keys in this chapter using the key element and key( ) function in tandem. You also learned how to use multiple keys, how to use parameters with those keys, and how to use multiple keys with multiple documents for a cross-reference effect. Finally, you saw how to group with keys using the Muenchian method. Although you have been introduced to the *usage* of keys, these simple examples do not fully demonstrate the *value* of keys—the benefits of performance gains that keys offer when processing large documents with many nodes.

In the following chapter, you'll learn how to process XML documents conditionally with XSLT using the if and choose elements.

CHAPTER 12

Conditional Processing

If you are familiar with programming or scripting languages, you have no doubt seen statements that allow a program to make decisions based on Boolean logic. Such statements execute when a given condition proves to be true or false.

Here's a brief illustration. If you started computing before the mouse and the graphical user interface were around, like me, you might recognize the following statement written in FORTRAN 77:

```
IF(POPULATION .GT. 10000000) THEN
   PRINT *, NAME
END IF
```

In plain English, this statements says: if the value of the variable POPULATION is greater than 10,000,000, print the value associated with the NAME variable.

You could expand this statement to optionally perform a step if the first statement is false:

```
IF(POPULATION .GT. 10000000) THEN
   PRINT *, NAME
ELSE IF(POPULATION .LT. 10000000) THEN
   PRINT *, MSG
   PRINT *, NAME
END IF
```

In this statement, if the POPULATION is not greater than 10,000,000, and is less than 10,000,000, the program will print the value in the MSG variable as well as the value in NAME.

In Java, you can write an if statement like this:

```
if (population > 10000000)
    System.out.println(name)
```

Or, to handle the situation when the first statement is not true, you could write:

```
if (population > 10000000) {
    System.out.println(name);
```

```
    } else if (population < 10000000) {
        System.out.println(msg);
        System.out.println(name);
    }
```

XSLT likewise offers several elements that allow you to perform Boolean logic inside stylesheets using the if and choose instruction elements. An if element works similarly to an if statement in Java, and a choose element, with its children when and otherwise, works like an if-else statement. I'll start out by exploring ways to use the if element. For more information on if and choose, see Section 9 of the XSLT specification.

The if Element

The XML document you'll process in this chapter is Example 12-1, *africa.xml*, found in *examples/ch12*. It's over 300 lines long, so only part of it is shown here.

Example 12-1. An excerpt of a document listing countries in Africa

```xml
<?xml version="1.0" encoding="ISO-8859-1"?>

<africa>
 <source>
  <title>CIA Factbook</title>
  <url>http://www.cia.gov/cia/publications/factbook/</url>
  <populations estimate="true" year="2002"/>
 </source>
 <nation>
  <name>Algeria</name>
  <capital>Algiers</capital>
  <population>32277942</population>
  <cc>dz</cc>
 </nation>
 <nation>
  <name>Angola</name>
  <capital>Luanda</capital>
  <population>10593171</population>
  <cc>ao</cc>
 </nation>
 <nation>
  <name>Benin</name>
  <capital>Porto-Novo</capital>
  <population>6787625</population>
  <cc>bj</cc>
 </nation>
 <nation>
  <name>Bostwana</name>
  <capital>Gaborone</capital>
  <population>1591232</population>
  <cc>bw</cc>
 </nation>
```

```
<nation>
 <name>Burkina Faso</name>
 <capital>Ouagadougou</capital>
 <population>12603185</population>
 <cc>bf</cc>
</nation>
<nation>
```

After some source information about the online CIA World Factbook where you can find this information, each of the 53 nations on the African continent is listed, along with the nation's capital city, population (an estimate as of midyear 2002), and two-letter country code. (You can find the factbook at *http://www.cia.gov/cia/publications/ factbook/.*)

The simple stylesheet *if.xsl*, shown in Example 12-2, uses the if element to process *africa.xml.*

Example 12-2. A stylesheet that checks to see if countries have populations over 10,000,000

```
<xsl:stylesheet version="1.0" xmlns:xsl="http://www.w3.org/1999/XSL/Transform">
<xsl:output method="text"/>

<xsl:template match="africa">
 <xsl:apply-templates select="nation"/>
</xsl:template>

<xsl:template match="nation">
 <xsl:text> * </xsl:text>
 <xsl:value-of select="name"/>
  <xsl:if test="population > 10000000">
   <xsl:text> (over 10M)</xsl:text>
  </xsl:if>
 <xsl:text>&#10;</xsl:text>
</xsl:template>

</xsl:stylesheet>
```

The first template in *if.xsl* matches the document element africa, and then applies templates to any nation element that is a child of africa. The template that matches nation elements writes the name of the nation to the result tree, preceded by a literal asterisk, which acts as a bullet in the plain text output.

Then comes the if element. The if element has one required attribute, test, which must contain an expression that produces a Boolean result (true or false). The content of an if element is a template. If test returns true, the template is instantiated; if false, the template is not instantiated. (You don't actually see the words *true* or *false* returned. Booleans are handled internally by the processor.)

In this instance, the test attribute contains an expression testing whether the population child of nation has content (converted implicitly to a number) that is greater than 10,000,000. If the number is greater than 10,000,000, the template inside the if element is instantiated—that is, the text (over 10M) is written to the result; if it is less than 10,000,000, the template is not instantiated.

Let's see what happens. Process *africa.xml* with this command:

```
xalan africa.xml if.xsl
```

to produce the following results (only the first 10 lines of the output are shown):

```
* Algeria (> 10M)
* Angola (> 10M)
* Benin
* Bostwana
* Burkina Faso (> 10M)
* Burundi
* Cameroon (> 10M)
* Cape Verde
* Central African Republic
* Chad
```

The African nations shown here that have populations greater than 10,000,000—Algeria, Angola, Burkina Faso, and Cameroon—are annotated with (> 10m).

Compare those results with that of *less.xsl*, shown in Example 12-3.

Example 12-3. Testing to see if a population is less than 10,000,000

```
<xsl:stylesheet version="1.0" xmlns:xsl="http://www.w3.org/1999/XSL/Transform">
<xsl:output method="text"/>

<xsl:template match="africa">
 <xsl:apply-templates select="nation"/>
</xsl:template>

<xsl:template match="nation">
 <xsl:text> * </xsl:text>
 <xsl:value-of select="name"/>
  <xsl:if test="population &lt;= 10000000">
   <xsl:text> (&lt;= to 10M)</xsl:text>
  </xsl:if>
 <xsl:text>&#10;</xsl:text>
</xsl:template>

</xsl:stylesheet>
```

Because it is in an attribute value, the less-than symbol (<) is represented by < in the value of the test attribute. (The need for predefined entities was explained in Chapter 2.) When you process *africa.xml* with *less.xsl* using:

```
xalan africa.xml less.xsl
```

you get the opposite effect, that is, results showing those nations whose populations are less than 10,000,000 are annotated (first 10 shown):

```
* Algeria
* Angola
* Benin (<= to 10M)
* Bostwana (<= to 10M)
* Burkina Faso
* Burundi (<= to 10M)
* Cameroon
* Cape Verde (<= to 10M)
* Central African Republic (<= to 10M)
* Chad (<= to 10M)
```

if.xsl and *less.xsl* are simple examples of the if element. You can just as easily perform similar conditional operations using predicates, without the if element. Example 12-4, *withoutif.xsl*, shows you one way you could process on the same conditions without using if.

Example 12-4. Testing using predicates instead of explicit if statements

```
<xsl:stylesheet version="1.0" xmlns:xsl="http://www.w3.org/1999/XSL/Transform">
<xsl:output method="text"/>

<xsl:template match="africa">
 <xsl:apply-templates select="nation"/>
</xsl:template>

<xsl:template match="nation[population &lt;= 10000000]">
 <xsl:text> * </xsl:text>
 <xsl:value-of select="name"/>
 <xsl:text> (&lt;= 10M)</xsl:text>
 <xsl:text>&#10;</xsl:text>
</xsl:template>

<xsl:template match="nation[population > 10000000]">
 <xsl:text> * </xsl:text>
 <xsl:value-of select="name"/>
 <xsl:text> (> 10M)</xsl:text>
 <xsl:text>&#10;</xsl:text>
</xsl:template>

</xsl:stylesheet>
```

In this stylesheet, the conditional testing for population numbers is done by predicates (see the bold lines). Applied to *africa.xml* with:

```
xalan africa.xml withoutif.xsl
```

this stylesheet will give you the following output (first 10 lines):

```
* Algeria (> 10M)
* Angola (> 10M)
* Benin (<= 10M)
* Bostwana (<= 10M)
```

```
* Burkina Faso (> 10M)
* Burundi (<= 10M)
* Cameroon (> 10M)
* Cape Verde (<= 10M)
* Central African Republic (<= 10M)
* Chad (<= 10M)
```

In Example 12-5, I'll show you how to use several if elements together in a useful way. The stylesheet is *comma.xsl*.

Example 12-5. A stylesheet using multiple if statements

```
<xsl:stylesheet version="1.0" xmlns:xsl="http://www.w3.org/1999/XSL/Transform">
<xsl:output method="text"/>

<xsl:template match="africa">
 <xsl:text>The nations of Africa are </xsl:text>
 <xsl:apply-templates select="nation"/>
</xsl:template>

<xsl:template match="nation">
 <xsl:value-of select="name"/>
  <xsl:if test="position() != last()">, </xsl:if>
  <xsl:if test="position() mod 5 = 0">
   <xsl:text>&#10;</xsl:text>
  </xsl:if>
  <xsl:if test="position() = (last() - 1)">and </xsl:if>
  <xsl:if test="position() = last()">.</xsl:if>
</xsl:template>

</xsl:stylesheet>
```

This stylesheet writes out the entire list of African nations, separating nearly all of them by commas and spaces. The first template writes some text at the beginning of the result tree. Then after printing the name of each African nation with value-of, *comma.xsl* considers the position of nation nodes with four instances of the if element. Each instance of if uses the position( ) function to test the condition of the current nation node:

- The first one tests to see whether the context node is the last of the nation nodes; if it is not the last, the template in if writes a comma to the result tree.

- The second uses the modulo operator mod to test whether the remainder of its operation is zero. If the remainder is zero, it means that five nation nodes have been written to the result tree and so, upon finding that condition, the processor adds a linefeed to the result tree.

- The third writes the word and to the result tree if the node is the next-to-last nation node.

- The fourth writes a period (.) if the node is the last nation node in the list.

To see the outcome, type the following on a command line:

```
xalan africa.xml comma.xsl
```

Here is the result. Note the placement of commas, line breaks, the word *and*, and the period (.):

```
The nations of Africa are Algeria, Angola, Benin, Bostwana, Burkina Faso,
Burundi, Cameroon, Cape Verde, Central African Republic, Chad,
Comoros, Congo, Congo, Democratic Republic of, Cote d'Ivoire, Djibouti,
Eqypt, Equatorial Guinea, Eritrea, Ethiopia, Gabon,
Gambia, Ghana, Guinea, Guinea-Bissau, Kenya,
Lesotho, Liberia, Libya, Madagascar, Malawi,
Mali, Mauritania, Maurutius, Morocco, Mozambique,
Namibia, Niger, Nigeria, Rwanda, Sao Tome and Principe,
Senegal, Seychelles, Sierra Leone, Somalia, South Africa,
Sudan, Swaziland, Tanzania, Togo, Tunisia,
Uganda, Zambia, and Zimbabwe.
```

This concludes your brief tour of the if instruction. You're ready to move on to using the choose element, which processes multiple conditions at one time, and to dealing with exceptions to those conditions.

The choose and when Elements

The difference between if and choose is that choose allows you to test one or more conditions in a single structure while if allows you to test only one condition at a time. A choose element has no attributes, but it must have one or more when children. Similar to if, the when element has a single required test attribute that returns a Boolean.

The combination of choose with a single when child works the same way that a lone if element works. Example 12-6 demonstrates this, in the stylesheet *choose.xsl*.

Example 12-6. Using choose rather than if

```
<xsl:stylesheet version="1.0" xmlns:xsl="http://www.w3.org/1999/XSL/Transform">
<xsl:output method="text"/>

<xsl:template match="africa">
 <xsl:apply-templates select="nation"/>
</xsl:template>

<xsl:template match="nation">
 <xsl:choose>
  <xsl:when test="population > 10000000">
   <xsl:value-of select="name"/>
   <xsl:text>&#10;</xsl:text>
  </xsl:when>
 </xsl:choose>
</xsl:template>

</xsl:stylesheet>
```

Apply this to *africa.xml*:

```
xalan africa.xml choose.xsl
```

and you will get a plain list of African nations with populations exceeding 10,000,000:

```
Algeria
Angola
Burkina Faso
Cameroon
Congo, Democratic Republic of
Cote d'Ivoire
Eqypt
Ethiopia
Ghana
Kenya
Madagascar
Malawi
Mali
Morocco
Mozambique
Niger
Nigeria
Senegal
South Africa
Sudan
Tanzania
Uganda
Zimbabwe
```

The stylesheet *when.xsl* adds another when element to the template in *choose.xsl* so that the stylesheet can test another condition: which nations have less than 10,000,000 inhabitants. Example 12-7 shows this stylesheet.

Example 12-7. Using two when elements

```
<xsl:stylesheet version="1.0" xmlns:xsl="http://www.w3.org/1999/XSL/Transform">
<xsl:output method="text"/>

<xsl:template match="africa">
 <xsl:apply-templates select="nation"/>
</xsl:template>

<xsl:template match="nation">
 <xsl:choose>
  <xsl:when test="population > 10000000">
   <xsl:text>&#10;</xsl:text>
   <xsl:value-of select="name"/>
   <xsl:text> </xsl:text>
  </xsl:when>
  <xsl:when test="population &lt;= 10000000">
   <xsl:text>[Skip] </xsl:text>
  </xsl:when>
```

Example 12-7. Using two when elements (continued)

```
  </xsl:choose>
</xsl:template>

</xsl:stylesheet>
```

When this stylesheet encounters population nodes whose content is greater than 10,000,000, the name of the nation is written to the result tree; when it encounters population nodes whose content is less than or equal to 10,000,000, only a bit of text is written ([Skip]).

Test this stylesheet with *africa.xml* using:

```
xalan africa.xml when.xsl
```

to get the following output:

```
Algeria
Angola [Skip] [Skip]
Burkina Faso [Skip]
Cameroon [Skip] [Skip] [Skip] [Skip] [Skip]
Congo, Democratic Republic of
Cote d'Ivoire [Skip]
Eqypt [Skip] [Skip]
Ethiopia [Skip] [Skip]
Ghana [Skip] [Skip]
Kenya [Skip] [Skip] [Skip]
Madagascar
Malawi
Mali [Skip] [Skip]
Morocco
Mozambique [Skip]
Niger
Nigeria [Skip] [Skip]
Senegal [Skip] [Skip] [Skip]
South Africa
Sudan [Skip]
Tanzania [Skip] [Skip]
Uganda [Skip]
Zimbabwe
```

The test attribute in the when elements checks whether certain nodes match certain criteria; if they do, the template in the when element is instantiated. The occurrences of [Skip] help you to see where nodes were skipped.

The otherwise Element

When programming, it's possible that none of the conditions you test are true, so the language has to handle that case. In FORTRAN 77, for example, a final ELSE statement provides an escape hatch when nothing else works:

```
IF(POPULATION .GT. 10000000) THEN
   PRINT *, NAME
ELSE IF(POPULATION .LT. 10000000) THEN
```

```
      PRINT *, MSG
      PRINT *, NAME
   ELSE
      GO TO 100
   END IF
100 STOP
   END
```

In this statement, if neither of the conditions are met (are true), execution jumps to the line labeled 100 in the program where execution stops, and the program ends.

In Java, you could write a similar statement as follows:

```
if (population > 10000000) {
    System.out.println(name);
} else if (population < 10000000) {
    System.out.println(msg);
    System.out.println(name);
} else {
    System.exit(1);
}
```

If both Booleans fail, the last statement executes and exits out of the program. The otherwise element in XSLT takes on the role of the escape hatch, just as the ELSE or else statements take on the role in FORTRAN or Java. The *otherwise.xsl* stylesheet, shown in Example 12-8, demonstrates how this is done.

Example 12-8. Using otherwise to terminate stylesheet execution

```
<xsl:stylesheet version="1.0" xmlns:xsl="http://www.w3.org/1999/XSL/Transform">
<xsl:output method="text"/>

<xsl:template match="africa">
 <xsl:apply-templates select="nation"/>
</xsl:template>

<xsl:template match="nation">
 <xsl:choose>
  <xsl:when test="population = 10000000">
   <xsl:value-of select="name"/>
   <xsl:text> = 10M</xsl:text>
   <xsl:text>&#10;</xsl:text>
  </xsl:when>
  <xsl:when test="population = 1000000">
   <xsl:value-of select="name"/>
   <xsl:text> = 1M</xsl:text>
   <xsl:text>&#10;</xsl:text>
  </xsl:when>
  <xsl:otherwise>
   <xsl:message terminate="yes">Not found!</xsl:message>
  </xsl:otherwise>
 </xsl:choose>
</xsl:template>

</xsl:stylesheet>
```

The test attributes on when elements check whether a population element has content that equals 10,000,000 or 1,000,000. None of the population elements in *africa.xml* will satisfy these tests, so the control in the choose structure drops down to the otherwise element.

At that point, the processor encounters a message element. A message element outputs a message to the screen (standard output), not to the result tree, and so it is a good way to create status or error messages. (The destination of such messages is left undefined in the XSLT spec, but generally XSLT processors send them to the screen.)

 Commonly, stylesheet developers use message elements inside fallback elements. Chapter 15 discusses how to use message and fallback elements together.

Processing More Than One Kind of Document

Imagine that you want to efficiently process several kinds of XML documents, each containing similar content, but each using a different vocabulary. The document *africa2.xml* is structured just like *africa.xml*, but uses verbose element names. Example 12-9 shows part of *africa2.xml*.

Example 12-9. A version of the African countries document using verbose markup

```
<?xml version="1.0" encoding="ISO-8859-1"?>

<continent.africa>
 <continent.africa.country>
  <continent.africa.country.name>Algeria</continent.africa.country.name>
  <continent.africa.country.capital>Algiers</continent.africa.country.capital>
  <continent.africa.country.population>32277942</continent.africa.country.population>
  <continent.africa.country.code>dz</continent.africa.country.code>
 </continent.africa.country>
 <continent.africa.country>
  <continent.africa.country.name>Angola</continent.africa.country.name>
  <continent.africa.country.capital>Luanda</continent.africa.country.capital>
  <continent.africa.country.population>10593171</continent.africa.country.population>
  <continent.africa.country.code>ao</continent.africa.country.code>
 </continent.africa.country>
 <continent.africa.country>
  <continent.africa.country.name>Benin</continent.africa.country.name>
  <continent.africa.country.capital>Porto-Novo</continent.africa.country.capital>
  <continent.africa.country.population>6787625</continent.africa.country.population>
  <continent.africa.country.code>bj</continent.africa.country.code>
 </continent.africa.country>
 <continent.africa.country>
  <continent.africa.country.name>Bostwana</continent.africa.country.name>
  <continent.africa.country.capital>Gaborone</continent.africa.country.capital>
  <continent.africa.country.population>1591232</continent.africa.country.population>
  <continent.africa.country.code>bw</continent.africa.country.code>
```

```
 </continent.africa.country>
 <continent.africa.country>
  <continent.africa.country.name>Burkina Faso</continent.africa.country.name>
  <continent.africa.country.capital>Ouagadougou</continent.africa.country.capital>
  <continent.africa.country.population>12603185</continent.africa.country.population>
  <continent.africa.country.code>bf</continent.africa.country.code>
 </continent.africa.country>
```

The document has a structure that is similar to *africa.xml* but uses long, structured element names. Using choose, when, and otherwise elements, Example 12-10, the stylesheet *dual.xsl*, can process similar elements in both *africa.xml* and *africa2.xml*, plus handle nonconforming documents that it encounters.

Example 12-10. A stylesheet that tests for multiple element names explicitly

```
<xsl:stylesheet version="1.0" xmlns:xsl="http://www.w3.org/1999/XSL/Transform">
<xsl:output method="text" encoding="ISO-8859-1"/>

<xsl:template match="africa | continent.africa">
 <xsl:apply-templates select="nation[10] | continent.africa.country[10]"/>
</xsl:template>

<xsl:template match="nation | continent.africa.country">
 <xsl:choose>
  <xsl:when test="name = 'Chad'">
   <xsl:apply-templates select="name"/>
  </xsl:when>
  <xsl:when test="continent.africa.country.name = 'Chad'">
   <xsl:apply-templates select="continent.africa.country.name"/>
  </xsl:when>
  <xsl:otherwise>
   <xsl:message terminate="yes">Not found!</xsl:message>
  </xsl:otherwise>
 </xsl:choose>
</xsl:template>

<xsl:template match="name | continent.africa.country.name">
 <xsl:value-of select="name( )"/>
 <xsl:text>: </xsl:text>
 <xsl:value-of select="."/>
 <xsl:text>&#10;</xsl:text>
</xsl:template>

</xsl:stylesheet>
```

The templates in *dual.xsl* can match parallel elements in either *africa.xml* or *africa2. xml*. The first template, for example, matches either an africa or a continent.africa element, the document elements of *africa.xml* and *africa2.xml*, respectively. The second template, which matches nation or continent.africa.country elements, uses choose and when to find the tenth matching child name or continent.africa.country. name node. If it finds one or the other of those nodes, it processes them with a third template, which inserts the node name and content into the result tree. If neither node is found, the stylesheet handles the problem with a message element inside an otherwise element. The message element also terminates processing.

I'll process this example with xsltproc. (You saw this processor once before in Chapter 10.) When I enter the following command line:

```
xsltproc dual.xsl africa.xml africa2.xml truncated.xml
```

it gives this result:

```
name: Chad
continent.africa.country.name: Chad
Not found!
```

Because it accepts a stylesheet first, then the XML documents after that, you can process more than one XML document at a time with xsltproc. You can see from the output that each document yields a different result. The document *truncated.xml* has only 10 nation elements, but none with a name child that matches Chad, so it generates the Not found! message.

This stylesheet should help you write other stylesheets that process more than one kind of document but produce similar results. This is just one way to get that job done. For illustration, Example 12-11 is a stylesheet that produces the same results, but it is written more tightly. It's called *dual2.xsl*.

Example 12-11. Refining Example 12-10

```
<xsl:stylesheet version="1.0" xmlns:xsl="http://www.w3.org/1999/XSL/Transform">
<xsl:output method="text" encoding="ISO-8859-1"/>

<xsl:template match="africa | continent.africa">
 <xsl:apply-templates select="nation[10] | continent.africa.country[10]"/>
</xsl:template>

<xsl:template match="nation | continent.africa.country">
 <xsl:choose>
  <xsl:when test="(name|continent.africa.country.name) = 'Chad'">
   <xsl:apply-templates select="name|continent.africa.country.name"/>
  </xsl:when>
  <xsl:otherwise>
   <xsl:message terminate="yes">Not found!</xsl:message>
  </xsl:otherwise>
 </xsl:choose>
</xsl:template>

<xsl:template match="name | continent.africa.country.name">
 <xsl:value-of select="name()"/>
 <xsl:text>: </xsl:text>
 <xsl:value-of select="."/>
 <xsl:text>&#10;</xsl:text>
</xsl:template>

</xsl:stylesheet>
```

The difference between *dual.xsl* and *dual2.xsl* is that *dual.xsl* has two when elements, whereas *dual2.xsl* has only one. The test attribute of the single when element in *dual2.xsl* returns true for either name or (|) continent.africa.country.name elements, depending on the source tree. So one when element, when used with |, does the job of two. Try it with this command:

```
xsltproc dual2.xsl africa.xml africa2.xml truncated.xml
```

and you will get the same result as you did with *dual.xsl*.

Summary

This chapter showed you how to use if, choose, when, and otherwise elements (as well as predicates) for conditional processing. It also introduced the message element, which will be discussed further in Chapter 15. In the next chapter, you'll learn how to work with multiple stylesheets and source trees.

CHAPTER 13

Working with Multiple Documents

This chapter explains how to use the include, import, and apply-imports elements, which work with stylesheets, and how to use the document( ) function, which works with source documents. These elements provide features that help you work with multiple stylesheets and source documents as modules so that they can be integrated or reused.

With the include element, you can integrate one or more external stylesheets within another stylesheet, as if they were all just one stylesheet. If you import external stylesheets into a stylesheet with the import element, certain rules go into effect, namely that templates are invoked based on the order in which they appear. This feature is called *import precedence*. You can override these precedence rules, however, by using the apply-imports element.

You can read about include and import in Sections 2.6.1 and 2.6.2 of XSLT specification; apply-imports is discussed in Section 5.6 of that specification.

You can also work with more than one source document by using the document( ) function. This means that you can transform nodes from more than one source document at a time. Earlier examples in this book have used document( ), but this chapter covers it in greater detail. The document( ) function is fully documented in Section 12.1 of the XSLT spec.

Including Stylesheets

XSLT allows you to use and manage stylesheets in a modular way with the include element. This means that you aren't limited to storing all your template rules in a single stylesheet, but that you can spread them around in as many stylesheets as you want. Included stylesheets must be complete stylesheets, however, not just template rules. You can also include third-party stylesheets, such as those from EXSLT (*http:// www.exslt.org*), which provide extended functionality to XSLT, such as dates, times, math, regular expressions, and much more. (You'll learn more about EXSLT in Chapter 15.)

The XML document in Example 13-1, *top.xml* (in *examples/ch13*), lists the three states in the U.S. whose populations were estimated to have grown the most between July 1, 2001 and July 2, 2002, according to the U.S. Census Bureau (see *http://eire. census.gov/popest/data/states/tables/ST-EST2002-02.php*).

Example 13-1. Fast-growing states in the U.S.

```
<?xml version="1.0"?>

<PopulationChange segment="Top 3">
 <State>
  <Name>California</Name>
  <Population>35116033</Population>
  <Rank>1</Rank>
  <Increase>515570</Increase>
  <PercentChange>1.5</PercentChange>
 </State>
 <State>
  <Name>Texas</Name>
  <Population>21779893</Population>
  <Rank>2</Rank>
  <Increase>408910</Increase>
  <PercentChange>1.9</PercentChange>
 </State>
 <State>
  <Name>New York</Name>
  <Population>19157532</Population>
  <Rank>3</Rank>
  <Increase>73182</Increase>
  <PercentChange>0.4</PercentChange>
 </State>
</PopulationChange>
```

The *include.xsl* stylesheet, shown in Example 13-2, processes *top.xml* with its own templates and with some whitespace-generating templates added by means of an include element (note the bold lines).

Example 13-2. A stylesheet that includes another stylesheet

```
<xsl:stylesheet version="1.0" xmlns:xsl="http://www.w3.org/1999/XSL/Transform">
<xsl:output method="text"/>
<xsl:include href="wspace.xsl"/>
<xsl:template match="PopulationChange">
 <xsl:text>Population Change: July 1, 2001 to July 1, 2002</xsl:text>
 <xsl:call-template name="n1"/>
 <xsl:text>Source: US Census Bureau</xsl:text>
 <xsl:call-template name="n2"/>
 <xsl:apply-templates select="State"/>
</xsl:template>

<xsl:template match="State">
 <xsl:text>State:</xsl:text>
 <xsl:call-template name="sp1"/>
```

Example 13-2. A stylesheet that includes another stylesheet (continued)

```
<xsl:value-of select="Name"/>
<xsl:call-template name="n1"/>
<xsl:text>Rank:</xsl:text>
<xsl:call-template name="sp1"/>
<xsl:value-of select="Rank"/>
<xsl:call-template name="n2"/>
</xsl:template>

</xsl:stylesheet>
```

The include element is a top-level element with only one required attribute, href, which references a stylesheet that you want to include—*wspace.xsl*, in this case. The value of href is a URI, which can be an absolute reference (as in *http://www.example. com/wspace.xsl* or *file:///C:/learningxslt/examples/ch13/wspace.xsl*) or a relative reference (as in *wspace.xsl*).

The reference to *wspace.xsl* in the value of href is a relative reference. This means that the XSLT processor will depend on the location of the including stylesheet *include.xsl* to determine the relative location of *wspace.xsl*. In other words, the processor establishes a *base URI* in relation to the location of the main stylesheet, and then uses that base URI (the main document's location in a filesystem or on the Web) to resolve any relative references that may be used.

All the templates that are called in *include.xsl* (those named sp1, n1, and n2) are stored in *wspace.xsl*, which is shown in Example 13-3.

Example 13-3. A stylesheet containing whitespace templates for use elsewhere

```
<xsl:stylesheet version="1.0" xmlns:xsl="http://www.w3.org/1999/XSL/Transform">

<xsl:template name="sp1">
 <xsl:text>&#32;</xsl:text>
</xsl:template>

<xsl:template name="sp2">
 <xsl:text>&#32;</xsl:text>
 <xsl:text>&#32;</xsl:text>
</xsl:template>

<xsl:template name="sp3">
 <xsl:text>&#32;</xsl:text>
 <xsl:text>&#32;</xsl:text>
 <xsl:text>&#32;</xsl:text>
</xsl:template>

<xsl:template name="n1">
 <xsl:text>&#10;</xsl:text>
</xsl:template>

<xsl:template name="n2">
```

```
  <xsl:text>&#10;</xsl:text>
  <xsl:text>&#10;</xsl:text>
</xsl:template>

<xsl:template name="n3">
  <xsl:text>&#10;</xsl:text>
  <xsl:text>&#10;</xsl:text>
  <xsl:text>&#10;</xsl:text>
</xsl:template>

</xsl:stylesheet>
```

This stylesheet contains only named templates that emit various amounts of whitespace. None of the templates, however, are invoked by matching patterns within *wspace.xsl*, so it does nothing on its own—it needs some help. Admittedly, *wspace.xsl* is trivial, but it is also useful and amenable to reuse in a variety of other stylesheets.

Apply *include.xsl* to *top.xml*:

```
xalan top.xml include.xsl
```

and you will get this output:

```
Population Change: July 1, 2001 to July 1, 2002
Source: US Census Bureau

State: California
Rank: 1

State: Texas
Rank: 2

State: New York
Rank: 3
```

You can have multiple `include` elements in a stylesheet, but it's an error for a stylesheet to include itself. (If you'd like, try this yourself and see what happens!) You can include a stylesheet multiple times with no effect other than having duplicate top-level elements.

Conflicts between such duplicates are resolved using the same conflict resolution rules that exist for any single stylesheet where, for example, the last conflicting template match wins (this is an error, but processors are allowed to recover from this error, with or without issuing a warning message). Having more than one template with the same name in its `name` attribute, however, is an error from which a processor cannot recover.

You can also chain stylesheets together. I'll show you how by chaining these three stylesheets together: *chain.xsl* (Example 13-4), *state.xsl* (Example 13-5), and *wspace.xsl* (Example 13-3).

This use of the term *chain* here refers to including a series of stylesheets together. Another more common sense of the term *chaining* has to do with processing multiple stylesheets in succession, as in a pipeline. Only the former sense is implied in this context.

Here's the first of the bunch, *chain.xsl*.

Example 13-4. A stylesheet containing an include statement, the start of the chain

```
<xsl:stylesheet version="1.0" xmlns:xsl="http://www.w3.org/1999/XSL/Transform">
<xsl:output method="text"/>
<xsl:include href="state.xsl"/>

<xsl:template match="PopulationChange">
 <xsl:text>Population Change: July 1, 2001 to July 1, 2002</xsl:text>
 <xsl:call-template name="n1"/>
 <xsl:text>Source: US Census Bureau</xsl:text>
 <xsl:call-template name="n2"/>
 <xsl:apply-templates select="State"/>
</xsl:template>

</xsl:stylesheet>
```

It's similar to *include.xsl*, but it doesn't have a template to match State elements. It needs such a template in order to work. That template is in *state.xsl*, which *chain.xsl* includes, shown in Example 13-5.

Example 13-5. The stylesheet meant for inclusion to process the state information

```
<xsl:stylesheet version="1.0" xmlns:xsl="http://www.w3.org/1999/XSL/Transform">
<xsl:include href="wspace.xsl"/>
<xsl:template match="State">
 <xsl:text>State:</xsl:text>
 <xsl:call-template name="sp1"/>
 <xsl:value-of select="Name"/>
 <xsl:call-template name="n1"/>
 <xsl:text>Rank:</xsl:text>
 <xsl:call-template name="sp1"/>
 <xsl:value-of select="Rank"/>
 <xsl:call-template name="n2"/>
</xsl:template>

</xsl:stylesheet>
```

The stylesheet *state.xsl* also includes *wspace.xsl*. This describes what I mean by chaining: *chain.xsl* includes *state.xsl*, which includes *wspace.xsl*. This makes all the templates available as if they were in one stylesheet instead of three.

As described in the XSLT specification, what happens when you include a stylesheet is that everything in the included stylesheet is taken into the XSLT processor's stylesheet representation (whatever it may use to create such a representation—a hash table or whatever), except the stylesheet element. The processor doesn't make a fuss about where a template or some other top-level element came from.

For all intents and purposes, while still honoring template priority (see Chapter 10), all included stylesheets are lumped together into the same pot with the stylesheet that includes them. Therefore, if you process *top.xml* with *chain.xsl*, you will get the same result as when you processed *top.xml* with *include.xsl*. Importing a stylesheet instead of including it has a different effect, as you will see in the next section.

Importing Stylesheets

Like include, the import element is also a top-level element with one required attribute, href. Importing is similar to inclusion except that template rules from imported stylesheets have a lower precedence than template rules in the stylesheet that is doing the importing. Imported stylesheets allow you, when required, to override one template rule with another.

You can see import at work in the stylesheet *import.xsl* (Example 13-6), where *imported.xsl* is imported.

Example 13-6. A stylesheet using an import element

```
<xsl:stylesheet version="1.0" xmlns:xsl="http://www.w3.org/1999/XSL/Transform">
<xsl:import href="imported.xsl"/>
<xsl:output method="text"/>

<xsl:template match="PopulationChange">
 <xsl:text>Population Change: July 1, 2001 to July 1, 2002</xsl:text>
 <xsl:call-template name="n1"/>
 <xsl:text>Source: US Census Bureau</xsl:text>
 <xsl:call-template name="n2"/>
 <xsl:apply-templates select="State"/>
</xsl:template>

<xsl:template match="State">
 <xsl:text>Rank:</xsl:text>
 <xsl:call-template name="sp1"/>
 <xsl:value-of select="Rank"/>
 <xsl:call-template name="n1"/>
 <xsl:text>State:</xsl:text>
 <xsl:call-template name="sp1"/>
 <xsl:value-of select="Name"/>
 <xsl:call-template name="n2"/>
</xsl:template>

</xsl:stylesheet>
```

Notice that the import element is the first child of stylesheet. This is a special requirement—that is, one or more import elements must *immediately* follow the stylesheet element.

The stylesheet, *imported.xsl,* is shown in Example 13-7.

Example 13-7. The imported stylesheet, which itself imports another stylesheet

```
<xsl:stylesheet version="1.0" xmlns:xsl="http://www.w3.org/1999/XSL/Transform">
<xsl:import href="wspace.xsl"/>
<xsl:template match="State">
 <xsl:text>State:</xsl:text>
 <xsl:call-template name="sp1"/>
 <xsl:value-of select="Name"/>
 <xsl:call-template name="n1"/>
 <xsl:text>Rank:</xsl:text>
 <xsl:call-template name="sp1"/>
 <xsl:value-of select="Rank"/>
 <xsl:call-template name="n2"/>
</xsl:template>

</xsl:stylesheet>
```

In turn, this stylesheet imports *wspace.xsl,* which you saw earlier in Example 13-3. When applied to *top.xml*:

```
xalan top.xml import.xsl
```

you get the following result:

```
Population Change: July 1, 2001 to July 1, 2002
Source: US Census Bureau

Rank: 1
State: California

Rank: 2
State: Texas

Rank: 3
State: New York
```

The outcome is identical to what you would expect from stylesheets included with include elements. The main difference, however, between include and import is that import establishes something called *import precedence.* Import precedence simply means that template rules in an importing stylesheet have precedence over any rules from a stylesheet that it imports, and that the order in which stylesheets are imported affects their import precedence in succession.

Import Tree

When you include a stylesheet using include, the top-level elements—all but stylesheet elements—are merged in with the top-level elements of the stylesheet that included it. When you import a stylesheet with import, that stylesheet is represented internally in something called an *import tree.* An import tree stores stylesheets in the order in which they were imported and includes the stylesheet element from each. If you import more than one stylesheet, each imported stylesheet is added to the import tree.

Just as a stylesheet can't include itself, a stylesheet can't import itself, either. You can import a stylesheet more than once, however, in which case any conflicts are worked out using the normal rules of template priority—the last of two or more conflicting templates wins.

The following stylesheets, Examples 13-8 through 13-10, will show you import precedence in action. The *precedence.xsl* stylesheet (Example 13-8) imports two stylesheets, *first.xsl* (Example 13-9) and *second.xsl* (Example 13-10).

Example 13-8. A stylesheet importing two other stylesheets

```
<xsl:stylesheet version="1.0" xmlns:xsl="http://www.w3.org/1999/XSL/Transform">
<xsl:import href="second.xsl"/>
<xsl:import href="first.xsl"/>
<xsl:output method="text"/>

<xsl:template match="PopulationChange">
 <xsl:text>Population Change: July 1, 2001 to July 1, 2002</xsl:text>
 <xsl:call-template name="n1"/>
 <xsl:text>Source: US Census Bureau</xsl:text>
 <xsl:call-template name="n2"/>
 <xsl:apply-templates select="State"/>
</xsl:template>

</xsl:stylesheet>
```

This stylesheet also attempts to apply a template that matches the State element; however, no such template exists in *precedence.xsl*. One such template, however, does exist in the imported stylesheet *first.xsl*.

Example 13-9. A stylesheet containing a template for processing the State element

```
<xsl:stylesheet version="1.0" xmlns:xsl="http://www.w3.org/1999/XSL/Transform">
<xsl:import href="wspace.xsl"/>

<xsl:template match="State">
 <xsl:text>Rank:</xsl:text>
 <xsl:call-template name="sp1"/>
 <xsl:value-of select="Rank"/>
 <xsl:call-template name="n1"/>
 <xsl:text>State:</xsl:text>
 <xsl:call-template name="sp1"/>
 <xsl:value-of select="Name"/>
 <xsl:call-template name="n2"/>
</xsl:template>

</xsl:stylesheet>
```

Another template exists in *second.xsl*, also imported into *precedence.xsl* (the differences between *first.xsl* and *second.xsl* are emphasized in bold).

Example 13-10. Another stylesheet containing a template for processing the State element

```
<xsl:stylesheet version="1.0" xmlns:xsl="http://www.w3.org/1999/XSL/Transform">
<xsl:import href="wspace.xsl"/>

<xsl:template match="State">
 <xsl:text>State:</xsl:text>
 <xsl:call-template name="sp1"/>
 <xsl:value-of select="Name"/>
 <xsl:call-template name="n1"/>
 <xsl:text>Rank:</xsl:text>
 <xsl:call-template name="sp1"/>
 <xsl:value-of select="Rank"/>
 <xsl:call-template name="n2"/>
</xsl:template>

</xsl:stylesheet>
```

In *first.xsl*, rank is displayed first, followed by the state; in *second.xsl*, the state is displayed first, followed by rank. Because *first.xsl* is the last stylesheet that is imported, its template, which matches State, is invoked first, rather than the template in *second.xsl*. The rank comes before state in the output. When applied to *top.xml* with:

```
xalan top.xml precedence.xsl
```

the processor yields the following output:

```
Population Change: July 1, 2001 to July 1, 2002
Source: US Census Bureau

Rank: 1
State: California

Rank: 2
State: Texas

Rank: 3
State: New York
```

If you were to change the order in which the stylesheets were imported, that is, to this order:

```
<xsl:import href="first.xsl"/>
<xsl:import href="second.xsl"/>
```

The import precedence would favor *second.xsl* and a transformation against that stylesheet would give you the states first, then the ranks:

```
Population Change: July 1, 2001 to July 1, 2002
Source: US Census Bureau

State: California
Rank: 1
```

```
State: Texas
Rank: 2

State: New York
Rank: 3
```

Now, I'll show you how to manipulate import precedence with `apply-imports`.

Applying Imports

The `apply-imports` instruction element has no attributes and is always empty, that is, it has no children. (In XSLT 2.0, however, `apply-imports` can have one or more `with-param` children.) It applies templates from imported stylesheets that normally would not be used (it's somewhat like calling a method with super in Java). Example 13-11, the stylesheet *apply-imports.xsl*—which produces XML output—imports *add.xsl* and uses the apply-imports element.

Example 13-11. A stylesheet using apply-imports

```
<xsl:stylesheet version="1.0" xmlns:xsl="http://www.w3.org/1999/XSL/Transform">
<xsl:import href="add.xsl"/>
<xsl:output method="xml" indent="yes"/>

<xsl:template match="PopulationChange">
 <xsl:element name="topStates">
  <xsl:apply-templates select="State"/>
 </xsl:element>
</xsl:template>

<xsl:template match="State">
 <xsl:element name="stateData">
  <xsl:element name="stateRank">
   <xsl:value-of select="Rank"/>
  </xsl:element>
  <xsl:element name="stateName">
   <xsl:value-of select="Name"/>
  </xsl:element>
  <xsl:apply-imports/>
 </xsl:element>
</xsl:template>

</xsl:stylesheet>
```

The *add.xsl* stylesheet, Example 13-12, also has a template that matches State elements.

Example 13-12. A stylesheet that will be applied through apply-imports

```
<xsl:stylesheet version="1.0" xmlns:xsl="http://www.w3.org/1999/XSL/Transform">

<xsl:template match="State">
 <xsl:element name="dataAdvice">
  <xsl:text>July 2002 estimated population was </xsl:text>
```

```
  <xsl:value-of select="Population"/>
  <xsl:text>.</xsl:text>
 </xsl:element>
</xsl:template>

</xsl:stylesheet>
```

Usually the template in *add.xsl* would be disregarded because the template matching State in *apply-imports.xsl* has precedence over the one in *add.xsl*. The inclusion of apply-imports, however, tells the XSLT processor to invoke the template matching State in *add.xsl*, in addition to the one in *apply-imports.xsl*. Processing *top.xml* with *apply-imports.xsl* with this command:

```
    xalan -i 1 top.xml apply-imports.xsl
```

produces the following output:

```
    <?xml version="1.0" encoding="UTF-8"?>
    <topStates>
     <stateData>
      <stateRank>1</stateRank>
      <stateName>California</stateName>
      <dataAdvice>July 2002 estimated population was 35116033.</dataAdvice>
     </stateData>
     <stateData>
      <stateRank>2</stateRank>
      <stateName>Texas</stateName>
      <dataAdvice>July 2002 estimated population was 21779893.</dataAdvice>
     </stateData>
     <stateData>
      <stateRank>3</stateRank>
      <stateName>New York</stateName>
      <dataAdvice>July 2002 estimated population was 19157532.</dataAdvice>
     </stateData>
    </topStates>
```

So apply-imports provides a way to apply more than one template to the same node, perhaps one for a general purpose and another for a special purpose. Now, we'll leave processing multiple stylesheets behind and move on to processing multiple XML documents with the document( ) function.

Using the document( ) Function

You have already been introduced to how the document( ) function works in examples from Chapters 5 and 9. This section will reintroduce some of the concepts discussed earlier, plus a few more. The following examples will focus on the text of the Book of Jonah, excerpted from the King James version of the Bible.

I'll start this discussion by showing you a stub of a document, *bible.xml*:

```
<?xml version="1.0" encoding="UTF-8"?>

<volume>
 <book/>
</volume>
```

There is not much to it. You can get *bible.xml* to do something interesting with Example 13-13, the stylesheet *jonah.xsl*.

Example 13-13. A stylesheet that copies in a separate document

```
<xsl:stylesheet version="1.0" xmlns:xsl="http://www.w3.org/1999/XSL/Transform">
<xsl:output method="xml" indent="yes"/>

<xsl:template match="volume">
 <xsl:copy>
  <xsl:attribute name="name">Old Testament</xsl:attribute>
  <xsl:apply-templates select="book"/>
 </xsl:copy>
</xsl:template>

<xsl:template match="book">
 <xsl:copy>
  <xsl:attribute name="name">Jonah</xsl:attribute>
  <xsl:copy-of select="document('jonah1.xml')"/>
 </xsl:copy>
</xsl:template>

</xsl:stylesheet>
```

Applying this stylesheet to *bible.xml* will produce the first chapter of Jonah in XML markup. It makes shallow copies of the volume and book nodes in *bible.xml*, adding name attributes to each. Then, using copy-of, it makes a deep copy of all the nodes in the document *jonah1.xml*, which contains the text of the first chapter of the Book of Jonah from the Old Testament, surrounded by XML elements. copy-of finds the nodes in *jonah1.xml* with the document( ) function.

The document( ) function must have at least one argument, but it can have two. The first argument must be an object, the second must be a node-set. The second argument of document( ) is rarely used. The first argument is usually a literal string that is the URI of the source document you are including, either as a relative filename or as a URI, or it is a node in the source document that contains a link to the required document.

In *jonah.xsl*, document( ) uses only one argument, the string jonah1.xml. The XSLT processor knows where to find the document *jonah1.xml* because it uses the location of the stylesheet as a base URI (the argument is a string). In other words, because it knows internally where the stylesheet is located on the filesystem, it looks for *jonah1.xml* relative to the location of the stylesheet, that is, in the same directory as the stylesheet. You could also use an absolute URI path for the file, as in document('file:///C:/learningxslt/examples/ch13/jonah1.xml').

Here are a few lines of *jonah1.xml*:

```
<chapter number="1">
<verse number="1">Now the word of the LORD came unto Jonah the son of Amittai,
saying,</verse>
<verse number="2">Arise, go to Nineveh, that great city, and cry against it; for
their wickedness is come up before me.</verse>
```

Apply *jonah.xsl* to *bible.xml* using this command:

```
xalan bible.xml jonah.xsl
```

You will get output that looks similar to the following (this is a clipped version of the output):

```
<?xml version="1.0" encoding="UTF-8"?>
<volume name="Old Testament">
<book name="Jonah">
<chapter number="1">
<verse number="1">Now the word of the LORD came unto Jonah the son of Amittai,
saying,</verse>
<verse number="2">Arise, go to Nineveh, that great city, and cry against it; for
their wickedness is come up before me.</verse>
```

The chapter and verse nodes are all pulled into the result tree using document( ).

Now look at the document *jonahMap.xml*:

```
<?xml version="1.0" encoding="UTF-8"?>

<volume name="Old Testament">
 <book name="Jonah">
  <chapter location="jonah1.xml"/>
  <chapter location="jonah2.xml"/>
  <chapter location="jonah3.xml"/>
  <chapter location="jonah4.xml"/>
 </book>
</volume>
```

The location attributes in *jonahMap.xml* contain the relative path names to the four files containing the four chapters of the Book of Jonah, respectively. The document( ) function can use the location attributes in the current context to find these files, as shown in Example 13-14, *jonahMap.xsl*.

Example 13-14. Applying the document() function to data from a source document

```
<xsl:stylesheet version="1.0" xmlns:xsl="http://www.w3.org/1999/XSL/Transform">
<xsl:output method="xml" indent="yes"/>

<xsl:template match="volume">
 <xsl:copy>
  <xsl:attribute name="name"><xsl:value-of select="@name"/></xsl:attribute>
```

```
  <xsl:apply-templates select="book"/>
 </xsl:copy>
</xsl:template>

<xsl:template match="book">
 <xsl:copy>
  <xsl:attribute name="name"><xsl:value-of select="@name"/></xsl:attribute>
  <xsl:apply-templates select="chapter"/>
 </xsl:copy>
</xsl:template>

<xsl:template match="chapter">
 <xsl:copy-of select="document(@location)"/>
</xsl:template>

</xsl:stylesheet>
```

In this instance of document( ), the object in the argument is an XPath location path for the location attributes on the chapter elements in the source tree. Also in this instance, the relative URI is interpreted as being relative to the base URI of chapter elements in the source document, not relative to the stylesheet.

When you apply *jonahMap.xsl* to *jonahMap.xml* with:

```
    xalan jonahMap.xml jonahMap.xsl
```

all the chapters of Jonah will appear in the result. (The stylesheet, by the way, also takes the values of the name attributes from volume and book and places these values in the result.)

In the next example, Example 13-15, the document( ) function is used in conjunction with nodes found in the accessed document (as shown earlier in the book). The *jonahVerse.xsl* stylesheet prints verses from any of the files *jonah1.xml*, *jonah2.xml*, *jonah3.xml*, or *jonah4.xml*.

Example 13-15. Extracting information using document() function and parameters

```
<xsl:stylesheet version="1.0" xmlns:xsl="http://www.w3.org/1999/XSL/Transform">
<xsl:include href="wspace.xsl"/>
<xsl:output method="text"/>
<xsl:strip-space elements="*"/>
<xsl:param name="chap" select="1"/>
<xsl:param name="ver" select="1"/>

<xsl:template match="volume/book">
 <xsl:choose>
  <xsl:when test="$chap = 1 and $ver &lt; 18">
   <xsl:call-template name="cite"/>
   <xsl:value-of select="document('jonah1.xml')/chapter/verse[@number=$ver]"/>
  </xsl:when>
  <xsl:when test="$chap = 2 and $ver &lt; 11">
   <xsl:call-template name="cite"/>
```

Example 13-15. Extracting information using document() function and parameters (continued)

```
  <xsl:value-of select="document('jonah2.xml')/chapter/verse[@number=$ver]"/>
 </xsl:when>
 <xsl:when test="$chap = 3 and $ver &lt; 11">
  <xsl:call-template name="cite"/>
  <xsl:value-of select="document('jonah3.xml')/chapter/verse[@number=$ver]"/>
 </xsl:when>
 <xsl:when test="$chap = 4 and $ver &lt; 12">
  <xsl:call-template name="cite"/>
  <xsl:value-of select="document('jonah4.xml')/chapter/verse[@number=$ver]"/>
 </xsl:when>
 <xsl:otherwise>Not found!</xsl:otherwise>
 </xsl:choose>
</xsl:template>

<xsl:template name="cite">
 <xsl:text>The Book of Jonah</xsl:text>
 <xsl:call-template name="n1"/>
 <xsl:text>Chapter </xsl:text>
 <xsl:value-of select="$chap"/>
 <xsl:text>, verse </xsl:text>
 <xsl:value-of select="$ver"/>
 <xsl:text>: </xsl:text>
 <xsl:call-template name="n2"/>
</xsl:template>

</xsl:stylesheet>
```

The stylesheet includes *wspace.xsl* so it can call templates from it (the ones named n1 and n2). The parameters chap and ver default to 1, that is, to Chapter 1, verse 1 of Jonah. The test attribute on the when elements checks to see what chapter you want to refer to and then uses that number to bring up a given file. It also makes sure that you don't request a verse that is out of range for a given chapter. If any of these tests return false, the otherwise element returns Not found! and the processor exits without doing anything else. If a verse is found, the cite template writes the citation and the verse to the result tree.

Try it. Enter the following command passing in values for the chap and ver parameters:

```
xalan -p chap '2' -p ver '8' bible.xml jonahVerse.xsl
```

which will return:

```
The Book of Jonah
Chapter 2, verse 8:

They that observe lying vanities forsake their own mercy.
```

 There are several other ways besides those shown to use document() with two arguments, but frankly, they are difficult to explain and are neither common nor very useful.

Summary

This chapter explained how you include and import stylesheets, and it discussed the difference between the two operations. You also saw how to use the `apply-imports` element. The following three ways to use document( ) are also the three most common ways to use the function:

document('file.xml')
>   With one argument that is a string object representing a file.

document(@location)
>   With one argument that is a node-set containing a URI for a document.

document('file.xml')/node
>   With one argument that is a string object representing a file, followed by a node-set from the file.

In the next chapter, you'll learn more details of how to use alternative stylesheets.

CHAPTER 14

Alternative Stylesheets

Up to this point, the XSLT stylesheets you've seen have had the stylesheet element as their document element and have been separate documents from the source documents. This chapter will show you several alternatives to this model.

The first alternative is called a *literal result element stylesheet*. (I'll sometimes call it a literal stylesheet in this book, just to be brief.) This simplified stylesheet (as XSLT 2.0 calls it), in essence, has a literal result element as its document element rather than stylesheet. You can read more about this kind of stylesheet in Section 2.3 of the XSLT specification.

The second alternative is called an *embedded stylesheet*, which embeds an XSLT stylesheet in the same document that it transforms. It's a sort of self-contained source and stylesheet combined. This requires the use of the id attribute on the stylesheet element. See Section 2.7 of the XSLT specification for more information on embedded stylesheets.

In addition, this chapter will discuss the namespace-alias element. This element allows you to swap a namespace aliased in a stylesheet with a different one in the result. You'll also see how to exclude unneeded namespaces with the exclude-result-prefixes attribute.

The opening example shows you how to use a literal stylesheet.

A Literal Result Element Stylesheet

Tired of the same old stylesheet? You can try a literal result element stylesheet. The original design idea behind a literal stylesheet was to provide a simple subset of XSLT for non-programmers who want to write fill-in-the-blank HTML pages.

First, we need something to transform. The document *scand.xml* found in *examples/ch14* will do fine:

```
<?xml version="1.0" encoding="UTF-8"?>

<europe>
 <scandinavia>
  <state>Finland</state>
  <state>Sweden</state>
  <state>Iceland</state>
  <state>Norway</state>
  <state>Denmark</state>
 </scandinavia>
</europe>
```

This document is just a short list of the five Scandinavian countries in northern Europe. The following simplified XML literal stylesheet, *literal.xsl*, transforms *scand.xml*:

```
<?xml version="1.0" encoding="UTF-8"?>

<scandinavia xsl:version="1.0"
 xmlns:xsl="http://www.w3.org/1999/XSL/Transform">
  <xsl:for-each select="europe/scandinavia/state">
  <country><xsl:value-of select="."/></country>
  </xsl:for-each>
</scandinavia>
```

There is no `stylesheet` element (I already mentioned that it would be absent in a literal stylesheet). You can't even find a `template` element. The reason why there are no `template` elements found in a literal stylesheet is because a literal stylesheet cannot contain any top-level XSLT elements. This means that elements such as `template`, `import`, `include`, and `output` aren't allowed in literal stylesheets.

A literal stylesheet, in fact, works like a single, implicit `template` element that matches the root node (/). Only instruction elements like `for-each`, `value-of`, and `copy-of` will work inside this implicit template. This stylesheet uses `for-each` to march through all the `state` nodes in the source tree.

An important trick to making a literal stylesheet work is to use the `xsl:version` attribute on the document element together with the namespace declaration for XSLT using `xmlns:xsl`. With the `xsl:version` attribute and the XSLT namespace declaration in place, an XSLT processor will know how to interpret instruction elements from the XSLT namespace that it may find later in the document.

To see how it works, transform *scand.xml* with the literal stylesheet using the following command line:

```
xalan -i 1 scand.xml literal.xsl
```

This transformation will give you this result:

```
<?xml version="1.0" encoding="UTF-8"?>
<scandinavia>
 <country>Finland</country>
 <country>Sweden</country>
 <country>Iceland</country>
 <country>Norway</country>
 <country>Denmark</country>
</scandinavia>
```

Pull and Push Stylesheets

Because they are limited by having only one template, literal stylesheets are reserved for pull transformations. A *pull stylesheet* might have one template rule that grabs input from the source tree with `value-of` or `for-each` in the order that is declared in the stylesheet, regardless of input order, but it will have few, if any, other template rules. A *push stylesheet*, on the other hand, uses lots of template rules and `apply-templates` so that the order of input, rather than the stylesheet, determines the order of the output.

It's hard to get `apply-templates` to work in a literal stylesheet. You can't use the `select` or `mode` attributes to select another template, because you have only one template (the implicit one that matches /). If you use `apply-templates` without an attribute, the literal stylesheet will process all the children of the root node, which may not be what you want. As a general rule, then, I suggest avoiding `apply-templates` in literal stylesheets.

Now on to an XHTML literal stylesheet that you can easily see in a browser.

A Literal XHTML Stylesheet

The literal stylesheet *xhtmlit.xsl* has the `html` element as its document element:

```
<?xml version="1.0" encoding="UTF-8"?>

<html xsl:version="1.0" xmlns:xsl="http://www.w3.org/1999/XSL/Transform"
 xmlns="http://www.w3.org/1999/xhtml">
<body>
<h3>Scandanavian Countries</h3>
 <ul>
  <xsl:for-each select="europe/scandinavia/state">
  <li><xsl:value-of select="."/></li>
  </xsl:for-each>
 </ul>
</body>
</html>
```

This stylesheet uses `xsl:version` and declares the XSLT namespace in its document element. It also declares the XHTML namespace as the default namespace (with no prefix). After some common XHTML elements, the stylesheet uses `for-each` to print list items from the `state` nodes in the source.

xhtmlit.xsl will not display directly in a browser; you have to transform it into regular HTML before it will display properly.

Process *scand.xml* with this stylesheet using the following:

```
xalan -i 1 -o scand.html scand.xml xhtmlit.xsl
```

This saves the file *scand.html* in the local directory. It looks like this:

```
<?xml version="1.0" encoding="UTF-8"?>
<html xmlns="http://www.w3.org/1999/xhtml">
 <body>
  <h3>Scandanavian Countries</h3>
  <ul>
   <li>Finland</li>
   <li>Sweden</li>
   <li>Iceland</li>
   <li>Norway</li>
   <li>Denmark</li>
  </ul>
 </body>
</html>
```

Figure 14-1 shows you how *scand.html* looks in the Netscape browser.

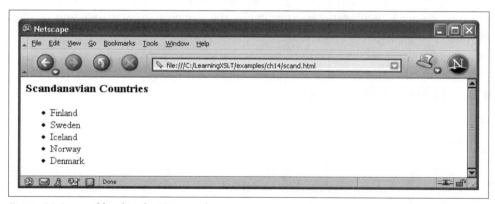

Figure 14-1. scand.html in the Netscape browser

An Embedded Stylesheet

Using a few tweaks and techniques, you can also embed a stylesheet in a document so that it's all stored in one package. An embedded stylesheet is a good idea when it's suitable to store both source and stylesheet in one convenient location. It's a convenience for situations when you write a stylesheet that will always be used with the same XML document, and it is distinct from stylesheets that might process a family of XML documents.

The stylesheet *scandinavia.xml*, shown in Example 14-1, uses this method to produce default HTML output.

Example 14-1. An XML document with an embedded stylesheet

```
<?xml version="1.0" encoding="UTF-8"?>
<?xml-stylesheet href="#scand" type="text/xsl"?>
<!DOCTYPE europe [
 <!ATTLIST xsl:stylesheet id ID #IMPLIED>
]>

<europe>
 <scandinavia>
  <state>Finland</state>
  <state>Sweden</state>
  <state>Iceland</state>
  <state>Norway</state>
  <state>Denmark</state>
 </scandinavia>

<!-- embedded stylesheet -->

<xsl:stylesheet id="scand" version="1.0" xmlns:xsl="http://www.w3.org/1999/XSL/Transform">

<xsl:template match="europe">
 <xsl:apply-templates select="scandinavia"/>
</xsl:template>

<xsl:template match="scandinavia">
 <html>
 <head><title>Scandanavian European States</title></head>
 <style type="text/css">
  h3,h4 {color: gray}
  body {font-family: sans-serif}
  span {color: red}
 </style>
 <body>
  <h3>Alphabetical List of Scandanavian European States</h3>
  <h4>Total Number of States:<xsl:text> </xsl:text>
   <span><xsl:value-of select="count(state)"/></span></h4>
  <ul>
   <xsl:apply-templates select="state">
    <xsl:sort/>
   </xsl:apply-templates>
  </ul>
 </body>
 </html>
</xsl:template>

<xsl:template match="state">
 <li><xsl:apply-templates/></li>
```

Example 14-1. An XML document with an embedded stylesheet (continued)

```
</xsl:template>

</xsl:stylesheet>

</europe>
```

What's a stylesheet doing inside a source document? This works because of the id attribute on the stylesheet element. The *scandinavia.xml* document has an XML stylesheet PI at the top. It's href pseudoattribute contains a relative fragment identifier, #scand, and the fragment identifier refers to the value of the id attribute on stylesheet. That's the trick that makes the transformation happen.

Note also that the id attribute is declared in the internal subset DTD. This is required by most processors in order for an embedded stylesheet to work. (Xalan and the XSLT processor in Mozilla work without it, for example, but others, such as Saxon, do not.)

One other thing to note is that the complete stylesheet lives inside the document element of the source document (europe). The stylesheet can be at the top, bottom or middle of the source tree. The exact location within the document element doesn't matter, as long as the stylesheet resides within the document element.

Try it using the -a option with Xalan (this option works with Saxon, too). The -a option instructs the XSLT processor to find the stylesheet using the XML stylesheet PI:

```
xalan -i 1 -a scandinavia.xml
```

Here's the result you'll see:

```
<html>
 <head>
  <META http-equiv="Content-Type" content="text/html; charset=UTF-8">
  <title>Scandanavian European States</title>
 </head>
 <style type="text/css">
  h3,h4 {color: gray}
  body {font-family: sans-serif}
  span {color: red}
 </style>
 <body>
  <h3>Alphabetical List of Scandanavian European States</h3>
  <h4>Total Number of States: <span>5</span>
  </h4>
  <ul>
   <li>Denmark</li>
   <li>Finland</li>
   <li>Iceland</li>
   <li>Norway</li>
   <li>Sweden</li>
  </ul>
 </body>
</html>
```

Because *scandinavia.xml* has an XML stylesheet PI, you can load the file directly with a browser that supports client-side XSLT such as Mozilla, Mozilla Firefox, and Netscape. The transformation will occur automatically, as it does in Netscape, shown in Figure 14-2.

Figure 14-2. scandinavia.xml in Netscape

 Loading an XML document with an embedded stylesheet does not work in IE 6.

Aliasing a Namespace

Another area of interest is namespace aliasing. This is a feature that allows you to use one namespace in the stylesheet and then swap it with another in the result tree. This is done with the namespace-alias element.

 namespace-alias makes the most sense if you are designing stylesheets whose purpose is to generate other stylesheets. You can achieve the same effect, however, by using element in place of literal result elements, as in <xsl:element name="xsl:stylesheet">.

The namespace-alias element may appear on the top level of a stylesheet. It has two attributes: stylesheet-prefix, which contains a prefix associated with a namespace in the stylesheet, and result-prefix, which holds a prefix also declared in the stylesheet but to be output in the result tree. If you want to refer to a default namespace declaration instead of a prefix, you can use #default as a value for either of these attributes. All this will make more sense with a practical example.

The stylesheet *alias.xsl* uses the namespace-alias element:

```
<xsl:stylesheet version="1.0" xmlns:xsl="http://www.w3.org/1999/XSL/Transform"
 xmlns="urn:wyeast-net:scandinavia"
 xmlns:sc="http://www.wyeast.net/scand">
<xsl:output method="xml" indent="yes" encoding="ISO-8859-1"/>
<xsl:namespace-alias stylesheet-prefix="sc" result-prefix="#default"/>

<xsl:template match="europe">
 <xsl:apply-templates select="scandinavia"/>
</xsl:template>

<xsl:template match="scandinavia">
 <sc:scandinavia>
  <xsl:apply-templates select="state">
   <xsl:sort/>
  </xsl:apply-templates>
 </sc:scandinavia>
</xsl:template>

<xsl:template match="state">
 <sc:country><xsl:value-of select="."/></sc:country>
</xsl:template>

</xsl:stylesheet>
```

The stylesheet produces XML. The literal result elements in the templates are pre-fixed with sc, which is associated with the namespace URI http://www.wyeast.net/scand. A default namespace is also declared using the URN urn:wyeast-net:scandanavia, but it isn't used in the stylesheet—it's intended for use in the result.

To demonstrate how this process works, apply *alias.xml* to *scand.xml* with MSXSL:

```
msxsl scand.xml alias.xsl
```

Here is the output from this transformation:

```
<?xml version="1.0" encoding="ISO-8859-1"?>
<scandinavia xmlns="urn:wyeast-net:scandinavia">
<country>Denmark</country>
<country>Finland</country>
<country>Iceland</country>
<country>Norway</country>
<country>Sweden</country>
</scandinavia>
```

With MSXSL, the sc prefix is dropped in the resulting elements. The default namespace urn:wyeast-net:scandinavia is used instead of the namespace associated with the sc prefix, that is, http://www.wyeast.net/scand. This is what I expected a processor to do, having read the spec on the issue (Section 7.1.1). Now, if you per-form the same transformation with Xalan:

```
xalan scand.xml alias.xsl
```

you get a different result:

```
<sc:scandinavia xmlns="urn:wyeast-net:scandinavia"
 xmlns:sc="urn:wyeast-net:scandinavia">
<sc:country>Denmark</sc:country>
<sc:country>Finland</sc:country>
<sc:country>Iceland</sc:country>
<sc:country>Norway</sc:country>
<sc:country>Sweden</sc:country>
</sc:scandinavia>
```

With Xalan, the prefix is retained in the output. The main difference is that the default namespace in the stylesheet is now associated with the prefix sc. Frankly, the MSXSL interpretation seems more logical to me, but the functionality displayed by Xalan and other processors like Saxon appear to be the norm.

> XSLT never specifies exactly what the prefix for elements and attributes in the result should be; it specifies only the namespace URI. A processor can use any prefix it likes. In most cases, XSLT processors choose the obvious prefix. But with namespace-alias, processors tend to choose a prefix that is convenient, hence giving varied results.

The most common reason to use namespace-alias is probably to create XSLT elements in the result tree. Without aliasing, any XSLT element will be interpreted as just that, an XSLT element. Sometimes, you just want to create XSLT elements in the result tree, and namespace aliasing will let you do it.

You can see how this works in Example 14-2, which shows the stylesheet *xslt.xsl*.

Example 14-2. A stylesheet using namespace aliasing

```
<xsl:stylesheet version="1.0" xmlns:xsl="http://www.w3.org/1999/XSL/Transform"
 xmlns="urn:wyeast-net:scandanavia"
 xmlns:sc="http://www.wyeast.net/scand"
 xmlns:t="http://www.wyeast.net/temp">
<xsl:output method="xml" indent="yes" encoding="ISO-8859-1"/>
<xsl:namespace-alias stylesheet-prefix="t" result-prefix="xsl"/>

<xsl:template match="europe">
 <t:stylesheet version="1.0">
 <t:output method="xml" indent="yes" encoding="ISO-8859-1"/>
 <t:namespace-alias stylesheet-prefix="sc" result-prefix="#default"/>
<xsl:text>&#10;&#10;</xsl:text>
<t:template match="{name( )}">
  <t:apply-templates select="scandinavia"/>
</t:template>
<xsl:text>&#10;</xsl:text>

<xsl:apply-templates select="scandinavia"/>

<xsl:apply-templates select="scandinavia/state[1]"/>
```

Example 14-2. A stylesheet using namespace aliasing (continued)

```
 <xsl:text>&#10;</xsl:text>

 </t:stylesheet>

</xsl:template>

<xsl:template match="scandinavia">
<xsl:text>&#10;</xsl:text>
 <t:template match="{name( )}">
  <sc:scandinavia>
   <t:apply-templates select="state">
    <t:sort/>
   </t:apply-templates>
  </sc:scandinavia>
 </t:template>
<xsl:text>&#10;</xsl:text>
</xsl:template>

<xsl:template match="state">
<xsl:text>&#10;</xsl:text>
 <t:template match="{name( )}">
  <sc:country>
   <t:value-of select="."/>
  </sc:country>
 </t:template>
<xsl:text>&#10;</xsl:text>
</xsl:template>

</xsl:stylesheet>
```

Now apply it to *scand.xml* with MSXSL:

```
msxsl -o newalias.xsl scand.xml xslt.xsl
```

When you look at *newalias.xsl*, you will see the following output, which is nearly identical to *alias.xsl*:

```
<?xml version="1.0" encoding="ISO-8859-1"?>
<xsl:stylesheet version="1.0" xmlns="urn:wyeast-net:scandanavia" xmlns:sc="http://
www.wyeast.net/scand" xmlns:xsl="http://www.w3.org/1999/XSL/Transform">
<xsl:output method="xml" indent="yes" encoding="ISO-8859-1" />
<xsl:namespace-alias stylesheet-prefix="sc" result-prefix="#default" />

<xsl:template match="europe">
<xsl:apply-templates select="scandinavia" />
</xsl:template>

<xsl:template match="scandinavia">
<sc:scandinavia>
<xsl:apply-templates select="state">
<xsl:sort />
```

```
  </xsl:apply-templates>
  </sc:scandinavia>
  </xsl:template>

  <xsl:template match="state">
  <sc:country>
  <xsl:value-of select="." />
  </sc:country>
  </xsl:template>

  </xsl:stylesheet>
```

The stylesheet effectively scanned the document and created a new stylesheet based on what it found. To complete the circle, now transform *scand.xml* with *newalias.xsl*:

```
msxsl scand.xml newalias.xsl
```

You'll get the same result you got with *alias.xsl*:

```
<?xml version="1.0" encoding="ISO-8859-1"?>
<scandinavia xmlns="urn:wyeast-net:scandanavia">
<country>Denmark</country>
<country>Finland</country>
<country>Iceland</country>
<country>Norway</country>
<country>Sweden</country>
</scandinavia>
```

Namespace aliasing, as you can see, is useful when you want to create new stylesheets from your old stylesheets.

Excluding Namespaces

Sometimes you will find that the result document contains namespace declarations that you don't want. You can use XSLT's exclude-result-prefixes attribute on the stylesheet element or xsl:exclude-result-prefixes on literal result elements to exclude such declarations from the result.

This attribute contains a whitespace-separated list of one or more namespace prefixes that you want to exclude from the result tree, provided that the namespace is not actually used. In other words, you can use this attribute to keep superfluous namespaces defined in the stylesheet from reaching the result tree. Any namespace node found in the stylesheet gets copied to the result.

 The exclude-result-prefixes attribute affects only namespaces copied by literal result elements.

The stylesheet *exclude.xsl* shows you how to use this attribute:

```
<xsl:stylesheet version="1.0" xmlns:xsl="http://www.w3.org/1999/XSL/Transform"
 xmlns:sc="http://www.wyeast.net/scand"
 xmlns:scand="http://www.wyeast.net/scandinavia"
 xmlns:nr="http://www.wyeast.net/scandinavia"
 exclude-result-prefixes="scand nr">
<xsl:output method="xml" indent="yes" encoding="ISO-8859-1"/>

<xsl:template match="europe">
 <xsl:apply-templates select="scandinavia"/>
</xsl:template>

<xsl:template match="scandinavia">
 <sc:scandinavia>
  <xsl:apply-templates select="state">
   <xsl:sort/>
  </xsl:apply-templates>
 </sc:scandinavia>
</xsl:template>

<xsl:template match="state">
 <sc:country><xsl:value-of select="."/></sc:country>
</xsl:template>

</xsl:stylesheet>
```

On the stylesheet element, two namespaces are declared, xmlns:scand="http://www.wyeast.net/scandinavia" and xmlns:nr="http://www.wyeast.net/scandinavia". They are desired in the stylesheet but are unnecessary in the result document. These namespaces are not written to the result tree because of the presence of the exclude-result-prefixes on stylesheet with scand and nr in its value.

See this attribute in action by performing the transformation:

```
xalan scand.xml exclude.xsl
```

which gives this result:

```
<?xml version="1.0" encoding="ISO-8859-1"?>
<sc:scandinavia xmlns:sc="http://www.wyeast.net/scand">
<sc:country>Denmark</sc:country>
<sc:country>Finland</sc:country>
<sc:country>Iceland</sc:country>
<sc:country>Norway</sc:country>
<sc:country>Sweden</sc:country>
</sc:scandinavia>
```

You get only the needed namespace. Without the exclude-result-prefixes attribute, all the namespaces nodes on the stylesheet element would be included in the result tree.

You can also use xsl:exclude-result-prefixes (when properly prefixed) on literal result elements. Example 14-3 shows an example, the stylesheet *excludeonlit.xsl*.

Example 14-3. An XSLT stylesheet that excludes some prefixes

```
<xsl:stylesheet version="1.0" xmlns:xsl="http://www.w3.org/1999/XSL/Transform"
 xmlns:sc="http://www.wyeast.net/scand">
<xsl:output method="xml" indent="yes" encoding="ISO-8859-1"/>

<xsl:template match="europe">
 <xsl:apply-templates select="scandinavia"/>
</xsl:template>

<xsl:template match="scandinavia">
 <sc:scandinavia
 xmlns:scand="http://www.wyeast.net/scandinavia"
 xmlns:nr="http://www.wyeast.net/scandinavia"
 xsl:exclude-result-prefixes="scand nr">

  <xsl:apply-templates select="state">
   <xsl:sort/>
  </xsl:apply-templates>
 </sc:scandinavia>
</xsl:template>

<xsl:template match="state">
 <sc:country><xsl:value-of select="."/></sc:country>
</xsl:template>

</xsl:stylesheet>
```

When used with *scand.xml*, you will get the same result with *excludeonlit.xsl* that you did with *exclude.xsl*.

Summary

There is more than one way to write a stylesheet. In addition to the traditional way, you can also create a stylesheet using literal result elements, though you get only one implicit template in such a case. Embedded stylesheets let you include a stylesheet within a source document. The namespace-alias element helps you hoodwink an XSLT processor, letting you, among other things, create XSLT elements in templates for inclusion on the result tree. You can also keep unnecessary namespace nodes out of a result tree with exclude-result-prefixes.

Now, on to an entirely different subject. Conveniently, XSLT lets itself be extended, allowing you to add your features or use someone else's enhancements. The next chapter covers XSLT extensions.

CHAPTER 15
Extensions

Extensibility defines the ways in which a language can be extended. XSLT is extensible, meaning that if you are a programmer, you can add your own functionality to a processor in the form of extension elements, attributes, and functions. The developers of XSLT realized that they couldn't please everyone with their first shot (who can?), so they made it possible for developers to both add features to their XSLT processors independently, and to share those features with others.

If you aren't going to write your own extensions, you still have a lot of extensions available to you through other processors. Most processors offer their own internal extensions, such as Xalan and Saxon. The EXSLT group also provides a number of extensions that can be supported directly by a processor or by pure XSLT 1.0 processors (see *http://www.exslt.org*). EXSLT organizes its extensions into modules, such as math and string modules. You can submit extension implementations and proposals to EXSLT; Xalan and Saxon also provide means to add your own external extensions and then integrate them in with the existing processor.

The EXSLT effort attempts to standardize and unify all XSLT 1.0 extensions. Saxon, for example, now implements many, but not all, EXSLT extension functions. It is good practice to use EXSLT extensions when available, if your processor supports them. It may be easier, however, to simply use a proprietary extension offered by your processor. XSLT 2.0 and XPath 2.0, discussed in the next chapter, offer many more functions than their predecessors, and will likely be the most successful at unifying previous extensions to XSLT 1.0 and XPath 1.0.

In this chapter, I'll provide a sample of available extensions and, to get you started, show you how to use some of them. This will include how to use the extension-element-prefixes attribute on the stylesheet element. I'll also show you how to test for extension availability and provide for fallback behavior using the fallback and message elements. In the first part of the chapter, I'll list extension functionality offered by three sources: Xalan, Saxon, and EXSLT.

Xalan, Saxon, and EXSLT Extensions

It would be overwhelming to list all available extensions from just these three sources. Thus, I have chosen to show a sampling of what's available from Xalan, Saxon, and EXSLT. Most processors offer their own documented extensions, but I will deal only with a handful of those offered by Saxon and EXSLT. Xalan offers only a few extension functions, so I'll show all those. The following tables list a number of extensions available from these sources.

Xalan C++ currently supports six internal extension functions, but it also has support for several EXSLT modules: common, math, set, and string (see *http://xml.apache.org/xalan-c/extensionslib.html*). Table 15-1 shows the extension functions that Xalan C++ offers directly.

 Xalan Java provides a different set of extensions than Xalan C++, including a set of SQL extensions. See *http://xml.apache.org/xalan-j/extensionslib.html* for more information.

Table 15-1. Sample of Xalan C++ extension functions

Extension	Description
`xalan:difference(node-set1, node-set2)`	Returns a node-set from nodes that exist in one node-set but not in another.
`xalan:distinct(node-set)`	Returns a node-set that contains nodes with distinct string values.
`xalan:evaluate(xpath-expression)`	Evaluates an XPath expression supplied at runtime as a string.
`xalan:hasSameNodes(node-set1, node-set2)`	Returns true if the two node-sets contain exactly the same set of nodes.
`xalan:intersection(node-set1, node-set2)`	Returns a node-set from nodes that exist in two different node-sets.
`xalan:nodeset(result-tree-fragment)`	Returns a node-set from a result tree fragment defined in a variable.

The current release of Saxon at the time of this writing (7.7 or later) provides partial support for XSLT 2.0 plus a large number of extension attributes, elements, and functions (see *http://saxon.sourceforge.net/* for more information). Other versions of Saxon, such as Instant Saxon 6.5.3, support only XSLT 1.0. As for EXSLT, Saxon supports the common, math, sets, dates/times, and functions modules. Some of Saxon's direct extensions are listed in Table 15-2.

Table 15-2. Sample of Saxon extensions

Extension	Type	Description
saxon:assignable	Attribute (variable element only)	Indicates whether a variable may have a new value assigned.
saxon:indent-spaces	Attribute (output or saxon:output element only)	Sets the number of indentation spaces used on the result tree.
saxon:assign	Element	Assigns a new value to an assignable variable.
saxon:output	Element	Outputs an additional result tree, saving it as a file.
saxon:while	Element	Iterates through a loop while a condition is true.
saxon:distinct(node-set-1, stored-expression?)	Function	Returns a node-set of nodes not duplicated in the optional stored-expression (current node list if not present).
saxon:evaluate(string)	Function	Evaluates an XPath expression.
saxon:has-same-nodes(node-set-1, node-set-2)	Function	Returns true if the two node-sets contain exactly the same set of nodes.
saxon:line-number( )	Function	Returns the line number of the current node in the source tree.

EXSLT currently proffers 74 extensions, most of them functions. Many of the functions offer a pure XSLT 1.0 solution using the call-template element that is using with-param children. Table 15-3 lists a single sample from each of the eight modules.

Table 15-3. Sample of EXSLT extensions

Extension	Module	Type	Description
date:date( )	Date and time	Function	Returns the current date.
dyn:evaluate(string)	Dynamic	Function	Evaluates an XPath expression.
exsl:node-set(object)	Common	Function	Returns a node-set from a result tree fragment defined in a variable.
func:function	Functions	Element	Declares an extension function.
math:lowest(node-set)	Math	Function	Returns the lowest value from a node-set.
regexp:test(string, string, string?)	Regular expressions	Function	Returns true if the string in the first argument matches the regular expression in the second argument (the third argument is an optional flag).
set:difference(node-set, node-set)	Sets	Function	Returns a node-set from nodes that exist in one node-set but not in another.
str:tokenize(string, string?)	Strings	Function	Breaks a string into tokens (the second argument is an optional delimiter).

Although these tables list only a sample of what's available, you may have noticed that there are some extensions that are implemented by more than one processor—the distinct( ) extension function, for example, is supported by both Xalan and Saxon. In XSLT 2.0, this extension function has evolved into the fn:distinct-values( ) function. You can learn more about these functions in the W3C specification for XPath 2.0 (and XQuery 1.0) functions and operators at *http://www.w3.org/TR/xpath-functions/*. You will also get an introduction to XSLT 2.0 and XPath 2.0 in Chapter 16.

Using a Saxon Extension Attribute

Remember how Xalan's -i option lets you set the exact number of spaces to indent child elements in the result tree? Saxon offers the same ability, but through an extension attribute, which goes in the stylesheet, rather than as a command-line option. As I walk you through this first extension example, I'll point out the basic requirements for getting a vendor extension to work.

Example 15-1, the sloppily indented document *keywords.xml*, in *examples/ch15*, contains a nonalphabetical list of keywords from Version 2.3 of the Python programming language.

Example 15-1. Python keywords in XML

```
<?xml version="1.0"?>

<python version="2.3">
      <keyword>while</keyword>
<keyword>continue</keyword>
  <keyword>def</keyword>
    <keyword>elif</keyword>
   <keyword>except</keyword>
 <keyword>from</keyword>
     <keyword>del</keyword>
        <keyword>break</keyword>
    <keyword>print</keyword>
   <keyword>exec</keyword>
 <keyword>raise</keyword>
<keyword>finally</keyword>
     <keyword>global</keyword>
       <keyword>if</keyword>
       <keyword>and</keyword>
     <keyword>is</keyword>
     <keyword>else</keyword>
  <keyword>import</keyword>
<keyword>in</keyword>
  <keyword>lambda</keyword>
    <keyword>not</keyword>
```

Example 15-1. Python keywords in XML (continued)

```
      <keyword>for</keyword>
 <keyword>class</keyword>
        <keyword>pass</keyword>
    <keyword>return</keyword>
      <keyword>try</keyword>
    <keyword>yield</keyword>
 <keyword>or</keyword>
    <keyword>assert</keyword>
</python>
```

Example 15-2, the stylesheet *indent.xsl*, aims to clean this document to make it more presentable. To do part of the job, it uses Saxon's extension attribute saxon:indent-spaces that was mentioned in Table 15-2.

Example 15-2. A stylesheet using a Saxon extension function

```
<xsl:stylesheet version="1.0" xmlns:xsl="http://www.w3.org/1999/XSL/Transform"
xmlns:saxon="http://icl.com/saxon" extension-element-prefixes="saxon">
<xsl:output method="xml" saxon:indent-spaces="2" indent="yes"/>
<xsl:strip-space elements="*"/>

<xsl:template match="python">
<xsl:copy>
 <xsl:attribute name="version"><xsl:value-of select="@version"/></xsl:attribute>
 <xsl:apply-templates>
  <xsl:sort/>
 </xsl:apply-templates>
</xsl:copy>
</xsl:template>

<xsl:template match="keyword">
 <xsl:copy-of select="."/>
</xsl:template>

</xsl:stylesheet>
```

There are two things you need to know before you can get saxon:indent-spaces to work:

1. You must declare the Saxon namespace with a prefix.
2. You must register the namespace as an extension namespace.

You are already familiar with the first step. The namespace name or URI http://icl.com/saxon is associated with the prefix saxon. You can use whatever prefix you want, but saxon is commonly used probably because it appears in the Saxon documentation. The namespace URI is important, too. This URI—http://icl.com/saxon—works with Instant Saxon Version 6.5.3. (Later versions of Saxon use http://saxon.sf.net/, but it won't work with Instant Saxon.)

Instant Saxon 6.5.3 is an XSLT 1.0 processor. Saxon 7.7 or greater is a partial implementation of XSLT 2.0. Many of Saxon extensions from earlier, 6.X versions have not been carried forward because these extensions have been incorporated into other functionality in XSLT 2.0.

The second step is new to you, or at least I haven't mentioned it yet: you must notify the processor of those namespaces that are used for extension elements (not attributes or functions) by supplying one or more whitespace-separated prefixes in the value of the `extension-element-prefixes` attribute. Once you have taken care of these two steps, you can start using extensions in your stylesheet and have confidence that they will be recognized as such.

The `saxon:indent-spaces` attribute appears on the output element. This attribute accepts an integer value, which represents the number of space characters that will be used to indent child elements in a result tree. In order to work correctly, the indent attribute must also be specified on output with a value of yes.

When you process *keywords.xml* with this stylesheet:

```
saxon keywords.xml indent.xsl
```

the output, shown in Example 15-3, is nicely indented by two spaces, thanks to Saxon's extension attribute.

Example 15-3. Formatted results produced by the saxon:indent-spaces attribute

```
<?xml version="1.0" encoding="utf-8"?>
<python version="2.3">
  <keyword>and</keyword>
  <keyword>assert</keyword>
  <keyword>break</keyword>
  <keyword>class</keyword>
  <keyword>continue</keyword>
  <keyword>def</keyword>
  <keyword>del</keyword>
  <keyword>elif</keyword>
  <keyword>else</keyword>
  <keyword>except</keyword>
  <keyword>exec</keyword>
  <keyword>finally</keyword>
  <keyword>for</keyword>
  <keyword>from</keyword>
  <keyword>global</keyword>
  <keyword>if</keyword>
  <keyword>import</keyword>
  <keyword>in</keyword>
  <keyword>is</keyword>
  <keyword>lambda</keyword>
  <keyword>not</keyword>
  <keyword>or</keyword>
  <keyword>pass</keyword>
```

```
    <keyword>print</keyword>
    <keyword>raise</keyword>
    <keyword>return</keyword>
    <keyword>try</keyword>
    <keyword>while</keyword>
    <keyword>yield</keyword>
</python>
```

The keyword elements are also sorted alphabetically, so the result is certainly more attractive than the source.

The Full Java Version of Saxon

Instant Saxon won't work if you are working on a Unix platform or on a Windows platform that doesn't have the Java Virtual Machine (JVM) installed. (Windows XP, for example, does not install a JVM by default.) You can use the full Java version on the command line instead. Assuming that the JAR file for Saxon Version 6.5.3 is available in the current directory (saxon.jar), and that a Java Runtime Environment (JRE 1.2 or later) is installed on your system, you can perform the transformation on *keywords.xml* using this line:

```
    java -jar saxon.jar keywords.xml indent.xsl
```

This should give you the same result you saw earlier. If the terms Java, JAR file, and runtime environment make you queasy, don't worry: just go to the appendix where you will find all the information you need to download and install Saxon and get Sun's Java interpreter as well. You'll learn about how to use other processors there, too.

Result Tree Fragment to Node-Set

As you learned in Chapter 7, a variable can hold a special XSLT type called a *result tree fragment*. Such a fragment can hold XML nodes, but it isn't natively treated as a node-set. Nonetheless, with Xalan's node-set( ) function or Saxon's nodeset( ), you can cast a result tree fragment as a node-set and manipulate it as such. The following example will apply node-set( ) from Xalan (note, however, that many processors now provide the EXSLT version of this function for portability).

Consider the document *escapes.xml*, which lists most of the string escapes offered by Python Version 2.3:

```
    <?xml version="1.0"?>

    <python version="2.3">
     <escape purpose="bell">\a</escape>
     <escape purpose="backspace">\b</escape>
     <escape purpose="formfeed">\f</escape>
```

```
<escape purpose="newline">\n</escape>
<escape purpose="carriage return">\r</escape>
<escape purpose="horizontal tab">\t</escape>
<escape purpose="vertical tab">\v</escape>
</python>
```

There are a few escapes missing from this list. The stylesheet *node-set.xsl* supplies the missing nodes in a result tree fragment, as shown in Example 15-4.

Example 15-4. Using the Xalan nodeset function to convert result tree fragments into node-sets

```
<xsl:stylesheet version="1.0" xmlns:xsl="http://www.w3.org/1999/XSL/Transform"
xmlns:xalan="http://xml.apache.org/xalan" exclude-result-prefixes="xalan">
<xsl:output method="xml" indent="yes"/>
<xsl:variable name="frag">
<python>
 <description>Python 2.3 String Escapes</description>
 <escape purpose="ignore EOL">\</escape>
 <escape purpose="backslash">\\</escape>
 <escape purpose="octal value">\ddd</escape>
 <escape purpose="hexadecimal">\xXX</escape>
 <escape purpose="other">\other</escape>
 <escape purpose="single quote">\'</escape>
 <escape purpose="double quote">\"</escape>
</python>
</xsl:variable>

<xsl:template match="python">
 <xsl:copy>
  <xsl:copy-of select="xalan:nodeset($frag)/python/*"/>
  <xsl:apply-templates select="escape"/>
 </xsl:copy>
</xsl:template>

<xsl:template match="escape">
 <xsl:copy-of select="."/>
</xsl:template>

</xsl:stylesheet>
```

The Xalan namespace and prefix are set up for use on the stylesheet element. Following that is a variable definition that contains a result tree fragment. It contains the Python string escapes missing from *escapes.xml*.

In the template matching python, the python element is copied into the result tree from the source tree, then copy-of uses xalan:node-set( ) in an expression to copy the result tree fragment with the node-set. Yes, copy-of could copy a result tree fragment into the result tree, but xalan:node-set( ) allows you to manipulate the fragment as a node-set. That's why it's possible to follow the function call with the XPath location steps /python/*, which grabs all the escape children in the fragment.

Although the function is called xalan:node-set( ), and the type of object the function returns is a node-set, the node-set that a result tree fragment contains is always a single root node, no matter what processor or extension you use. In this example, the python element is a child of this root node in the fragment. To demonstrate this, try doing count(xalan:node-set($frag))—the result will be 1, regardless of the contents of the fragment.

The second template copies all the escape nodes in the source tree into the result tree, joining them with nodes cast from frag. The following command:

```
xalan -i 2 escapes.xml node-set.xsl
```

gives you this combined output:

```
<?xml version="1.0" encoding="UTF-8"?>
<python>
  <description>Python 2.3 String Escapes</description>
  <escape purpose="ignore EOL">\</escape>
  <escape purpose="backslash">\\</escape>
  <escape purpose="octal value">\ddd</escape>
  <escape purpose="hexadecimal">\xXX</escape>
  <escape purpose="other">\other</escape>
  <escape purpose="single quote">\'</escape>
  <escape purpose="double quote">\"</escape>
  <escape purpose="bell">\a</escape>
  <escape purpose="backspace">\b</escape>
  <escape purpose="formfeed">\f</escape>
  <escape purpose="newline">\n</escape>
  <escape purpose="carriage return">\r</escape>
  <escape purpose="horizontal tab">\t</escape>
  <escape purpose="vertical tab">\v</escape>
</python>
```

That's an example of a Xalan function; now, I'll demonstrate an EXSLT function.

Using EXSLT

You'll get to use several EXSLT extensions in the following example. Here is a simple order for oats from a feed store represented in XML (*order.xml*), shown in Example 15-5.

Example 15-5. An order for oats, in XML

```
<?xml version="1.0"?>

<order id="TDI-983857">
 <store>Prineville</store>
 <product>feed-grade whole oats</product>
 <package>sack</package>
 <weight std="lbs.">50</weight>
```

Example 15-5. An order for oats, in XML (continued)

```
<quantity>23</quantity>
<price cur="USD">
 <high>5.99</high>
 <regular>4.99</regular>
 <discount>3.99</discount>
</price>
<ship>the back of Tom's pickup</ship>
</order>
```

The EXSLT extensions in Example 15-6, the stylesheet *order.xsl*, augment the order with date and time.

Example 15-6. A stylesheet that does mathematical computations using the EXSLT math functions

```
<xsl:stylesheet version="1.0" xmlns:xsl="http://www.w3.org/1999/XSL/Transform"
xmlns:date="http://exslt.org/dates-and-times" xmlns:math="http://exslt.org/math">
<xsl:output method="xml" indent="yes" encoding="ISO-8859-1"/>
<xsl:strip-space elements="*"/>

<xsl:template match="order">
 <xsl:copy>
  <xsl:attribute name="id"><xsl:value-of select="@id"/></xsl:attribute>
  <date><xsl:value-of select="date:date( )"/></date>
  <time><xsl:value-of select="date:time( )"/></time>
  <xsl:copy-of select="product|package|weight|quantity"/>
  <price cur="{price/@cur}"><xsl:value-of select="math:lowest(price/*)"/></price>
  <total><xsl:value-of select="format-number(math:lowest(price/*)*quantity,'#,###.00')"/>
</total>
  <xsl:copy-of select="ship"/>
 </xsl:copy>
</xsl:template>

</xsl:stylesheet>
```

Using the date:date( ) and date:time( ) functions from the dates and times module, and the math:lowest( ) function from the math module, *order.xsl* transforms and improves upon the information in the original *order.xml*. The date:date( ) and date: time( ) functions provide the system date and time to the result tree respectively. The math:lowest( ) function takes a node-set as an argument. The function then selects the node having the lowest value, in this case 3.99.

Instant Saxon supports these EXSLT functions, so you can get results by issuing the following command:

```
saxon order.xml order.xsl
```

This will produce the following results:

```
<?xml version="1.0" encoding="ISO-8859-1"?>
<order id="TDI-983857">
   <date>2003-05-09</date>
   <time>09:00:39-07:00</time>
```

```
    <product>feed-grade whole oats</product>
    <package>sack</package>
    <weight std="lbs.">50</weight>
    <quantity>23</quantity>
    <price cur="USD">3.99</price>
    <total>91.77</total>
    <ship>the back of Tom's pickup</ship>
</order>
```

EXSLT's exsl:node-set Function

Like Saxon, EXSLT also has a function for converting result tree fragments into node-sets. It's called exsl:node-set(). The *enode-set.xsl* stylesheet shown in Example 15-7 is very similar to *node-set.xsl*.

Example 15-7. A stylesheet using the EXSLT node-set() function

```
<xsl:stylesheet version="1.0" xmlns:xsl="http://www.w3.org/1999/XSL/Transform"
xmlns:exsl="http://exslt.org/common" extension-element-prefixes="exsl">
<xsl:output method="xml" indent="yes"/>
<xsl:variable name="frag">
<python>
 <description>Python 2.3 String Escapes</description>
 <escape purpose="ignore EOL">\</escape>
 <escape purpose="backslash">\\</escape>
 <escape purpose="octal value">\ddd</escape>
 <escape purpose="hexadecimal">\xXX</escape>
 <escape purpose="other">\other</escape>
 <escape purpose="single quote">\'</escape>
 <escape purpose="double quote">\"</escape>
</python>
</xsl:variable>

<xsl:template match="python">
 <xsl:copy>
  <xsl:copy-of select="exsl:node-set($frag)/python/*"/>
  <xsl:apply-templates select="escape"/>
 </xsl:copy>
</xsl:template>

<xsl:template match="escape">
 <xsl:copy-of select="."/>
</xsl:template>

</xsl:stylesheet>
```

The only differences are the namespace and prefix. If you apply this against *escapes.xml* with Saxon, you will get the same result you got when using *node-set.xsl*. Saxon supports many but not all EXSLT extensions; however, Saxon's documentation states that it prefers that users work with EXSLT's extensions over Saxon's (see *http://saxon.sourceforge.net/saxon6.5.2/extensions.html* or *http://saxon.sourceforge.net/saxon7.5/extensions.html*).

Many EXSLT extensions are also implemented as pure XSLT 1.0, meaning that they use imported templates in tandem with call-template to implement the functionality (nevertheless, some extensions like node-set( ) cannot be implemented in XSLT 1.0 alone). The call-template element acts as a function call. These pure implementations, however, are several years old, and I could not get a number of them to work as advertised, try as I may. Therefore, I won't be exploring them here.

Fallback Behavior

What happens if you use a stylesheet that has a Saxon extension element with another processor? It's hard to predict what might happen, except that it's likely you'll get an error stating that the extension element can't be found. You can prepare for this by specifying fallback behavior for extension elements in your stylesheet using the fallback and message elements together.

 fallback works only with extension elements. You can test for the availability of extension elements with the XSLT function element-available( ). To test for extension functions, use function-available( ). These functions are demonstrated in the section "Checking for Extension Availability," later in this chapter.

The *output.xsl* stylesheet shown in Example 15-8 uses the XSLT elements fallback and message to deal with the possibility of a processor other than Saxon encountering it.

Example 15-8. A stylesheet using fallbacks

```
<xsl:stylesheet version="1.0" xmlns:xsl="http://www.w3.org/1999/XSL/Transform"
xmlns:saxon="http://icl.com/saxon" extension-element-prefixes="saxon">
<xsl:output method="text" encoding="ISO-8859-1"/>
<xsl:strip-space elements="*"/>

<xsl:template match="python">
 <!-- to result tree as text -->
 <xsl:text>Python 2.3 Keywords&#10;&#10;</xsl:text>
 <xsl:apply-templates select="keyword" mode="text">
  <xsl:sort/>
 </xsl:apply-templates>
 <!-- save as HTML, too -->
 <saxon:output href="keywords.html" method="html" indent="yes"
   saxon:indent-spaces="1">
  <xsl:fallback>
   <xsl:message terminate="yes">ERROR: saxon:output not available!</xsl:message>
  </xsl:fallback>
  <html>
  <body>
  <h3>Python 2.3 Keywords</h3>
  <ol>
```

Example 15-8. A stylesheet using fallbacks (continued)

```
    <xsl:apply-templates select="keyword" mode="html">
     <xsl:sort/>
    </xsl:apply-templates>
   </ol>
  </body>
  </html>
  </saxon:output>
</xsl:template>

<xsl:template match="keyword" mode="html">
 <li><xsl:value-of select="."/></li>
</xsl:template>

<xsl:template match="keyword" mode="text">
 <xsl:value-of select="."/>
 <xsl:choose>
 <xsl:when test="not((position( ) mod 5)=0) and not(position( )=last( ))">
  <xsl:text>&#09;</xsl:text>
 </xsl:when>
 <xsl:otherwise>
  <xsl:text>&#10;</xsl:text>
 </xsl:otherwise>
 </xsl:choose>

</xsl:template>
</xsl:stylesheet>
```

Using the saxon:output element, this stylesheet produces two result trees: a normal result tree as text and an additional HTML result tree saved as a file in the current directory. The saxon:output element has many of the same attributes as XSLT's output element, such as method, indent, encoding, and so forth. Two important differences are:

1. saxon:output has a required attribute, href, whose value names the filename for the additional result tree. XSLT's output has no such attribute.

2. saxon:output can contain a template, as you can see in *output.xsl*. XSLT's output is an empty element.

In the initial template, the one that matches python, some title text is created for the result tree, then templates are applied for keyword elements in the text mode. In addition, the keyword elements are sorted. The template whose mode is text prints a keyword, followed by a tab (	) or a linefeed (
), depending on the position of the word in the source tree.

After that, the same template (the one matching python) uses saxon:output to write an HTML version of the result tree to the file *keywords.html*. It uses the saxon: indent-spaces attribute, and, yes, it is not allowed on saxon:output without a namespace prefix. It also employs ordinary HTML tags, sorts the keyword elements, and applies the mode html template to print list items (li).

This functionality is provided in XSLT 2.0 in a rather different form using the new result-document instruction element. You'll learn about XSLT 2.0 and result-document in the next chapter.

The text result tree is printed on standard output, and the HTML result is written to a file. Perform the transformation by using:

```
saxon keywords.xml output.xsl
```

or using:

```
java -jar saxon.jar keywords.xml output.xsl
```

Here is the text output you will get:

```
Python 2.3 Keywords

and     assert break   class  continue
def     del    elif    else   except
exec    finally for    from   global
if      import in      is     lambda
not     or     pass    print  raise
return  try    while   yield
```

This is the HTML that is saved to *keywords.html*:

```
<html>
 <body>
  <h3>Python 2.3 Keywords</h3>
  <ol>
   <li>and</li>
   <li>assert</li>
   <li>break</li>
   <li>class</li>
   <li>continue</li>
   <li>def</li>
   <li>del</li>
   <li>elif</li>
   <li>else</li>
   <li>except</li>
   <li>exec</li>
   <li>finally</li>
   <li>for</li>
   <li>from</li>
   <li>global</li>
   <li>if</li>
   <li>import</li>
   <li>in</li>
   <li>is</li>
   <li>lambda</li>
   <li>not</li>
   <li>or</li>
   <li>pass</li>
   <li>print</li>
```

```
      <li>raise</li>
      <li>return</li>
      <li>try</li>
      <li>while</li>
      <li>yield</li>
    </ol>
  </body>
</html>
```

Invoking the Fallback Behavior

Immediately following saxon:output in output.xsl is the fallback element, followed by an instance of message. (This isn't the first time in this book that you've seen fallback and message working together.) A fallback element provides a fail-safe mechanism that will let you know when a processor can't accept an extension element. You must use fallback right after an extension element in order for it to work; it contains a template.

A message element can be used in any template, not just in fallback. It generally prints a message to standard output, but not, however, to the result tree (this behavior—where the message appears—is undefined in the XSLT spec, however). It has a single required attribute, terminate, which lets you specify whether, once encountered, processing should stop. The value of terminate must be yes or no.

You've run this stylesheet successfully with Saxon. Now you'll see what happens when you try it with another processor. Why not try MSXSL for a switch?

```
msxsl keywords.xml output.xsl
```

This command works only on Windows, by the way. MSXSL will give you this error report:

```
Python 2.3 Keywords

and      assert  break  class  continue
def      del     elif   else   except
exec     finally for    from   global
if       import  in     is     lambda
not      or      pass   print  raise
return   try     while  yield

Error occurred while executing stylesheet 'output.xsl'.

Code:   0x80004005
ERROR: saxon:output not available!
```

MSXSL performed the regular transformation, but when it encountered saxon: output, it hiccupped. If saxon:output were first in the top template, the MSXSL processor would just blurt out its error messages, including your custom message, then terminate.

The error message that *output.xsl* produces, however, isn't all that different from the behavior you would get if you didn't include `fallback`. An interesting case would be to write an empty `fallback` element, which would silently ignore the error; then you just wouldn't get the second output file! You can try it by transforming *keywords.xml* with *nofall.xsl* in *examples/ch15* (not shown here).

Checking for Extension Availability

XSLT provides two functions that allow you to check for the availability of extension elements or functions. Both the `element-available( )` and `function-available( )` functions take a single argument, a string identifying the element or function by QName. Example 15-9, *check.xsl*, uses both these functions in a simple way.

Example 15-9. A stylesheet testing for the availability of extensions

```
<xsl:stylesheet version="1.0" xmlns:xsl="http://www.w3.org/1999/XSL/Transform"
xmlns:saxon="http://icl.com/saxon"
xmlns:msxsl="urn:schemas-microsoft-com:xslt"
xmlns:date="http://exslt.org/dates-and-times"
xmlns:math="http://exslt.org/math"
xmlns:xalan="http://xml.apache.org/xalan">
<xsl:output method="text" encoding="UTF-8"/>
<xsl:param name="avail"/>

<xsl:template match="/">
<xsl:choose>
 <xsl:when test="element-available($avail)">
  Element <xsl:value-of select="$avail"/> is available with this processor.
 </xsl:when>
 <xsl:when test="function-available($avail)">
  Function <xsl:value-of select="$avail"/> is available with this processor.
 </xsl:when>
 <xsl:otherwise>
  The element or function you requested is not available with this processor.
 </xsl:otherwise>
</xsl:choose>

</xsl:template>

</xsl:stylesheet>
```

check.xsl tests to see whether a particular extension element or function is available with a given processor. There isn't much to this stylesheet by itself, but it could easily be included with another stylesheet using the `include` mechanism.

Here's a simple test (use any XML document on the command line you like; it doesn't really matter):

```
saxon keywords.xml check.xsl avail=date:date
```

This command line tests to see if the Instant Saxon processor (saxon) can support the EXSLT function date:date( ). The result should be:

```
Function date:date is available with this processor.
```

Now try a Saxon extension function:

```
saxon keywords.xml check.xsl avail=saxon:assign
```

The answer is as follows:

```
Element saxon:assign is available with this processor.
```

Finally, try an MSXSL function:

```
saxon keywords.xml check.xsl avail=msxsl:node-set
```

The news you'll get back won't be unexpected:

```
The element or function you requested is not available with this processor.
```

Summary

This chapter has highlighted a sample of extensions offered by Xalan, Saxon, and EXSLT. You learned how to use several extensions (including an extension attribute and extension element) and several extension functions. You also learned how to use the fallback element, along with informative messages, which responds as directed if a processor does not support a given extension element. You can also test for extension functions and elements using the function-available( ) and element-available( ) functions from XSLT.

This chapter did not explore how to write your own extensions, but that's because it is beyond the scope for an introductory text and is somewhat different for every processor. Chapter 8 in Doug Tidwell's *XSLT* (O'Reilly) provides some guidance on writing extensions if you are interested in learning how to do this.

The next chapter presents a brief introduction to XSLT 2.0 and XPath 2.0.

CHAPTER 16

XSLT 2.0 and XPath 2.0

Although XSLT 2.0 and XPath 2.0 are still working drafts at the time of this writing, they are nearing completion, and there are some partial implementations available for these specs, such as Saxon 7.7 (check *http://saxon.sourceforge.net* for the latest version). This chapter attempts to summarize some of the more interesting features in these specifications, and demonstrates a few of them, too. But it won't be an exhaustive review of XSLT 2.0 or XPath 2.0, partly because these specs are still changing, and partly because an exhaustive review would take up a whole book by itself.

 The material in this chapter is based on the May 2003 working drafts of XSLT 2.0 and XPath 2.0, so it is possible that things will change in those drafts by the time you read this.

First of all, I'll highlight some of the changes that have been made since XSLT 1.0 and XPath 1.0, and I'll also mention a few of the features that have been added. Then I'll show you how you can put some of this new stuff to work today.

Rather than just two specifications, as is the case with XSLT 1.0 and XPath 1.0, the next versions of these specs are broken into five documents. Three new documents have been broken out for those features of XSLT and XPath that also support the XML Query Language (see *http://www.w3.org/TR/xquery/*).

XSL Transformations (XSLT) Version 2.0 (see http://www.w3.org/TR/xslt20/)
This evolution of the XSLT 1.0 specification is about twice as long as its predecessor. Although it's lengthy, I think this spec is clearer than 1.0, and it even sports a glossary.

XML Path Language (XPath) 2.0 (see http://www.w3.org/TR/xpath20/)
XPath has also evolved; the data model and functions are now documented in separate specifications.

XQuery 1.0 and XPath 2.0 Data Model (see http://www.w3.org/TR/xpath-datamodel/)
XPath has an upgraded data model that applies to XQuery as well. The terminology used to describe the data model has been changed and refined, so although

the data model for XSLT 2.0 is technically very similar to XPath 1.0, it is now described in more formal language.

XQuery 1.0 and XPath 2.0 Functions and Operators (see http://www.w3.org/TR/xpath-functions/)

Many functions that also support XQuery have been added to XPath. The function library has tripled in size, from under 30 functions in 1.0 to over 100 in 2.0 (counting functions in all signatures).

XSLT 2.0 and XQuery 1.0 Serialization (see http://www.w3.org/TR/xslt-xquery-serialization/)

This description of how result trees are serialized, which was previously an integral part of the XSLT spec, has been pulled out into a separate document so that it can be used in non-XSLT environments such as XQuery.

New XSLT 2.0 Features

Listed below are some of the new features added to the XSLT 2.0 specification:

Terminology changes

XSLT makes a number of refinements to terminology, and a glossary is now available at the end of the specification. For example, the term *result tree fragment* has been replaced by the term *temporary tree*. A temporary tree is natively a sequence of nodes, obviating the need for an extension function for node-sets to cast a result tree fragment to a node-set. Another example: a template is now known as a *sequence constructor*. A sequence can contain nodes or atomic values.

XHTML output

In addition to xml, html, and text, XSLT 2.0 adds the xhtml output method (see Section 20 of XSLT 2.0 and Section 5 of the serialization specification).

Multiple result trees

One of the most welcome new features in XSLT 2.0 is the ability to produce multiple result trees, rather than just one. This is accomplished through the result-document element. This element is similar to the saxon:output element you saw in the last chapter, though it has somewhat different attributes. You will see an example of this in the section "Multiple Result Trees," later in this chapter. Also see Section 19.1 of XSLT 2.0.

Regular expressions

A regular expression describes text with a pattern made up of characters that have special meaning within the expression. The analyze-string element, together with matching-substring and non-matching-substring child elements, allows you to analyze a string using a regular expression. The XPath 2.0 functions matches( ), replace( ), and tokenize( ) also make use of regular expressions. See "Using Regular Expressions" later in this chapter for an example. See also Section 15 of XSLT 2.0.

Validation support for XML Schema

A schema-aware XSLT processor supports validation using W3C XML Schema. This support is not required, however. There is also a conformance level for a basic XSLT processor that does not support validation. See Section 21 of XSLT 2.0. XML Schema support, in fact, goes well beyond just validation (in the sense of rejecting invalid documents). Once a source document has been processed by a schema, you can use information about the types of different nodes. For example, you could write a template rule that processes any attribute of type date.

Date format

Just as numbers could be formatted with the `format-number( )` function and the `decimal-format` element in XSLT 1.0, a date may be formatted with the `format-date( )` function used with the `date-format` element. See Section 16.5 of XSLT 2.0.

Character maps

A new character map declaration using the `character-map` element enables a stylesheet to support sets of characters for output. Similarly, the `output-character` element maps a single character to a string for output. This functionality is an improvement over the `disable-output-escaping` attribute functionality in XSLT 1.0. See Section 20.1 of XSLT 2.0.

Grouping

Using the new `for-each-group` element, XSLT 2.0 now offers a built-in grouping feature, rather than depending on common yet nonstandard approaches used in XSLT 1.0. See "Grouping in XSLT 2.0" in this chapter as well as Section 14 of XSLT 2.0.

Parameters in new places

You can pass a parameter to the template rule having the highest import precedence using `with-param` as a child of the `apply-imports` element. You can also pass parameters using the `next-match` element, which matches other template rules beside the current one (that also happens to have the highest priority). See Section 6.7 of XSLT 2.0.

New elements

Besides those already mentioned, XSLT 2.0 adds a half dozen other elements:

`function` *element*

Defines a stylesheet function. Stylesheet functions are similar to named templates, except that rather than invoking them using a `call-template` instruction, you can invoke them using a function call anywhere in an XPath expression. This makes them more versatile than templates—for example, you can write a function to compute a sort key.

`import-schema` *element*

Imports an XML Schema for validation by a schema-aware XSLT processor.

`namespace` *element*

Creates a namespace node. This is useful (in rare cases) when you need to decide at runtime which namespaces to include in the result tree.

`next-match` *element*

Overrides a template rule with another rule of lower priority or precedence; works with the current or imported stylesheets.

`sequence` *element*

Constructs a sequence of nodes or atomic values.

`sort-key` *element*

Declares a named sort key; holds one or more sort elements.

New attributes on existing elements

A number of new attributes appear on elements that have existed since XSLT 1.0 and are listed here:

`as` *attribute*

Added to `key`, `param`, `template`, and `variable`, this attribute specifies the required type for the result.

`collation` *attribute*

Identifies a named collation for ordering strings; this attribute has now been added to the `key` and `sort` elements.

`copy-namespaces` *attribute*

Available on the `copy` and `copy-of` elements with a value of yes or no. The default is yes.

`disable-output-escaping` *attribute*

Now appears on `attribute`; it appeared only on `text` and `value-of` in XSLT 1.0.

`type` *attribute*

Appears on `attribute`, `copy`, `copy-of`, and `element` in order to associate with the item type from a schema.

`undeclare-namespaces` *attribute*

Appears on `output` to specify whether to undeclare namespaces in the output. This feature anticipates support for XML Namespaces 1.1, which allows namespaces to be undeclared.

`validation` *attribute*

Appears on `attribute`, `copy`, `copy-of`, and `element`, with one of four possible values: `lax`, `preserve`, `strict`, or `strip`. This is closely associated with the type attribute.

New attributes on output

A number of new attributes also have been added to the output element:

`escape-uri-attributes` *attribute*

Specifies whether a processor escapes URIs in HTML and XHTML; value must be yes or no.

`include-content-type` *attribute*

Specifies whether to add a `meta` element in HTML and XHTML output; value must be either yes or no.

name *attribute*

> An output declaration may now be labeled with a name attribute. This is used in conjunction with result-document which allows multiple result trees; these can either all use the same output format or use a variety of different output formats.

normalize-unicode *attribute*

> Indicates whether, yes or no, the Unicode output should use Normalization Form C (see *http://www.unicode.org/unicode/reports/tr15/*).

use-character-maps *attribute*

> Identifies a named character map defined by the character-map element.

That's just a few of the new features in XSLT 2.0; next, I'll discuss some of the new ones found in XPath 2.0.

New XPath 2.0 Features

Following are just a handful of some of the new features added to the XPath 2.0 specification:

Improved terminology

> XPath has tightened up its terminology, and a glossary will be available at the end of the specification in later drafts. For example, the result of an expression is now considered a sequence of zero or more items, and an item is either a node or an atomic value, such as an integer, as defined by XML Schema datatypes (see *http://www.w3.org/TR/xmlschema-2/*). This is much more than a terminology change. You can now have sequences of integers or strings (there are many more datatypes) as well as sequences of nodes.

New functions

> XPath 2.0 has over 100 functions, compared with 27 in XPath 1.0 (I'm counting functions with the same name but different signatures or argument lists as one function). They are too numerous to list in this book, but you can peruse them in the new functions and operators specification (see *http://www.w3.org/TR/xpath-functions/*).

Strongly typed

> XPath 2.0 has grown into a strongly typed language. It recognizes datatypes from XML Schema and also its own datatypes, such as xdt:anyAtomicType. See Section 2.4 of XPath 2.0.

New kind tests

> New kind tests are now offered that test kinds of nodes, such as document-node( ), element( ), and attribute( ); for example, document-node( ) matches the document node (root node in XSLT 1.0). You can also test with empty( ) and item( ). The occurrence indicators ? (zero or one), * (zero or more), and + (one or more) are also in the mix; for example, item( )* matches zero or more atomic values or nodes. See 2.4 in XPath 2.0.

Sequences and ranges

Sequence expressions allow you to specify a sequence of items that can be atomic values or nodes; for example, (100, 101, 102) will return a sequence of the atomic values 100, 101, and 102, in that order. Range expressions let you represent a range of items; for example, (100 to 110) is a range from 100 to 110. See Section 3.3 of XPath 2.0. You can also combine sequences of nodes with the union, intersect, and except operators. See Section 3.3.2 of XPath 2.0.

Comparison

XPath 2.0 adds new comparison operators, such as eq, ne, lt, le, gt, and ge, but you can still use =, !=, < as <, <= as <=, >, and >=. The node comparison operators is and isnot have also been added as well. Also new are << and >>, which test the order of nodes. The new operators are stricter about the type conversions they allow, and they should be faster and safer as a result. Strong typing means your errors are more likely to be reported at compile time rather than simply give you the wrong output. See Section 3.5 of XPath 2.0.

For and conditional expressions

For expressions make it possible to process a range of values in one step. For example, sum(for $i in //item return $i/price * $i/quantity) computes the sum of the value of price times quantity over all items. See Section 3.7 in XPath 2.0. Also, you can now use a construct such as if (value[1] gt value[2]) then value[1] else value[2] in expressions. See Section 3.8 in XPath 2.0.

Quantified expressions

XPath 2.0 has new keywords such as some, every, and satisfies, which allow you to test for partial or complete compliance with a given item; for example, if (every $i in //item satisfies $i < 1000) then.... See Section 3.9 of XPath 2.0.

Working with types

You can now test whether an item is an instance of a type; you can cast as a type (change the type) and check whether an item is castable (its type can change); for example, if ($x castable as xs:date) tests whether the string in $x is a valid date; you can also treat as a type (meaning temporarily treat a type as another type).

This is by no means a complete review of all the changes and additions to XSLT 2.0 or XPath 2.0—it's just a quick discussion of a good number of them. These are working drafts; it is possible that they will change somewhat before they become recommendations. Fortunately, you can start playing with some of the new features today by using Saxon 7.7 (or later), which is an experimental implementation of XSLT 2.0 and XPath 2.0. The remaining sections of this chapter will try out some of these features, the first of which is result-document element.

Multiple Result Trees

In the last chapter, you used the saxon:output extension element to create more than one result tree from a single stylesheet. XSLT 2.0 has integrated this functionality into the mainstream of the specification with the result-document element. The following example shows you how to use this element to produce three result trees from one source tree.

Example 16-1, the document *functions.xml* in *examples/ch16*, describes the new context-related functions from XPath 2.0.

Example 16-1. A document describing XPath 2.0 functions

```
<?xml version="1.0"?>

<functions type="context">
 <function>
  <name>fn:context-item( )</name>
 <description>Returns the context item.</description>
 </function>
 <function>
  <name>fn:position( )</name>
  <description>Returns the position of the context item within the sequence of items
currently being processed.</description>
 </function>
 <function>
  <name>fn:last( )</name>
  <description>Returns the number of items in the sequence of items currently being
processed.</description>
 </function>
 <function>
  <name>fn:current-dateTime( )</name>
  <description>Returns the current xs:dateTime.</description>
 </function>
 <function>
  <name>fn:current-date( )</name>
  <description>Returns the current xs:date.</description>
 </function>
 <function>
  <name>fn:current-time( )</name>
  <description>Returns the current xs:time.</description>
 </function>
 <function>
  <name>fn:default-collation( )</name>
  <description>Returns the value of the default collation property from the static
context.</description>
 </function>
 <function>
  <name>fn:implicit-timezone( )</name>
  <description>Returns the value of the implicit timezone property from the evaluation
context.</description>
 </function>
</functions>
```

The descriptions of the functions are from the specification. The `fn:position( )` and `fn:last( )` functions are the same as the `position( )` and `last( )` functions from XPath 1.0. The `fn:context-item( )` function is similar to the `current( )` function available from XSLT 1.0 and XSLT 2.0. Usually, a context item is the same as the current item, except when a predicate is involved.

 You don't need to worry about the namespace prefix `fn:` for functions, because you won't need to use it in XSLT. It's there because XPath can be used from other environments besides XSLT, and some may use different function libraries, so it's useful to use namespaces to distinguish the functions as being from different libraries.

Example 16-2, the *context.xsl* stylesheet, produces four result trees based on *functions.xml*. The default result tree is text, and the three others are for XML, HTML, and XHTML output, respectively.

Example 16-2. An XSLT 2.0 stylesheet that produces four kinds of output

```
<xsl:stylesheet version="2.0" xmlns:xsl="http://www.w3.org/1999/XSL/Transform">
<xsl:output method="text"/>
<xsl:output name="xml" method="xml" indent="yes"/>
<xsl:output name="html" method="html" indent="yes"/>
<xsl:output name="xhtml" method="html" indent="yes"/>
<xsl:param name="dir">file:///C:/LearningXSLT/examples/ch16</xsl:param>

<xsl:template match="functions">
 <xsl:text>XPath 2.0 Context Functions&#10;</xsl:text>
 <xsl:text>Date: </xsl:text>
 <xsl:value-of select="current-date( )"/>
 <xsl:text>&#10;</xsl:text>
 <xsl:apply-templates select="function" mode="text"/>
 <xsl:result-document format="xml" href="{$dir}/context.xml">
 <xsl:message terminate="no">Printing text result tree...</xsl:message>
  <list>
   <description>XPath 2.0 Context Functions</description>
   <date><xsl:value-of select="current-date( )"/></date>
    <xsl:message terminate="no">Printing XML result tree in functions.xml...</xsl:message>
    <xsl:apply-templates select="function" mode="xml"/>
  </list>
 </xsl:result-document>
 <xsl:result-document format="html" href="{$dir}/context.html">
  <xsl:message terminate="no">Printing HTML result tree in functions.html...</xsl:message>
  <html>
  <body>
  <h2>XPath 2.0 Context Functions</h2>
  <h3>Date: <xsl:value-of select="current-date( )"/></h3>
  <ul>
   <xsl:apply-templates select="function" mode="html"/>
  </ul>
  </body>
  </html>
```

Example 16-2. An XSLT 2.0 stylesheet that produces four kinds of output (continued)

```
  </xsl:result-document>
  <xsl:result-document format="xhtml" href="{$dir}/context-x.html">
   <xsl:message terminate="no">Printing XHTML result tree in functions-x.html...</xsl:
message>
   <html xmlns="http://www.w3.org/1999/xhtml">
   <body>
   <h2>XPath 2.0 Context Functions</h2>
   <h3>Date: <xsl:value-of select="current-date( )"/></h3>
   <ol>
    <xsl:apply-templates select="function" mode="xhtml"/>
   </ol>
   </body>
   </html>
  </xsl:result-document>
</xsl:template>

<xsl:template match="function" mode="text">
 <xsl:text> - </xsl:text>
 <xsl:value-of select="name"/>
 <xsl:text>&#10;</xsl:text>
</xsl:template>

<xsl:template match="function" mode="xml">
 <function><xsl:value-of select="name"/></function>
</xsl:template>

<xsl:template match="function" mode="html">
 <li><xsl:value-of select="name"/></li>
</xsl:template>

<xsl:template match="function" mode="xhtml">
 <li xmlns="http://www.w3.org/1999/xhtml"><xsl:value-of select="name"/></li>
</xsl:template>

</xsl:stylesheet>
```

The version attribute on stylesheet shows the 2.0 version number. There are four output elements, three of which are named. This allows a result-document element to reference an output element by name, hence to use the information in it. A global parameter named dir holds the name of the directory where three of the result trees are written as files. This information is referenced by the attribute value template {$dir} in the href attributes on the result-document elements. You could pass in a new value for the dir parameter if you want to change the destination of the output.

The template matching functions creates a text result tree, plus three other result trees inside result-document elements. Each result tree issues its own message using the message element. Each result tree also applies templates to a template matching function, though each in a different mode (text, xml, html, and xhtml). The different modes for each result help create an appropriate tree for each of the given formats. The new current-date( ) function is called in each result tree, too.

To get this to work, you need to use a full Java version of Saxon, preferably Version 7.7 or later, available from *http://saxon.sourceforge.net* or in the *examples/ch16* directory as saxon7-7.zip (the JAR file saxon7.jar has already been extracted from saxon7-7.zip). For specific instructions on how to download, install, and use Saxon with the Java interpreter, see the appendix.

Once everything is installed and working, you can type this command:

```
java -jar saxon7.jar functions.xml context.xsl
```

and you will get the following text result tree, plus messages about the other three:

```
Printing text result tree...
Printing XML result tree in context.xml...
Printing HTML result tree in context.html...
Printing XHTML result tree in context-x.html...
XPath 2.0 Context Functions
Date: 2003-08-26
 - fn:context-item( )
 - fn:position( )
 - fn:last( )
 - fn:current-dateTime( )
 - fn:current-date( )
 - fn:current-time( )
 - fn:default-collation( )
 - fn:implicit-timezone( )
```

The files that the three result-document elements produced contain the other result trees. The first one is *context.xml*:

```
<?xml version="1.0" encoding="UTF-8"?>
<list>
   <description>XPath 2.0 Context Functions</description>
   <date>2003-10-03</date>
   <function>fn:context-item( )</function>
   <function>fn:position( )</function>
   <function>fn:last( )</function>
   <function>fn:current-dateTime( )</function>
   <function>fn:current-date( )</function>
   <function>fn:current-time( )</function>
   <function>fn:default-collation( )</function>
   <function>fn:implicit-timezone( )</function>
</list>
```

The second is *context.html*, an HTML document that uses an unordered (bulleted) list:

```
<html>
   <body>
      <h2>XPath 2.0 Context Functions</h2>
      <h3>Date: 2003-10-03</h3>
      <ul>
         <li>fn:context-item( )</li>
         <li>fn:position( )</li>
         <li>fn:last( )</li>
         <li>fn:current-dateTime( )</li>
```

```
        <li>fn:current-date( )</li>
        <li>fn:current-time( )</li>
        <li>fn:default-collation( )</li>
        <li>fn:implicit-timezone( )</li>
      </ul>
    </body>
  </html>
```

And the third is *context-x.html*, an XHTML document that uses an ordered (numbered) list:

```
<html xmlns="http://www.w3.org/1999/xhtml">
  <body>
    <h2>XPath 2.0 Context Functions</h2>
    <h3>Date: 2003-10-03</h3>
    <ol>
      <li>fn:context-item( )</li>
      <li>fn:position( )</li>
      <li>fn:last( )</li>
      <li>fn:current-dateTime( )</li>
      <li>fn:current-date( )</li>
      <li>fn:current-time( )</li>
      <li>fn:default-collation( )</li>
      <li>fn:implicit-timezone( )</li>
    </ol>
  </body>
</html>
```

As you can see, result-document provides a great convenience creating more than one result tree from just one stylesheet. Next is an example that uses regular expressions.

Using Regular Expressions

Regular expressions allow you to define specific patterns for searching strings of text. XML Schema supports regular expressions, and XSLT 2.0 relies on XML Schema–style regular expressions. Table 16-1 shows a sampling of symbols used in regular expressions that XSLT 2.0 supports. The table represents only a few of the possibilities.

Table 16-1. Sample of regular expression symbols

Regular Expression	Description
.	Matches any character except a newline or carriage return.
*	Matches any character.
?	Matches any single character.
\s	Matches any whitespace character, including a space, tab, newline, or carriage return.
\S or [^\s] or [^#x20\t\n\r]	Matches any character except a whitespace character.
\d or [0-9]	Matches any digit.
\d{3}	Matches any three digits.

Table 16-1. Sample of regular expression symbols (continued)

Regular Expression	Description
\D or [^\d] or [^0-9]	Matches any character except a digit.
^	Matches the beginning of a line.
$	Matches the end of a line.
\Ll{5}	Matches any five lowercase letters.
\Lu{6}	Matches any six uppercase letters.
\P{1}	Matches any single punctuation character.

In regular expressions, you can mix these symbols with actual characters to form a search string. For example, using these symbols, you could match:

- A U.S.-style 9-digit ZIP code, such as 10048-1000 with \d{5}-\d{4}
- A U.S.-style 10-digit phone number, such as (800)555-1234 with (\d{3})\d{3}-\d{4}
- The word *The* at the beginning of a line, followed by a whitespace character, followed by any character, with the expression ^The\s*

XPath 2.0 adds three new functions for use with regular expressions: matches( ), replace( ), and tokenize( ). For more information on these new functions, see Section 7.5 of the functions and operators specification for XPath 2.0 and XQuery 1.0 at *http://www.w3.org/TR/xpath-functions/*. XSLT 2.0 offers the new analyze-string element. See Section 15 of the XSLT 2.0 spec at *http://www.w3.org/TR/xslt20/* for more information on that. I'll show you examples of the matches( ) and replace( ) functions, and the analyze-string element.

 The tokenize( ) function is not demonstrated in this chapter. It breaks a string into tokens. The tokens are separated by a regular expression such as by one or more spaces (\s+).

The matches( ) Function

The function matches( ) is new in XPath 2.0. This function returns an xs:boolean value that indicates whether the value in the first argument matches the regular expression in the value of the second argument. The stylesheet *match.xsl*, in Example 16-3, uses the matches( ) function to test whether a string matches a regular expression.

Example 16-3. A stylesheet matching on a regular expression

```
<xsl:stylesheet version="2.0" xmlns:xsl="http://www.w3.org/1999/XSL/Transform">
<xsl:output method="xml" indent="yes"/>

<xsl:template match="functions">
 <xsl:element name="list">
  <xsl:element name="description">XPath 2.0 Context Functions</xsl:element>
  <xsl:element name="date">
   <xsl:value-of select="current-date( )"/>
  </xsl:element>
   <xsl:apply-templates select="function"/>
 </xsl:element>
</xsl:template>

<xsl:template match="function">
 <xsl:copy>
  <xsl:if test="matches(name,'^fn:')">
   <xsl:value-of select="substring(name, 4)"/>
  </xsl:if>
 </xsl:copy>
</xsl:template>

</xsl:stylesheet>
```

The first template rule uses a new XPath 2.0 function, `current-date( )`, to insert the current date into a `date` element in the result tree, then it applies templates for `function` elements. In the second template rule, the first argument of `matches( )` is `name`—a child node of `function`. The content of `name` is the string that this function attempts to match. The second argument is a regular expression. `^fn:` looks for the letters *fn:* at the beginning of the line (`^`). If `matches( )` finds `^fn:` and returns true, the `value-of` element in the template of `if` writes a substring from the content of `name` beginning from the fourth character, thus eliminating `fn:`.

Transform *functions.xml* with *match.xsl* with:

```
java -jar saxon7.jar functions.xml match.xsl
```

and you will see this result:

```
<?xml version="1.0" encoding="UTF-8"?>
<list>
    <description>XPath 2.0 Context Functions</description>
    <date>2003-10-03</date>
    <function>context-item( )</function>
    <function>position( )</function>
    <function>last( )</function>
    <function>current-dateTime( )</function>
    <function>current-date( )</function>
    <function>current-time( )</function>
    <function>default-collation( )</function>
    <function>implicit-timezone( )</function>
</list>
```

The replace( ) Function

The new replace( ) function in XPath 2.0 returns the value of the first argument with every substring matched by the regular expression in the second argument, replaced by the string in the third argument. Example 16-4, the stylesheet *replace.xsl*, will show you how it works.

Example 16-4. A stylesheet replacing regular expressions

```
<xsl:stylesheet version="2.0" xmlns:xsl="http://www.w3.org/1999/XSL/Transform">
<xsl:output method="xml" indent="yes"/>

<xsl:template match="functions">
 <xsl:element name="list">
  <xsl:element name="description">XPath 2.0 Context Functions</xsl:element>
  <xsl:element name="date">
   <xsl:value-of select="current-date( )"/>
  </xsl:element>
   <xsl:apply-templates select="function"/>
 </xsl:element>
</xsl:template>

<xsl:template match="function">
 <xsl:copy>
  <xsl:value-of select="replace(name, '^fn:', '')"/>
 </xsl:copy>
</xsl:template>

</xsl:stylesheet>
```

The first argument of replace( ) is the name element, meaning the content of the name element. The second argument is the regular expression you are looking for, and the third argument is the string you want to replace the second argument with. If you process *functions.xml* with:

```
java -jar saxon7.jar functions.xml replace.xsl
```

it will produce the same output as *match.xsl*.

The analyze-string Element

Finally, the instruction element analyze-string is also new in XSLT 2.0. This element allows you to select a string using the select attribute, and then search that string with a regular expression defined in a regex attribute. Two children can then follow analyze-string: matching-substring to define what happens when analyze-string finds a matching substring, and can follow non-matching-substring to define what happens when analyze-string finds a non-matching substring. You can use either matching-substring or non-matching-substring or both. (Also, analyze-string accepts fallback as a child.)

The *regex.xsl* stylesheet, Example 16-5, uses analyze-string to handle some text in a node.

Example 16-5. A stylesheet performing more complex regular expressions processing

```
<xsl:stylesheet version="2.0" xmlns:xsl="http://www.w3.org/1999/XSL/Transform">
<xsl:output method="xml" indent="yes"/>

<xsl:template match="functions">
 <xsl:element name="list">
  <xsl:element name="description">XPath 2.0 Context Functions</xsl:element>
  <xsl:element name="date">
   <xsl:value-of select="current-date()"/>
  </xsl:element>
   <xsl:apply-templates select="function"/>
 </xsl:element>
</xsl:template>

<xsl:template match="function">
 <xsl:copy>
 <xsl:analyze-string select="name" regex="^fn:">
  <xsl:matching-substring></xsl:matching-substring>
  <xsl:non-matching-substring>
   <xsl:value-of select="."/>
  </xsl:non-matching-substring>
  </xsl:analyze-string>
 </xsl:copy>
</xsl:template>

</xsl:stylesheet>
```

The second template searches the content of function elements in the source tree. When analyze-string finds the string fn: at the beginning of a line, it replaces the matching substring with nothing in the result tree and outputs the matching substring as is using value-of.

Execute the transformation with this command:

```
java -jar saxon7.jar functions.xml regex.xsl
```

and you will get the following result:

```
<?xml version="1.0" encoding="UTF-8"?>
<list>
    <description>XPath 2.0 Context Functions</description>
    <date>2003-08-26</date>
    <function>context-item()</function>
    <function>position()</function>
    <function>last()</function>
    <function>current-dateTime()</function>
    <function>current-date()</function>
    <function>current-time()</function>
    <function>default-collation()</function>
    <function>implicit-timezone()</function>
</list>
```

This same effect can be achieved by using replace( ) or even matches( ), as you saw earlier. The main reason for using analyze-string is when the replacement text contains elements—for example, you could use analyze-string to replace a line break by a br tag.

These examples give you a taste of what is possible using regular expressions. For more information on the regular expressions used by XML Schema, and XSLT 2.0 by association, see *http://www.w3.org/TR/xmlschema-0.html#regexAppendix* and *http://www.w3.org/TR/xmlschema-2.html#regexs*.

Grouping in XSLT 2.0

Grouping in XSLT is the process by which you can group nodes based on a given criterion. In XSLT 1.0, the process is a little complicated and requires somewhat elaborate expressions, often employing the preceding-sibling axes to check whether a node belongs to a group. You could also group nodes with a key using the Muenchian method, which was demonstrated in Chapter 11. You can also read about how to do XSLT 1.0 grouping in Chapter 6 of Doug Tidwell's *XSLT* (O'Reilly) or in Chapter 9 of Michael Kay's *XSLT Programmer's Reference, Second Edition* (Wrox). I prefer grouping in XSLT 2.0 because it is *much* simpler and easier to explain, the ease of which probably grew out of my experience with grouping in Version 1.0.

Grouping in XSLT 1.0 usually brings the for-each instruction element into service. XSLT 2.0 has a new instruction element called for-each-group that makes grouping a relative snap. I'll show you how in the following example.

Glance at *group2.xml*, in Example 16-6, which lumps the XPath 2.0's context-related functions into two piles by labeling them with a type attribute.

Example 16-6. A list of XPath 2.0 context-related functions

```
<?xml version="1.0"?>

<list>
 <description>XPath 2.0 Context Functions</description>
 <date>2003-10-03</date>
 <function type="new">context-item( )</function>
 <function type="new">current-date( )</function>
 <function type="new">current-dateTime( )</function>
 <function type="new">current-time( )</function>
 <function type="new">default-collation( )</function>
 <function type="new">implicit-timezone( )</function>
 <function type="legacy">last( )</function>
 <function type="legacy">position( )</function>
</list>
```

The eight functions in this list are either legacy or new functions. The *group2.xsl* stylesheet, in Example 16-7, groups the functions in *group2.xml* according to the content of the type attribute.

Example 16-7. A stylesheet grouping elements using XSLT 2.0

```
<xsl:stylesheet version="2.0" xmlns:xsl="http://www.w3.org/1999/XSL/Transform">
<xsl:output method="xml" indent="yes"/>

<xsl:template match="list">
<xsl:copy>
 <xsl:for-each-group select="function" group-by="@type">
  <functions type="{@type}">
   <xsl:value-of select="current-group()" separator=", "/>
  </functions>
 </xsl:for-each-group>
</xsl:copy>
</xsl:template>

</xsl:stylesheet>
```

The for-each-group function selects the node-set to group with the select attribute—all function children of list, that is. The group-by attribute determines the key for grouping, which, in this case, is the content of the type attribute in the source. The functions literal result element uses an attribute value template to reflect the value of the type attribute.

The value-of element's select attribute uses the current-group( ) function—also a new kid on the block in XSLT 2.0—to keep track of which group is which. The separator attribute is also a new addition to XSLT 2.0. It tells the XSLT 2.0 processor to write a comma followed by a space after each found node is sent to the result tree.

 In XSLT 1.0, value-of outputs only the first node of a returned node-set in string form; in XSLT 2.0, all nodes can be returned, so you have to plan accordingly.

You might guess correctly that for-each-group has several other attributes, which it does, namely, group-adjacent, group-starting-with, group-ending-with, and collation. I'm not going to cover them here, but you can read more about for-each-group and its attributes in Section 14 of the XSLT 2.0 specification.

Use this command to transform *group.xml*:

```
java -jar saxon7.jar group2.xml group2.xsl
```

The result is two lists of functions, grouped and comma-separated, in functions elements:

```
<?xml version="1.0" encoding="UTF-8"?>
<list>
   <functions type="new">context-item( ), current-date( ), current-dateTime( ),
current-time( ), default-collation( ), implicit-timezone( )</functions>
   <functions type="legacy">last( ), position( )</functions>
</list>
```

This example should give you a feel of how to group nodes in XSLT 2.0. In the example that follows, you will learn how to use the new top-level function element.

Extension Functions

You learned about external extension functions in the last chapter. You can now add extension functions on the stylesheet level in XSLT 2.0 using the function element. These are called *stylesheet functions*, but they work like any extension function in an expression. The difference is that they are completely portable between one XSLT 2.0 processor and another.

Example 16-8, *function.xsl*, uses function to declare a stylesheet function.

Example 16-8. Creating extension functions in XSLT 2.0

```
<xsl:stylesheet version="2.0" xmlns:xsl="http://www.w3.org/1999/XSL/Transform"
xmlns:xs="http://www.w3.org/2001/XMLSchema-datatypes"
xmlns:wy="http://www.wyeast.net/functions">
<xsl:output method="text"/>
<xsl:function name="wy:kilometers">
 <xsl:param name="miles" as="xs:decimal"/>
 <xsl:sequence select="$miles * 1.609347"/>
</xsl:function>

<xsl:template match="/">
 <xsl:apply-templates select="trip"/>
</xsl:template>

<xsl:template match="trip">
 <xsl:apply-templates select="distance"/>
</xsl:template>

<xsl:template match="distance">
 <xsl:text>The distance from </xsl:text>
 <xsl:value-of select="location"/>
 <xsl:text> to </xsl:text>
 <xsl:value-of select="destination"/>
 <xsl:text> is </xsl:text>
 <xsl:value-of select="round(wy:kilometers(miles))"/>
 <xsl:text> kilometers.&#10;</xsl:text>
</xsl:template>

</xsl:stylesheet>
```

When I tested this, it appeared that stylesheet functions must have at least one argument, but this may not be the case, given that 2.0 is still in the early stages. Stylesheet functions must also be identified with a QName that uses a prefix (this is to ensure that user-defined functions don't clash with system-defined functions). The namespace URI and prefix associated with the QName in this example is `http://www.wyeast.net/functions` and `wy:`, respectively. It's declared on the `stylesheet` element.

The `function` element must be on the top level and declares the stylesheet function named `wy:kilometers()`. The function performs a simple conversion of miles to kilometers by accepting a single parameter, `miles`. Parameters for stylesheet functions are defined with `param` elements but cannot have default values. The new `as` attribute on `param` declares the value of miles as an `xs:decimal` value, according to the boundaries set by XML Schema datatypes (the namespace is declared on the document element).

The new XSLT 2.0 `sequence` element adds a sequence of nodes or atomic values to the result tree. In this case, it returns a product (a single atomic value) and works much like `value-of`. In other situations, you can add existing nodes to a sequence with this element, not just new ones. The factor for converting miles to kilometers (1.609347) comes from the National Institute of Standards and Technology (NIST), and is based on the U.S. survey foot (see *http://physics.nist.gov/Pubs/SP811/appenB8.html*).

The `wy:kilometers()` function is called later in the stylesheet in a `value-of` element. It takes a miles node as an argument, and its return value is rounded up or down with the `round()` function. The result is output as text, embedded in a sentence formed from the nodes in the source tree.

Soon, you'll apply this stylesheet to *trip.xml,* shown in Example 16-9, which holds the road mileage between several U.S. cities.

Example 16-9. Mileage between selected U.S. cities

```
<?xml version="1.0"?>

<trip>
 <distance>
  <location>Tucson</location>
  <destination>Flagstaff</destination>
  <miles>253</miles>
 </distance>
 <distance>
  <location>Portland</location>
  <destination>Medford</destination>
  <miles>272</miles>
 </distance>
 <distance>
  <location>Denver</location>
  <destination>Colorado Springs</destination>
  <miles>67</miles>
 </distance>
</trip>
```

Perform the transformation with:

```
java -jar saxon7.jar trip.xml function.xsl
```

You will see this outcome on your screen:

```
The distance from Tucson to Flagstaff is 407 kilometers.
The distance from Portland to Medford is 438 kilometers.
The distance from Denver to Colorado Springs is 108 kilometers.
```

The wy:kilometers( ) stylesheet function may be reused as often as you need it in this stylesheet. A stylesheet function can also be included or imported from another stylesheet.

Summary

XSLT 2.0 and XPath 2.0 offer an almost overwhelming number of new features. Some have complained about the new versions of XSLT and XPath on this count. Personally, I like most of the new offerings and, fortunately, no one is forced to adopt all the new functionality. Nevertheless, the terminology will definitely require devotees to plow deeply into the new specifications in order to get a grip on it.

This chapter lightly introduced you to many highlights from these new technologies. It also walked you through how to output multiple result documents, define and use regular expressions, use grouping, and create stylesheet functions.

The next chapter shows programmers how to use APIs to write your own interface to an XSLT processor.

CHAPTER 17

Writing an XSLT Processor Interface

You've had a chance to use a number of XSLT processors in this book, such as Xalan C++ and Instant Saxon. Now you'll get the opportunity to write your own Java or C# XSLT processor with a simple command-line interface. Actually, you won't be writing an XSLT processor from scratch, but rather an interface to a processor that is available through Application Programming Interfaces (APIs).

This chapter assumes that you are already an experienced programmer in either or both of these languages. The nice thing about writing your own processor at the API level is that you have control over the interface and how things work. Of course, such a task requires much more effort on your part, but if a high level of control matters enough to you, the effort will be worthwhile.

The first part of the chapter walks through the creation of a Java XSLT processor using Sun's Java API for XML Processing (JAXP). The second part guides you in creating a processor with C# using Microsoft's .NET Framework 1.1 SDK. You don't need an interactive development environment (IDE) to work with these examples— they require only a text editor and the javac or csc compilers. I'll show you where to get those compilers if you don't already have them.

Running an XSLT Processor from Java

JAXP comes standard with Java Version 1.4 or enterprise edition. JAXP includes the APIs you'll need to create an XSLT processor. You must use Version 1.4 or a later Java Runtime Environment (JRE) to run this example as it is described (more on this later). You can download the latest Java JRE or Software Development Kit (SDK) from *http://java.sun.com*.

To write a processor with JAXP, you need two extension packages: javax.xml. transform and javax.xml.transform.stream. There are other packages available to help you do more things in XSLT, but we'll focus on these packages for the sake of simplicity. You can consult the API documentation for these packages at *http://java. sun.com/j2se/1.4/docs/api/index.html*.

The Moxie Source Code

In *examples/ch17*, you will find the source code for the Moxie XSLT processor, *Moxie.java*. This program has only 68 lines because the heavy lifting is done by classes from Java extension packages.

Example 17-1 lists the source code.

Example 17-1. The Moxie code for running an XSLT processor

```
/*
 * Moxie JAXP XSLT processor
 */

import java.io.File;
import java.io.FileOutputStream;
import javax.xml.transform.OutputKeys;
import javax.xml.transform.Transformer;
import javax.xml.transform.TransformerFactory;
import javax.xml.transform.stream.StreamResult;
import javax.xml.transform.stream.StreamSource;

public class Moxie {

    public static void main(String[] args) throws Exception {

        /* Output file flag */
        boolean file = false;

        /* Default system property for Xalan processor */
        System.setProperty("javax.xml.transform.TransformerFactory",
            "org.apache.xalan.processor.TransformerFactoryImpl");

        /* Usage strings */
        String info = "Moxie JAXP XSLT processor";
        String usage = "\nUsage: java -jar moxie.jar";
        String parms = " source stylesheet [result]";

        /* Test arguments */
        if (args.length == 0) {
            System.out.println(info + usage + parms);
            System.exit(1);
        } else if (args.length == 3) {
            file = true;
        } else if (args.length > 3) {
            System.out.println("Too many arguments; exit.");
            System.exit(1);
        }

        /* XML source document and stylesheet */
        File source = new File(args[0]);
        File stylesheet = new File(args[1]);
```

Example 17-1. The Moxie code for running an XSLT processor (continued)

```
        /* Set up source and result streams */
        StreamSource src = new StreamSource(source);
        StreamSource style = new StreamSource(stylesheet);
        StreamResult out;
        if (file) {
            FileOutputStream outFile = new FileOutputStream(args[2]);
            out = new StreamResult(outFile);
        } else {
            out = new StreamResult(System.out);
        }

        /* Create transformer */
        TransformerFactory factory = TransformerFactory.newInstance( );
        Transformer xf = factory.newTransformer(style);

        /* Set output encoding property */
        xf.setOutputProperty(OutputKeys.ENCODING, "US-ASCII"); // encoding
        xf.setOutputProperty(OutputKeys.INDENT, "yes");        // indent

        /* Perform the transformation */
        xf.transform(src, out);

    }

}
```

To an experienced Java programmer, this code should readily make sense, but just to make sure the code is comprehensible, I've provided the following discussions that dissect each part of the program.

Looking at the Moxie Code

Moxie imports seven classes at the beginning of the program:

```
import java.io.File;
import java.io.FileOutputStream;
import javax.xml.transform.OutputKeys;
import javax.xml.transform.Transformer;
import javax.xml.transform.TransformerFactory;
import javax.xml.transform.stream.StreamResult;
import javax.xml.transform.stream.StreamSource;
```

The first two classes are from the java.io package. The three classes that follow are from the javax.xml.transform extension package, and the two after that are from javax.xml.transform.stream.

The File class handles the input files (the source XML document and the stylesheet), and FileOutputStream helps write an output file from the result tree of the transformation. TransformerFactory assists in creating a new instance of Transformer class, which actually performs the transformations. OutputKeys lets you submit values to the transformer that normally come from attributes on the output element, such as the method or encoding attributes. The remaining classes, StreamResult and StreamSource, are holders for streams representing the result and source trees, respectively.

Next in the program, the class Moxie is defined as well as the main( ) method that makes everything happen. The first thing that's done is to create a boolean called file that acts as a flag to tell the processor whether output will be sent to a file:

```
/* Output file flag */
  boolean file = false;
```

This flag is set to true if a third argument appears on the command line (explained shortly).

The next thing that you see in the program is a call to the setProperty( ) method from the System class:

```
/* Default system property for the Xalan processor */
System.setProperty("javax.xml.transform.TransformerFactory", "org.apache.xalan.
processor.TransformerFactoryImpl");
```

This method is not required, but I've included it to illustrate a point. The Xalan processor from Apache is the default XSLT engine underneath JAXP's hood. This system property sets the transformation engine to Xalan for JAXP explicitly, but it is already done automatically, so it is unnecessary. It is there so that if you want to change the system property, you can easily do so. The system property for Xalan is org.apache.xalan.processor.TransformerFactoryImpl. You can change the property to Saxon Version 7 or above with the property net.sf.saxon.TransformerFactoryImpl, or you can change it to jd.xslt with jd.xml.xslt.trax.TransformerFactoryImpl. If you change the system property to Saxon 7, you have to add *saxon7.jar* to the classpath; if you change it to jd.xslt, you need to add *jdxslt.jar*.

The arguments to main( ) are evaluated with an if statement. The three possible command-line arguments all represent files:

1. The first argument (args[0]) represents the XML source document that you want to transform.

2. The second argument (args[1]) is the XSLT stylesheet for performing the transformation.

3. The third argument (args[2]) is optional and, if used, represents the name of the file where the result tree will be stored. If absent, the result tree will appear on System.out (standard output or the screen). The file variable is of type boolean and indicates whether this third argument is present; if so, file is set to true (false by default) and a file will be written for the result tree.

These arguments are interpreted as files with the help of two File class constructors. Constructors for two StreamSource objects and two StreamResult objects are then called:

```
StreamSource src = new StreamSource(source);
StreamSource style = new StreamSource(stylesheet);
StreamResult out;
if (file) {
    FileOutputStream outFile = new FileOutputStream(args[2]);
    out = new StreamResult(outFile);
} else {
    out = new StreamResult(System.out);
}
```

This tells the program to interpret the input files as streams for the benefit of the transformer. (You could also represent these files as DOM documents by using the DOMSource class from javax.xml.transform.dom, or as SAX events with SAXSource class from javax.xml.transform.sax.) An if-else statement provides a little logic using the Boolean file that either sends the result stream to the screen or to a file.

After that, a factory is used to call a constructor and then create a new transformer:

```
TransformerFactory factory = TransformerFactory.newInstance( );
Transformer xf = factory.newTransformer(style);
```

Notice that the new transformer takes the stylesheet as an argument (style).

Next, the output encoding for the result tree is set to US-ASCII, and indention is set to yes by calling the setOutputProperty( ) method twice:

```
xf.setOutputProperty(OutputKeys.ENCODING, "US-ASCII"); // encoding
xf.setOutputProperty(OutputKeys.INDENT, "yes");         // indent
```

The setOutputProperty( ) method comes from the Transformer class. The OutputKeys class, discussed earlier, provides fields, such as ENCODING and INDENT, that correlate with the attributes of the XSLT output element (like encoding and indent). These method calls have the same effect as using the output element in a stylesheet like this:

```
<xsl:output encoding="US-ASCII" indent="yes"/>
```

Calling setOutputProperty( ) with ENCODING and a value of US-ASCII, and calling INDENT with yes, replaces the values of the encoding and indent attributes on the stylesheet's output element.

Finally, the program performs the actual transformation using the transform( ) method of the Transformer class:

```
xf.transform(src, out);
```

The first argument, src, is the source stream derived from the input file, and the second argument is the result tree. The stylesheet has already been associated with the instance of Transformer earlier in the code.

Running Moxie

To run Moxie, you need to have at least a JRE installed for Version 1.4 or later. A JRE is a Java Runtime Environment, a Java Virtual Machine (JVM) with core classes. If you want to change the code in *Moxie.java* and then recompile it, you need a Java 2 1.4 SDK to get the javac compiler, but to only run it, you just need a JRE.

To find out what version your JRE is, type the following line at a command-line prompt:

```
java -version
```

When I type this on my system, I get the following response:

```
java version "1.4.1_01"
Java(TM) 2 Runtime Environment, Standard Edition (build 1.4.1_01-b01)
Java HotSpot(TM) Client VM (build 1.4.1_01-b01, mixed mode)
```

If you get back something like this, it means you're in good shape. Now, while in *examples/ch17*, type this line:

```
java -jar moxie.jar
```

or this line:

```
java Moxie
```

You will get some usage information in response:

```
Moxie JAXP XSLT processor
Usage: java -jar moxie.jar source stylesheet [result]
```

If you've gotten this far without errors, you are ready to perform a transformation. The document *test.xml* contains a list of methods from the Transformer class, and *test.xsl* transforms it:

```
java -jar moxie.jar test.xml test.xsl
```

The result should look like this:

```
<?xml version="1.0" encoding="US-ASCII"?>
<methods>
<method>clearParameters( )</method>
<method>getErrorListener( )</method>
<method>getOutputProperties( )</method>
<method>getOutputProperty(String name)</method>
<method>getParameter(String name)</method>
<method>getURIResolver( )</method>
<method>setErrorListener(ErrorListener listener)</method>
<method>setOutputProperties(Properties oformat)</method>
<method>setOutputProperty(String name, String value)</method>
<method>setParameter(String name, Object value)</method>
<method>setURIResolver(URIResolver resolver)</method>
<method>transform(Source xmlSource, Result outputTarget)</method>
</methods>
```

By default, the transformer uses UTF-8 for output encoding, but setOutputProperty( ) overrides the default with US-ASCII, as you can see in the XML declaration of the result tree. The setOutputProperty( ) method also turns on indentation—without it, all elements in the result would run together.

If you'd like, you can also send the result tree to a file rather than to the screen. To accomplish this, you must submit a filename as the third argument on the command line, as you see here:

```
java -jar moxie.jar test.xml test.xsl moxie.xml
```

When you enter this line, Moxie writes the result tree to a file in the current directory using the FileOutputStream class.

You will also find a pair of files in *examples/ch17* that will help you: *moxie.bat* is a Windows batch file and *moxie.sh* is a Unix shell script. You can use either of them to reduce typing. For example, to perform the previous transformation at a Unix shell prompt, just type:

```
moxie.sh test.xml test.xsl moxie.xml
```

Or, at a Windows command prompt, type:

```
moxie test.xml test.xsl moxie.xml
```

You can alter the source file *Moxie.java* to your heart's content. For more information on JAXP, check the Javadocs for the following packages: javax.xml.parsers, javax.xml.transform, javax.xml.transform.dom, javax.xml.transform.sax, and javax. xml.transform.stream.

Compiling Moxie

If you alter *Moxie.java*, you will have to recompile it in order to get the new version to run. With Java Version 1.4 SDK installed, the Java compiler javac should be available to you if the compiler is in your path variable. Find out whether javac is there by typing the following on a command line:

```
javac
```

If the compiler is available, you will see usage information on the screen:

```
Usage: javac <options> <source files>
where possible options include:
  -g                        Generate all debugging info
  -g:none                   Generate no debugging info
  -g:{lines,vars,source}    Generate only some debugging info
  -O                        Optimize; may hinder debugging or enlarge class file
  -nowarn                   Generate no warnings
  -verbose                  Output messages about what the compiler is doing
  -deprecation              Output source locations where deprecated APIs are used
  -classpath <path>         Specify where to find user class files
  -sourcepath <path>        Specify where to find input source files
```

```
-bootclasspath <path>      Override location of bootstrap class files
-extdirs <dirs>            Override location of installed extensions
-d <directory>             Specify where to place generated class files
-encoding <encoding>       Specify character encoding used by source files
-source <release>          Provide source compatibility with specified release
-target <release>          Generate class files for specific VM version
-help                      Print a synopsis of standard options
```

To compile Moxie, enter:

```
javac Moxie.java
```

If the program compiles without errors, the compilation produces the class file *Moxie.class*. This class file contains the byte codes that the JRE interprets to run the program on your particular platform. You can then run the program by using this line:

```
java Moxie test.xml test.xsl
```

You can also recreate your JAR file with the jar tool using this command:

```
jar cfm moxie.jar META-INF/MANIFEST.MF Moxie.class
```

This line uses the jar tool to create (c) a new file (f) moxie.jar with a manifest file (m) called META-INF/MANIFEST.MF and with the class file *Moxie.class*. The manifest file conveys information to the Java interpreter when, for example, the interpreter is run with the -jar option. One such bit of information is what class holds the main( ) method. This information is passed on with the following field and value pair from the manifest file:

```
Main-Class: Moxie
```

You need this field and value in order for this command to work:

```
java -jar moxie.jar
```

Actually, there is an easier way to perform all these steps at once by using the Ant build tool.

Using Ant

Ant is a Java-based build tool sponsored by Apache (see *http://ant.apache.org*). Ant is easy to use and a time saver. If you are not familiar with Ant but would like to give it a try, go to *http://ant.apache.org/resources.html* for a list of FAQs, articles, presentations, and books that will help you get up to speed. A build file called *build.xml* is in *examples/ch17* and is available to you for building Moxie with Ant.

The file *build.xml* also depends on the *ant.properties* file (which is also in *examples/ch17*) to provide the location of the base directory where the builds take place. The base directory on Windows is assumed to be base.dir=c:/learningxslt/examples/ch17/; change the base directory to the correct location.

Assuming that you have downloaded Ant (I'm using Version 1.5.3), installed it, and placed it in your path, you should be able to type the following on a command line:

```
ant -version
```

You will get this information on your screen:

```
Apache Ant version 1.5.3 compiled on April 9 2003
```

If you type the word ant alone on a command line on Windows, while the current directory is *examples/ch17*, Ant automatically picks up the build file *build.xml* and performs the build, reporting the following to the screen:

```
Buildfile: build.xml

init:
    [delete] Deleting: C:\learningxslt\examples\ch16\moxie.jar

compile:
    [javac] Compiling 1 source file

jar:
      [jar] Building jar: C:\LearningXSLT\examples\ch16\moxie.jar

java:
     [java] Moxie JAXP XSLT processor
     [java] Usage: java -jar moxie.jar source stylesheet [result]
     [java] Java Result: 1

zip:
      [zip] Building zip: C:\LearningXSLT\examples\ch16\moxie.zip

finish:
     [copy] Copying 1 file to C:\LearningXSLT\examples\ch16\Backup

BUILD SUCCESSFUL
Total time: 7 seconds
```

In just one step, the build process defined by *build.xml* performs the following tasks:

1. Deletes the old *moxie.jar* file.
2. Compiles *Moxie.java*, if it has changed since the last build.
3. Builds a new JAR file for Moxie (*moxie.jar*).
4. Runs the Moxie program without arguments.
5. Creates a zip file that stores all of Moxie's resources in one spot (*moxie.zip*).
6. Copies *moxie.zip* to the directory *examples/ch17/Backup*.

Ant is growing in popularity and is being integrated into IDEs like jEdit, VisualAge, and even WebSphere (for links, see *http://ant.apache.org/manual/ide.html*). Ant also has tasks that do XSLT processing. Check it out at *http://ant.apache.org/manual/CoreTasks/style.html*. If you work much with Java, learning Ant will be well worth your time.

Other Java Resources

Eric Burke's *Java and XSLT* (O'Reilly) is a good place to turn for help with using XSLT with JAXP. Brett McLaughlin's *Java & XML, Second Edition* (O'Reilly) provides solid help with using Java APIs such as JAXP, SAX, DOM, JDOM, with XML. I also recommend that you get acquainted with Elliotte Rusty Harold's Java API XML Object Model or XOM, available for download from *http://www.xom.nu*. XOM is simple, easy to learn, and has taken many lessons from earlier APIs. XOM also has a package (nu.xom.xslt) for connecting to XSLT processors that support JAXP.

I'll now turn my attention to writing a simple XSLT processor with C#.

Writing an XSLT Processor with C#

C# is Microsoft's evolution of C++ and Java. It's similar to Java, so I've found it easy to learn. C# takes some interesting forks from Java, such as its use of properties, delegates, and so forth. However, exploring the virtues and foibles of C# is not my mission here. I'm just going to show you how to create an XSLT processor in C#—really only a simple command-line interface to .NET's underlying XSLT engine. It's easy to do after you have the right pieces.

C# comes as part of Microsoft's .NET Framework 1.1 SDK. You can download the Framework by following the .NET download link on *http://www.microsoft.com/net*. It's well over 100 megabytes, so it takes some time to download, especially if you don't have a fast Internet connection. This example uses Version 1.1 of the .NET Framework SDK. You need Windows 2000 or Windows XP for the Framework to even install, so either one is required for this exercise. .NET applications will run on other Windows operating systems, but that requires extra steps that I won't go into here.

 The Mono Project includes an open source version of C# that was declared code complete about mid-2003. The Mono version of C# runs on Windows, Linux, FreeBSD, and Mac OS X. I have not tested the C# code in this chapter with Mono, but it's likely to work.

The Pax Code

In *examples/ch17/Pax.cs*, you will also find the C# source code for the Pax XSLT processor, shown in Example 17-2.

Example 17-2. The Pax code for running an XSLT processor

```
/*
 * Pax C# XSLT Processor
 */

using System;
using System.IO;
```

Example 17-2. The Pax code for running an XSLT processor (continued)

```csharp
using System.Text;
using System.Xml;
using System.Xml.XPath;
using System.Xml.Xsl;

public class Pax
{

    public static void Main(String[ ] args)
    {

        // Output file flag
        bool file = false;

        // Usage strings
        string info = "Pax C# XSLT processor";
        string usage = "\nUsage: Pax source stylesheet [result]";

        // Test arguments
        if (args.Length == 0) {
            Console.WriteLine(info + usage);
            Environment.Exit(1);
        } else if (args.Length == 3) {
            // Third argument = output to file
            file = true;
        } else if (args.Length > 3) {
            Console.WriteLine("Too many arguments; exit.");
            Environment.Exit(1);
        }

        // Create the XslTransform
        XslTransform xslt = new XslTransform( );

        // Load the XML document, create XPathNavigator for transform
        XPathDocument doc = new XPathDocument(args[0]);
        XPathNavigator nav = doc.CreateNavigator( );

        // Load a stylesheet
        xslt.Load(args[1]);

        // Create the XmlTextWriter
        XmlTextWriter writer;
        if (file) {
            // Output to file with ASCII encoding
            writer = new XmlTextWriter(args[2], Encoding.ASCII);
        } else {
            // Output to console
            writer = new XmlTextWriter(Console.Out);
        }

        // Write XML declaration
        writer.WriteStartDocument( );
```

Example 17-2. The Pax code for running an XSLT processor (continued)

```
        // Set indentation to 1
        writer.Formatting = Formatting.Indented;
        writer.Indentation = 1;

        // Transform file
        xslt.Transform(nav, null, writer, null);

        // Close XmlTextWriter
        writer.Close( );

    }

}
```

Right away, you should notice that the code for *Pax.cs* and *Moxie.java* are very similar. A C# programmer should be able to figure out this code in a few glances, but again, if you're not familiar with C#, you can read the following section, which walks through the program nearly line by line.

Looking at the Pax Code

C# uses similar comment characters to Java. Instead of packages, C# uses namespaces, declaring them at the very beginning of the program with the reserved word using:

```
using System;
using System.IO;
using System.Text;
using System.Xml;
using System.Xml.XPath;
using System.Xml.Xsl;
```

You can't import individual classes in C# as you can in Java: you have to use the namespace name, such as System.Xml.Xsl, which exposes the entire object to the program.

Following this, the Pax class is defined and the Main( ) method is invoked. The command-line arguments to Main( ) are, as in *Moxie.java*, evaluated with an if statement. The three possible arguments represent files:

1. The first argument (args[0]) represents an XML source document that you want to transform.

2. The next argument (args[1]) represents the XSLT stylesheet for the transformation.

3. The optional third argument (args[2]) represents the name of the file where the result tree will be stored, if it is used. If it is absent, the result tree will appear on Console.Out (C#'s name for standard output or the screen). The file variable (of

type bool) indicates whether the third argument is present. file is set to false by default, but if the third argument is on the command line, file is set to true, and the program will know that a file should be written for the result tree.

The XslTransform class comes from the System.Xml.Xsl namespace. This line instantiates a transformer named xslt:

```
XslTransform xslt = new XslTransform( );
```

The classes that follow are in the System.Xml.Xpath namespace:

```
XPathDocument doc = new XPathDocument(args[0]);
XPathNavigator nav = doc.CreateNavigator( );
```

An XPathDocument provides a cache for performing the transformation, and the CreateNavigator( ) method from XPathDocument creates an XPathNavigator for navigating the cached document.

The Load( ) method from XslTransform loads the stylesheet from the second argument (args[1]) to the program:

```
xslt.Load(args[1]);
```

In C#, the XmlTextWriter class from the System.Xml namespace creates a writer for XML output:

```
XmlTextWriter writer;
if (file) {
    // Output to file with ASCII encoding
    writer = new XmlTextWriter(args[2], Encoding.ASCII);
} else {
    // Output to console
    writer = new XmlTextWriter(Console.Out);
}
```

If a third argument is present on the command line, file is set to true, and the output from the program will be written to a file encoded as US-ASCII. Encoding is a property from System.Text. Some other possible values for this property are UTF8 for UTF-8 output, Unicode for UTF-16 output, and BigEndianUnicode for UTF-16BE. If file is false, the output will be written to the console using IBM437 output, based on the codepage for a Windows command prompt.

The following line tells the writer to use an XML declaration in the output:

```
writer.WriteStartDocument( );
```

Without this line, no XML declaration is written. These lines of code set the indentation of the output to a single space per child element:

```
writer.Formatting = Formatting.Indented;
writer.Indentation = 1;
```

Formatting and Indentation are properties from the XmlTextWriter class. The next line performs the actual transformation:

```
xslt.Transform(nav, null, writer);
```

The XslTranform instance xslt loaded the stylesheet earlier with its Load( ) method. The first argument to Transform( ) provides the name of an instance of an XpathNavigator object, and the third argument is the name of an instance of an XmlTextWriter object. The second argument, which is null, can use an XsltArgumentList to provide a list of parameters or extension objects to the transform. The final statement in the program closes the XmlTextWriter object writer, automatically closing any element or attributes that might still be open:

```
writer.Close( );
```

Running Pax

A compiled version of Pax is in *examples/ch17* (*Pax.exe*). To run Pax, type the following line at a Windows 2000/XP command prompt:

```
pax
```

If all is well, the program will return some usage information to you:

```
Pax C# XSLT processor
Usage: Pax source stylesheet [result]
```

To transform *test.xml* with *test.xsl*, type:

```
pax test.xml test.xsl
```

With this command, you will get the following results:

```
<?xml version="1.0" encoding="IBM437"?>
<methods>
 <method>clearParameters( )</method>
 <method>getErrorListener( )</method>
 <method>getOutputProperties( )</method>
 <method>getOutputProperty(String name)</method>
 <method>getParameter(String name)</method>
 <method>getURIResolver( )</method>
 <method>setErrorListener(ErrorListener listener)</method>
 <method>setOutputProperties(Properties oformat)</method>
 <method>setOutputProperty(String name, String value)</method>
 <method>setParameter(String name, Object value)</method>
 <method>setURIResolver(URIResolver resolver)</method>
 <method>transform(Source xmlSource, Result outputTarget)</method>
</methods>
```

The output encoding is set to IBM437 for screen output. You can also save the output to a file using:

```
pax test.xml test.xsl pax.xml
```

The output encoding in *pax.xml* is US-ASCII as set by the Encoding.ASCII property. If you want to alter this program, you'll also need to know how to recompile it.

Compiling Pax

With the .NET Framework Version 1.1 downloaded and installed on your system, you should be able to access the C# complier csc. If you type csc at a command prompt with no options, you should see this:

```
Microsoft (R) Visual C# .NET Compiler version 7.10.2292.4
for Microsoft (R) .NET Framework version 1.1.4322
Copyright (C) Microsoft Corporation 2001-2002. All rights reserved.

fatal error CS2008: No inputs specified
```

To view the many options available with csc, enter:

```
csc /help
```

To compile Pax, type this command:

```
csc Pax.cs
```

Upon success, the compiler will produce a new version of *Pax.exe*. For more information on C#, study the vast documentation provided with the Version 1.1 Framework download. You can access the documentation by clicking on the Documentation link under Microsoft .NET Framework SDK v1.1 under Programs or All Programs on the Start menu.

Summary

If you are a programmer, this chapter has given you a leg up for creating your own interface to an XSLT processor in either Java or C#. I hope that the code and explanations were simple enough that you got the basic concepts down, and perhaps you were inspired to try some coding yourself. It certainly isn't that difficult to get started if you have a programming background. There is only one more chapter to go, and it's a short one.

CHAPTER 18

Parting Words

It's time for us to part company. If you have read the whole book, I trust you are fairly competent using XSLT and XPath by now. You should be proud of yourself for sticking with it to the end.

Whatever the case, this book is only an introduction to XSLT and XPath. You can now branch out and discover or rediscover some additional resources that are available for these technologies. Some of these I have mentioned before, but it will be nice to present all these resources in one place for your convenience. Here's the list:

XSL Transformations (XSLT) Version 1.0
> This is the original XSLT recommendation from the W3C. You'll find it at *http://www.w3.org/TR/xslt*. It first appeared in November 1999, and it is under 100 pages long.

XML Path Language (XPath) Version 1.0
> This concise little XPath recommendation is at *http://www.w3.org/TR/xpath*. It was introduced on the same day as the XSLT spec.

XSL Transformations (XSLT) 2.0
> Here is XSLT 2.0 in working draft form, available at *http://www.w3.org/TR/xslt20*. It is over twice as long as the original XSLT 1.0 spec, but it offers plenty of new features.

XML Path Language (XPath) 2.0
> The latest working draft of the 2.0 specification is available at *http://www.w3.org/TR/xpath20*. Like the XSLT 2.0 draft, it is considerably longer than its predecessor, and packed with all kinds of new features, not all of which are certain to make it into the final recommendation.

Michael Kay's XSLT Programmer's Reference, Second Edition (Wrox)
> At over 900 pages, Michael Kay's standard volume on XSLT weighs in heavily, but there is no fluff or waste. I have the first two editions of this book, and I count on them as a second-tier resource next to the XSLT specification itself. In fact, Michael's book helps clarify and expand on the spec. If you are serious about XSLT, I suggest that you invest in this book.

Doug Tidwell's XSLT (O'Reilly)

Doug Tidwell has a brisk and fun writing style that makes quick work of XSLT. I especially like the element and function reference appendixes at the end of the book. If you look up a particular element or function in the appendixes, you will find a complete stylesheet that demonstrates how to use that particular element or function.

Sal Mangano's XSLT Cookbook (O'Reilly)

Sal's popular book appeared at the end of 2002. The book crisply addresses just over 100 problems that can be addressed with XSLT recipes. If you do anything serious with XSLT, you'll be glad to have Sal's book on your shelf.

XSL-List

This active mail list maintained by Mulberry Technologies, Inc. is *the* place to go with your questions about XSLT. To subscribe, go to *http://www.mulberrytech.com/xsl/xsl-list/index.html*. The list archive, complete with search capability, is available at *http://www.biglist.com/lists/xsl-list/archives/*. Incidentally, Mulberry Tech also offers quick reference cards in PDF form for both XSLT and XPath at *http://www.mulberrytech.com/quickref/index.html*.

Robin Cover's Coverpages for XSLT

Robin Cover provides broad and accurate coverage of a number of XML-related topics, including XSLT. Hosted by OASIS, the Coverpages are updated regularly and are considered by some as the resource of last resort when looking for technical information related to XML. See *http://xml.coverpages.org/xsl.html*.

Dave Pawson's XSLT FAQ

Dave Pawson's FAQ for XSLT is at *http://www.dpawson.co.uk/*. Dave has nicely organized the FAQ into categories. I find it easy to use, and it certainly has helped me pry a few rusty bolts off my stylesheets, so to speak.

Jeni Tennison's site

Jeni Tennison is a top XSLT consultant and author whose web site (*http://www.jenitennison.com*) offers plenty of helpful information, including advice on how to perform grouping in XSLT 1.0.

Be sure to check the appendix, which follows this chapter, for references to XSLT processor resources. One last tool I'll mention is a simple Java package I've written called Ox.

The Ox Documentation Tool

Although this book provides a glossary, it doesn't provide alphabetical references for XSLT and XPath, partly because the other books I recommend, such as those written by Doug Tidwell and Michael Kay, have already provided excellent reference material. Short of that, you can still easily get the reference information you need about XSLT and XPath by using the glossary in this book and the Ox documentation tool that is provided with this book's resources.

Ox is a small, extensible, open source command-line Java tool that quickly and easily provides brief, syntax-based documentation on a given topic. You can find the tool in the *examples/Ox* directory of the example archive that you downloaded with this book. Ox accepts one or more terms on a command line and then returns brief documentation on each term. At this time, Ox supports only XSLT 1.0 and XPath 1.0.

Give it a try. While in the directory *examples/Ox*, type the following command where the term is the name of an XSLT element. Ox is case sensitive, and all XSLT element names must be given in lowercase, as shown here:

```
java -jar ox.jar xsl:apply-templates
```

Ox will return the following information to you on standard output:

```
xsl:apply-templates XSLT instruction element
 Applies templates, processing a node-set (the matching
 node and its children, if any).

Attributes:
 select = An expression [optional]
 mode = The mode [optional]

Content:
 template
 <xsl:sort/> [optional]
 <xsl:with-param/> [optional]

Example:
 <xsl:template match="/">
  <xsl:apply-templates/>
 </xsl:template>

See Also: xsl:sort, xsl:value-of
```

You can also submit multiple terms to Ox, as shown in the following line:

```
java -jar ox.jar xsl:template xsl:apply-templates
```

This whitespace-separated list on the command line produces documentation on both terms:

```
xsl:template XSLT top-level element
 Container for an XSLT template.

Example:
 match = pattern [optional if name attribute present]
 mode = QName for mode [optional]
 name = QName for template [optional if match attribute present]
 priority = number for template's priority, the higher the number,
 the higher the priority [optional]

Content:
 template
 xsl:param [zero or more]
```

```
Examples:
 <xsl:template match="/">
  <xsl:apply-templates/>
 </xsl:template>
```

```
See Also: xsl:apply-templates
```

```
---------
```

```
xsl:apply-templates XSLT instruction element
 Applies templates, processing a node-set (the matching
 node and its children, if any).
```

```
Attributes:
 select = An expression [optional]
 mode = The mode [optional]
```

```
Content:
 template
 <xsl:sort/> [optional]
 <xsl:with-param/> [optional]
```

```
Example:
 <xsl:template match="/">
  <xsl:apply-templates/>
 </xsl:template>
```

```
See Also: xsl:sort, xsl:value-of
```

You can also submit one or more prefixed terms to Ox by using the -xsl switch:

```
java -jar ox.jar -xsl template apply-templates
```

This line will return the same output at the previous, prefixed example.

In addition to element names, you can also submit definitional terms to Ox, like *XSLT*:

```
java -jar ox.jar XSLT
```

Ox will return with:

```
XSLT
Extensible Stylesheet Language Transformations
```

Phrased terms that contain spaces must be enclosed in quotes, as shown in the following line:

```
java -jar ox.jar "literal result element"
```

With this term, Ox will give you:

```
XSLT literal result element
A non-XSLT element, defined literally in a template, that creates
an element in the result tree.
```

If you submit a term that Ox doesn't know, such as an XSLT 2.0 element name:

```
java -jar ox.jar xsl:result-document
```

Ox barks back, but also gives you a venue where to issue a complaint:

```
Term "xsl:result-document" not found.
```

If enough people show interest in Ox, it will grow and expand to meet the demand. Ox uses Java properties files to store its documentation. The Ox package includes a template (*template.ox*) that you can use to create your own documentation package or simply add terms on your own. All you have to do is add your properties file to the Ox JAR file (*ox.jar*), and you will have access to the terms from the command line.

Signing Off

Once again, the appendix provides information on where to download XSLT processors, and how to install and run them. There also is a glossary at the end of the book where you can look up XML, XSLT, and XPath terms. All the terms in the glossary are also available in the Ox tool, though the terms in Ox may be updated more regularly than those in the book.

As with any new technology, once you get past the jargon and barriers of entry, XSLT can be fun to learn and use. If you are doing anything with XML, it's likely that you will have a reason to use XSLT, too. I hope this book has helped make the learning process go quickly for you. Now that you know what you're doing, go ask your boss for a promotion.

XSLT Processors

Throughout this book, I have used or mentioned a variety of XSLT processors. This appendix provides some detail in one location on how to download, install, and use seven processors. It also supplies some basic information on working the Java programming environment, which is essential to using several of the processors discussed in this book (Saxon and jd.xslt). In addition to those processors actually used in this book, I also list several others that may be of interest to readers.

Table A-1 lists and describes a dozen readily available XSLT processors. This is by no means a complete list of what's available, but it provides you with a wide variety of choices from among the most commonly used processors. If the XSLT processor's name is italicized, that means that it is demonstrated in this appendix. All of the processors support only version 1.0 of XSLT and XPath, unless otherwise noted. A much longer list of processors exists at *http://xml.coverpages.org/xslSoftware.html*.

Table A-1. XSLT processors

XSLT processor	URL	Notes
Cocoon	*http://cocoon.apache.org/*	Apache's XML publishing environment with central XSLT support.
Cooktop	*http://www.xmlcooktop.com*	Victor Pavlov's free XML editor that includes support for XSLT transformations.
Instant Saxon	*http://saxon.sourceforge.net*	Michael Kay's Windows-executable XSLT processor.
jd.xslt	*http://www.aztecrider.com/xslt/*	Written and maintained by Johannes Döbler. Supports the now withdrawn XSLT 1.1 draft.
MSXSL	*http://msdn.microsoft.com/downloads*	Microsoft's command-line XSLT processor, based on MSXML 4.0.
Saxon	*http://saxon.sourceforge.net*	Michael Kay's full Java version of Saxon that offers partial support for XSLT 2.0 and XPath 2.0.
Stylus Studio	*http://www.sonicsoftware.com*	An XML development environment with an XSLT editor and debugger.
Xalan	*http://xml.apache.org*	Apache's open source processor available in C++ and Java versions.

Table A-1. XSLT processors (continued)

XSLT processor	URL	Notes
xmlspy	*http://www.xmlspy.com*	Altova's popular and well-featured XML development environment, which includes, among may other things, a built-in XSLT processor and debugger.
xRay2	*http://architag.com/xray/*	An XML editing environment that supports XSLT.
xsltproc	*http://xmlsoft.org/XSLT/*	Daniel Veillard's XSLT processor based on his libxml/libxslt libraries.
XT	*http://www.blnz.com/xt/index.html*	Originally written by James Clark, XT is now maintained by Bill Lindsey.

Installing and Running XSLT Processors

The following sections provide detailed information about how to download, install, and run five popular XSLT processors with command-line interfaces: Instant Saxon, Saxon, MSXSL, Xalan C++, and jd.xslt.

You also learn how to transform XML documents using the graphical tools xmlspy and xRay2. Both xmlspy and xRay2 are XML editors with XSLT capabilities and run only on Windows.

Installing and Running Java

As a first step, you need to get the latest version of the Java Runtime Environment (JRE) or SDK (which includes a JRE) on your machine. To do so, go to *http://java.sun.com/downloads*. A JRE provides a Java virtual machine (JVM), a Java interpreter (java), and other necessities, but not tools like the Java compiler javac or a JAR (Java Archive) tool such as jar. To get the JRE from the Sun Java site, search for *Java VM*, click it, and then click the download button that appears. This will automatically download and install the latest JRE. If you already have the latest JRE installed, this will be detected and you will be alerted about it.

You can test to find out whether a JRE is working on your machine by typing this command at a command or shell prompt:

```
java -version
```

If you get something back like the following, you are in good shape:

```
java version "1.4.1_01"
Java(TM) 2 Runtime Environment, Standard Edition (build 1.4.1_01-b01)
Java HotSpot(TM) Client VM (build 1.4.1_01-b01, mixed mode)
```

To get a Java SDK, search for the download of your choice on the Sun Java site, such as J2SE 1.4.1, and then select *All platforms* in the text pull-down box. Click the *Go* button. Under the SDK columns, click the Download link for the appropriate platform, such as *Linux self-extracting file*. Fill out the information form if you wish, or just click the download link again. Accept the license by clicking the *Accept* button. Finally, click the download link, and save the archive to the directory of your choice. After downloading the archive file, follow the installation instructions provided by Sun. (These instructions may vary over time.)

Setting the path variable

After the installation is complete, you must place the Java *bin* directory in your path environment variable. You can add the location to the path using one of the following methods.

The path environment variable on Windows. Supposing the *bin* directory is located at *C:\Java\j2sdk1.4.1_01\bin*, on Windows, you could temporarily set the path environment variable at a command prompt with this line:

```
path %path%;c:\Java\j2sdk1.4.1_01\bin
```

This command adds the path *C:\Java\j2sdk1.4.1_01\bin*, which contains the executable file *javac.exe*, to your current path variable, represented by the substitution variable *%path%*.

Another method for amending your path variable is adding this command line to your *autoexec.bat* file so that the new path is set each time you boot your computer.

On Windows 2000 or XP Professional, you can also set the path variable by choosing Start → Control Panel → System → Advanced → Environment Variables, and then adding the path to your user or system variables in the Environment Variables dialog box.

The path environment variable on Unix. Supposing that the *bin* directory is located at */usr/mike/j2sdk1.4.1_01/bin* on a Unix system, you could temporarily set the path environment variable at a bash shell prompt with this line:

```
path="/usr/mike/j2sdk1.4.1_01/bin:$PATH"
```

This command adds the path */usr/mike/java/j2sdk1.4.1_01/bin*, which contains the executable file *javac.exe*, to your current path variable, represented by the substitution variable *$PATH*.

You could also add this command line to your */etc/profile* or *~/.profile* file, so that the new path is set each time you boot your computer.

Running the Java compiler

With the *bin* directory in the path variable, you are ready to put its content to use. Type the following at a command prompt or shell:

```
javac
```

If the path is working right, it will return advice that looks somewhat like this:

```
Usage: javac <options> <source files>
where possible options include:
  -g                         Generate all debugging info
  -g:none                    Generate no debugging info
  -g:{lines,vars,source}     Generate only some debugging info
  -O                         Optimize; may hinder debugging or enlarge class file
  -nowarn                    Generate no warnings
  -verbose                   Output messages about what the compiler is doing
  -deprecation               Output source locations where deprecated APIs are used
  -classpath <path>          Specify where to find user class files
  -sourcepath <path>         Specify where to find input source files
  -bootclasspath <path>      Override location of bootstrap class files
  -extdirs <dirs>            Override location of installed extensions
  -d <directory>             Specify where to place generated class files
  -encoding <encoding>       Specify character encoding used by source files
  -source <release>          Provide source compatibility with specified release
  -target <release>          Generate class files for specific VM version
  -help                      Print a synopsis of standard options
```

Using the Classpath

When dealing with Java, you also have to deal with the classpath. The classpath is the path that enables a Java interpreter to see the classes that it is trying to execute. When running Java from the command line, Java classes can be included using the -cp or -classpath command-line options.

For example, you could place the jar file *saxon7.jar* in the classpath with something like this:

```
java -cp c:\lib\saxon7.jar net.sf.saxon.Transform test.xml test.xsl
```

You can also place a JAR file in the classpath using this command on Windows:

```
set CLASSPATH=".;c:\lib\saxon7.jar;%CLASSPATH%"
```

The dot (.) refers to the current directory (the Java interpreter needs to be told explicitly to look in the current directory for classes). %CLASSPATH% adds the current classpath to the new value of CLASSPATH.

Or type something like this command on Unix:

```
classpath="/usr/lib/saxon7.jar:$CLASSPATH"
```

Another convenient way to handle the classpath is to place a copy of the desired JAR file in the *jre/lib* directory where your JRE is installed. For example, if your JRE is installed under C:\j2sdk1.4.1_01, it will have the subdirectory *jre/lib*, which holds various resources.

The jar method

If you use the `-jar` option, however, you can just use a regular path or the path environment variable to find a JAR file. For example, if the JAR file were in the current directory, you could simply type:

```
java -jar saxon7.jar
```

Or, if it were in *C:\Temp*, you could use:

```
java -jar c:\lib\saxon7.jar
```

This assumes that the manifest file in the JAR has a `Main-Class` field that tells the Java interpreter where the class holding the `main( )` method is. For more information on running JAR-package software, see *http://java.sun.com/docs/books/tutorial/jar/basics/run.html*.

If you would like more help understanding how the Java classpath works and how Java finds classes to run, see *http://java.sun.com/j2se/1.4.1/docs/tooldocs/findingclasses.html*. For help setting the classpath for Windows, see *http://java.sun.com/j2se/1.4.1/docs/tooldocs/windows/classpath.html*; for help setting the classpath for Solaris or a similar Unix system, see *http://java.sun.com/j2se/1.4.1/docs/tooldocs/solaris/classpath.html*.

Installing and Running Instant Saxon

Saxon is a free, open source XSLT processor created and maintained by Michael Kay and hosted at *http://saxon.sourceforge.net*. Instant Saxon is a Windows 32 executable version of Saxon, that is, in essence, a parcel of Java classes packaged together in an *.exe* file. The last release of Instant Saxon at this writing was Version 6.5.3 (August 2003).

Michael Kay's Saxon, including Instant Saxon, was the first compliant XSLT 1.0 processor and was released 17 days after the XSLT and XPath recommendations were published in late 1999. Michael Kay is the current editor of the XSLT 2.0 specification, and he's one of the editors of XPath 2.0. Both programs are under development at the W3C. (Blessedly, he was also a technical editor for this book.)

 You can find the archive for Instant Saxon 6.5.3 in *examples/ch07*, or you can use the directions for downloading the archive that follow.

Downloading Instant Saxon

Follow these steps (they may vary over time):

1. Using a web browser, go to *http://saxon.sourceforge.net*.

2. Search for *Instant Saxon 6.5.3* and, after finding it, click on *Download* just below.

3. Select a mirror download server, then save the zip file *instant-saxon6_5_3.zip* to the directory of your choice.

4. When the download is complete, unzip the *instant-saxon6_5_3.zip*. Two files are extracted, namely, *instant.html* and *saxon.exe*.

5. The installation is complete.

6. You can use *saxon.exe* by copying it to your current directory, copying it to another location that is already in the path (such as *C:\Windows* or *C:\WINNT*), or adding its location to the path environment variable (see "Setting the path variable" earlier in this appendix).

Running Instant Saxon

Display usage information for Instant Saxon by entering the following at a Windows command prompt:

```
saxon
```

Without any parameters, you should see this usage synopsis:

```
No source file name
SAXON 6.5.3 from Michael Kay
Usage: saxon [options] source-doc style-doc {param=value}...
Options:
  -a            Use xml-stylesheet PI, not style-doc argument
  -ds           Use standard tree data structure
  -dt           Use tinytree data structure (default)
  -o filename   Send output to named file or directory
  -m classname  Use specified Emitter class for xsl:message output
  -r classname  Use specified URIResolver class
  -t            Display version and timing information
  -T            Set standard TraceListener
  -TL classname Set a specific TraceListener
  -u            Names are URLs not filenames
  -w0           Recover silently from recoverable errors
  -w1           Report recoverable errors and continue (default)
  -w2           Treat recoverable errors as fatal
  -x classname  Use specified SAX parser for source file
  -y classname  Use specified SAX parser for stylesheet
  -?            Display this message
```

Normally, Instant Saxon expects at least two parameters: the name of the source document followed by the name of the stylesheet. Supply the names of the document and stylesheet discussed earlier on the command line, like this:

```
saxon test.xml test.xsl
```

Any file named *test*, regardless of the file suffix, is fictitious and used only as an example in this appendix.

To direct Instant Saxon's output to a file, use the -o option:

```
saxon -o test.out test.xml test.xsl
```

To use an XML document that contains an XML stylesheet PI, use the -a option, followed by the filename:

```
saxon -a test.xml
```

The XML stylesheet PI contains a reference to a stylesheet and will look something like:

```
<?xml-stylesheet href="test.xsl" type="text/xsl"?>
```

For version and timing information, try the -t option:

```
saxon -t test.xml test.xsl
```

If the source document has an associated DTD, you can validate it at runtime with the -v option:

```
saxon -v test.xml test.xsl
```

A DTD will be associated with the XML document by a document type declaration, which will look something like:

```
<!DOCTYPE test SYSTEM "test.dtd">
```

Installing and Running Saxon (Full Java Version)

Saxon is a free, open source XSLT processor that, like Instant Saxon, was created by Michael Kay and hosted at *http://saxon.sourceforge.net*. The recommended version of Saxon for XSLT 1.0 is Version 6.5.3. The latest version at the time of this writing is 7.7, which partially supports the working drafts for XSLT 2.0 and XPath 2.0. By the time you read this, Saxon may have gone beyond Version 7.7.

 You can find the archive for Saxon 7.7 in *examples/ch16*, or you can get the latest version by using the directions for downloading the archive that follow.

Downloading Saxon

To download Saxon, follow these steps (which may vary over time):

1. Using a web browser, go to *http://saxon.sourceforge.net*.
2. Search for *Saxon 7.7* or later and, after finding it, click on *Download* just below.
3. Select a mirror download server, then save the zip file *saxon7-7.zip* to the directory of your choice.
4. When the download is complete, unzip the *saxon7-7.zip*. Many files will be extracted, including *saxon7.jar*.
5. The installation is complete.

You can use the full Java version of Saxon on any platform that supports Java, including Windows or a Unix environment such as Linux, Solaris, or Mac OS X. This requires that you have at least a JRE or JVM installed for Version 1.4 or higher. If you don't have Java on your system, you can download an SDK or JRE from *http://sun.java.com*. You will find installation instructions earlier in this appendix in the section, "Installing and Running Java."

Running Saxon

You can download Saxon from *http://saxon.sourceforge.net*, or copy the file *saxon7.jar* from *C:\LearningXSLT\examples\ch16* (Version 7.7 of *saxon7.jar* exists in *examples/ch16*, but you may want a more recent version, if one is available). Placing the JAR file in your working directory obviates the need to deal with the classpath (see "Using the Classpath," earlier in this appendix).

This file contains the Java class files that will enable you to transform documents using Saxon. Assuming that *saxon7.jar* is in your current directory, you can enter the line:

```
java -jar saxon7.jar
```

This should yield the following output if you used no arguments:

```
No source file name
SAXON 7.7 from Michael Kay
Usage:  java net.sf.saxon.Transform [options] source-doc style-doc {param=value}...
Options:
  -a           Use xml-stylesheet PI, not style-doc argument
  -ds          Use standard tree data structure
  -dt          Use tinytree data structure (default)
  -im modename Start transformation in specified mode
  -o filename  Send output to named file or directory
  -m classname Use specified Emitter class for xsl:message output
  -r classname Use specified URIResolver class
  -t           Display version and timing information
  -T           Set standard TraceListener
  -TJ          Trace calls to external Java functions
  -TL classname Set a specific TraceListener
  -u           Names are URLs not filenames
  -v           Validate source document
  -w0          Recover silently from recoverable errors
  -w1          Report recoverable errors and continue (default)
  -w2          Treat recoverable errors as fatal
  -x classname Use specified SAX parser for source file
  -y classname Use specified SAX parser for stylesheet
  -?           Display this message
  param=value  Set stylesheet parameter
  !option=value Set serialization option
```

You can use *saxon7.jar* with the same arguments as you did with Instant Saxon. For example, to transform *test.xml* with *test.xsl*, type the following:

```
java -jar saxon7.jar test.xml test.xsl
```

To send output to a file, use the -o option:

```
java -jar saxon7.jar -o test.out test.xml test.xsl
```

If a document contains an XML stylesheet PI, you can use the -a option:

```
java -jar saxon7.jar -a test.xml
```

The XML stylesheet PI contains a reference to a stylesheet and will look something like:

```
<?xml-stylesheet href="test.xsl" type="text/xsl"?>
```

For version and timing information, use the -t option:

```
java -jar saxon7.jar -t test.xml test.xsl
```

If the source document has an associated DTD, you can validate it at runtime with the -v option:

```
java -jar saxon7.jar -v test.xml test.xsl
```

A DTD will be associated with the XML document by a document type declaration, which will look something like this:

```
<!DOCTYPE test SYSTEM "test.dtd">
```

Using a Windows batch file with Saxon

You can use a batch file on Windows to run Saxon's full Java version. You can copy the following lines and place them in a batch file named *sp.bat*:

```
@echo off
java -jar "C:\LearningXSLT\examples\ch16\saxon7.jar" %1 %2 %3 %4 %5 %6 %7 %8 %9
```

This assumes that you have set up the directory *C:\LearningXSLT\examples\ch16* (among other directories) for the example files. You can change the location of *saxon7.jar* in the batch file to match your own directory structure. If you are working on Windows 2000 Professional or XP Professional, you can delete the replaceable parameters *%1* thorough *%9* and use *%** in their place. You could then run Saxon by typing:

```
sp test.xml test.xsl
```

Using a Unix shell script with Saxon

If you're on a Unix system, you could copy the following into a file named *sp.sh*:

```
#! /bin/sh
java -jar ~/learningxslt/examples/saxon/saxon.jar $*
```

This script assumes that you have set up a directory called *learningxslt* in your home directory (something like */usr/mike*, which is represented by *~/*). You can change the location of *saxon7.jar* in the batch file to match your own set up. You could then run Saxon by typing:

```
sp.sh test.xml test.xsl
```

Installing and Running MSXSL

MSXSL is Microsoft's free command-line XSLT processor, available at *http://msdn.microsoft.com/downloads/*. MSXSL is a Windows 32 executable that requires MSXML 4.0 (*msxml4.dll*). This processor is incredibly small (25 KB) and is one of the fastest around, probably because it is compiled natively on Windows and uses the XSLT library included in MSXML. You can also download the source code.

By default, MSXSL uses UTF-16 output. You have to use the `encoding` attribute on an output element in a stylesheet to override this, which you probably will want to do because UTF-16 doesn't always produce very attractive output in a command window.

Downloading MSXSL

Follow these steps (they may vary over time):

1. Using a browser, go to *http://msdn.microsoft.com/downloads/*.
2. Under *Search for Developer Downloads*, search for MSXSL.
3. Click on the link provided to MSXSL.
4. The DLL *msxml4.dll* must also be installed for MSXSL to run. If it isn't installed, follow the link provided to the MSDN Online XML Developer Center, then download and install it according to the instructions provided.
5. Find the link for *msxsl.exe* and click it.
6. Save *msxsl.exe* to a directory of your choice.
7. The installation is complete.
8. You can use *msxsl.exe* by copying it to your current directory, copying it to another location that is already in the path (such as *C:\Windows* or *C:\WINNT*), or adding its location to the path environment variable (see "Setting the path variable" earlier in this appendix).

Running MSXSL

To see the display usage information for MSXSL, enter the following at a Windows command prompt:

```
msxsl -?
```

With the -? option, you will see this usage information:

```
Microsoft (R) XSLT Processor Version 4.0

Usage: MSXSL source stylesheet [options] [param=value...] [xmlns:prefix=uri...]

Options:
    -?              Show this message
    -o filename     Write output to named file
    -m startMode    Start the transform in this mode
```

```
-xw          Strip non-significant whitespace from source and stylesheet
-xe          Do not resolve external definitions during parse phase
-v           Validate documents during parse phase
-t           Show load and transformation timings
-pi          Get stylesheet URL from xml-stylesheet PI in source document
-u version   Use a specific version of MSXML: '2.6', '3.0', '4.0'
-            Dash used as source argument loads XML from stdin
-            Dash used as stylesheet argument loads XSL from stdin
```

MSXSL takes at least two arguments: the name of the XML source document followed by the name of the stylesheet. On the command line, type:

```
msxsl test.xml test.xsl
```

To direct output to a file, use the -o option:

```
msxsl -o test.out test.xml test.xsl
```

To transform an XML document that contains an XML stylesheet PI, use the -pi option, followed by an appropriate filename:

```
msxsl -pi test.xml
```

The XML stylesheet PI contains a reference to a stylesheet and will look something like:

```
<?xml-stylesheet href="test.xsl" type="text/xsl"?>
```

For timings, try the -t option:

```
msxsl -t test.xml test.xsl
```

If the source document has a DTD, you can validate it with the -v option:

```
msxsl -v test.xml test.xsl
```

A DTD will be associated with the XML document by a document type declaration, which will look something like:

```
<!DOCTYPE test SYSTEM "test.dtd">
```

Installing and Running Xalan C++

Xalan C++ is an open source XSLT processor hosted by Apache. To run, Xalan C++ also requires the C++ version of Apache's XML parser Xerces. Both Xerces C++ and Xalan C++ are available for download from the Apache site (*http://xml.apache.org*).

Downloading and installing Xalan C++

Follow these steps (which may vary over time) to install Xalan C++:

1. Using a web browser, go to *http://xml.apache.org/dist/xerces-c/stable/*.
2. Select the latest distribution archive for your platform, such as the recent versions *xerces-c2_2_0-win32.zip* or *xerces-c2_2_0-linux8.0gcc32.tar.gz*.
3. Save the archive to the directory of your choice.

4. After the download is complete, extract the files from the archive using either the *unzip* or *tar* utility.

5. The directory *xerces-c2_2_0* is extracted to the current directory or another directory of your choice. All files from Xerces are stored under this directory.

6. The installation of Xerces C++ is complete. Now you must also install Xalan C++.

7. Using a browser, go to *http://xml.apache.org/dist/xalan-c/stable/*.

8. Select the latest distribution archive for your platform, such as *Xalan-C_1_5-win32.zip* or *Xalan-C_1_5-linux7.2Proton.tar.gz*.

9. Save the archive to the directory of your choice.

10. After the download is complete, extract the files from the archive using either the *unzip* or *tar* utility.

11. The directory *xml-xalan* is extracted to the current directory or another directory of your choice. All files from Xalan C++ are stored under this directory.

12. The installation of Xalan C++ is complete.

To use *xalan.exe*, you need to add its location to the path, as well as to the location of the Xerces *bin* directory. If you are working on Windows, follow the instructions in the section "Setting the path variable for Xalan on Windows." If you are working on a Unix platform, see "Setting the path variable for Xalan on a Unix platform."

Setting the path variable for Xalan on Windows

If, for example, you installed (actually unzipped) the Xalan C++ archive in the root directory on Windows (*C:*), the location for *xalan.exe* would be something like *C:\xml-xalan\c\Build\Win32\VC6\Release*. So in order to add this to the path, you could enter the following line:

```
path %path%;"C:\xml-xalan\c\Build\Win32\VC6\Release"
```

This command appends the path *C:\xml-xalan\c\Build\Win32\VC6\Release*, which contains the executable file *xalan.exe*, to your current path variable, represented by the substitution variable *%path%*. If you want, you could add this command line to your *autoexec.bat* file, so that the new path is set each time you boot your computer.

The C++ version of Xerces must also be in the path. If you unzipped Xerces in the root directory, the location for the Xerces dynamic-link libraries would be at *C:\xerces-c2_2_0-win32\bin*. Add this location to your path as you did with Xalan.

On Windows 2000 or XP Professional, you can also set the path variable by choosing Start → Control Panel → System → Advanced → Environment Variables, and then adding the path to your user or system variables in the Environment Variables dialog box. With *xalan.exe* in the path variable, you are ready to put it to use.

Setting the path variable for Xalan on a Unix platform

If you installed or unzipped the Xalan C++ in your home directory on a Unix platform (such as in */usr/mike*), the location for *xalan.exe* would be something like */usr/mike/xml-xalan/c/Build/Win32/VC6/Release*. To add this location to the path, enter the following line:

```
path="/usr/mike/xml-xalan/c/Build/Win32/VC6/Release:$PATH"
```

This command adds */usr/mike/xml-xalan/c/Build/Win32/VC6/Release*, which contains the executable file *xalan.exe*, to your current path variable. (The path variable is represented by $PATH.) If you want, you could add this command line to your */etc/profile* or *~/.profile* file, so that the new path is set each time you boot your computer.

Xerces must also be in the path in order for Xalan to work. If you unzipped Xerces in your home directory on Unix, the location for the Xerces dynamic-link libraries would be at something like */usr/mike/xerces-c2_2_0-win32/bin*. Add this location to your path as you did Xalan, and you'll be ready to run.

Running Xalan C++

With Xalan C++ and Xerces C++ installed and the proper directories in the path, you can begin using Xalan. To start, just type the name of the program on a command line:

```
xalan
```

If Xalan works, you will see the following usage information on the screen:

```
Xalan version 1.5.0
Xerces version 2.2.0
Usage: Xalan [options] source stylesheet
Options:
  -a                  Use xml-stylesheet PI, not the 'stylesheet' argument
  -e encoding         Force the specified encoding for the output.
  -i integer          Indent the specified amount.
  -m                  Omit the META tag in HTML output.
  -o filename         Write output to the specified file.
  -p name expression  Sets a stylesheet parameter.
  -u                  Disable escaping of URLs in HTML output.
  -v                  Validates source documents.
  -?                  Display this message.
  -                   A dash as the 'source' argument reads from stdin.
  -                   A dash as the 'stylesheet' argument reads from stdin.
                      ('-' cannot be used for both arguments.)
```

Xalan takes at least two parameters: the name of the source document followed by the name of the stylesheet, like this:

```
xalan test.xml test.xsl
```

To direct Xalan's output to a file, use the -o option:

```
xalan -o test.out test.xml test.xsl
```

Use an XML document that contains an XML stylesheet PI, and then use the -a option, followed by the filename:

```
xalan -a test.xml
```

The XML stylesheet PI contains a reference to a stylesheet and will look something like:

```
<?xml-stylesheet href="test.xsl" type="text/xsl"?>
```

To set the number of spaces used for the indentation of output, use the -i option, followed by an integer (2 means the output will be indented by two spaces for each element level of the XML document):

```
xalan -i 2 test.xml test.xsl
```

If the source document has an associated DTD, you can validate it at runtime with the -v option:

```
xalan -v test.xml test.xsl
```

A DTD will be associated with the XML document by a document type declaration, which will look something like:

```
<!DOCTYPE test SYSTEM "test.dtd">
```

Using jd.xslt

The jd.xslt XSLT processor was written by Johannes Döbler of Munich, Germany. This processor supports XSLT Version 1.1 (see *http://www.w3.org/TR/xslt11*). XSLT 1.1 was withdrawn by the W3C in favor of XSLT 2.0, which is now under development. Nevertheless, Version 1.1 offers several interesting features, including the script element, not available under XSLT Version 1.0. The script element allows you to define extensions within a stylesheet, something like the function element in XSLT 2.0. You can read more about the jd.xslt processor at *http://www.aztecrider.com/xslt/*.

Downloading and installing jd.xslt

Follow these steps (which may vary over time) to download and install jd.xslt:

1. Using a browser, go to *http://aztecrider.com/xslt/download.html*.
2. Click on *http://aztecrider.com/xslt/jdxslt.zip*.
3. Save the file *jdxslt.zip* to the directory of your choice.
4. When the download is complete, extract the file from the archive using an *unzip* utility.
5. The installation is complete.

Running jd.xslt

One option is to copy the JAR file *jdxslt.jar* from the *lib* directory of the archive to one of the chapter directories under *C:\LearningXSLT\examples* directory. Placing the JAR in a working directory obviates the need to deal with the Java classpath (see "Using the Classpath," earlier in this appendix).

Test to see if jd.xslt works by typing the following line at a command prompt:

```
java -jar jdxslt.jar
```

This should give you:

```
jd.xslt processor version 1.5.2

Usage: java jd.xml.xslt.Stylesheet [options] xml [xsl...]

xml                     the uri of an input xml document, "-" for STDIN
xsl...                  zero or more uris of stylesheets - if their number is
                        = 0: use the associated stylesheets of the xml document
                        = 1: transform the input with that stylesheet
                        > 1: chain the transformations
                        the uri "urn:jdxslt:identity" denotes the identity
                        transformation
options:
-entityresolver <cls>   set a sax EntityResolver
-errorstack             show the java call stack in case of an error
-media <media>          filter associated stylesheets by their media attribute
-msglistener <class>    set a message listener
-out <file>             write the output to the file (default is System.out)
-out:<prop> <value>     set the value of a xsl:output property
-param <name> <expr>    set the value of a toplevel parameter (expr is a context-
                        free XPath expression). Multiple parameters are allowed
-parser <class>         set a sax parser
-parserxml <class>      set a sax parser for input xml documents
-parserxsl <class>      set a sax parser for the stylesheet
-proxy <url>            set a proxy host
-repeat <number>        repeat the transformation n times
-security <class>       set a XsltSecurityManager
-title <title>          filter associated stylesheets by their title attribute
-trace                  create trace output
-uriresolver <class>    set a UriResolver
-validate               validate xml documents
-verbose                turn on verbose mode to display transformation info
-w0                     recover silently from recoverable errors
-w1                     report recoverable errors and continue (default)
-w2                     treat recoverable errors as fatal
java -jar saxon7.jar test.xml test.xsl
```

To transform a file, use the following:

```
java -jar jdxslt.jar test.xml test.xsl
```

To transform a source file with more than one stylesheet, use the following line:

```
java -jar jdxslt.jar test.xml test1.xsl test2.xsl test3.xsl
```

To send output to a file, use the -out option:

```
java -jar jdxslt.jar -out test.out test.xml test.xsl
```

Set an output property (based on the attributes of the output element) using the -out: option:

```
java -jar jdxslt.jar -out:indent yes test.xml
```

For verbose output, use the -verbose option:

```
java -jar jdxlst.jar -verbose test.xml test.xsl
```

If the source document has an associated DTD, you can validate it at runtime with the -validate option:

```
java -jar jdxslt.jar -validate test.xml test.xsl
```

A DTD will be associated with the XML document by a document type declaration, which will look something like:

```
<!DOCTYPE test SYSTEM "test.dtd">
```

Using xmlspy

Altova's xmlspy is available for download from *http://www.xmlspy.com*. You can get a free trial before purchasing a license. (This is the only XSLT processor I am demonstrating that isn't free.) I should note, however, that xmlspy runs only on the Windows platform.

Assuming that you have successfully installed xmlspy, follow these steps.

1. Launch the xmlspy application.
2. Choose Window → All on/off. This closes the Project, Info, and Entry Helper windows.
3. Open the file *message.xml* with File → Open from the working directory *C:\LearningXslt\examples\ch01* (or something similar, depending on how you've set things up).
4. Choose View → Text view.
5. Open the file *message.xsl* with File → Open in the same location as *message.xml*.
6. Choose View → Text view again. At this point, xmlspy should appear as it does in Figure A-1.
7. Click on the *message.xml* window to give it the focus.
8. Choose XSL → XSL Transformation or press F10. A dialog box appears.
9. Click the Window button, select the file *message.xsl*, and click OK. The dialog box should appear as shown in Figure A-2.
10. Click OK once more and another HTML window appears showing you the result of the transformation, as in Figure A-3.

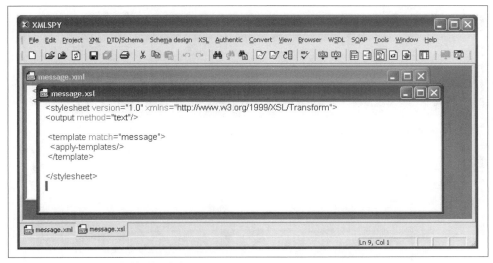

Figure A-1. xmlspy with files loaded

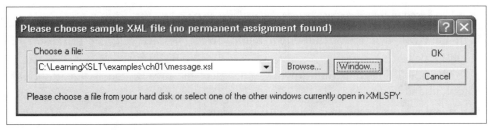

Figure A-2. xmlspy dialog box

Using xRay2

Architag's xRay2 is a free, graphical XML editor with XSLT processing capability. It is available for download from *http://www.architag.com/xray*. xRay2, like xmlspy, runs only on the Windows platform.

Assuming that you have successfully downloaded and installed xRay2 according to the easy instructions provided by Architag, follow these steps to process a source document with a stylesheet.

1. Launch the xRay2 application.
2. Open the file *message.xml* with File → Open from the working directory *C:\ LearningXSLT\examples\ch01* (or something similar).
3. Open the file *message.xsl* with File → Open in the same location.
4. Choose File → New XSLT Transform.

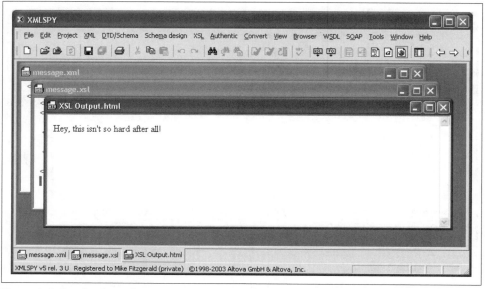

Figure A-3. Result of transforming message.xml with message.xsl

5. In the XML Document pull-down menu, select *message.xml* (see the result in Figure A-4).

6. In the XSLT Program pull-down menu, select *message.xsl* (see what it should look like in Figure A-5).

7. If it is not already checked, check Auto-update.

8. The result of the transformation should appear in the transform window (see Figure A-6).

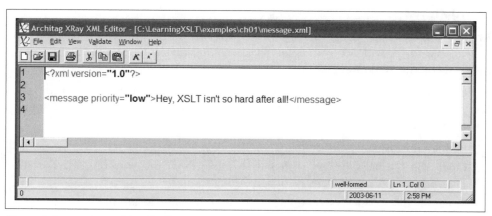

Figure A-4. message.xml in xRay2

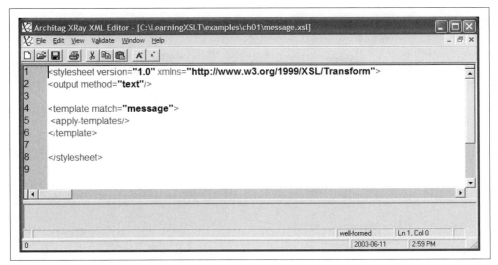

Figure A-5. message.xsl in xRay2

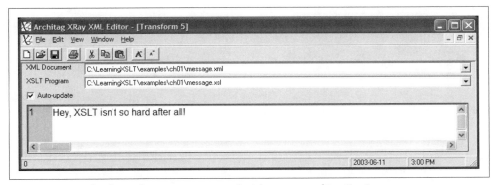

Figure A-6. Result of transforming message.xml with message.xsl in xRay2

Glossary

Abbreviated syntax
　　See "Location path."

Absolute location path
　　See "Location path."

Ancestor
　　See "Parent-child relationship."

Ancestor axis
　　See "Axes."

Ancestor-of-self axis
　　See "Axes."

Ant
　　Ant is a Java-based build tool sponsored by Apache (see *http://ant.apache.org*). Ant is a timesaver and easy to use. See *http://ant.apache.org/resources.html* for a list of FAQs, articles, presentations, and books on Ant. Ant was used in this book to build the JAXP-based processor discussed in Chapter 17.

Attribute
　　A name/value pair that modifies an element. In the attribute specification `<name type="first">`, type is the attribute and first (in double quotes) is the value of the attribute. Attributes can appear on start-tags or on empty element tags. Each attribute can only appear once on a tag (no duplicates), and the order of attributes is not preserved in XML processing. An attribute value must be surrounded by matching single or double quotes. See "Node."

Attribute axis
　　See "Axes."

Attribute-list declaration
　　In a DTD, a declaration for a valid attribute comes in the form `<!ATTLIST date type CDATA #IMPLIED>`, where date is the element name for which the attribute is declared, type is the name of the attribute, CDATA is the type of the attribute (a string), and #IMPLIED means that the attribute is optional; it may also be #REQUIRED or #FIXED (a fixed attribute must always have its default value). In XML 1.0, there are several types available for valid attributes such as CDATA, ID, IDREF, IDREFS, and so forth. Attribute-list declarations can also contain enumerations, and default values, in the form `<!ATTLIST date day (Monday|Wednesday|Friday) "Monday">`, where Monday, Wednesday, and Friday, separated by a | (union operator implying *or*) and enclosed in parentheses, make up the enumeration and Monday (in quotes) is the default value. See "ID."

Attribute node
　　See "Node."

Attribute set
　　A named set of attributes, defined in XSLT with the top-level attribute-set element. An attribute set may be reused by referencing its name in a use-attribute-sets attribute value on attribute-set, element, or copy instruction elements.

Attribute value template

In XSLT, an expression that is surrounded by braces and contained in an attribute value. For example, the following literal result element has an attribute value that contains an attribute value template: `<days number="{3 + $week}">`. days is the element name, number is the attribute name, and the attribute value template, in braces, is evaluated to 3 plus the value of the week variable. (See "Variable.") Attribute value templates may be found in the attribute value of literal result elements and in XSLT elements that allow them, such as in the name attribute of the element or attribute instruction elements.

Axes

Nodes in an XML document fall within one or more of 13 distinct axes defined by the XPath data model. The axes are ancestor, ancestor-or-self, attribute, child, descendant, descendant-or-self, following, following-sibling, namespace, parent, preceding, preceding-sibling, and self. Axes can be forward or reverse: the ancestor, ancestor-or-self, preceding, and preceding-sibling axes are reverse axes; all other axes are forward axes. Axis identifiers are said to be in unabbreviated syntax when used with a name, name test, or node test, and separated by the connector `::`. Some location path examples that use the unabbreviated syntax: `child::date`, `child::days/attribute::number`, `self::node( )`.

Base URI

The base URI is the internal, base location of a node, based on the location of the source document or stylesheet. (This can also be set explicitly with `xml:base`, where supported.) Relative URIs are relative to this base location that is set according to the rules in Section 3.2 of the XSLT specification at *http://www.w3.org/TR/xslt/*.

Boolean

An XPath datatype whose value can be either true (1) or false (0). Some expressions return Boolean values, testing whether a condition is true or false, such

as an expression contained in the test attribute of the if or when XSLT instruction elements.

Built-in template rules

In XSLT, built-in template rules match nodes without an explicit rule. Each of the seven node types has a built-in rule that will be instantiated in the absence of an explicit template rule in a stylesheet. Commonly, an apply-templates element will trigger the built-in template rule for text nodes.

C#

See ".NET Framework."

CDATA section

Provides a way to hide character data from an XML processor so that the processor will ignore its contents as markup. For example, entering `<![CDATA[O'Reilly & Associates]]>` would display the ampersand (&). Without a CDATA section, the & could not properly be displayed. In XSLT, the cdata-section-elements attribute on the output element specifies a list of the names of elements whose text node children should be output using CDATA sections.

Character reference

See "Entity."

Child axis

See "Axes."

Child element

See "Parent-child relationship."

Client-side XSLT

Support for XSLT transformations that is embedded in the browser (the client). Late versions of IE, Mozilla, Mozilla Firebird, and Netscape all support client-side XSLT.

Comments

Comments provide a way for documenting what is in an XML or DTD document or for hiding text or markup from the XML processor. Anything contained in a comment is ignored by the XML processor. Comments begin with <! and end with > and cannot contain except at the end of the comment. You can create comments in a result tree by using the comment instruction element in a stylesheet. The comment node is one of seven node types in the XPath data model.

Context node

According to XPath, the node being currently processed. Compare with "Current node."

Context position

The position of the context node within the current node list. See "Current node list."

Context size

The number of nodes in the current node list. See "Current node list."

Current node

The current node is the same as the context node, except when a predicate is being evaluated. This is the only time the context node (defined by XPath) and the current node (defined by XSLT) are different. When a predicate is evaluated, the node in the predicate momentarily becomes the current node. See "Context node" and "Current node list."

Current node list

A list of nodes, each one of which will in turn be the current node a processing progresses. See "Current node."

Current template rule

The template rule currently being processed. See "Template rule."

Default namespace

See "Namespaces."

Descendant axis

See "Axes."

Descendant element

See "Parent-child relationship."

Descendant-or-self axis

See "Axes."

Document element

The first element in an XML document, the parent of all other elements within a given document. The html element, for example, is the document element of an

XHTML document. The document element is also called the *root element*.

Document entity

An entity representing the XML document where an XML processor logically begins processing.

Document node

In XPath 2.0, the *root node* is called the document node.

Document order

The order in which nodes appear in the source document that is being processed by an XSLT processor.

Document type declaration

A document type declaration in an XML document declares either a document type definition (DTD) internally (called the internal subset) or declares the name or location of an external document definition (the external subset). An example of an external subset declaration is: `<!DOCTYPE date SYSTEM "date.dtd">`. An example of an internal subset declaration is: `<!DOCTYPE date [ <!ELEMENT date (#PCDATA)> ]>`. Internal and external declarations may also be combined.

Document type definition

A document type definition, or DTD, is a document that contains the definitions or markup declarations for XML elements, attributes, and so on. If an XML document has a DTD associated with it, an XML processor can validate the XML document against the DTD. In other words, the XML processor may be directed to check that an XML document follows the rules outlined in an associated DTD, in addition to checking for compliance with the normal rules of XML well-formedness. See "Attribute-list declaration," "Element-type declaration," and "Markup declaration."

DTD

See "Document type definition."

Element

The most common structure in an XML document. An element may be empty, contain a string (parsed character data) or other elements, or have mixed content (elements and strings mixed together). For example, `<date>2003-12-31</date>` is an example of an element (date) with parsed character data as content (2003-12-31). See "Node."

Element node

A node representing an element and its contents. See "Node."

Element-type declaration

An element-type declaration refers to the markup declaration for an element that appears in a DTD for valid XM. For example, in `<!ELEMENT date (#PCDATA)>`, an element date is declared to have parsed character data content. In `<!ELEMENT date (month,day,year)>`, the element date is declared to have one month child element, one day, and one year. An element can also have mixed content. See "Mixed content."

Embedded stylesheet

A stylesheet that is embedded in the document element of an XML document and referenced by a fragment identifier in the href attribute of an XML stylesheet processing instruction. The fragment identifier references an attribute of type ID on the stylesheet element of the embedded stylesheet. Compare with "Literal result element stylesheet."

Empty element

An element that has no content is empty; that is, it does not have text or other content such as other elements between a start-tag and an end-tag. An example of an empty element in XHTML is `<br />`. In XML, an empty elements tag looks like `<date today="2003-10-03"/>` where date is an element and today is an attribute, but there is no element content in date.

Encoding

Refers to the character set in use in an XML document, such as UTF-8 or ISO-8859-1. In XSLT, you can control encoding with the encoding attribute on the output element. See "Encoding declaration."

Encoding declaration

Appears in an XML declaration to declare the encoding for an XML document, in the form `encoding="UTF-8"`. See "XML declaration."

Entity

An XML storage unit. Often, an entity structure that provides replacement text wherever a reference is given in an XML document. Character and general entity references begin with an ampersand (&) and end with a semicolon (;). For example, the reference to the predefined XML entity `&lt;` stands for the less-than (<) sign, and wherever `&lt;` appears in an XML document, it will be replaced by < when the XML document is displayed in a browser or processed in some other way. Several general entities are built into or predefined in XML: `&lt;` (less-than [<]), `&gt;` (greater-than [>]), `&amp;` (ampersand [&]), `&apos;` (apostrophe [']), and `&quot;` (quote ["]). Character references provide replacement text for single characters. General entities can replace characters or strings. Parameter entities, delimited by a percent sign (%)—not an ampersand—and a semicolon, provide a way to reuse declaration and other text in DTDs.

Entities can be internal and external. This means that an entity could be internally defined within the XML document's DTD, or it could be defined externally in a separate file, even in a file out on the Web somewhere. Entities can also be parsed or unparsed. An unparsed entity is ignored by the XML processor and is some resource other than XML text, such as a JPEG graphic file, or even an HTML file. All other entities are considered parsed, that is, the XML processor processes them normally. See "Document entity."

Entity reference

See "Entity."

Escape characters

You can escape characters in XML with character entities and CDATA sections. See "Entity" and "CDATA section."

Expression

Defined by XPath, expressions contain node names (location paths), arithmetic, functions, and so forth, and can resolve to a node-set, number, string, Boolean, or, as defined in XSLT, a result tree fragment. Expressions appear only in attribute values, such as the select attribute of apply-templates or value-of. A pattern is a subset of an expression. See "Location path" and "Pattern."

EXSLT

See "Extension."

Extensible Hypertext Markup Language

XHTML is a vocabulary defined by the W3C that brings together XML and HTML. XHTML is defined by an XML DTD rather than an SGML DTD. XHTML must be well-formed XML, and must use all lowercase tag names. XHTML 1.0 became a W3C recommendation in early 2000; since then, other XHTML specs have appeared, and XHTML has been modularized. See *http://www.w3.org/MarkUp/*.

Extensible Markup Language (XML)

XML is a language that allows you to create your own markup language. It has an inherent, logical structure that you can use to label document content and data. This, in turn, makes XML an ideal language for storing interoperable data. In addition, XML is open, nonproprietary, platform independent, and license free. See *http://www.w3.org/TR/REC-xml.html*.

Extensible Stylesheet Language (XSL)

Provides a way to apply formatting to XML documents using stylesheets. It is similar to CSS but is actually written in XML, and applies specifically to XML documents, whereas CSS can apply to either HTML or XML. XSL is more extensive than CSS, and is commonly referred to as *XSL-FO* (*FO* stands for formatting objects). See *http://www.w3.org/TR/xsl/*.

Extensible Stylesheet Language Transformations (XSLT)

Allows you to transform XML documents into new XML, XHTML, HTML, or text documents. An XSLT stylesheet uses templates to match patterns in a source document and then outputs a result tree that may be serialized. XSLT relies on XPath syntax to match patterns. XSLT also allows you to add new markup to a result, such as new elements, attributes, comments, and so forth, by using instruction elements. See *http://www.w3.org/TR/xslt/*.

Extension

You can extend XSLT by adding extension elements and functions (which requires programming and processor support). You can also use the extensions already provided by existing XSLT processors such as Xalan and Saxon. One common extension function in XSLT 1.0 is the node-set( ) function, which can coerce a result tree fragment into a set of nodes. EXSLT is a group that is attempting to standardize XSLT extensions for portability and consistency (*http://www.exslt.org*).

External entity

See "Entity."

Fallback

In XSLT, processing may fall back in case an extension element or function is not supported by a given processor. For extension elements, this is performed using the fallback element, often in combination with a message element. You can also use the element-available( ) function to test for the availability of extension elements, or the function-available( ) function to test for extension functions. See "Extension."

Fragment identifier

A fragment identifier is preceded by a # in a URI, as in *http://www.example.com/index.html#top*. In HTML, #top refers to named anchor (<a name="top">) in the document *index.html*. An embedded stylesheet uses a fragment identifier. See "Embedded stylesheet" and "URI."

Following axis

See "Axes."

Following-sibling axis

See "Axes."

Function

Used in XPath expressions, functions perform specialized operations and appear only in XSLT attribute values that can contain expressions (such as select or value-of). Both XPath and XSLT define functions. Examples of functions are substring() (XPath) and document() (XSLT).

General parsed entity

See "Entity."

Global variable

A variable or parameter that is defined on the top level of a stylesheet and so is visible to (in scope for) the entire stylesheet. See "Local variable" and "Variable."

ID

An attribute type in XML 1.0. The value of an attribute of type ID is an identifier that is unique within an XML document and must not be duplicated. This associates an ID with an element. You can reference an ID from an attribute of type IDREF or multiple IDs from an attribute of type IDREFS (a whitespace-separated list of IDs). IDs must not start with a number in order to be valid XML.

Import

The ability to import stylesheets into another stylesheet, thus imposing rules of import precedence. Imported stylesheets are retained in an import tree. An import element (or more than one) must be the first child of the stylesheet element. See "Import precedence."

Import precedence

Imported template rules and top-level declarations have a lower precedence than those rules and declarations that exist in an importing stylesheet. In other words, rules and declarations in the importing stylesheet have higher precedence than those in an imported stylesheet. Import precedence is established by the order in which stylesheets are imported, and, therefore, how they are stored in the import tree. See "Import."

Include

You can include external stylesheets in a stylesheet using the include element. Template rules and declarations from the included stylesheet are mixed in with those of the including stylesheet as if they were one stylesheet. Compare with "Import."

Instance

An instance is an XML document that matches a particular DTD or schema, making it an instance of that schema. It is, also, any occurrence of a given structure.

Instantiation

The process of writing out the content of a template (sequence constructor in XSLT 2.0) based on a successful match of the template rule.

Instruction element

In XSLT, an element that is contained in a template, and not the top level. For example, element, attribute, copy, copy-of, and value-of are examples of instruction elements. Some elements, such as variable, may be used as instruction elements and as top-level elements.

Internal entity

See "Entity."

JAXP

Sun's Java API for XML Processing (JAXP) provides many resources for the programmer who wants to process XML or to write an XSLT processor (or more accurately an interface to one). The extension packages javax.xml.transform and javax.xml.transform.stream help get the job done. See *http://java.sun.com/j2se/1.4docs/api/index.html*.

Key

XSLT offers keys (a method of associating data with a name) that improve performance and efficiency. You declare a key at the top level of a stylesheet with a key element, and later you can employ the declared key with the key() function.

Literal result element

Literal elements, attributes, text, and other items in a template that, when instantiated, produce new elements, attributes, text and so forth in a result tree. Literal result elements are subject to the rules of XML well-formedness.

Literal result element stylesheet

A simplified stylesheet whose document element is html or an XML element that contains a single template. Compare with "Embedded stylesheet."

Local variable

A variable or parameter that is defined locally within a template rule and is visible to (in scope for) that rule alone. See "Global variable" and "Variable."

Location path

In XPath, a location path is an expression that identifies a node or nodes. It may consist of one or more steps. A step in a location path is separated by slashes. An absolute location path always begins with a slash and evaluates to or begins at the root node. A relative location path evaluates to or begins with the context node. An example of an abbreviated location path with two steps is date/month, which locates a date element relative to the context node, followed by a month element. In unabbreviated syntax, you use the axis specifiers with connectors like child::date/child::month, which gives you the same result as the unabbreviated syntax. Following are a few more comparisons of abbreviated and unabbreviated syntax, each pair having the same meaning: @type and attribute::type, child::* and *, @* and attribute::*, and self::node( ), and parent::date and /date.

Location step

See "Location path."

Markup

Includes element tags plus attributes, processing instructions, XML declarations, stylesheet declarations, document type declarations, and entity references. For example, <date>, </date>, <?xml-stylesheet href="date.xsl" type="text/xsl"?>, and > are all considered markup.

Markup declaration

Declarations in a DTD, such as <!ELEMENT date (#PCDATA)> and <!ATTLIST date type CDATA #IMPLIED>, are markup declarations. See "Attribute-list declaration" and "Element-type declaration."

Mixed content

Mixed content in an XML element consists of a mixture of text and child elements. In a DTD, it is declared <!ELEMENT date (#PCDATA | month | day | year)*>. See "Element-type declaration."

Modes

Normally, you can't match nodes with more than one template rule in a stylesheet. Modes allow you to apply more than one rule to a pattern by using the mode attribute on both the template and apply-template elements simultaneously with identical values. Each identical mode attribute value identifies a distinct mode. Modes are useful for visiting the same pattern repeatedly, each time with a different effect.

Name characters

Name characters are those ISO/IEC 10646-1 or Unicode characters that are legal for use in XML names. These characters must match the production Name-Char in section 2.3 of the XML specification. The legal name characters are too numerous to list here, but some common examples include the Latin characters A-Z, a-z, hyphen (-), colon (:), period or full-stop (.), and underscore (_).

Named templates

A template element may have a name attribute on it. You can then use call-template to invoke the named template. Calling a named template does not change the context; you can call the named template as often as you like. Named templates may also be invoked by matching a pattern because a template element may have both a name and match attribute.

Namespace axis

See "Axes."

Namespaces

An approach to qualifying elements and attributes so that they are unique from all other element and attribute names. You identify a namespace by associating an element with a URI (with either a URL or a URN) and optionally a prefix. A default namespace declaration associates a namespace with an element and its children without a prefix. The XML namespace specification became a W3C recommendation in 1999. It is available at *http://www.w3.org/tr/REC-xml-names/*. Namespace URI identify only the namespace; they do not point to the location of a schema or other resource that describes or defines the namespace. See "Node," "NCName," and "Qualified name (QName)."

NaN

Stands for "Not a number." Used by the XSLT top-level element `decimal-format`.

NCName

An NCName is an XML name that does not contain a colon. The element `<date>` is an example of an element that uses an NCName. It is sometimes called a noncolonized name. An NCName also does not have a namespace prefix associated with it. See "Qualified name (QName)."

.NET Framework

Microsoft's .NET Framework provides a programming and web development environment that includes programming languages such as VB.NET, ASP.NET, and C#. C# has strong support of XML and XSLT, and a variety of APIs provide the programmer easy access to these resources. You can write an XSLT processor (or actually an interface to one) in just a few lines of code using C#'s `System.Xml`, `System.Xml.XPath`, and `System.Xml.Xsl` namespaces. See *http://www.microsoft. com/net*.

Node

According to the XSLT 1.0 data model, a node is one of seven distinctive parts of an XML document, namely, the root node, element nodes, attribute nodes, text nodes, comment nodes, processing instruction nodes, and namespace nodes. *Node* comes from the Latin *nodus*, which is a knot in a rope.

Node-set

A set of unordered nodes of possible different types that may be empty. See "Node."

Node test

An XPath method that tests for given nodes. For example, the node tests that are listed here, `comment( )`, `node( )`, `processing-instruction( )`, and `text( )`, test for nodes of a given type (any given type in the case of `node( )`).

Output

The serialization of XSLT output is controlled by the top-level `output` element. This element has a number of attributes that can control the output method (`xml`, `html`, or `text`), encoding, XML declaration, indentation, CDATA sections, document type declaration, and so forth. You can have more than one `output` element in a stylesheet.

Output escaping

The `text` and `value-of` elements have an optional attribute: `disable-output-escaping`. It can have a value of yes or no (default). By default, `&lt;` will be output escaped, that is, as `&lt;`. If you disable output escaping with a value of yes, you will get `<` instead. The output method should be `xml` or `html` for this to work. See "Output."

0x

Ox is a compact command-line documentation tool written in Java that provides quick reference material for XSLT 1.0 and XPath 1.0. It is discussed in Chapter 18.

Parameter

In XSLT, you can bind a name with a default value using the `param` element. This parameter can be declared on the top or global level (scope is the whole stylesheet) or on the local level (scope is the template where the local parameter is declared). You can pass parameters into a stylesheet using a mechanism provided by an XSLT processor or into a template using the `with-param` element. See "Variable."

Parent-child relationship

XML elements have a relationship to each other, which forms the structure of an XML document. These relationships are parent, child, ancestor, descendant, and sibling. A child element is contained in the content of its parent element. The document element, for example, is the ancestor of all other elements in a document. A descendant is a child element and can be removed by more than one generation (or level of structure). If a parent element has more than one direct child, these children are called siblings.

Path expression

A path expression selects a node-set from a source document and may consist of location steps. See "Location path."

Pattern

A pattern is a subset of an XPath expression. It can contain location paths for nodes that are along the child or attribute axes only, but it can also contain predicates, `id( )`, and `key( )` functions. The `match` attribute of `template`, for example, can contain a pattern for matching nodes as part of a template rule. See "Location path."

Preceding axis

See "Axes."

Preceding-sibling axis

See "Axes."

Predicate

A filter containing an expression enclosed in square brackets. A predicate can be associated with nodes where either patterns or expressions may appear. A predicate returns a Boolean. For example, `date[.='2003-12-31']` returns true if a `date` element contains the string `2003-12-31`.

Processing instruction

A special instruction issued to an application processing XML. A processing instruction, or PI, is always enclosed by an angle bracket-question mark (`<?`) and ended by a question mark-angle bracket (`?>`) combination. A target name, such as `xml-stylesheet`, must immediately follow the `<?` with no intervening space. An XML stylesheet PI contains pseudoattributes such as `href` and `type`, which help associate an XML document with a stylesheet; for example, `<?xml-stylesheet href= "test. xsl" type="text/xsl"?>`. See "Node."

Prolog

Structures that appear before the document element. A prolog can include an XML declaration, a document type declaration, and processing instructions, comments, and whitespace. See "XML declaration," "Document type declaration," and "Processing instruction."

Qualified name (QName)

A qualified name or QName is an XML name that is qualified with a namespace. It may use a namespace prefix and a colon in its name. The element `xsl:element` is an example of an element that uses a QName with a prefix. See "Namespaces" and "NCName."

RELAX NG

Appearing in late 2001, RELAX NG is a simple yet elegant schema language created under the auspices of OASIS. It is easier to learn than XML Schema and has a sound theoretical basis (it is based on ideas from tree automata). You can learn more about RELAX NG at *http://www. relaxng.org/*. Compare with "XML Schema."

Relative location path

See "Location path."

Repetition operator

A repetition operator in an XML 1.0 DTD or a regular expression indicates the frequency with which an element or expression may be repeated in an instance. These operators are: a comma (,) for exactly one (DTDs); an asterisk (*) for zero or more; a plus sign (+) for one or more; and a question mark (?) for zero or one.

Result tree

The result of an XSLT transformation upon an XML source document is called a result tree. A result tree may be, and usually is, serialized to the screen or to a file.

Result tree fragment

A result tree fragment is defined in the element content of the `variable` element. This fragment may contain fragments of text or even well-formed XML. In XSLT 1.0, it can be manipulated as a node-set using a `node-set( )` extension function. In XSLT 2.0, a result tree fragment is called a temporary tree and intrinsically is a node-set.

Root element

See "Document element."

Root node

Refers to a way of addressing an entire document in the XPath data model. See "Node."

Sibling element

See "Parent-child relationship."

SGML

Standard Generalized Markup Language is a complex ISO/IEC standard from which XML was derived. XML is a simplified, restricted subset of SGML. HTML uses an SGML DTD.

Source tree

The original XML document from which a new document or result tree is derived. See "Extensible Stylesheet Language Transformations (XSLT)."

Standalone declaration

See "XML declaration."

Template

See "Template rule."

Template priority

See "Template rule."

Template rule

Consists of a matching pattern and template or sequence constructor (XSLT 2.0 term). When a template rule matches a pattern, its sequence constructor—the body of the template instructions—is instantiated, or written out. Some XSLT elements can contain templates but not template rules. For example, the element instruction can contain a template but does not match a pattern. Template rules

have a built-in priority scheme that can be explicitly controlled using the `priority` attribute on `template`.

Temporary tree

See "Result tree fragment."

Text declaration

A text declaration occurs in an external parsed entity and allows you to declare the encoding for the entity. It is similar to the XML declaration but it does not require version information. An example of a text declaration is `<?xml encoding= "UTF-8"?>`.

Text node

See "Node."

Top-level elements

In XSLT, a top-level element is a child of the `stylesheet` element and usually provides declarations that are global for the entire stylesheet. `attribute-set`, `variable`, and `template` are a few top-level elements.

Tree

An XML document has a tree structure. Starting from the document element (imagine it as the trunk of a tree), its branches grow out in the form of elements and other nodes. An XSLT processor analyzes and organizes its input and output into a tree structure. See "Source tree," "Result tree," and "Parent-child relationship."

Unabbreviated syntax

See "Location path."

Unicode

An international standard of character definitions that, in concert with ISO/IEC 10646-1, attempts to codify all the writing systems of all languages in the world. See *http://www.unicode.org*.

Unparsed entity

See "Entity."

URI

An acronym for Uniform Resource Identifier, a naming scheme for identifying resources on the Internet. The term URI encompasses the subset terms Uniform

Resource Locator (URL) and Uniform Resource Name (URN). A URL is a representation of a resource that indicates where the resource is located on a network. A URN is a name that must remain globally unique and must persist. For example, urn:wyeast-net:date is a valid URN. For complete details on URIs, see *http://www.ietf.org/rfc/rfc2396.txt.*

URL

See "URI."

URN

See "URI."

Valid XML

XML is considered valid when it has an associated document type definition (DTD) or other schema. With a DTD in tow, an XML processor can validate elements, attributes, and so forth against the DTD or schema, insuring that the XML document is going by the rules. Compare "Well-formed XML." See "Document type declaration" and "Document type definition."

Variable

A name bound to a value. Generally refers to variables declared by the variable and param elements. You refer to a variable with a variable reference that consists of the variable name preceded by a $—for example, $date. A value defined with variable cannot change, but the value of a variable defined with param is a default value that can change. Variables can be empty. See "Parameter."

Version information

See "XML declaration."

Vocabulary

An XML vocabulary is a collection of XML elements and attributes. For example, one such vocabulary is MathML, an XML-based markup language that allows you to render mathematical symbols and equations. See *http://www.w3.org/Math*

W3C

See "World Wide Web Consortium (W3C)."

Well-formed XML

Follows the general rules of XML but is not necessarily valid according to a document type definition (DTD) or some other schema. Some of those general rules include always opening an XML element with a start-tag and closing it with an end-tag, placing attributes in matching quotation marks, making sure that tags use uppercase and lowercase identically, and so forth. Compare "Valid XML."

World Wide Web Consortium (W3C)

Established in 1994, the World Wide Web Consortium (*http://www.w3.org*) is an international body headed by the inventor of the World Wide Web, Tim Berners-Lee. W3C forms committees of interested parties—companies and individuals—that jointly develop specifications and recommendations for the web engineering community at large. While not without controversy or detractors, the recommendations of W3C are highly regarded by industry; however, although the W3C produces recommendations, it does not claim to be a national and international standards organizations.

XML

See "Extensible Markup Language (XML)."

XML declaration

When included, the XML declaration is the first line of an XML document, and is part of the prolog (see "Prolog"). An example of an XML declaration is as follows: <?xml version="1.0" encoding="UTF-8" standalone="yes"?>. The version information indicates the XML specification version number; the encoding declaration indicates the type, such as UTF-8; a standalone declaration indicates the presence of references to external definition documents, such as a DTD (see "Document type definition") or other external entity.

XML namespace

See "Namespaces."

XML processor

Every application that looks at XML documents must have an accompanying program called the XML processor. This processor picks apart the XML document to make sure its contents are well-formed, and when a DTD is present, it may also check for validity. If the XML document is not well-formed, the XML processor must generate a fatal error and stop processing the document, though it can continue to look for other fatal errors in the document and report them. If a processor finds a validity error in a valid XML document, it must report that error, but it need not stop processing.

XML Path Language (XPath)

A W3C recommendation that provides a grammar for addressing parts of an XML document. For example, the location path child::* selects all the children of an element. XPath was designed for use with XSLT and XPointer, which addresses the inner structure of an XML document. The XPath 1.0 recommendation is available at *http://www.w3.org/TR/xpath.*

XML Schema

An XML vocabulary for defining XML documents. It is more powerful than the DTD because of its richer datatypes and more straightforward XML syntax, among other things. The XML Schema specs are: *http://www.w3.org/TR/xmlschema-0/ http://www.w3.org/TR/xmlschema-1/ http://www.w3.org/TR/xmlschema-2/ .*

XML stylesheet processing instruction

See "Processing instruction."

XPath

See "XML Path Language (XPath)."

XSL

See "Extensible Stylesheet Language (XSL)."

XSLT

See "Extensible Stylesheet Language Transformations (XSLT)."

XSLT processor

A processor that transforms XML documents according to the rules outlined in the XSLT specification. Xalan C++ and Instant Saxon are examples of command-line XSLT processors. xmlspy and xRay2 are graphical XML editors with XSLT processing capability. See the appendix.

XHTML

See "Extensible Hypertext Markup Language."

Index

Symbols

& (ampersand), 20
&quot and &apos entities, 21
< and > (angle brackets), 2, 20
  entity references for, 100
' (apostrophe), 21
@* (at-asterisk), 117
$ (dollar sign), 127
// (double forward slashes), 167
&gt (entity reference), 100
&lt (entity reference), 100
= (equals sign), 8
/ (forward slash), 2, 5, 83
-- (hyphens, doubled), 37
&#10 vs. &#13 (line-end vs. carriage return characters), 20
<? and ?> (PI start and end tags), 8
" (quotes, double), 8, 21
  (see also quotes)
' (quotes, single), 8, 203
  (see also quotes)
| (union operator), 88, 128

A

add.xsl, 234
africa2.xml, 221
africa.xml, 212
alias.xsl, 248
alphabetical lists, 158–161
alternative stylesheets, 241–253
amount element, 83
ampersand (&), 20
analyze-string element (XSLT 2.0), 282, 284

ancestor.xsl, 95
angle brackets (< and >), 2, 20
Ant and Moxie processor building, 298
any.xsl, 173
Apache, XML parser, 11
apostrophe ('), 21
apply-imports element, 225, 234–235
apply-imports.xsl, 234
apply-templates element, 9, 11
  sort element as child of, 139
Architag xRay2, 13, 327
as attribute (XSLT 2.0), 274
ascending sorts, 137–142
ASCII, 50
ascii-treeview.xsl, 79
attribute nodes, 79
attribute value templates, 29
attributes, 8
  quotes, including in values, 21
  reusing, 34–37
attribute-set element, 34
axes, 92–96

B

base URI, 8
better.xsl, 168
bible.xml, 236
binary coding, viewing files in, 54
blank.xsl, 195
BOM (Byte Order Mark), 52
  Windows and, 53
Boolean functions, 104
Boolean logic, 211

We'd like to hear your suggestions for improving our indexes. Send email to *index@oreilly.com*.

Boolean.xsl, 100
browsers
    cllient-side XSLT processing, 6–9
    handling of whitespace in text, 19
    XSLT support, 7
built-in templates, 6, 117
    built-in template rules, 194–198
        behavior at each node, 198
built-in.xsl, 196
Byte Order Mark (BOM), 52

C

C#, 73
    processor interface
            programming, 300–305
        .NET framework, downloading, 300
        Pax, 300–305
call-template element, 186
call.xsl, 186
canada.xml, 153
case-order attribute (sort element), 152
CDATA sections, 62
cdata.xsl, 63
chain.xsl, 228
character encoding, 49–54
    Unicode, 50
character map, 53
character references, 20
child elements, 9
child nodes, 9
choose element, 217
choose.xsl, 217
client-side XSLT processing, 6–9
code pages, 53, 74
code points, 50
collation attribute (XSLT 2.0), 274
comma.xsl, 216
comment nodes, 79
comments, 37
concat( ) function, 31, 108
conditional processing, 211–224
    of multiple kinds of documents, 221–224
context nodes, 81
context position, 82
context size, 82
contexts, 81
context.xsl, 278
control.xsl, 19

copy element, 113–118
    attributes, adding, 116
    identity transforms, 117
    shallow copies, 115
    templates and, 117
copy-namespaces attribute (XSLT 2.0), 274
copy-of element, 118–122
copy-of.xsl, 118
copy.xsl, 114
cougar.xsl, 197
count( ) function, 121
count attribute (number element), 156
count.xsl, 156
Cover, Robin, 307
Cowan, John, 108
csharp.xsl, 71
current nodes, 81
current-group( ) function (XSLT 2.0), 287
Cygwin, 189
    xxd utility, 54

D

data-type attribute (sort element), 145
data.xml, 170
data.xsl, 171
date:date( ) and date:time( ) functions,
        EXSLT, 263
decimal-format element, 175–179
    attributes, 176
deep copies, 118
    shallow copies, compared to, 118
default-html.xsl, 46
default-xml.xsl, 47
delaware.xml, 187
descending sorts, 142–144
disable-output-escaping attribute, 20–23
disable-output-escaping attribute (XSLT
        2.0), 274
DOCTYPE keyword, 59
doctype-public.xsl, 61
document( ) function, 120, 129, 225,
        235–239
    arguments, 236
document element, 2
document order, 82
document type declarations, 59–63
    public identifiers, 61
    validation with transformation, 60

document type definitions (DTDs), 56, 59
documents
    examples, download web site, 2
    multiple documents, working
        with, 235–239
    processing more than one kind, 221–224
dollar sign ($), 127
dot.xsl, 164
doubled hyphens (--), 37
DTDs (document type definitions), 56, 59
dual2.xsl, 223

E

ECMA-94, 50
edges, 77
element element, 31–33
    namespace attribute, 32
ELEMENT keyword, 59
element nodes, 79
element tags
    attributes, 8
elements
    child elements, 9
    literal result elements, 23–31
    template-containing elements, 40
    top-level elements, 5
embedded stylesheets, 244–247
    compatible browsers, 247
    location in document, 246
empty element tags, 2
encoding declarations, 26, 49–54
entities, 55–58
entity references for < and >, 100
entity.xml, 56
equals sign (=), 8
escapes.xml, 260
escape-uri-attributes attribute (output
        element, XSLT 2.0), 274
escape.xml, 21, 22
escape.xsl, 22
escaping of special characters, 21
europe.xml, 137
eu.xml, 113
excludeonlit.xsl, 252
exclude-result-prefixes attribute, 251
exclude.xsl, 252
expressions, 99–101
expressions (in XPath), 83, 99–101
EXSLT group, 254
Extensible Markup Language (see XML)

Extensible Stylesheet Language (XSL), 1
Extensible Stylesheet Language
        Transformations (see XSLT)
extensions, 254–270
    EXSLT extensions, 256, 262–265
        exsl:node-set function, 264–265
    extension elements, testing for
        availability, 265
    fallback behavior, 265–269
        invoking, 268
    Saxon extension attributes, 257–260
    Saxon extension functions, 255
    Xalan C++ extension functions, 255
    XSLT 2.0 developments, 288–290
external entities, 56
external subsets, 59

F

fallback behavior for extension
        elements, 265–269
    invoking, 268
fallback element, 265
files, viewing in hexadecimal or binary, 54
final.xml and final.xsl, 42
first.xsl, 232
fn:position( ), fn:last( ), and fn:context-item( )
        functions (XSLT 2.0), 278
for-each-group function (XSLT 2.0), 287
format attribute (number element), 155, 157
format-number( ) function, 129, 175–179
forward slash (/), 2, 5, 83
fragment.xsl, 133
FreeBSD, .NET implementation, 73
from attribute (number element), 174
function element (XSLT 2.0), 273, 288
functions, 102–112
    Boolean functions, 104
    node-set functions, 106
    node-tests, compared to, 102
    number functions, 107
    string functions, 108–112
functions.xml, 277
function.xsl, 288

G

generate-id( ) function, 111
generate-id.xsl, 111
greet.xml, 105
greet.xsl, 105

grouping with keys, 206–209
grouping, XSLT 2.0 developments, 286–288
grouping-separator attribute (number element), 164
grouping-size attribute (number element), 164
group.xml, 206, 286
group.xsl, 287

H

hexadecimal coding, viewing files in, 54
href attribute
    import element, 230
    include element, 227
    result-document element, 279
    saxon:output element, 266
href pseudoattribute, 8, 38, 246
HTML
    literal result elements, 26–28
    outputting, 64–70
HTTP (Hypertext Transfer Protocol)
    META tag and, 27
hyphens, doubled (--), 37

I

IBM437 character set, 74
id( ) function, 106
identity transforms, 117
identity.xml, 117
id.xsl, 106
if element, 212–217
    position( ) function, use of, 216
    test attribute, 213
    use of several at once, 216
if.xsl, 213
import element, 225, 230–234
import precedence, 225, 231
    manipulating, 234
import trees, 231
imported.xsl, 231
import-schema element (XSLT 2.0), 273
import.xsl, 230
include element, 225–230
    href attribute, 227
include-content-type attribute (output element, XSLT 2.0), 274
included stylesheets, 225
    self inclusion, problems with, 228
include.xsl, 226

indent.xsl, 258
Instant Saxon, 129, 315–317
    downloading, 315
    passing in parameters, 131
    requirements for use with Unix and Windows, 260
    running, 316
instantiation, 5
instruction element, 9, 17
internal subsets, 56, 59
ISO-8859, 50–51
ISO/IEC 10646-1, 49
ISO/IEC 8859, 50

J

Java
    classpath, 314–315
    downloading, 312
    installing and running, 312–315
    Java Runtime Environment (JRE), 312
    path variable, setting in Windows and Unix, 313
    processor interface programming, 291–300
        additional resources, 300
        Ant, 298
        javac, 297
        JAXP (Java API for XML Processing), 291
        JRE version verification, 296
        Moxie, 292–300
        Moxie source code, 292
    running the compiler, 313
    SDK, 312
jd.xslt, 324–326
jonah.xsl, 236
JRE (Java Runtime Environment), 312

K

Kay, Michael, 306
keys, 199–209
    cross-referencing with, 204
    grouping with, 206–209
    key( ) function, 201
    key elements, 201
    parameters, using with, 203
keys.xsl, 202
keywords.xml, 257

L

lang( ) function, 105
lang attribute
    number element, 175
    sort element, 152
last.xsl, 181
Latin-1, 50, 50–51
leaf nodes, 77
left angle-brackets (<), 20
less.xsl, 214
letter-value attribute (number element), 175
level attribute (number element), 165–173
    three numbering levels, 165
lf.xsl, 17
limerick.xsl, 109
line-end vs. carriage return characters (&#10
        vs. &#13), 20
Linux
    Mono Project and, 300
    .NET implementation, 73
    Saxon, Java version support, 317
    Xalan C++ support, 11
    XSLT support in browsers, 7
    xsltproc, 189
    xxd utility, 54
lists
    alphabetical lists, 158–161
    numbered lists, 153–179
    roman numeral order, 162–163
list.xsl, 151
literal result element stylesheets, 241–244
    in XHTML, 243
literal result elements, 23–31
    for HTML, 26–28
    for XHTML, 28–31
literal-cdata.xsl, 64
literal.xml, 23
literal.xsl, 242
location paths, 82
location steps, 82

M

Mac OS X, .NET implementation, 73
Macintosh, XSLT support in browsers, 7
mailing list, XSLT, 307
mammals.xml, 194
Mangano, Sal, 307
markup, 2
match attribute, template element, 5
matches( ) function (XPath 2.0), 282

match.xsl, 282
math:lowest( ) function (EXSLT), 263
math.xml, 99
math.xsl, 99
media-type attribute, output element, 75
member.xml, 145
message element, 265
META tag, 27
method attribute, output element, 4
Microsoft
    C# (see C#)
    code pages, 53
    file path, conversion to Unix, 109
    Internet Explorer, XSLT compatible
        versions, 6
    MSXSL, 13, 320–321
    .NET (see .NET)
MIME (Multipurpose Internet Mail
        Extensions) types, 75
mixed content, 39
Mono Project, 300
Moxie XSLT processor, 292–298
    Ant, building with, 298
    compiling, 297
    imported classes, 293
    JRE version verification, 296
    source code, 292
Mozilla browser, compatible versions, 6
msg-pi.xml document, 6
msg.xml document, 2
msg.xsl stylesheet, 3
MSXSL, 320–321
    downloading, 320
    running, 320
Muench, Steve, 207
Muenchian method, 207–209
multiple result trees (XSLT 2.0), 272,
        277–281
multiple sorts, 148–152

N

name( ) function, 31
name attribute (output element, XSLT
        2.0), 275
name attribute (template element), 186
name tests, 96–98
namespace aliasing, 247–251
namespace declarations, 3, 30
namespace element (XSLT 2.0), 273
namespace nodes, 79

namespace prefixes, 4, 23–26
namespace-alias element, 247–251
    attributes, 247
namespaces, excluding, 251–253
name.xml, 46
NCNames, 25
.NET, 73
    C# XSLT processor, creating, 300
    Pax, compiling, 305
    required Windows versions, 300
Netscape Navigator, XSLT compatible
            versions, 6
newalias.xsl, 250
next-match element (XSLT 2.0), 274
nodes, 5, 77
    children, 9
    copying from two documents, 120–122
node-set functions, 106
node-sets, 82
node-set.xsl, 261
nodes.xml, 77
    xml:lang attribute, usage of, 81
node-tests, 68, 83, 96–98
    functions, compared to, 102
noescape.xsl, 22
non-colonized names, 25
normalize-space( ) function, 109
normalize-unicode attribute (output element,
            XSLT 2.0), 275
notalone.xsl, 57
notsotedious.xsl, 24
number element, 155–158
    count attribute, 156
    format attribute, 155, 157
    from attribute, 174
    lang and letter-value attributes, 175
    level attribute, 165–173
        three numbering levels, 165
    multiple level counting, 166–173
        counting on any level, 173
        for section and item element, 167
        more depth, 170–172
    value attribute, 163
number functions, 107
numbered lists, 153–179
    counting on multiple levels, 166
    (see also number element)
number.xsl, 155
numerical sorts, 145–148

O

omit.xsl, 49
order attribute (sort element), 142
order.xml, 262
otherwise element, 219–221
outline.xml, 166
outline.xsl, 166
output
    of comments, 37
    controlling (see output element)
    of processing instructions, 38–41
    of text, 16
output element, 4, 45–76
    cdata-section-element attributes, 62
    doctype-system attributes, 60
    encoding declarations, 49–54
    HTML output and, 64–70
    media type attributes, 75
    method attribute, 46–48
        default HTML output, 46
        default vs. explicit method
            specification, 48
        default XML output, 47
    new attributes, XSLT 2.0, 274
    QName output method, 74
    text declarations, 55
    text output and, 70–74
    version attribute, XML, 58
    XHTML, validating, 62
    XML declaration, 48–52
    XML output, 48–64
    XSLT processors, adherence to, 45
output.xsl, 265
Ox documentation tool, x, 307–310

P

param element, 123–124, 130–132, 190
parameters, 123–136
    Instant Saxon, passing in using, 131
    keys, using with, 203
    stylesheets, passing in to, 203
    templates, using with, 190–192
    Xalan, passing in using, 131
param.xsl, 130
parsed character data, 9
parsed entities, 56
patterns, 84
    matching multiple nodes using, 88–93
pattern.xsl, 87

Pawson, Dave, 307
Pax, 300–305
   compiling, 305
   running, 304
   source code, 300–302
      C# namespaces, 302–304
PIs (processing instructions), 38–41
   creating and using, 41
   processing instruction nodes, 79
poem.xml, 108
position( ) function, 154
position.xsl, 154
precedence.xsl, 232
predefined entity references, 21
predicates, 85–88
pretty.xsl, 140
price.dtd, 127
price.xml, 127
priority attribute (template element), 182
priority.xsl, 182
processing instruction nodes, 79
processing instructions (see PIs)
provinces.xml, 97
pseudoattributes, 8
public identifiers, 61
pull stylesheets, 243
push stylesheets, 243

Q

QNames, 25, 96
qualified names, 25
quotes, 8, 21
   including in attribute values, 21
   key( ) function and, 201
   select attribute, usage in, 125

R

recent.xsl, 146
regex.xsl, 285
regular expressions (XSLT 2.0), 281–286
relative references, 227
RELAX NG, 97
replace( ) function (XPath 2.0), 282, 284
replace.xsl, 284
result tree fragments, 84, 133
   casting as a node-set, 260–262
result trees, 5

result-document element (XSLT 2.0), 272, 277
result-prefix attribute (namespace-alias element), 247
reusing attributes, 34–37
RFC 1766 (Tags for the Identification of Languages), 81
rhodeisland.xml, 188
right angle brackets (>), 21
ri.xml, 181
roman numeral lists, 162–163
root elements, 2
root nodes, 5, 79
round( ) function, 107

S

Saxon, 317–319
   differences between versions, 259
   downloading, 317
   extension attributes, using, 257–260
   extension functions, 255
   indentation depth, 27
   nodeset( ), 260
   running, 318
   start tags, 27
   Unix and Windows requirements for Instant Saxon, 260
   Unix shell scripts, using with, 319
   Windows batch files, using with, 319
saxon:indent-spaces attribute, 266
saxon:indent-spaces extension attribute, 258–260
saxon:output element, 266
SC Unipad, 55
scand.html, 244
scandinavia.xml, 245
scand.xml, 242
second.xsl, 232
select attribute (for-each element), 167
select attribute (sort element), 148
sequence constructors, 4
sequence constructors (XSLT 2.0), 272
sequence element (XSLT 2.0), 274, 289
setProperty( ) method, 294
SGML and XML, 21
shallow copies, 115
   deep copies, compared to, 118
shopping.xsl, 149
shutoff.xsl, 197

single quotes (' '), 203
sort element, 137–152
   apply-templates, as child of, 139
   ascending sorts, 137–142
   case-order attribute, 152
   data-type attribute, 145
   descending sorts, 142–144
   lang attribute, 152
   multiple sorts, 148–152
   numerical sorts, 145–148
   order attribute, 142
   select attribute, 148
sort-key element (XSLT 2.0), 274
sort.xsl, 138
source document validation, 60
source trees, 5
splat.xsl, 97
standalone declarations, 56
standalone.xml, 57
state.xsl, 228
string functions, 108–112
string-length( ) function, 68
stylesheet element, 3
stylesheet-prefix attribute (namespace-alias
    element), 247
stylesheets, 3
   chaining together, 228
   embedded stylesheets, 244–247
    compatible browsers, 247
   examples web site, 2
   excluding namespaces, 251–253
   literal result element stylesheets, 241–244
   multiple stylesheets, working
     with, 225–235
   namespace aliasing, 247–251
   pull stylesheets, 243
   push stylesheets, 243
substring( ) function, 67, 109
sum( ) function, 107
SYSTEM keyword, 56

T

tab.xsl, 157
tags, 2
   empty element tags, 2
   META tag, 27
   reserved characters, 20
   XHTML syntax, 29
   XML, 2

Tags for the Identification of Languages (RFC
    1766), 81
tedious.xsl, 23
template element, 4
   instantiation, 5
   match vs. name attributes, 186
   name and match attributes, 187
   name attribute, 186
   priority attribute, 182
template pattern conflicts
   modes, solving with, 192
   template priority, solving with, 181–186
template rules, 4, 39
   patterns, 85
template-containing element, 40
templates, 5, 9, 180–198
   built-in template rules, 194–198
   built-in templates, 117
   import precedence, 225
   invocation by name, 20, 186
   order of, impact on output, 41
   parameters using with, 190–192
   template priority, 181–186
temporary trees (XSLT 2.0), 272
Tennison, Jeni, 307
test attribute (if element), 213
test attribute (when element), 219
text declarations, 55
text element, 17
   disable-output-escaping attribute, 20–23
text method, 70
text nodes, 9, 79
text output, 16
   and whitespace, 17–20
text.xml, 16
thanks.xsl, 164
Tidwell, Doug, 307
tokenize( ) function (XPath 2.0), 282
top-level elements, 5
top.xml, 226
transform element, 3
translate( ) function, 109
tree-view.xsl, 80
trip.xml, 289
txt.xsl, 17
type attribute (XSLT 2.0), 274
type pseudoattribute, 8, 38

U

UCS Transformation Format (UTF), 51
UCS (Universal Multiple-Octet Coded Character Set), 49
undeclare-namespaces attribute (XSLT 2.0), 274
Unicode, 10, 49
union operator (|), 88, 128
UniPad, 55
Universal Multiple-Octet Coded Character Set (UCS), 49
URIs (Uniform Resource Identifiers), 3
US-ASCII, 50
USC (Universal Multi-Octet Character Set), 10
use-attribute-sets attribute (copy element), 116
use-character-maps attribute (output element, XSLT 2.0), 275
UTF-8 and UTF-16, 51

V

validation attribute (XSLT 2.0), 274
value attribute (number element), 163
variable element, 123–124, 127–130
variable names and element names, 128
variable-alt.xsl, 129
variables (XSLT), 123–136
vendor attribute, 83
version attribute, stylesheets, 3
version.xsl, 58

W

W3C Markup Validation Service, 62
welcome.dtd, 111
welcome.xml, 111
welcome.xsl, 112
well-formed XML, 2
wg.xml, 64
wg.xsl, 66
when element, 217
    test attribute, 219
when.xsl, 218
whitespace and text output, 17–20
whitespace.xsl, 18
Windows
    batch files and Saxon, 319
    BOM and, 53
    code pages, changing, 53

Instant Saxon compatibility, 129, 260
Java classpath, setting, 314
Java path enviroment variable, setting, 313
.NET (see .NET)
Xalan C++ support, 11
Xalan, setting the path variable for, 322
XSLT support in browsers, 7
XSLT support, Internet Explorer, 7
Windows Character Map utility, 53
withoutif.xsl, 215
with-param element, 123–124, 192
with-param.xsl, 132
wspace.xsl, 227

X

Xalan, 11
    C++ extension functions, 255
    indentation depth, 27
    indentation features, 47
    META tag and head element, 27
    passing in parameters, 131
    start tags, 27
    -v and -i options, 128
Xalan C++, 12, 321–324
    C++ extension functions, 255
    downloading and installing, 321
    path variable, setting, 322
    running, 323
xalan:node-set( ) function, 260–262
Xerces, 11
Xerces C++, 321
XHTML
    literal result elements, 28–31
    tags, syntax of, 29
    validating, 62
xhtmlit.xsl, 243
Ximian open source .NET implementation, 73
xls:exclude-result-prefixes attribute, 251
XML declaration, output element, 48–52
XML (Extensible Markup Language), 1
    attributes and pseudoattributes, 8
    declarations, 9
    document comments, 37
    documents, 2
    element tags and attributes, 8
    predefined entity references, 21
    SGML and, 21
    stylesheet processing instructions, 7–9

XML (*continued*)
  tags, 2
  Unicode and, 10
  versioning information via output
      element, 58
XML Path Language (see XPath)
xml:lang attribute, 81
  lang( ) function, 105
xmlns attributes, 3
xmlspy, 326
XmlTextWriter object, 73
XPath (XML Path Language), ix, 1
  @* (at-asterisk), 117
  additional resources, 306
  axes, 92–96
  data model, 77–82
  expressions, 83, 99–101
  forward slash (/), 5
  functions, 102–104
      Boolean functions, 104
      node-set functions, 106
      number functions, 107
      position( ), 154
      string functions, 108–112
  location paths, 82
  name and node-tests, 96–98
  node type examples, 117
  nodes, 78–79
  operators, 100
  unabbreviated syntax, 94
  V. 2.0 developments, 271, 275–276
      for and conditional expressions, 276
      matches( ) function, 282
      new comparison operators, 276
      new functions, 275
      new kind tests, 275
      new terminology, 275
      replace( ) function, 284
      sequences and ranges, 276
      strong typing, 275
  viewing of trees, 79
xRay2, 13, 327–329
XSL (Extensible Stylesheet Language), 1
XSL-FO, 1
XSLT (Extensible Stylesheet Language
      Transformations), ix, 1
  additional resources, 306
  browsers, support in, 7
  C# programming, 71
  client-side processing, 6–9
  extensions (see extensions)

functions, 102, 104
  node-set functions, 106
  string functions, 108–112
mailing list, 307
parameters, 123–136
patterns, 84
processing multiple kinds of
      documents, 221–224
stylesheets (see stylesheets)
V. 2.0 developments, 271–290
  analyze-string element, 284
  character maps, 273
  date format, 273
  extension functions, 288–290
  grouping, 286–288
  multiple result trees, 277–281
  new attributes on old elements, 274
  new elements, 273
  new terminology, 272
  parameters in new places, 273
  regular expressions, 281–286
  xhtml output method, 272
  XML Schema, validation support
      for, 273
variables, 123–136
XSLT graphical user interfaces, 13
XSLT namespace, 3
XSLT processors, 11–14, 311–329
  available processors, 311
  built-in template rules, 194–198
  writing a C# interface, 300–305
  installing and running, 312–329
      Instant Saxon, 315–317
      Java, 312–315
      jd.xslt, 324–326
      MSXSL, 320–321
      Saxon (full Java version), 317–319
      Xalan C++, 321–324
      xmlspy, 326
      xRay2, 327–329
  writing a Java interface, 291–300
  output element, adherence to, 45
  Xalan, 11
  xRay2, 13
xsltproc, 189
xslt.xsl, 249
xxd utility, 54

Y

year.xsl, 147

About the Author

Michael Fitgerald is principal of Wy'east Communications (*http://www.wyeast.net*). He is a contributor to XML.com, and, in addition to *Learning XSLT*, he is the author of *Building B2B Applications with XML* and *XSL Essentials*, both published by Wiley.

Colophon

Our look is the result of reader comments, our own experimentation, and feedback from distribution channels. Distinctive covers complement our distinctive approach to technical topics, breathing personality and life into potentially dry subjects.

The animal on the cover of *Learning XSLT* is a Marabou stork (*Leptoptilos crumeniferus*). Among the largest flying birds in the world, the Marabou stork's flight capability is facilitated by hollow toe bones, which are an important adaptation for flight, considering its large size. The adult male's wingspan is approximately 9.5 feet (2.9 meters). He can stand up to 5 feet tall (1.5 meters) and weigh 20 pounds (9 kilograms). The size and wingspan of females are generally smaller.

Native to the marshes and savannahs of Africa, Marabou storks can also be found near landfills, abattoirs, and fishing villages. Marabous have adapted well to human growth and activity, which has benefited the thriving species. Because they ingest bacterial waste, Marabou storks help humans by reducing the spread of disease, and thus, they are important predators. Their powerful beaks break through the rough hides of rotting mammal carcasses, which speeds up the decomposition process and enables weaker scavengers to feast on the dead fleash. Marabous are attracted to grass fires, where they hunt the small animals fleeing from the blaze. They will eat almost any kind of animal, dead or alive, from caterpillars to flamingos to elephants. These hefty protein diets are necessary for adult Marabous; they require over 25 ounces (700 grams) of food a day.

Marabous are large carnivores, notoriously ugly, not only because of their unsavory habits, including squirting excrement onto their own legs, but also because of their featherless, scabby, pink heads and necks speckled with dark pigmentation spots. Interestingly, Marabous evolved bald heads to avoid getting their feathers soiled by the bloody carnage of successful scavenging expeditions. In breeding season, the bare neck turns a pale blue-green, and the spots on the head and neck become encrusted with dried blood. Although the birds are generally considered unsightly, their soft, white tail feathers, called marabou, were once fashionable as trim for hats and gowns.

Marabou storks are colonial breeders, and they will return to the same community nesting site year after year. The male Marabou stork arrives at the nesting site first, in order to establish his territory. As he treats all newcomers with hostility, the courting female responds with submission, waiting to be accepted as his mate. Like lobsters, penguins, and most bird species, Marabou storks mate for life. Females usually lay 2 to 3 eggs during a breeding season that both parents will help incubate for 29 to 31 days. Marabous nest in the dry season when low water levels make it easier to catch prey, such as frogs and small fish, to feed their young. The relatively long pre-fledgling period lasts 95 to 115 days. Marabous reach sexual maturity at approximately four years of age. In zoos, and possibly in the wild, Marabou storks can live up to 25 years.

Marlowe Shaeffer was the production editor and copyeditor for *Learning XSLT*. Mary Brady was the proofreader. Emily Quill and Claire Cloutier provided quality control. John Bickelhaupt wrote the index.

Ellie Volckhausen designed the cover of this book, based on a series design by Edie Freedman. The cover image is a 19th-century engraving from the Dover Pictorial Archive. Emma Colby produced the cover layout with QuarkXPress 4.1 using Adobe's ITC Garamond font.

David Futato designed the interior layout. This book was converted by Joe Wizda to FrameMaker 5.5.6 with a format conversion tool created by Erik Ray, Jason McIntosh, Neil Walls, and Mike Sierra that uses Perl and XML technologies. The text font is Linotype Birka; the heading font is Adobe Myriad Condensed; and the code font is LucasFont's TheSans Mono Condensed. The illustrations that appear in the book were produced by Robert Romano and Jessamyn Read using Macromedia FreeHand 9 and Adobe Photoshop 6. The tip and warning icons were drawn by Christopher Bing. This colophon was written by Marlowe Shaeffer.